Naval Powers in the Indian Ocean and the Western Pacific

A vital component of the interdependent global economy, maritime transit routes are nowhere more critical than those traversing the Indian Ocean and the Western Pacific. Previously, areas of the Indian Ocean and Western Pacific have been viewed as separate and discrete political, economic, and military regions. In recent years, however, a variety of economic, political, and military forces have created a new understanding of these maritime expanses as one zone of global interaction.

This book complements the material presented in its companion volume, *Maritime Security in the Indian Ocean and the Western Pacific*, by analysing the perceptions, interests, objectives, maritime capabilities, and policies of the major maritime powers operating in the Indian Ocean and the Western Pacific. In addition, the book also assesses the contemporary maritime challenges and opportunities that confront the global community within what is rapidly becoming recognised as an integrated zone of global interaction.

A valuable study for researchers and policymakers working in the fields of maritime security; military, security and peace studies; conflict resolution; and Asian affairs.

Howard M. Hensel is Professor of Politico-Military Affairs at the USAF Air War College, USA.

Amit Gupta is Associate Professor of International Security Studies at the USAF Air War College, USA.

Naval Powers in the Indian Ocean and the Western Pacific

Edited by Howard M. Hensel
and Amit Gupta

LONDON AND NEW YORK

First published 2018
by Routledge
2 Park Square, Milton Park, Abingdon, Oxon OX14 4RN

and by Routledge
711 Third Avenue, New York, NY 10017

Routledge is an imprint of the Taylor & Francis Group, an informa business

© 2018 selection and editorial matter, Howard M. Hensel and Amit Gupta; individual chapters, the contributors

The right of Howard M. Hensel and Amit Gupta to be identified as the authors of the editorial material, and of the authors for their individual chapters, has been asserted in accordance with sections 77 and 78 of the Copyright, Designs and Patents Act 1988.

All rights reserved. No part of this book may be reprinted or reproduced or utilised in any form or by any electronic, mechanical, or other means, now known or hereafter invented, including photocopying and recording, or in any information storage or retrieval system, without permission in writing from the publishers.

Trademark notice: Product or corporate names may be trademarks or registered trademarks, and are used only for identification and explanation without intent to infringe.

British Library Cataloguing-in-Publication Data
A catalogue record for this book is available from the British Library

Library of Congress Cataloging-in-Publication Data
Names: Hensel, Howard M., editor of compilation. | Gupta, Amit, 1958– editor of compilation.
Title: Naval powers in the Indian Ocean and the Western Pacific / edited by Howard M. Hensel and Amit Gupta.
Description: Abingdon, Oxon ; New York, NY : Routledge, [2018] | Includes bibliographical references and index.
Identifiers: LCCN 2017052836 | ISBN 9781138303669 (hardback) | ISBN 9780203730874 (e-book)
Subjects: LCSH: Sea-power—Pacific Area. | Sea-power—Indian Ocean Region. | Navies—Asia. | Pacific Area—Strategic aspects. | Indian Ocean Region—Strategic aspects. | Pacific Ocean—Strategic aspects. | Indian Ocean—Strategic aspects.
Classification: LCC VA620 .N38 2018 | DDC 359/.03091824—dc23
LC record available at https://lccn.loc.gov/2017052836

ISBN: 978-1-138-30366-9 (hbk)
ISBN: 978-0-203-73087-4 (ebk)

Typeset in Times New Roman
by Apex CoVantage, LLC

Contents

List of figures and tables   vii
List of contributors   viii
Introduction   x

1 **The United States and security issues in the IO-WestPac maritime region**   1
   WILLIAM L. DOWDY

2 **China's naval strategy**   22
   YVES-HENG LIM

3 **Russian maritime strategy since the Ukrainian crisis**   36
   ALEXANDR BURILKOV

4 **Contemporary Europe in the Indian Ocean and the Western Pacific**   55
   DOUGLAS CARL PEIFER

5 **Japanese maritime perspectives, interests, objectives, and policies**   69
   TAKUYA SHIMODAIRA

6 **The Republic of Korea navy: capabilities, confrontations and potential outcomes**   86
   KEVIN W. MADDEN

7 **Strategic and "everyday" maritime security challenges in Southeast Asia**   120
   MARIA ORTUOSTE

8 **Australia's maritime strategy**   138
   ALAN BLOOMFIELD AND SHIRLEY V. SCOTT

Contents

9   A New Zealand view: anchored in *Oceania* – reaching out to Asia   154
CAROL ABRAHAM

10   India's maritime strategy: aspirations and reality   172
AMIT GUPTA

11   Iran's maritime aims: persistent strategy, changing capabilities   195
NATHAN GONZÁLEZ MENDELEJIS

12   The Arab Gulf States: contemporary maritime perspectives, interests, objectives, and policies in the Gulf Cooperation Council   207
JOSEPH A. KÉCHICHIAN

13   South Africa and maritime security: interests, objectives, policies and challenges   230
THEO NEETHLING

Conclusion   247
HOWARD M. HENSEL

Index   254

Figures and tables

Figures

6.1 Locations of Key ROK Navy Headquarters — 89
6.2 DPRK West Sea Military Demarcation Line (September 1999) — 99

Tables

6.1 Approximate strengths of Northeast Asia's regional navies — 108
7.1 Security challenges in Southeast Asia — 121
11.1 Balance of naval forces in the Persian Gulf — 203

Contributors

Carol Abraham: B.Sc. (Hons), University of Canterbury, New Zealand; MSS. (Merit), Victoria University of Wellington, New Zealand; MSS (Grand Strategy), Air University. Group Captain, Royal New Zealand Air Force; Head New Zealand Defense Staff, Defense Advisor Canberra, Australia.

Alan Bloomfield: B.A./LLB; University of Western Australia; MA UNSW; Ph.D. Queens University. Lecturer, University of Western Australia.

Alexandr Burilkov: B.A., University of Florida; D.Phil., University of Hamburg. Research Fellow, C4SS, Metropolitan University of Prague, Czech Republic and Research Fellow, German Institute of Global and Area Studies (GIGA), Hamburg, Germany.

William L. Dowdy: B.A., Duke University; M.A. and Ph.D., Tulane University. Professor of Political Science (retired), Alabama State University, USA.

Nathan González Mendelejis: B.A., University of California, Los Angeles; Master of International Affairs, Columbia University; Ph.D., University of California, Los Angeles. Assistant Professor of National Security Studies eSchool of Graduate PME, Air University, USA

Amit Gupta: B.A., Delhi University; M.A., Jawaharlal Nehru University; M.A., Australian National University; Ph.D., University of Illinois. Associate Professor of International Security Studies, USAF Air War College, USA.

Howard M. Hensel: B.A., Texas A&M University; M.A. and Ph.D., University of Virginia. Professor of Politico-Military Affairs, USAF Air War College, USA.

Joseph A. Kéchichian: B.A. Immaculate Heart College; M.A., Monterey Institute of International Studies; Ph.D. University of Virginia. Senior Fellow, King Faisal Center for Research and Islamic Studies, Saudi Arabia.

Yves-Heng Lim: B.A., Institute of Political Science, Lyon, France; M.A, Defense and International Security, University of Grenoble, France; Ph.D., University of Lyon, France. Lecturer, Department of Security Studies and Criminology, Macquarie University, Australia.

Kevin W. Madden: B.S., Northern Illinois University; M.A., University of Washington; M.S., University of Canberra, Australia. Defense Intelligence Chair, Air University, USA.

Theo Neethling: B.A. and M.A., Potchefstroom University of CHE (North-West University); DLitt et Phil., University of South Africa. Professor of Political Science, University of the Free State, South Africa.

Maria Ortuoste: B.A. and M.A., University of the Philippines; Ph.D., Arizona State University. Associate Professor of Political Science, California State University East Bay, USA.

Douglas C. Peifer: B.A., Miami University; M.A. and Ph.D., University of North Carolina at Chapel Hill. Professor of Strategy and History, USAF Air War College, USA.

Shirley V. Scott: B.Mus., B.A. (Hons) and Ph.D. University of Queensland; M.H.Ed., University of New South Wales. Head of School of Humanities and Social Sciences UNSW, Canberra, at the Australian Defence Force Academy; Head of School and Professor of International Relations, University of New South Wales, Canberra, Australia.

Takuya Shimodaira: B.S., National Defense Academy; M.A., University of Tsukiba; Ph.D., Kokushikan University. Naval Captain, JMSDF; Senior Research Fellow, The National Institute for Defense Studies, Tokyo, Japan; Former Visiting Military Professor, U.S. Naval War College, USA.

Introduction

Howard M. Hensel and Amit Gupta

Maritime transit is a vital component in sustaining the interdependent, global economy of the twenty-first century. Nowhere are maritime transit routes more critical than those that traverse the Indian Ocean and the Western Pacific. Indeed, the ships that pass through these waters carry a wide variety of important goods and raw materials, among the most vital of which are oil and liquefied natural gas. These cargos are necessary, in turn, in fueling the economies of the world, as well as, more broadly, in providing comfort and convenience to the various societies that compose the global community.

This book is part of a series of companion works designed to analyze and assess the heritage, contemporary maritime challenges, and national and international responses to those challenges by the littoral states, as well as those non-littoral powers with interests in the Indian Ocean basin and the Western Pacific region. The first of these companion works, *Maritime Security in the Indian Ocean and the Western Pacific*, examined: the maritime heritage of the Indian Ocean and the Western Pacific; the scope and significance of maritime transit routes through these waters, with special emphasis concerning the transit of oil and liquefied natural gas through critical chokepoints, including the Suez Canal, the Bab el-Mandeb, the Strait of Hormuz, and the Strait of Malacca; and the challenges confronting the global community in maintaining security at these critical chokepoints, as well as in the Red Sea, the Persian Gulf, the South China Sea and the East China Sea.

Complementing the material presented in the aforementioned companion volume, this volume[1] focuses on the ways in which a number of key regional powers in the Indian Ocean and the Western Pacific, as well as the United States, Great Britain, and France, see themselves within the context of the various sub-regions of the Indian Ocean and the Western Pacific, as well as within the larger area east of Suez. In addition, the various chapters examine the ways in which these powers perceive the contemporary challenges and opportunities confronting them and the ways in which they define their national interests and their resulting regional objectives with respect to the Indian Ocean basin and the Western Pacific region. Finally, the various chapters analyze the naval capabilities and deployment patterns of the respective states and assess the maritime policies and strategies of these states that are, in turn, designed to address the challenges and opportunities that currently confront them and, in doing so, promote their respective objectives and secure their national interests.

It is our hope that these two companion volumes, separately or jointly, will help scholars, statesmen, members of the military, and leaders of the global economy to better understand the heritage, complexity, and interrelationships between the various sub-regions within the broader Indian Ocean basin and the Western Pacific, such as the Red Sea, the Persian Gulf, the South China Sea, and the East China Sea, as well as the vital importance of the interconnecting maritime transit routes traversing these waters. In addition, these volumes also hope to highlight the historical and contemporary significance of the Indian Ocean basin and the Western Pacific as an interconnected economic and geo-strategic whole. In doing so, these companion volumes will, hopefully, emphasize the importance of formulating policy predicated upon this increasingly compelling reality.

Finally, we would like to express our thanks to the contributors to this volume, as well as to the staff of Routledge Publishing for their help and support throughout the course of this project. In addition, we would like to express our thanks to the U.S. Department of Defense for a Minerva research grant which helped to make this volume and its companion volume possible. Finally, we would like to extend our special thanks to Kirstin Howgate, Robert Sorsby, and Claire Maloney for their continuous cooperation and encouragement as we moved throughout the publication process.

Note

1 The opinions, conclusions, and/or recommendations expressed or implied within the chapters contained in this volume are solely those of the authors who are entirely responsible for the contents of their respective works and should not be interpreted as representing the views of any academic institution, the Air War College, the Air University, the United States Air Force, the U.S. Department of Defense, any other U.S. Government agency, any other government, multinational agency, or non-governmental organization.

1 The United States and security issues in the IO-WestPac[1] maritime region

William L. Dowdy

Introduction

With the rise of China and India, the development of nuclear weapons and ballistic missiles by North Korea, and ongoing territorial and maritime sovereignty disputes – all in the complicating context of economic globalization – U.S. policy makers have important choices to make regarding America's current and prospective role in the Indian Ocean and Western Pacific maritime region – choices involving both challenges and opportunities.

Because of its strategic geography, the United States since its founding has been a *maritime nation*. With continental expansion to the Pacific coast, the purchase of Alaska, seizure of the Hawaiian Islands, and "inheritance" of Spain's Pacific empire, the United States gradually became a *Pacific power*. As a maritime trading nation with the world's largest economy, the United States has a vital concern for freedom of navigation in the Pacific as elsewhere, and an abiding interest in access to Asian markets and resources. Finally, as the victorious naval power in the Pacific in World War II, and during the Cold War with its engagements in Korea and Vietnam, the United States has maintained a continuous naval presence in the Western Pacific for over 70 years.[2]

During this same period, the Indian Ocean (IO) became an arena of superpower competition[3] between the United States and the Soviet Union which, in part as a consequence of the Cuban Missile Crisis of 1962, embarked on a massive naval expansion in the 1960s and 1970s.[4] With British withdrawal from "east of Suez" in the late 1960s, and because of the dramatically increasing strategic importance of Persian Gulf oil from 1973 onward, the U.S. Navy greatly increased its operations in the Indian Ocean.[5] Its impactful presence there has been maintained through a succession of events including the Iranian Revolution, the Iran-Iraq War, the Iraqi invasion of Kuwait, U.S. wars in Iraq and Afghanistan, and the increasing Sino-Indian geopolitical rivalry in the IO.[6] It also remains engaged in actions against the Islamic State (ISIL/ISIS) in the region.

The coming of Trump

From the origins of President Barack Obama's "Pivot" or "Rebalancing" policy[7] in 2011, the United States was engaged in the execution of a coherent strategy toward the IO-WestPac maritime region. However, the campaign of Donald Trump for President and the early months of his administration placed in doubt the future course of U.S. Asia policy. On the one hand, Trump's "America First" rhetoric, accompanied by an apparent transactional approach toward alliance diplomacy and a zero-sum view of international trade, seemed to bode ill for the ongoing pivot toward Asia that reflected Obama's strong preference for multilateralism in both international security arrangements and in economic trade agreements. On the other hand, early Trump actions suggested more policy continuity with the pivot strategy than discontinuity.

The new president, backing away from campaign rhetoric about ungrateful and free-riding allies, dispatched Vice President Mike Pence, Secretary of State Rex Tillerson, and Defense Secretary James Mattis to reassure America's Asian allies such as Japan and South Korea that the United States remains committed to their security, especially at a time of increased North Korean bellicosity and Pyongyang's escalation of its nuclear weapons development program. This message of support was reinforced during a spring 2017 visit to the United States by Japanese Prime Minister Shinzo Abe. Subsequently, President Trump hosted China's President Xi Jinping in pursuit of a productive working relationship, especially vis-à-vis North Korea.

But if early indicators suggested *continuity in the security dimension* of Trump's Asia policy, then stark *discontinuity in economic policy* was signaled by his almost immediate executive order withdrawing U.S. support for the Trans-Pacific Partnership – painstakingly negotiated by the Obama Administration – thus effectively leaving the field of multinational economic institution-building to Chinese domination by removing the principal alternative to the Regional Comprehensive Economic Partnership (RCEP) championed by Beijing.

On the whole, countries with smaller economies in East and Southeast Asia had seen the Trans-Pacific Partnership

> as a great opportunity to increase the benefits of economic relations with the United States and to mitigate overdependence on China. Absent a replacement [of the TPP], those states might have little choice but to tie themselves economically even closer to Beijing.[8]

It is beyond the scope of this chapter to analyze economic issues confronting U.S. policy makers in Asia. Writ large, security issues do have significant economic dimensions, some of which will be indirectly addressed in this chapter. However, the focus here is on the maritime – and specifically naval – dimensions of security issues in the Indian Ocean and Western Pacific maritime region.

U.S. national interests

American naval presence and operations in the in the IO-WestPac region are of course in support of U.S. national *interests* – both global interests and those specific to that maritime region itself. According to the Obama Administration's

2015 National Security Strategy, the enduring national interests of the United States are:

- "The security of the United States, its citizens, and U.S. allies and partners;
- A strong, innovative, and growing U.S. economy in an open international economic system that promotes opportunity and prosperity;
- Respect for universal values at home and around the world; and
- A rules-based international order advanced by U.S. leadership that promotes peace, security, and opportunity through stronger cooperation to meet global challenges."[9]

The maintenance and advancement of those national *interests* in the Indian Ocean and Western Pacific will rest ultimately on achieving identifiable *objectives* through the application of carefully crafted and flexible region-specific *policies* and *strategies*. Such strategies will be implemented with military (principally naval), diplomatic, and economic instruments available to the United States in its foreign policy toolbox.

U.S. national objectives in the IO-WestPac region

In the regional context of the Indian Ocean and Western Pacific, the *first objective* of U.S. maritime policy is to bolster American security by deterring or defeating attacks on the homeland (most plausibly by nuclear-armed China or North Korea), ensuring the safety of American citizens in the region, and strengthening the security of U.S. allies and partners there.

Second, access to markets and resources is an *objective* serving the national interest in sustaining a strong and growing U.S. economy. Access is dependent on continuing to secure maritime lines of communication (LOCs) and safe passage through chokepoints such as the Bab el-Mandeb, Hormuz, Malacca, and Taiwan straits. Serious challenges to LOCs and chokepoint passages have been rare because all trading states share an interest in freedom of the seas.

Problems have occasionally arisen in the form of piracy attacks on shipping and as a consequence of attempts at over-reach by some littoral states in their sovereignty claims in order to expand territorial waters. Concerted actions by the navies of aggrieved trading nations have virtually eliminated the modern-day piracy threat. But national sovereignty claims persist to challenge freedom of navigation and maritime access.

A *third objective* of U.S. policy in the IO-WestPac region is to achieve acceptance of a rules-based international system, though such acceptance is now far from universal there. For example, the authority of, and a recent decision by, the international tribunal charged with adjudicating claims arising under the United Nations Convention on the Law of the Sea (UNCLOS) was vociferously repudiated in July 2016 by the People's Republic of China.[10]

The U.S. objective of upholding and promoting a "rules-based international system" extends well beyond international treaty law to legal practices established by international custom, as well as by many bilateral and multilateral agreements applying to parties in the IO-WestPac region. For example, in April 2014, the United States, China, and nearly 20 Western Pacific states signed the Conduct for Unplanned Encounters at Sea (CUES) protocol intended to avoid inadvertent confrontations that could lead to conflict. While non-binding, not applying to encounters in disputed waters, and covering only naval (not coast guard) forces, CUES nevertheless is a positive contribution to a "rules-based" system.[11] Another promising development has been institutionalized cooperation among navies of the IO-WestPac region in humanitarian assistance and disaster relief operations (HADR).[12] Such missions, for example in dealing with the aftermath of tsunamis, typhoons, and earthquakes, may help to facilitate constructive relations among navies and thereby enhance regional security.

A *fourth* U.S. *objective* of encouraging "respect for universal values," including human rights, applies to the domestic treatment of the citizens of the respective states of the IO-WestPac region as well as to relations among states. The traditional stance of China on the question of human rights and civil liberties within individual societies is that such matters are issues of national sovereignty and thus beyond the purview of outside states and international law. Other authoritarian states agree. U.S. policy opposes that view, just as it supports the right of democracies and nascent democracies in the IO-WestPac region to be free of external hegemony and coercion.

A *fifth* U.S. *objective* of promoting cooperation among IO-WestPac governments in meeting global challenges has long been evident in the cases of battling piracy, stemming pandemics, and policing human trafficking and international criminal activity such as terrorism and the illicit drug trade. So too has the United States been active in promoting cooperative efforts to curb the proliferation of weapons of mass destruction. Such bilateral and multilateral cooperation is useful in its own right, but it also serves to promote positive relations among states that are adversaries on other issues.

U.S. maritime policy and strategy for the IO-WestPac region

The erstwhile overarching *policy* to sustain U.S. national *interests* by achieving the *objectives* set forth above was first enunciated by the Obama Administration in 2011. Originally called a "pivot" to Asia, it was later characterized as a "rebalance" of American attention, from its long-term emphasis on European affairs and its prolonged preoccupation with the Middle East, to a focus on and a shift of resources to the Indo-Asia-Pacific region – toward what former Assistant Secretary of State Campbell called "an arc of ascendance."[13] Campbell further stated that "a crucial and enduring component of the Pivot [would] be to bend the arc of the Asian Century more toward the imperatives of Asian peace and prosperity and long-standing American interests."[14] Such a focus represented a new commitment of "the scarcest of all government resources – top-level time and attention."[15] This grand *strategy* of rebalance encompassed several subsidiary strategies:

- to increase the forward presence of U.S. naval assets in the region;
- to work with allies, friends, and potential adversaries to promote constructive bilateral and multilateral relations;

- to work toward amelioration of or solutions to ongoing disputes that, if left unresolved, could lead to increasing instability and insecurity in the region;
- to pursue a "nuanced China policy that displays resolve" to prevent "the emergence of a dominating hegemon in Asia" while, at the same time, "unambiguously invit[ing] cooperation" with Beijing to maintain stability in the region.[16]

Whether the Trump Administration pursues the general thrust of President Obama's rebalancing strategy, whatever Trump chooses to label it, remains to be seen. Assuming that U.S. *national interests*, as inventoried above, are more or less immutable, it is likely that President Trump's *objectives* will track relatively closely with those previously discussed. However, the Trump Administration *policies* and implementing *strategies* may well be repackaged and altered in content. As of this writing, it is too early to judge.

Increased regional presence of U.S. naval assets

In his February 2016 testimony before the Senate's Armed Services Committee, Admiral Harry B. Harris, Jr., Commander, U.S. Pacific Command (USPACOM), stated that "the tyranny of distance and short indications and warnings timelines place a premium on robust, modern, and agile foreign-stationed forces at high levels of readiness."[17] Admiral Harris's "combatant command" responsibilities include most U.S. Navy and Marine Corps (as well as Army and Air Force) assets in the "area of responsibility" (AOR) that includes most of the Pacific and Indian Oceans.[18]

A recent U.S. Department of Defense (DoD) report asserts that "the cornerstone of our forward presence will continue to be our presence in Japan," which hosts "the only forward-stationed Carrier Strike Force in the world, as well as . . . [the Third] Marine Expeditionary Force and significant Air Force assets."[19] "In an effort to ensure that this presence is sustainable" – an apparent reference to problematic community relations on Okinawa – "the Department of Defense will be able to shift its concentrated presence on Okinawa toward a more distributed model that includes Australia, Hawaii, Guam, and mainland Japan," as well as "new training ranges in . . . the northern Mariana Islands to enhance the readiness of our forward forces to respond to regional crises."[20]

"Over the next five years," the report states, "the U.S. Navy will increase the number of ships assigned to [the] Pacific Fleet outside of U.S. territory by approximately 30 percent, greatly improving our ability to maintain a more regular and persistent maritime presence in the Pacific. And by 2020, 60 percent of naval and overseas air assets will be home-ported in the Pacific region."[21]

In further support of the emphasis on forward presence, the United States has negotiated the bilateral Force Posture Agreement (FPA) with Australia, providing for the rotational presence of Marines in northern Australia and also negotiated the Enhanced Defense Cooperation Agreement (EDCA) with the Philippines, allowing for periodic use of extant facilities in Subic Bay.[22] Moreover, DoD "is on track to achieve its stated goal of simultaneous rotation of 4 Littoral Combat Ships (LCS) through Singapore by 2017, which will provide the first persistent U.S. naval presence in Southeast Asia in more than 20 years."[23]

The U.S. maritime presence in Guam will be modernized and expanded as part of "efforts to develop Guam into a strategic hub for our joint military presence in the region," including forwarded-stationing a fourth attack submarine to Guam and a submarine tender; a new "Zumwalt class" of stealth destroyers and unmanned reconnaissance drones may also be based out of Guam in the future.[24] Because Guam is U.S. sovereign territory, its status as an operating base will be unencumbered by political constraints.

Meanwhile, it is likely that a third carrier strike force will continue to operate in the northern Indian Ocean sectors of PACOM and of the U.S. Central Command (CENTCOM), especially in light of continuing Islamic State activities and the ongoing necessity to patrol LOCs to and from Persian Gulf oil fields. While naval assets in that region will probably rotate for operational control between PACOM and CENTCOM, depending on missions assigned, they will be available for contingencies arising in either of the two AORs.

U.S. naval forces enjoy developed port facilities on Bahrain Island in the Persian Gulf, location of Fifth Fleet Headquarters and CENTCOM's naval component command, and in British-owned Diego Garcia, a purpose-built lagoon base with a long airstrip in an archipelago off the southwest coast of India. American naval vessels are also welcome in most Indian Ocean littoral states where they call periodically for crew rest and to conduct naval diplomacy.

One additional point regarding "forward presence" is worthy of mention. It is a speculative observation for which there is no authoritative open-source evidence. However, considering the U.S. strategic nuclear doctrine based on the "Triad," it is possible, even likely, that U.S. strategic missile submarines (SSBNs or "boomers") have operational areas in the Indian Ocean and Western Pacific within range of potential adversaries that are either nuclear-armed or are threshold nuclear states. The very possibility of such patrols should be a cause for restraint in confrontational situations. The incentives should be extraordinarily high in the minds of potential adversaries to avoid first use of nuclear weapons and to avoid military conflicts that could escalate out of control. One can only hope that the logic of nuclear deterrence that prevailed for 40 years of the Cold War will continue to prevail, especially in Pyongyang.

Working with allies, friends, and potential adversaries

Reference has already been made to recent agreements with Australia, the Philippines, and Singapore. Long-standing defense treaties with South Korea, the Philippines, Thailand, and Japan also remain in force, although U.S.-Thailand relations are currently somewhat strained because of the anti-democratic coup that brought that country's present government to power. Washington continues to pursue closer relationships with Indonesia, Malaysia, and Vietnam. And the U.S. opening to Myanmar (Burma) received a boost from the 2016 visit to that country by President Obama.

In the Indian Ocean, the United States has had a long-term partnership based on mutual interests with Saudi Arabia, recently reinforced by a visit to the Kingdom by President Trump during his first trip abroad as President. Washington has also maintained good relations with the Arab Gulf states – Kuwait, Bahrain, Qatar, the UAE, and Oman. Kenya has been a reliable East Africa partner, and Djibouti hosts U.S. military forces. The U.S. operations base at Djibouti, "Camp Lemonnier," was established in 2003 to support special forces units and drone missions against jihadist groups in the Horn of Africa/Red Sea area.

Arguably, of greatest potential importance to the U.S. strategic objectives in the IO-WestPac region is the world's biggest democracy, with the world's second largest population and a growing naval capability, namely India. Former U.S. National Security Council official, Peter Lavoy, believes that "the evolving relationship between the United States and India . . . presents a 'tremendous opportunity'." Lavoy cites "habits of cooperation about every major problem" including freedom of navigation and overflights in the South China Sea. Noting that one-third of bulk cargo and two-thirds of petroleum exports pass through the IO, Lavoy asserts that the U.S. partnership with India needs to be deepened and broadened. [25] Commander of the U.S. Pacific Command, Admiral Harry Harris, echoes the sentiment: "our bilateral relationship with India represents USPACOM's most promising strategic opportunity." The Admiral underscored that view by making reference to the "Joint Strategic Vision of the Asia-Pacific and Indian Ocean Region" signed by President Obama and Prime Minister Modi in January 2015, and to the ten-year "Defense Framework Agreement" between the two countries of June 2015. Admiral Harris remains hopeful regarding India's role:

> USPACOM aims to build a powerful quadrilateral partnership framework of the most powerful democracies in the Indo-Asia-Pacific. India, Japan, Australia, and the U.S. working together will be a force for the maintenance of the regional rules-based order, counterbalancing and deterring coercion and unrestrained national ambitions.[26]

The regional adversaries with which the United States seeks to work constructively if possible are the PRC and the People's Democratic Republic of (North) Korea (PDRK). The American strategy is to cooperate with them when possible to achieve regional stability and security, and to confront them when necessary. North Korea has repeatedly shunned efforts at cooperation by the United States as well as by its neighbors. China is in a transitional stage, liberalizing economically, repressing internal political dissent, and rising as a regional and world power. Traditionally resistant to "Western-biased" international law and to any outside interference with what it deems to be its "internal affairs," China is becoming increasingly nationalistic as its global influence rises. Its leadership is still resentful and influenced by historical memories of Western interventions in the nineteenth and early twentieth centuries and the PRC consequently is demanding changes in the international system to reflect its new power status. The United States, meanwhile, (despite its revolutionary beginnings) is the world's leading status quo power and advocate of a rules-based international order. Therein lies the profound challenge inherent in U.S. – China relations.

Managing disputes that threaten peace and security

At this writing, the most portentous challenges to peace and stability in the IO-WestPac region are: 1) North Korea's nuclear program and its threats against U.S. treaty partners South Korea and Japan, and ultimately to the United States itself; 2) East China Sea islands in dispute between Japan and China; 3) the ongoing Taiwan status issue; 4) South China Sea territorial claims and unilateral coercive actions there by China; 5) the future of relations between the nuclear states of India and Pakistan; and, 6) the Islamic State and Islamist radicalism throughout the region. While all six issues significantly impinge on U.S. interests, the first four issues involve a strong maritime component, unlike the last two, and thus will be those discussed in order below.

Deterring North Korea

The U.S. Navy has a major role to play in deterring or defeating a conventional attack by North Korea on South Korea and, above all, in deterring North Korea from following through on its repeated threats to attack South Korea, Japan, and even the United States with nuclear weapons. U.S. Navy assets could blunt and help to defeat a conventional invasion of the South by using carrier-based aircraft (principally F/A18 "Hornets") and surface ship- and submarine-launched "Harpoon" and "Tomahawk" missiles in concert with South Korean armed forces and U.S. air and land forces based on the Korean peninsula and elsewhere in WestPac.

Moreover, the demonstrated capability to destroy short or medium range ballistic missiles in their mid-course or terminal phases – including missiles mounting nuclear warheads – has long been deployed for deterrence (and defense) purposes on board U.S. warships operating in the Sea of Japan and Northern Pacific. Specifically, the Aegis ballistic missile defense (BMD) system is installed on *Ticonderoga*-class guided missile cruisers and on *Arleigh Burke*-class guided missile destroyers. Aegis technology has been made available by the United States to South Korea and Japan, and both states have BMD-equipped ships at sea to reinforce deterrence and, if necessary, provide defense in the face of increasing North Korean nuclear capabilities and threats.[27]

Finally, in the spring of 2017, the South Korea government accepted deployment by the United States of Terminal High Altitude Area Defense (THAAD) missile systems on the peninsula to deter or defeat a missile attack from North Korea. China opposed the deployment on the grounds its radar could be used to spy into Chinese territory. Meanwhile, the newly elected South Korean president, Moon Jae-in, has called for a review of the THAAD deployment.[28]

East China Sea islands dispute between Japan and China

Arguably the most dangerous threat to Indo-WestPac peace and security is the sustained tension between Japan and China involving a group of islands located northeast of Taiwan. Called the Senkaku Islands by Japan and the Diaoyu Islands by China, they are currently owned and/or administered by Japan. Also claimed by China, their disputed history is complicated by intense nationalism on both sides and by evidence of the likelihood of petroleum deposits in the area.

Former State Department official Kurt Campbell believes that "these islands represent one of the few maritime disputes that could escalate to the level of a US-China conflict."[29] PACOM Commander, Admiral Harris, has testified that "China seeks to challenge Japan's administrative control over the islands by deploying warships into the area, sailing coast guard ships inside the territorial waters surrounding the Senkakus, and intercepting Japanese reconnaissance flights."[30] According to Campbell, "the United States takes no position on the ultimate sovereignty of the islands, but it does recognize Japan's administrative control over them," having returned the islands to Japan as part of its post-war occupation in 1971.[31]

Periodic crises have flared between Japan and China over the Senkakus. In 2013,

> China brashly declared a ADIZ [Air Defense Identification Zone] over the entire East China Sea and over disputed islands, setting off a major crisis. . . . China required all aircraft flying over them to alert China before doing so, at risk of being shot down. Japan condemned the ADIZ and refused to comply with it, and the United States publicly challenged it by flying two unarmed B-52 bombers through the ADIZ without notifying Beijing.[32]

Subsequently, "record numbers of Chinese maritime patrol vessels, fishing ships, fighter aircraft, and unauthorized landings" occurred to challenge Japan's claims; Tokyo responded with its own maritime patrols and by scrambling large numbers of fighter planes.[33] Such maneuvers raise the prospect of confrontations that could lead to conflict.

President Obama and his secretaries of defense and state repeatedly made the U.S. position clear that the United States continued to recognize Japanese administration of the Senkakus. President Trump and his secretary of defense have recently made the same commitment. During his early 2017 visit to the United States, Japanese Prime Minister Abe received personal assurances from President Trump that U.S. treaty guarantees to Japan, including those that cover the Senkaku island chain, remain in place.[34] China, therefore, should have no doubt regarding the U.S. position on its Senkaku/Diayou dispute with Japan.

Another long-standing U.S. commitment involves the security and self-determination of the island of Taiwan.

The Taiwan issue

In 1979, the United States and the People's Republic of China normalized relations. Taiwan was effectively "de-recognized" as a sovereign state, but there was no mood among many in the American electorate to abandon it altogether. The Taiwan Relations Act of 1979 incorporating a U.S. security guarantee, arms sales to Taiwan for self-defense, acceptance of a permanent "Taiwan Affairs Office" in Washington, and general diplomatic support together constituted a sort of consolation package for the Republic of China because of its past loyalty as an ally and to help offset its reduction in status.

Since then, and indeed during the Cold War, there have been periodic Taiwan crises, usually stimulated by the perception that the PRC was on the verge of attempting to force Taiwan into unification with the mainland as part of "one China." As recently as 1995–96, President Bill Clinton felt compelled to send two aircraft carrier battle groups to the area, ordering one carrier to transit the Taiwan Strait itself to deter what appeared to be preparations by Beijing to invade Taiwan. Notwithstanding President Clinton's firm response, the Chinese government continues periodically to threaten Taiwan militarily and to demand unification on Beijing's terms.

There have been periods of relatively good relations between Taiwan and the PRC that included mutually beneficial trade and cultural, educational, and people-to-people exchanges. Such was the state of relations during eight years of the Taiwan government of former president Ma Ying-jeou, leader of the Kuomintang (KMT) Party.[35] But since the election of Ma's successor, Tsai Ing-wen, leader of the Democratic Progressive Party (DPP) – which also won a legislative majority – the PRC government has once again hardened its approach to the question of Taiwan's status. In her victory speech in January 2016, President Tsai said she would "work to maintain the status quo for peace and stability across the Taiwan Strait."[36] Implicit in her notion of the status quo is the continuing self-governance of democratic Taiwan without declaring independence (previously advocated by the DPP), but also without unification. The status quo has been based on a 1992 agreement that there is only "one China." From the perspective of Taipei, that meant each side keeps its own interpretation of "one China," whereas for Beijing the two sides do not attempt to define its meaning.[37]

Following the inauguration of President Tsai in May of 2016, that status quo apparently is no longer is acceptable to President Xi of China. Chinese "state propaganda under Xi has shifted subtly in tone, hinting that force may be used to compel unification, and not just to prevent a declaration of independence [by Taiwan]."[38] Beijing has reportedly suspended official and semi-official cross-Strait talks.[39] The absence of official contacts, if protracted, could well lead to dangerous misunderstandings between the two parties.

Then President-Elect Trump created a major diplomatic flap and received a sharp rebuke from China after he accepted a congratulatory phone call from Taiwan President Tsai, thus implying an impending reversal in the status of Taiwan and hinting at the possible use of the issue as bargaining leverage on trade disputes with Beijing. However, Mr. Trump, on becoming president, soon offered a pledge to China's President Xi Jinping that the United States would respect the long-established "One China Policy."[40]

Meanwhile, the United States is not advocating any particular future for Taiwan, provided its future status is accepted by a majority of its citizens. For now, at least, "there are good reasons for Beijing to think that Washington might well come to Taipei's assistance in the event that it is attacked, and these [reasons] are likely to continue to deter China from any precipitate military aggression against Taiwan." But "the long-term durability of Taiwan's de facto independence may be questionable,"[41] especially given China's increasingly powerful navy.

Currently and for the indefinite future the Chinese navy is no match for the U.S. Navy.[42] However, as China continues to enhance its submarine force and its anti-ship missile capabilities, American aircraft carriers are likely to become increasingly vulnerable to Chinese attack if employed to defend Taiwan from a cross-Strait attack from the mainland. U.S. countermeasures to China's area-denial capabilities are already under development, but operational doctrine for carriers will need to adjust to an altered threat environment. Meanwhile, Beijing certainly knows that attacking a U.S. aircraft carrier in international waters would be tantamount to starting a war with the United States.

South China Sea territorial and jurisdictional disputes

The South China Sea is the portion of the Western Pacific Ocean that links it to the Indian Ocean. It is semi-enclosed by China to the north, Malaysia to the South, Vietnam to the west, and the Philippines to the east.[43] China has historically claimed most or all of the South China Sea, but such a claim directly conflicts with the United Nations Convention on the Law of the Sea (UNCLOS) which China has ratified. The Convention grants national sovereignty over waters up to 12 nautical miles from a country's coastline, and special economic rights to all littoral countries up to 200 miles from their coasts in an area called their exclusive economic zone (EEZ). Moreover, UNCLOS protects freedom of navigation of transiting ships seeking peaceful passage through both national waters and EEZs.

The Law of the Sea Treaty thus effectively has turned the South China Sea into a patchwork of claims – some overlapping – by several countries in addition to China that border the Sea or have unresolved claims to various islands and low-tide outcroppings scattered throughout the South China Sea. A recent UNCLOS Permanent Court of Arbitration ruling on a case brought by the Philippines in 2013 has rejected China's expansive claims to all or most of the South China Sea, as well as its claim to territorial sovereignty over reefs and rock outcroppings within the South China Sea which, the Court determined, are not islands (and therefore incapable of supporting claims *by any state* to 12-mile territorial seas surrounding them). The question of who owns the Spratly land features – and thus who can legally claim sovereignty over them – was not addressed by the Court's decision.[44]

In fact, China's claims to ownership of islands and other features in the South China Sea (some of them 800 miles from the Chinese mainland) and their surrounding territorial waters are contested by five other state claimants. Specifically, in the case of the *Spratlys*, which include more than 200 geographic features, China, Taiwan, and Vietnam claim sovereignty over *all s*uch features, while the Philippines, Malaysia, and Brunei each claim sovereignty over *certain* land features in the Spratly group. Vietnam and Malaysia have yet to fully stipulate exactly what their maritime claims are with respect to *some* geographic features in the South China Sea. Similarly, there are three claimants to the *Paracel Islands*, another South China Sea grouping located east of Vietnam and south of China's Hainan Island: China, Taiwan, and Vietnam. *Scarborough Reef*, a separate feature, is closest to the Philippine coast and claimed by the Philippines, China, and Taiwan. Finally, China's claim to the *Pratas Islands*, located in the northeastern sector of the Sea, is contested by Taiwan.[45]

Prior to the decision of the Court of Arbitration announced in July 2016, the United States Navy had conducted freedom of navigation operations (FONOPS) near the disputed "islands" in the South China Sea. In October 2015, the American guided missile destroyer, *USS Lassen* passed inside of 12 nautical miles off Subi Reef in the Spratlys. Even if China's ownership claims had been sustained by the Court, the right of innocent passage through the 12-mile territorial seas would not have been affected. Subsequently, in January 2016, the guided missile destroyer *USS Curtis Wilbur* transited within 12 miles of Triton Island in the Paracels group to assert innocent passage rights.[46] More recently, according to press reports, the guided missile destroyer *USS Decatur* in October 2016 sailed close to Triton and Woody Islands, the latter of which hosts a Chinese military airbase. And in May 2017, *USS Dewey* became the first U.S. Navy ship to conduct a FONOP in the South China Sea under the Trump Administration, passing within 12 nautical miles of Mischief Reef in the Spratly Islands.[47]

Perhaps in anticipation of an adverse decision by the Arbitration Court, China unilaterally changed the status quo by creating artificial geographic features. To place China's island building efforts into context, it has reclaimed or created in the past three years more than 3,000 acres of artificial land. By contrast, four other claimants (Vietnam, Malaysia, the Philippines, and Taiwan) have together over the past 45 years reclaimed only 115 acres. In addition to flouting the authority of the UNCLOS Arbitrations Court, China has rejected charges of serious damage to the fragile ecosystem of the South China Sea resulting from its engineering projects.[48]

In rejecting the UNCLOS Court's decision,

> Chinese leaders seem to believe that, through coercion, intimidation, and force, they can bypass accepted methods of dispute resolution. They have demonstrated this not only through aggressive artificial island building, but also by growing a fleet of 'white hull' ships and fishing vessels whose purpose is to dominate the area without the appearance of overt military force. China is now turning the artificial island projects into operating bases for forward-staging military capabilities.[49]

According to Commander PACOM, Admiral Harris,

> the U.S. takes no position on competing sovereignty claims in the South China Sea, but we encourage all countries to uphold international law, as

reflected in the Law of the Sea Convention, which ensures unimpeded lawful commerce, freedom of navigation and overflight, and peaceful dispute resolution.[50]

Mincing no words, the Admiral asserted that "the U.S. will sail, fly, and operate wherever international law allows."[51] Indications are that the U.S. Navy will conduct more frequent freedom of navigation operations and overflights in the South China Sea, and will encourage American allies to do the same; Japan and Australia have announced intentions to do so; U.S. carrier battle groups have also operated routinely in the South China Sea.[52]

U.S. strategies toward implementing a nuanced China policy

U.S. policy has been to influence the rise of China in such a way as to preserve a rules-based international order while shaping and defending that order in ways favorable to American interests, those of U.S. allies, and ultimately – Washington has argued – favorable to China's own interests. That requires demonstrating to Chinese leadership the benefits of rising into the international order as an influential player versus the costs resulting from attempting to overturn the international order.

In a recent "strategic dossier," International Institute of Strategic Studies (IISS) analysts opined that for over four decades U.S. policy "reflected a combination of engaging with China to encourage its transformation into a 'responsible stakeholder' [in the international system] whilst hedging against the enormous uncertainty inherent in China's rise."[53] The analysts state that "Beijing's actions [have] raised questions in the U.S. [about] the accuracy of . . . assumptions . . . that economic interdependence and a rising Chinese middle class would lead to a convergence of values or interests."[54]

Capabilities have always been more transparent than intentions – even more so in the age of satellite monitoring and modern information-gathering technology. The dramatic increase in the size and capabilities of the People's Liberation Army's Navy (PLAN) has tended to reinforce the worst fears of many Western and regional analysts regarding China's intentions. China skeptics also point to cyber espionage, currency manipulation, and even bad manners (e.g., withholding from President Obama a rolling stairway and a red carpet upon his arrival in Beijing for the 2016 G-20 Conference) as additional evidence of China's malign intent.

A second "school of thought" about China is that it has no grand strategic design to supplant the United States or to become a regional hegemon. Beijing's assertiveness has resulted from "uncertainties, fears, insecurities, and a certain level of opportunism" bolstered by the natural tendency to employ new capabilities "to address the potential threat [Beijing sees in the long-standing U.S.] dominance in the Asia-Pacific region."[55] The U.S. rebalance strategy, such analysts aver, may have contributed to China's insecurities and consequent assertiveness.

A third school of thought remains agnostic as to China's intentions, suggesting it is still too early to understand President Xi Jinping's ultimate objectives. But such agnosticism does not provide an excuse for complacency, nor obviate the need to be prepared for any eventuality. It is this third school of analysis that seems to have been prevalent in official U.S. policy making and defense establishment circles during the Obama Administration. And it clearly continues to animate U.S. naval strategy in the IO-WestPac region.

There has been a sustained effort by the U.S. military in general, and by senior Navy officials in particular, to reach out to their Chinese counterparts to promote understanding and to encourage professional interaction.[56] In a July 2016 visit by U.S. Chief of Naval Operations (CNO) Admiral John Richardson, he stated:

> I appreciate the opportunity to . . . meet with [PLAN Commander] Admiral Wu [Shengli] in person. There is no substitute for these types of face-to-face meetings. My goal is to forge a relationship based on frankness and cooperation. Given the responsibilities that our navies have, we must work together and speak candidly – when we agree as well as when we have differing opinions.[57]

This meeting of the two navy chiefs occurred one year after the PLAN for only the second time accepted the U.S. invitation to participate in the annual American-led Rim of the Pacific (RIMPAC) multilateral exercises.[58]

In a 2016 report by The National Institute for Defense Studies in Japan, the author places the PLAN's current size and capabilities in historical context, arguing that China's navy today is the result of long-term development dating from its establishment in 1949.[59] It is only from the early 2000s that offshore defense has been combined with "open seas defense," as the PLAN has developed a blue-water navy with global reach.[60] The salient point demonstrated by the Japanese study is that the Chinese navy did not suddenly appear in the twenty-first century, but has undergone long-term, evolutionary development commensurate with China's evolving status as a global trading power, albeit accelerated evolution over the past two decades.

The PLAN has steadily expanded the scope of its routine operations into the Indian Ocean, including the dispatch of 21 task forces through 2015 to participate in international counter-piracy operations off the Horn of Africa.[61] It has also undertaken naval diplomacy missions to Persian Gulf states and monitored LOCs along which much of China's oil imports pass. China has negotiated naval access to a number of Indian Ocean ports located variously in Myanmar, Sri Lanka, Bangladesh, Yemen, Oman, and the Seychelles.[62] New access rights at Djibouti, strategically located on the Horn of Africa, have recently drawn attention and speculation, especially since the U.S. military has operated out of Djibouti for nearly 15 years.[63]

Perhaps the most strategically located and best developed Chinese IO foothold is the deep-water port at Gwadar on the edge of Pakistan's Arabian Sea coastline across from the Strait of Hormuz. Resupply and maintenance facilities there can be expected to extend the PLAN's reach and staying power in the Indian Ocean. Gwadar is likely to serve as a catalyst for closer connections between the Chinese and Pakistani navies, as well as further cement U.S – Indian naval relations.[64]

Finally, China has undertaken steps to explore and mine the Indian Ocean seabed off the coast of Africa beyond the EEZs of the littoral states. The International Seabed Authority, established under auspices of the UNCLOS treaty, has approved China's application for rights to mine seabed minerals (often in the form of pure nodules) in a 10,000 square kilometer area in the southwest Indian Ocean. Such operations would provide the rationale for continuous Chinese naval presence in that sector of the IO.[65]

India has been increasingly concerned by China's sustained interest in the Indian Ocean and by its diplomatic and economic engagement with many littoral states. Indeed, Chinese naval operations in the Indian Ocean arguably have led directly to increased investment in India's own navy, as well as to increased cooperation between it and other Indian Ocean navies.

In 2008, New Delhi founded and hosted the Indian Ocean Naval Symposium (IONS) to foster greater interaction among the region's 35 maritime services. Subsequently, every two years, IONS has convened at different venues to coordinate efforts to promote Indian Ocean maritime security.[66]

Meanwhile, India, despite its excellent mainland ports, has developed naval facilities on its offshore islands in the Bay of Bengal – on the Andaman and Nicobar Islands strategically located near the approaches to the Strait of Malacca. Washington sees India's navy as a helpful balancer in the Indian Ocean.[67] New Delhi has been receptive to U.S. overtures for closer naval cooperation, having long since lost its Soviet naval aid and tutelage, and now concerned with Chinese naval capacity and assertiveness. Closer U.S. political and economic relations with India were well advanced before the mutually recognized benefits of closer maritime coordination began to be more seriously pursued.[68]

Admiral Harris remains hopeful regarding India's role:

> USPACOM aims to build a powerful quadrilateral partnership framework of the most powerful democracies in the Indo-Asia-Pacific. India, Japan, Australia, and the U.S. working together will be a force for the maintenance of the regional rules-based order, counterbalancing and deterring coercion and unrestrained national ambitions.[69]

Increasingly with India and Australia (both a Pacific *and* an Indian Ocean state), the United States has held combined naval exercises and developed close navy-to-navy relationships.[70]

What about other state actors in the Indo-WestPac region? Clearly China has caused resentment and alarm by its aggressive naval actions, especially among its South China Sea neighbors. The Association of Southeast Asian Nations (ASEAN) has been characteristically indecisive about taking any concerted actions, but bilateral and multilateral security agreements have resulted from China's actions, and a new willingness to accept and even invite U.S. naval presence in the area is apparent.

Japan, recently freed by its parliament from some constitutional constraints on its use of security forces, and itself the subject of Chinese bullying (in a reversal of historical roles) will be a key actor going forward. Its maritime "self-defense" force constitutes in reality a modern, well-equipped, national navy capable of combined operations with the U.S. Navy.[71] Japan's maritime self-defense force is larger than both the French and British navies and operates four huge helicopter carriers.[72]

Conclusion

Both China and the United States have *policy* and *strategy* decisions to make regarding their respective maritime postures and operations in the IO-WestPac region. So too do other regional actors. The American post-World War II role in the world, and the sets of U.S. *interests* and *objectives* discussed at the beginning of this chapter are well established and likely to remain essentially unchanged for the foreseeable future, subject to the vagaries of U.S domestic politics, clearly more problematic with the election of President Trump. How to uphold those interests and achieve those objectives is the challenge facing policy makers at a time when liberal internationalism is under assault in Washington.

China's view of its role and its strategic interests remains opaque. And North Korea's is even more so. Will China embrace a cooperative and constructive role in the region and the world? Will it choose to help curb North Korea's nuclear weapons program? Will it accede to "membership" in the established, rule-based global order, deciding that its security and its national aspirations can best be achieved in an environment of stability, peace, and predictability? Or will it continue playing the recently re-adopted role of revisionist power that seeks to reshape the strategic environment in ways more favorable to what China deems to be its proper place as a great power? Will China's economic growth, relatively tranquil domestic politics (the result of prosperity or repression?), and burgeoning naval capacity extend reliably into the future?

Will President Xi Jinping – arguably the most powerful Chinese leader since Mao Tse-tung, having himself assumed all top state and party official positions – overplay his hand? Having just won a second five-year leadership term during the 2017 Party Conference, will Xi's successful efforts in early 2018 to eliminate the constitution's two-term limit result in a domestic backlash? Can President Xi sustain the assertive Chinese nationalism and aggressive foreign policy of recent years by continuing to evoke cultural memories of imperial glory? Or will rising demands for political participation monopolize the future attention of PRC leadership, distracting it from international ambitions? All of these imponderables clearly will influence China's role in the IO-WestPac region and in the world.

Finally, it is worth noting that the future of the region is not only about the choices China makes. It is also about multilateral cooperative actions and relationships and about security institution-building – sometimes including China, sometimes counterbalancing China – to achieve peace, prosperity, and self-determination of peoples in the region. The United States has for over 70 years been an essential stabilizing actor in the IO-WestPac region whose future role is in question under the Trump Administration. A careful, nuanced course would seem to be optimal for the future – fostering cooperation when possible, confronting bad actors like North Korea when necessary; encouraging China to take its place in the sun, yet restraining it when it seeks to cast a malign shadow over U.S. interests, allies, and friends.

Notes

1. "IO-WestPac" is a more economical short-hand term for "Indo-Asia-Pacific" which is often used in official circles. It is also more accurate in describing and limiting the maritime region addressed in this essay. Finally, "IO" is often employed by Indian Ocean specialists, and "WestPac" is terminology long-used by West Coast-based American sailors. This shortened acronym will be used throughout this chapter.
2. Ironically, the degree of international order and stability maintained by robust and persistent U.S. naval presence in the Pacific for 70 years arguably has created conditions favorable to economic development of countries in the region, not least to China's explosive economic growth.
3. See, for example, Dowdy and Trood, 1985.
4. For analysis of Soviet Navy expansion during this period, see the books and articles of the late Michael K. MccGwire, the preeminent Western scholar on the subject and the first to discern the radical departure in Soviet naval strategy.
5. A small flotilla of U.S. Navy vessels, known as the Middle East Force, had conducted forward presence and naval diplomacy operations from 1949–71 in the Persian Gulf and Indian Ocean prior to the 1970s build-up. The author of this chapter served as Aide and Flag Lieutenant to Rear Admiral Ed R. King, one of the succession of Middle East Force commanders.
6. See Dowdy, 2012.
7. Campbell, 2016. The conceptual origins of the U.S. policy "pivot" toward Asia are traced to Hillary Clinton's State Department by her former Assistant Secretary for East Asia and Pacific Affairs, Kurt Campbell. In an October 2011 article in *Foreign Affairs*, Secretary of State Clinton wrote that "the United States stands at a pivot point" as it winds down the wars in Iraq and Afghanistan. "With that simple turn of phrase, the administration's Asia policy gained a name," Campbell recalls (p. 11).
8. Huxley, T. and Schreer, B., 2017. There have been persistent reports that the other 11 members of the TPP will try to sustain the organization for their mutual benefit, but also perhaps long enough for a more favorably disposed American Administration to decide to take the U.S. back into the TPP.
9. United States Government, The White House, 2015, p. 2. The Trump Administration's National Security Strategy of December 2017 was published while this chapter was in press. Its four "pillars" are very similar to Obama's four strategic interests, albeit with a more nationalistic tone and less emphasis on multilateralism. (See United States Government, The White House, 2017, pp. v–vi.)
10. See Rapp-Hooper, 2016.
11. International Institute for Strategic Studies, 2016a, pp. 156–57.
12. International Institute for Strategic Studies, 1016a, p. 157.
13. Campbell, 2016, p. 11.
14. Campbell, 2016, p. 9.
15. Campbell, 2016, p. 9.
16. Campbell, 2016, p. 9, 8, 9: content of fourth bullet point only.
17. Harris, 2016, p. 7.
18. PACOM covers by far the largest combatant command area of responsibility. It includes virtually the entire Pacific Ocean, except in the far northern latitudes, and about half of the Indian Ocean lying east of 68 degrees 34 minutes west longitude. West of that

longitude the Indian Ocean AOR is divided between the U.S. Central Command, north of 10 degrees 40 minutes south latitude, and the U.S. Africa Command, south of 10 degrees 40 minutes south latitude.
19 U.S. Department of Defense, 2015, p. 22.
20 U.S. Department of Defense, 2015, pp. 22–23.
21 U.S. Department of Defense, 2015, p. 22.
22 U.S. Department of Defense, 2015, p. 23. The FPA provides for up to 2,500 Marines.
23 U.S. Department of Defense, 2015, p. 23.
24 U.S. Department of Defense, 2015, p. 23.
25 Grady, 2016.
26 Harris, 2016.
27 For more information of the Aegis ABM system see Galdorisi and Truver, 2013.
28 Maresca, T., 2017.
29 Campbell, 2016, p. 180.
30 Harris, 2016, p. 4.
31 Campbell, 2016, p. 180.
32 Campbell, 2016, p. 182.
33 Campbell, 2016, p. 182.
34 Collison and Gaouette, 2017.
35 International Institute for Strategic Studies, 2016b, p. 130.
36 International Institute for Strategic Studies, 2016c, p. 1.
37 International Institute for Strategic Studies, 2016b, p. 131.
38 International Institute for Strategic Studies, 2016c, p. 3.
39 International Institute for Strategic Studies, 2016c, p. 1.
40 Collison and Gaouette, 2017.
41 International Institute for Strategic Studies, 2016b, pp. 140–41.
42 Comparative orders-of-naval-battle of major combatants are: PRC > 1 aircraft carrier; 61 submarines; 19 destroyers; 54 frigates; and 47 amphibious landing ships / United States > 10 aircraft carriers; 71 submarines; 22 cruisers; 62 destroyers; 4 frigates; 30 principal amphibious vessels (source: International Institute for Strategic Studies, 2016d, pp. 242–43; 41). Qualitatively, the US Navy advantage is even greater based on superior technology, operational experience, and over two centuries of modern seafaring tradition.
43 It is estimated that US$ 5.3 trillion in commerce passes though the South China Sea annually (IISS). More than half of the world's annual fleet tonnage passes through the South China Sea, as does half of global LNG trade and one third of global crude oil flows (DoD). Moreover, the U.S. Energy Information Administration estimates that the South China Sea floor could contain up to 22 billion barrels of crude oil and 290 trillion cubic feet of natural gas. See www.eia.gov/beta/international/regions-topics.cfm?RegionTopicID=SCS.
44 The 500-page Permanent Court of Arbitration report, issued July 16, 2016, was definitive in its rejection of China's claims of historical rights in the South China Sea; it ruled that China's construction of artificial islands and its abuse of fishing rights and petroleum extraction rights constituted illegal acts inside the Philippines exclusive economic zone. The United States strongly supported the Court's ruling even though UNCLOS has yet to be ratified by the U.S. Senate, an inconvenient fact undermining U.S. moral authority on law of the sea issues. (See Rapp-Hooper's discussion of these issues, 2016.)
45 The respective national territorial claims described in this paragraph were compiled from various sources, primarily, U.S. Department of Defense, 2015.
46 Information on the two FONOPS cited is taken from Huxley and Choong, 2016, p. 11 and p. 59. In addition, the aircraft carrier *USS John Stennis* and its escort ships completed three months of operations in the South China Sea in early 2016 (*USA Today*, June 29, 2016).
47 Situation Report, 2017.

48 Harris, 2016, p. 5.
49 Harris, 2016, p. 5. Chinese and Russian naval forces in September 2016 added a new complication to China's island-building activities by conducting eight days of exercises in the South China Sea reported to feature "island landing operations" (CNN, 12 Sept 2016). These and other regular naval exercises with China serve as a reminder of Russia's interests as a Pacific littoral state, though its strategic focus remains firmly on its European east.
50 Harris, 2016, p. 5.
51 Harris, 2016, p. 5.
52 See Harris, 2017, *passim* and International Institute for Strategic Studies, 2016e.
53 International Institute for Strategic Studies, 2016b, p. 7.
54 International Institute for Strategic Studies, 2016b, p. 7.
55 International Institute for Strategic Studies, 2016b, pp. 7–8, citing the views of analyst Michael D. Swaine. From the U.S. perspective, it could be argued that 70 years of American dominance in the region has allowed China and other Asian states to flourish economically in a relatively stable environment.
56 USPACOM executed over 50 bilateral, and numerous multilateral, engagements with China in 2015 according to Admiral Harris, 2016, p. 15. This official policy of engagement has drawn criticism as "appeasement" and rewarding Chinese bad behavior in the East and South China Seas (Fanell, 2016, p. 12).
57 Navy News Service, 2016a (July 18).
58 RIMPAC, hosted by the U.S. since 1971, is the largest military exercise in the world. When China participated for the first time in 2014, a total of 22 nations provided assets, including 49 surface ships, 6 submarines, and over 200 aircraft (United States Department of Defense, 2015, p. 25).
59 Japanese National Institute for Defense Studies, 2016.
60 Japanese National Institute for Defense Studies, 2016, p. 7.
61 Japanese National Institute for Defense Studies, 2016, p. 11.
62 Dowdy, 2012, pp. 13–15.
63 The U.S. base in Djibouti covers about 570 acres, has about 4,000 troops assigned, and currently has $1.4 billion of upgrades underway. The Chinese began building their "support facility" in 2016. Initially modest in size – 90 acres – it is thought to be the first of several Chinese outposts likely to be established in the Indian Ocean during the next decade. The United States in 2014 extended its Camp Lemonnier lease for 20 years at a cost of $70 million annually. Meanwhile, China's agreement with Djibouti is $20 million annually for 10 years with an option for 10 more years. The Chinese outpost will likely station only 300 troops, with a maximum potential of 2,000 (Page, 2016).
64 Khan, 2017.
65 Dowdy, 2012, pp. 16–17.
66 Dowdy, p. 20.
67 Dowdy, p. 20.
68 Pant and Joshi, 2015. Annual naval exercises were restarted by India and the United-States in 2002 with a series now code-named "Malabar." Japan participated at India's invitation in the July 2014 Malabar exercises in the Western Pacific. Moreover, Indian naval ships have been calling regularly on ports in Australia, Vietnam, and Indonesia. Despite India's naval interactions, these two analysts believe it will remain a "cautious" and "hedging" naval security partner, given domestic political constraints including the fact that the Indian navy has little political clout in a defense establishment that has been fixated on land threats to the north.
69 Harris, 2016, p. 16; see also Harris, 2017, p. 25.
70 Harris, 2016, p. 16.
71 For detailed information on Japan's naval assets and those of all IO-WestPac maritime forces, see International Institute for Strategic Studies, 2017, pp. 209–303 for Japan and various other country sections for other states *The Military Balance* is an annual

publication of IISS. See also the *International Navies* issue of U.S. Naval Institute *Proceedings* published in March each year.
72 International Institute for Strategic Studies, 2016d.

References

Campbell, K. M., 2016. *The Pivot: The Future of Statecraft in Asia*. New York: Twelve.
Cole, D. B., 2013. *Asian Maritime Strategies: Navigating Troubled Waters*. Annapolis, MD: U.S. Naval Institute Press.
Collison, S., and Gaouette, N., 2017. Donald Trump's Asia Pivot. *CNN*. 23 February.
Dombrowski, P., and Winner, A. C. eds., 2014. *The Indian Ocean and U.S. Grand Strategy*. Washington, DC: Georgetown University Press.
Dowdy, W. L., 2012. *Chinese and Indian Geopolitical Competition in the Indian Ocean Region*. Paper presented at Madrid world congress, International Political Science Association. Copy of paper available on request at wldowdy@aol.com.
Dowdy, W. L., and Trood, R. B., 1985. *The Indian Ocean: Perspectives on a Strategic Arena*. Durham, NC: Duke University Press.
Erickson, A. S., Goldstein, L. J., and Li, N. eds., 2010. *China, the United States and 21st Century Seapower: Defining a Maritime Security Partnership*. Annapolis, MD: U.S. Naval Institute Press.
Fanell, J., 2016. *Stop Engagement at All Costs*. U.S. Naval Institute Proceedings, 142(9), p. 12.
Galdorisi, G., and Truver, S., 2013. *Leading the Way in Ballistic Missile Defense*. U.S. Naval Institute Proceedings, 139(12), pp. 33–38.
Gompert, D. C., 2013. *Seapower and American Interests in the Western Pacific*. Santa Monica, CA: Rand Corporation.
Grady, J., 2016. NSC Official: U.S. India Security Relationship 'tremendous opportunity' for Next Administration. *U.S. Naval Institute News*, October 12. Available at: https://news.usni.org/2016/10/12/nsc-official-u-s-india-security-relationship-tremendous-opportunity-next-administration.
Haddick, R., 2014. *Fire on the Water: China, America, and the Future of the Pacific*. Annapolis, MD: U.S. Naval Institute Press.
Harris, Harry B., 2016. Statement before the Senate Armed Services Committee on U.S. Pacific Command Policy, (23 February 2016). *Reconfirmed* 13 October 2016. Available at: www.pacom.mil/Media/Speeches-Testimony/Article/671265/statement-before- the-senate-armed-services-committee/.
———, 2017. Statement of Harry B. Harris, Jr., U.S. Navy, Commander U.S. Pacific Command Before the House Armed Services Committee. *U.S. Pacific Command Posture*, 26 April. Available online.
Huxley, T., and Choong, W. eds., 2016. *Asia-Pacific Regional Assessment 2016*. London: The International Institute for Strategic Studies.
Huxley, T., and Schreer, B., 2017. Trump's missing Asia strategy. *Survival*, 59(3), June-July, pp. 81–89.
International Institute for Strategic Studies, 2016a. Naval-Capacity Development in the Asia- Pacific. In: *Asia-Pacific Regional Security Assessment 2016*. London: IISS.
———, 2016b. Relations Across the Taiwan Strait: Still a Major Political and Security Problem. In: *Asia-Pacific Regional Security Assessment 2016*. London: IISS.
———, 2016c. Turbulence in the Taiwan Strait. In: *IISS Strategic Comments*, August.
———, 2016d. *The Military Balance*. London: Routledge.

———, 2016e. China's Assertiveness in the South China Sea. In: *IISS Strategic Comments*, November 2016.
———, 2017. *The Military Balance*. London: Routledge.
Japan National Institute for Defense Studies, 2016. *China Security Report 2016*. Tokyo: NIDS. Available at: www.nids.go.jp.
Kaplan, R. D., 2010. *Monsoon: The Indian Ocean and the Future of American Power*. New York, NY: Random House.
———, 2015. *Asia's Cauldron: The South China Sea and the End of a Stable Pacific*. New York, NY: Random House.
Khan, M. A., 2017. Pakistan's Port is Pivotal. U.S. Naval Institute Proceedings, 143(3), March, pp. 50–54.
Lendon, B., and Hunt, K., 2016. China, Russia Begin Joint Exercises in South China Sea. *CNN*, 13 September. Available at: http://edition.cnn.com/2016/09/12/asia/china-russia-south- china sea-exercises/.
Manicom, J., 2014. *Bridging Troubled Waters: China, Japan, and Maritime Order in the East China Sea*. Washington, DC: Georgetown University Press.
Maresca, T., 2017. THAAD Frustrates Many S. Koreans. *USA Today*, 28 May.
Moran, D., and Russell, J. A. eds., 2016. *Maritime Strategy and Global Order: Markets, Resources, Security*. Washington, DC: Georgetown University Press.
Navy News Service, 2016 (July 18). *Chiefs of US and Chinese Navies Agree on Need for Cooperation*. Available at: www.navy.mil/submit/display.asp?story_id=95748.
Page, J., 2016. China Builds First Overseas Outpost. *Wall Street Journal*, 19 August online edition. Available at www.wsj.com/articles/china-builds-first-overseas-military-outpost-1471622690.
Pant, H. V., and Joshi, Y., 2015. The American "pivot" and the Indian navy: It's Hedging all the Way. *Naval War College Review*, 68(1).
Parello-Plesner, J., and Duchatel, M., 2015. *China's Strong Arm: Protecting Citizens and Assets Abroad*. New York: Routledge (for IISS Adelphi series).
Rapp-Hooper, M., 2016. Parting the South China Sea: How to Uphold the Rule of Law. *Foreign Affairs*, 95(5), pp. 76–82.
Shambaugh, D., 2013. *China Goes Global: The Partial Power*. New York: NY: Oxford University Press.
Situation Report, 25 May 2017. Setting Sail. *Foreign Policy*, online report [accessed 5 June 2017].
U.S. Naval Institute Proceedings, 2016. *International Navies Issue*, 142(3). Annapolis, MD: U.S. Naval Institute.
United States Department of Defense, 2015. *The Asia-Pacific Maritime Security Strategy: Achieving U.S. National Security Objectives*. Reconfirmed website, 13 October 2016 Available at www.defense.gov/Portals/1/Documents/pubs/NDAA%20A- P_Maritime_ SecuritY_Strategy-08142015–1300-FINALFORMAT.PDF.
United States Naval Postgraduate School, ca., 2014. *The Asia-Pacific Rebalance: Impact on U.S. Naval Strategy*. Lexington, KY: s.n.
United States Government, the White House, 2015 (Feb). *National security strategy*. Available at www.whitehouse.gov/sites/default/files/docs/2015_national_security_strategy.pdf.
United States Government, the White House, 2017 (Dec). National security strategy. Available at www.whitehouse.gov/wp-content/uploads/2017/12/NSS-Final-12-18-2017-0905.pdf.

2 China's naval strategy

Yves-Heng Lim

On May 26, 2015, the Information Office of the State Council[1] released the ninth edition of its White Paper on China's defense. Aside from noticeable variations in the title,[2] the document included a significant change for observers of the Chinese Navy. While previous editions had insisted on "the requirements of offshore defense strategy"[3] or on the PLA Navy's responsibility "for safeguarding its maritime security and maintaining its sovereignty over its territorial seas along with its maritime rights and interests",[4] the 2015 China's Military Strategy stated that "the PLA Navy (PLAN) will gradually shift its focus from 'offshore waters defense' to the combination of 'offshore waters defense' with 'open seas protection,' and build a combined, multi-functional and efficient marine combat force structure".[5] The event was not so much that Beijing had altered its position regarding the purposes of its naval forces, it had done so in the past as in the 2013 White Paper which largely read as a variation on Jintao's new historic missions. What appeared of more significance was that, in Beijing's eyes, Chinese naval forces had now to graduate from a purely local – or regional – and defensive role and look well beyond their traditional geographic horizon. As clearly put by the White Paper, however, the new oceanic role of the PLA Navy does not come as a replacement for its traditional role in the defense of the "near seas".[6] Rather, the Chinese naval forces would have, from now, to walk on two legs, each obeying its proper logic.

'Offshore water defense': China's naval posture in the Western Pacific

The origins of the first component of China's contemporary naval strategy can be traced back to a relatively precise period – the mid-1980s – and to one prominent actor – Liu Huaqing. In its first 30 years of existence, the PLA Navy had played a strictly subordinate role in the Chinese armed forces and was confined to a strategy of coastal defense[7] with its "key mission" defined as "accompany[ing] the ground forces in war actions".[8] As he ascended to the post of commander of the PLA Navy and was tasked to engineer a new naval strategy, Liu Huaqing[9] elaborated the concept of "active defense, near-seas operations". Though the first term of the new strategy was a naval variation on an old Maoist theme, Liu gave it a distinctive offensive coloratura, stating that the PLA Navy would "follow the guiding principle of responding to the enemy offensive by our own offensive".[10] The second term dramatically expanded the PLA Navy's area of operations. As reported in his Memoirs:

> In the past the PLA Navy had defined her operating zone as extending up to 200 nautical miles from the shore as "near seas". I emphasized we had to abide by the directions given by Comrade Deng Xiaoping to elaborate a unified concept of "near seas". "Near Seas" include the Yellow Sea, the East Sea, the South Sea, the Spratlys and Taiwan, the waters within and immediately beyond the Okinawa Islands chain, as well as the northern part of the Pacific Ocean.[11]

One of the major strengths of Liu Huaqing's redefinition of China's naval strategy was its flexibility, which has allowed an increasingly powerful PLA Navy to develop variations within this overarching framework. Though it found a geographical expression, the concept of near seas was not to be considered as a geographical limit. Liu explained that as "China's level of economic and technological [development] continuously improves, the power of our navy will progressively increase, and its area of naval operations will gradually expand in the Northern Pacific up to the 'second island chain'".[12] In other words, Liu anticipated that the PLA Navy would – in fact, should – expand its area of operations eastward as soon as it had the means to do so.

Recent years have reignited interest in Liu's idea as the rapid technological progress of the PLA Navy allowed the Chinese naval forces to enter the 'informationized (*xinxihua*) era'. Informationization has imposed a new set of constraints on Chinese naval forces as the PLA Navy will be able to achieve its traditional mission of defending Chinese near seas "only if it progressively enlarges the space within which China".[13] Chinese strategists have consequently adapted and expanded their views of China's naval chessboard to include "the maritime space that the enemy might use to threaten China's security militarily",[14] a considerable geographical expansion of the PLAN's area of operation if we keep in mind that Beijing views the United States – and its allies – as its most likely adversary.

In a perhaps unexpected way, the emphasis on the old Maoist motto of 'active defense' has also shown great flexibility in the naval domain over the last three decades. Here again, the flexibility of Liu's concept has proved useful for Chinese naval strategists who have seen the trend toward informationization impact the offense/defense equilibrium in a way much favorable to offense.[15] Under informationized conditions, Chinese naval forces will have to "carry out offensive operations actively" as "the destruction of enemy forces and the efficient protection of our own forces are an objective requirement to obtain the initiative in the naval theater".[16]

In addition, informationization creates new temporal constraints on operations. For at least some Chinese observers, the extraordinary power, precision and range of informationized weapons create conditions in which a first, successful offensive move could cripple an opponent to the point that it become simply unable to fight, ending the war before it even starts.[17] This creates considerable incentives to strike the enemy as early as possible and possibly preemptively. Accordingly, and still in a context where the United States remains the most likely adversary, Chinese strategists emphasize that seizing and retaining the initiative will require Chinese naval forces to strike enemy forces while on their way to the main theater of operations – i.e. East Asian waters – rather than to fight them once they are deployed.[18]

In the Western Pacific, these trends have pushed China toward an area-denial/anti-access naval doctrine. Pitted against a presumably superior power, Chinese naval forces will try to prevent opposing forces from reaching the region and dramatically degrade the combat efficiency of forces that make it through or are already present in the theater of operations. This doctrine might prove useful in a wide array of scenarios involving a Chinese use of force in the near seas.

The material and conceptual modernization of the PLA Navy has often been considered as stemming largely from China's irredentism regarding Taiwan. Should Beijing decide that the time has come for unification to be imposed on the reluctant island, it would have to make sure that the United States cannot intervene freely in a large section of the Western Pacific. Taiwan is, however, far from being the only regional scenario in which the PLA Navy might be put to use. The rise of China's assertiveness in the South China Sea and its provocative posture in the East China Sea[19] have increased the likelihood of a naval confrontation with some of China's neighbors.

Though the United States might not wish to be involved in each and every skirmish between Beijing and other East Asian players, Washington has also made clear that it would not sit on the sideline as China attempts to transform the near seas into a Chinese lake. Hillary Clinton stated in 2010 that "[t]he United States has a national interest in freedom of navigation, open access to Asia's maritime commons and respect for international law in the South China Sea",[20] and President Obama made clear four years later that the Senkaku/Diaoyutai fell within the scope of the U.S.-Japan alliance.[21] After a period of uncertainty, President Trump followed in the steps of the Obama administration, allowing Freedom of Navigation Operations in May and July 2017.[22] For China, this means that imposing Beijing's favored solution to opposing parties in the East Asian region will probably require neutralizing U.S. capacity to project forces in the East Asian theater. In this context, Beijing's preference for a naval area-denial/anti-access doctrine obviously makes sense as it maximizes Chinese chances to impede U.S. power projection.

The reengineering of China's naval doctrine would not be of much significance if it had not been accompanied by a sustained effort to develop the means allowing for its implementation. Area-denial in the near seas has long been a primary focus of the PLA Navy which has today the means to make naval operations in East Asian seas extremely difficult and risky for any opponent. China has today the largest fleet of diesel-electric submarines in the world with around 50 boats, and about 40 of them of modern design – Kilo, Song, Yuan.[23] Diesel attack submarines have an inherent advantage in what Milan Vego called "narrow seas",[24] as shorter distance diminishes the need to snorkel and the complex sound environment makes detection particularly difficult. Though the 13 Song and the 15 Yuan suffered from the relative short range of the YJ-82 anti-ship missile (ASM), it appears highly likely that they will be refitted with the brand-new YJ-18 ASM – the Chinese version of the formidable Russian *Klub* – which will literally increase their attack range ten-fold.[25] In addition, the latest generations – i.e. post-2000 – of major Chinese surface combatants[26] as well as smaller units such as the Houbei-class missile boat or the Jiangdao-class corvette – first launched in 2012[27] – are also equipped with potent, long-range ASM, and could hold at risk forces deployed within the first island chain. China might also leverage its land-based air and missile forces to deal with forces deployed within striking range. Chinese Su-30MKK2, JH-7, J-10 and J-16 – and presumably the new generation of J-20 and J-31 – are reportedly capable of delivering a wide array of high-performance anti-ship missiles of Russian and domestic designs.[28]

China has rapidly built forces that can reach beyond their relatively traditional area-denial role. The PLA Navy launched three improved Shang-class SSN in the spring 2015 which are expected to have at least partly improved their level of quietness and will likely be equipped with the abovementioned YJ-18.[29] It has also been confirmed that Yuan-class SSK have been fitted with an Air-Independent Propulsion system which significantly extends their submerged range.[30] The role of Chinese surface and air forces would be limited by their vulnerability and/or their combat radius in any confrontation beyond the near seas, but China has devoted important efforts to the development of long-range missile systems that could play a major role in an anti-access campaign. The DF-21D – a 1,500–2,000 km-range anti-ship ballistic missile – reportedly reached initial operational capability around the end of 2010[31] and a longer-range (3,000 to 4,000 km) DF-26 was put on display in the autumn 2015.[32] In parallel, China has developed a long-range anti-ship cruise missile. The 2015 ONI report confirmed that the YJ-62 also came in a 1,200-km range version and Chinese media have mentioned the existence of an anti-ship version for the CJ-10 with a potential range up to 2,500 km.[33] It is not yet clear whether China possesses the overarching architecture that is needed to support these systems, but with the rapid deployment of a vast constellation of observation and tracking satellites, Beijing is increasingly able to put together the links of a chain going from detection to strike. When put together, these 'sectorial' developments point to considerable improvements in the PLA's capacity to interdict access to the East Asian region, and to turn a sizeable part of the Western Pacific into 'contested'[34] waters.

'Open seas protection': China's naval posture in the Indian Ocean

The transformation of the PLAN into a blue-water navy has been discussed and anticipated for at least two decades.[35] Such a transformation is not tantamount to a simple geographical expansion of the PLAN's area of operation but implies a significant change in the logic of China's naval outlook. To put it simply, Beijing's need for a blue-water navy reflects what James Holmes and Toshi Yoshihara[36] termed a "turn to Mahan". Mahan's often-quoted axioms, that "[t]he necessity of a navy, in the restricted sense of the word, springs, therefore, from the existence of a peaceful shipping",[37] can be applied without much change to contemporary China. The Chinese economy has grown considerably dependent on international maritime trade routes over the last three decades and any interruption of traffic could have a disastrous impact on China's growth rate. As a result, China has a strong incentive to build a navy that could protect its sea lines of communication against potential threats.

The spectacular rise of China as the largest trading nation worldwide[38] has been accompanied by a growing dependence on oceanic trade routes – an unsurprising correlation considering that more than 80 percent of world trade is seaborne.[39] In 2014, less than 8 percent of China's foreign trade was conducted with its immediate land neighbors,[40] meaning that the remaining 92 percent had to travel by air and, mainly, by sea. In 2000, the only Chinese ports to rank in the top ten container ports worldwide were Hong Kong (1) and Shanghai (6). In 2016, seven of the ten largest container ports in the world were located in China.[41]

The sector of China's foreign trade that has attracted most attention has, naturally, been China's surging dependence on foreign oil supplies and the potential vulnerability it creates. It has taken barely two decades for China to 'rise' from self-sufficiency to a heavy addiction to foreign oil. According to the Energy Information Agency, Chinese oil imports reached the stunning figure of 6.1 million barrels per day (mbpd) in 2014[42] – which covered 60 percent of its domestic consumption – making China the largest net oil importer ahead of the United States. Of these, more than half came from Middle East and around one fifth from Africa.[43] In spite of Chinese efforts to diversify its suppliers, China's dependence on these two sources is likely to grow over the next few decades, with the OPEC forecasting a 10-mbpd gap between Chinese consumption and production in 2025 – growing to 15 mbpd in 2040 – with no obvious alternative supply available.[44] In two decades, China could have to import as much as 80 percent of the oil it needs with the largest part of this oil provided by traditional Middle Eastern and African suppliers.

The obvious problem for Beijing is that the oceanic routes travelled by tankers bound to Chinese ports are not under the control of the PLA Navy. Some relatively minor annoyance results from the existence of non-traditional actors – i.e. pirates – which sparked the dispatch of an anti-piracy flotilla to the Gulf Aden in December 2008.[45] The deployment constituted an opportunity – or a pretext – for a long-term deployment of the PLAN in the Indian Ocean. Since 2009, the PLA has maintained continuous presence in these waters – with the 23rd flotilla leaving port in April 2016.[46]

Anti-piracy and other low-intensity missions – such as the dispatch of a Jiangkai-II frigate to supervise the evacuation of Chinese nationals from Libya in 2011[47] – have undoubtedly gained salience over the last few years. However, the main focus of many Chinese strategists in the Indian Ocean remains the threat of disruption of Chinese maritime supply lines by some hostile power(s) – i.e. the United States and its allies. Chinese concerns regarding the vulnerability of seaborne supplies have been expressed under various forms. In the early 2000s, at least part of the discussions on sea power among Chinese navalists revolved around the question of "control of communications".[48]

To a certain extent, the need for a change of maritime perspective gained official endorsement by the end of 2003 when Hu Jintao coined the expression "Malacca dilemma" to depict the problematic role of the strait as a major chokepoint for Chinese oil (and trade) routes.[49] The concept has subsequently been abundantly discussed in the press and more specialized outlets.[50] Zhang Jie[51] discussed the dilemma in nightmarish scenarios – for China – observing that a shutdown of the traffic in the Malacca Strait could prove attractive for the United States under two broad sets of conditions:

> (1) The pace of China's rise is considered by the United States as a challenge to its pivotal position in the Asia-Pacific Region, and consequently the United States adopts a containment strategy against China. (2) An explosive incident occurs, for instance China faces a state of emergency in its internal affairs, i.e. if the Taiwan issue requires a solution through non-peaceful means, and the United States decides to intervene militarily in Chinese internal affairs or imposes economic sanctions.

In a book published in 2007, Wang Lidong[52] argued "the security of strategic maritime routes is related to China's supplies of strategic resources and to the construction go the Chinese economy as a whole", pointing out that "Indian Ocean maritime routes have become a lifeline for China in terms of energy supply". In this context, Wang[53] concluded, the PLAN would have to "protect key straits and maritime routes of communication" which include "some of the important international navigation routes in the Pacific and Indian Oceans".[54] An article published in 2013 in the authoritative *China Military Science* went a step farther arguing that Chinese anti-piracy operations in the Gulf of Aden suffered from the absence of Chinese bases in the region,[55] implicitly calling for the acquisition overseas basing rights. As explained in the introduction to this chapter, China's "turn to Mahan" became part of official policy, as the 2015 White Paper officially highlighted the PLAN's new mission "open seas protection".[56]

In many ways, the PLA Navy is still far from being able to gain and maintain control over distant seas. In this sense, the emergence of the PLA Navy's new missions is probably best conceived as a medium-term horizon, setting a new standard against which the progress of Chinese naval forces will be measured. The PLA Navy has nonetheless already devoted significant efforts to the development of the type of forces it will need to implement its new 'sea control' mission. China commissioned its first aircraft carrier – the *Liaoning*, ex-*Varyag* – in 2012 and a larger indigenously built Type-001A in 2017.[57] China has, at the same time, developed its "own" carrier aircraft, the J-15 – a copy of the Su-33, and PLAN Air Force pilots have been reportedly abundantly training at sea.[58] China will need to learn how to conduct complex carrier operations and current Chinese carriers do not offer the same set of possibilities, notably in terms of power projection, as current U.S. carriers.[59] However, even with these limited capabilities, Chinese carriers might be good fit for SLOCs protection as the 2015 ONI report mentioned that the *Liaoning* is "better suited to fleet air defense missions, where it could extend a protective envelope over a fleet operating in blue water".[60]

In parallel, Chinese naval forces are progressively patching their most glaring vulnerabilities. While PLAN's surface combatants suffered from a quasi-exclusive focus on anti-surface warfare for the clearest part of their history, things have begun to change around the turn of the millennium. Progress has been more noticeable in air defense capabilities. The generation of destroyers – Luyang I – and frigates – Jiangwei II – that was commissioned just before 2005 showed increased interest for capable AAW platform with the integration of reversed-engineered version of the French Crotale – the HHQ-7.[61] An even more significant step was taken with the launch of Luyang II/III and Jiangkai II frigates which have been respectively equipped with 100 km-range HHQ-9 and 30 km-range HHQ-16 SAM systems (both vertically launched), and give the PLA Navy the area air defense capability it had been lacking.[62] The clearest sign that air defense ranks high on the priority list of the Chinese navy is that both Luyang III and Jiangkai II have since been put in large-scale production.[63] China has also made progress, albeit at a more moderate pace, in anti-submarine warfare.[64] In August 2014, *Jane's Defence Weekly* reported that some of the Jiangkai II as well as some of the brand-new Type 056 corvette had been equipped with variable-depth sonars,[65] with later reports indicating that newly built Luyang III also carried VDS.[66] China ASW remains capacity limited by the weakness of its airborne ASW platforms, but in 2014, the PLA Navy acquired a new ASW-version of the Z-18 which has been integrated to the *Liaoning* air wing, though its size prevents it from being accommodated on Chinese destroyers and frigates.[67] Advanced anti-air and anti-submarine capabilities have been integrated on one single surface combatant, the latest Type-055 cruiser launched in 2017,[68] which will presumably become a pivotal part of future carrier battle groups.

On perhaps a less glamorous, but essential note, China has also significantly expanded its fleet of supply ships – part of which was on display during anti-piracy operations conducted in the Gulf of Aden and in the waters east of Somalia. Six improved Fuchi-class replenishment ships have been launched since 2012.[69] In December 2015, *Jane's Defence Weekly* reported that a new class of very large supply ship – 45,000–50,000 tons – was under construction. The first Type-901, which appears tailor-made for refueling aircraft carriers, was built in record time and joined the PLA Navy in December 2015.[70]

Finally, China has lifted the veil on its actual ambitions regarding overseas basing. Beijing obtained a first link for its 'maritime road' in early 2016, as it confirmed that it had reached an agreement with Djibouti.[71] Whether this evolves into a rekindled version of the "string of pearls"[72] in the Indian Ocean region remains to be seen, but China's activism along its 'maritime road' suggests that the Djibouti deal is only the first piece of a much larger puzzle. Neither the development of new, more capable warships nor the rapid build-up of a fleet of support and supply ships, nor even the opening of overseas naval infrastructures or bases mean that China would be a peer competitor to the U.S. Navy any time soon – if only because having all the pieces of the puzzle is not the same thing as actually putting them together. But when considered from a broader perspective, these elements suggest quite clearly that China has decided to acquire the means to further the expansion of its naval ambitions in the Indo-Pacific region.

Conclusion

Recent developments in China's naval strategy and forces unambiguously reflect Beijing's growing and changing maritime ambitions. They, however, also add to the already abundant set of dilemmas faced by the PLA. China's attempt to make its navy walk on two legs – anti-access/area-denial in the near seas and sea control in the far seas – creates two objectives that might become difficult to reconcile. Though one might arguably hypothesize that China has recently raised 'open seas protection' as a priority of the PLAN because it is already satisfied with its ability to achieve 'offshore water defense' in East Asian waters, it remains quite probable that the enormous requirements imposed by the build-up of a truly 'blue-water' navy will put the A2/AD objectives – and forces – under increased pressure – a thorny carrier vs. ASBM trade-off to somewhat caricature the dilemma. This appears even more likely when one takes into consideration the kind of challenges and adversaries – i.e. the U.S. Navy and India playing in its own maritime backyard – China will face in its efforts to control its sea lines of communication. In this sense, the next strategic hurdle that China has delineated for its own naval forces is significantly higher than those the PLA Navy cleared over the last two decades, making China's turn to Mahan a challenge for the future rather than a short-term achievable objective.

Notes

1 Information Office of the State Council, 2015.
2 White papers from 1998 to 2010 bear the title "China's National Defense", the one published in 2013 was entitled "The Diversified Employment of China's Armed Forces", and the last version to date has been renamed "China's Military Strategy".
3 Information Office of the State Council, 2011.
4 Information Office of the State Council, 2013.
5 Information Office of the State Council, 2015.
6 Li, 2011.
7 Cole, 2010.
8 Xiao Jingguang quoted in Kondapalli, 2001.
9 Liu Huaqing, 2007, p. 434.
10 Ibid.
11 Ibid.
12 Liu Huaqing, 2007, p. 437.
13 Tang, Wang and Wang, 2011, p. 36.
14 Huo, 2006, p. 242.
15 Zhang, Liu and Xia, 2010, p. 50.
16 Zhang, Yu and Zhou, 2006, p. 97.
17 Zhang, Liu and Xia, 2010.

18 Zhang, Yu and Zhou, 2006, p. 97.
19 Yahuda, 2013; Roy, 2015; Tiezzi, 2015.
20 Hillary Clinton quoted in Landler, 2010.
21 Panda, 2014.
22 Panda, 2017, Valencia, 2017.
23 International Institute for Strategic Studies 2016. The Yuan class – of which a second AIP version has been introduced – is still in production.
24 Vego, 2003; Vego, 2010.
25 Office of Naval Intelligence, 2015.
26 As of early 2016, this included four Sovremenny, two Luzhou and ten Luyang-class destroyers as well as ten Jiangwei II and twenty-two Jiangkai-class frigates (IISS, 2016).
27 Tate, 2016a.
28 Jackson, 2012.
29 Gady, 2015. The improved version of the Shang has a vertical launching system which will allow it to carry larger, longer-range missiles.
30 Department of Defense, 2013.
31 Collins and Erickson, 2016.
32 Erickson, 2015.
33 Office of Naval Intelligence, 2015; Xu, 2013.
34 Posen, 2003.
35 Yung, 1996.
36 Holmes and Yoshihara, 2007, see also Kane, 2002.
37 Mahan, 2007, p. 26.
38 In 2014, China ranked first among exporters accounting for 12,3% of total world exports, and second among importers – behind the United States – for a share of 10,2% of total world imports (World Trade Organization, 2015).
39 United Nations Conference on Trade and Development, 2015.
40 National Bureau of Statistics of China, 2014.
41 World Shipping Council, 2016.
42 Energy Information Agency, 2016.
43 Energy Information Agency, 2016.
44 Organization of the Petroleum Exporting Countries, 2014, p. 73.
45 Erickson, 2010.
46 *People's Daily*, 2016.
47 Collins and Erickson, 2011.
48 Zhen and Liu, 2002; Wang, 2002; Huang, 2003.
49 Storey, 2006.
50 Zhang, 2005; *People's Daily*, 2004; China Daily, 2004.
51 Zhang, 2005, p. 23.
52 Wang, 2007, p. 183.
53 Wang, 2007, p. 189.
54 Wang, 2007, p. 261; Xu, 2004.
55 Liu, 2013, p. 151.
56 Information Office of the State Council, 2015.
57 Dominguez, 2017.
58 Majumdar, 2015.
59 Office of Naval Intelligence, 2015; Majumdar, 2016. China's second carrier seems to have also adopted a ski-jump design which limits the payload that can be carried by onboard aircraft.
60 Office of Naval Intelligence, 2015, p. 23.
61 Cordesman, Hess and Yarosh, 2013, p. 168; O'Rourke, 2016, pp. 30–35.
62 The HHQ-9 has a reported maximal range of 55 nm (80 nm for some versions according to IISS estimates), against 40 nom for the HHQ-16 (Office of Naval Intelligence

2015, p. 15). China's Luyang II has sometimes been dubbed "Chinese Aegis" (O'Rourke, 2016, p. 31; International Institute for Strategic Studies, 2016, p. 225).
63 This contrast sharply with the approach adopted in the 1990s and 2000s when China experimented with different designs and built only a couple of units of each type of large surface combatants. As of early 2016, China has built six Luyang II and at least two Luyang III with ten more of the latest expected by the end of 2018. Twenty Jiangkai II have been built and four more are expected (O'Rourke, 2016; International Institute for Strategic Studies, 2016).
64 Goldstein, 2015.
65 Tate, 2014a. Eighteen Type-056 corvettes had been commissioned as of early 2016 (International Institute for Strategic Studies, 2016) but as many as 60 could be built in the next few years (Department of Defense, 2016, p. 27).
66 Tate, 2016b.
67 Tate, 2014b.
68 Tate, 2017.
69 Dominguez, 2016. The PLA Navy deployed two 20,500-ton Fuchi-class AOR in the early 2000s. The new version appears 15% larger (Erickson and Carlson, 2016).
70 Tate, 2015; Erickson and Carlson, 2016.
71 Tiezzi, 2016.
72 Holmes, 2014.

References

Chen D., and Shi, Y., 2016. Zhongguo Haijun di Ershisan Pai Huhuang Biandui Fu Yadingwan Tuzhong Kaizhan Fanhaidao Yanlian [The 23rd escort flotilla sails to the Gulf of Aden to carry out antipiracy drills]. *People's Daily* [online]. Available at: http://fj.people.com.cn/n2/2016/0412/c350372-28129589.html [accessed 15 August 2016].

Cole, C., 2010. *The Great Wall at Sea: China's Navy in the Twenty-First Century*. 2nd ed. Annapolis: Naval Institute Press.

Collins G., and Erickson, A. S., 2011. Missile Frigate Xuzhou Transits Suez Canal, to Arrive off Libya ~Wednesday 2 March. *China SignPost* [online]. Available at: www.chinasignpost.com/2011/02/28/missile-frigate-xuzhou-transits-suez-canal-to-arrive-off-libya-wednesday-2-march-chinas-first-operational-deployment-to-mediterranean-addresses-libyas-evolving-security-situation/ [accessed 15 August 2016].

———, 2016. China Deploys World's First Long-Range, Land-Based 'Carrier Killer': DF-21D Anti-Ship Ballistic Missile (ASBM) Reaches 'Initial Operational Capability (IOC). *China SignPost* [online]. Available at: www.chinasignpost.com/2010/12/26/china-deploys-worlds-first-long-range-land-based-carrier-killer-df-21d-anti-ship-ballistic-missile-asbm-reaches-initial-operational-capability-ioc/ [accessed 15 August 2016].

Cordesman, A. H., Hess, A., and Yarosh, N. S., 2013. *Chinese Military Modernization and Force Development: A Western Perspective*. Washington, DC: CSIS.

Department of Defense. *Annual Report to Congress: Military and Security Developments Involving the People's Republic of China 2013* [online]. Available at: www.defense.gov/pubs/2013_China_Report_FINAL.pdf [accessed 15 August 2016].

———, *Annual Report to Congress: Military and Security Developments Involving the People's Republic of China 2016* [online]. Available at: www.defense.gov/Portals/1/Documents/pubs/2016%20China%20Military%20Power%20Report.pdf [accessed 15 August 2016].

Dominguez, G., 2016. Two New Supply Ships Join China's South Sea Fleet. *Jane's Defence Weekly* [online]. Available at: https://janes.ihs.com/Janes/Display/1774091 [accessed 15 August 2016].

———, 2017. China Launches First Indigenously Built Aircraft Carrier. *Jane's Defence Weekly* [online]. Available at: https://janes.ihs.com/Janes/Display/jdw65486-jdw-2017 [accessed 12 August 2017].

Energy Information Administration, 2016. *China* [online]. Washington, DC. Available at www.eia.gov/beta/international/analysis.cfm?iso=CHN [accessed 15 August 2016].

Erickson, A. S., 2010. Chinese Sea Power in Action: The Counter Piracy Mission in the Gulf of Aden and Beyond. In: R. Kamphausen, D. Lai and A. Scobell, eds., *The PLA at Home and Abroad*. Carlisle: US Army War College, pp. 295–376.

———, 2015. Showtime: China Reveals Two 'carrier-killer' Missiles. *The National Interest* [online]. Available at: http://nationalinterest.org/feature/showtime-china-reveals-two-carrier-killermissiles-13769 [accessed 15 August 2016].

Erickson, A. S., and Carlson, C., 2016. Sustained Support: The PLAN Evolves its Expeditionary Logistics Strategy. *Jane's Navy International* [online]. Available at: https://janes.ihs.com/Janes/Display/1764589 [accessed 15 August 2016].

Gady, F.-S., 2015. China's 'new' Carrier-Killer Subs. *The Diplomat* [online]. Available at: http://thediplomat.com/2015/04/chinas-new-carrier-killer-subs/ [accessed 15 August 2016].

Goldstein, L. J., 2015. A Frightening Thought: China Erodes America's Submarine Advantage. *The National Interest* [online]. Available at: http://nationalinterest.org/feature/frightening-thought-china-erodes-americas-submarine-13592?page=3 [accessed 15 August 2016].

Holmes, J. R., 2014. China Could Still Build 'String of Pearls'. *The Diplomat* [online]. Available at: http://thediplomat.com/2014/11/china-could-still-build-string-of-pearls/ [accessed 15 August 2016].

Holmes, J. R., and Yoshihara, T., 2007. *Chinese Naval Strategy in the 21st Century: The Turn to Mahan*. London: Routledge.

Huang, J., 2003. Lun Xiandai Zhihaiquan [On Modern Mastery of the Seas]. *Zhongguo Junshi Kexue*, 16(2), pp. 23–29.

Huo, X., 2006. *Junzhong Zhanlue Xue* [Science of Armed Services Strategy]. Beijing: National Defense University Press.

Information Office of the State Council, 2011. *China's National Defense* [online]. Available at www.china.org.cn/government/whitepaper/node_7114675.htm [accessed 15 August 2016].

———, 2013. *The Diversified Employment of China's Armed Forces* [online]. Available at www.china.org.cn/government/whitepaper/node_7181425.htm, [accessed 15 August 2016].

———, 2015. *China's Military Strategy* [online]. Available at: www.china.org.cn/china/2015-05/26/content_35661433.htm [accessed 15 August 2016].

International Institute for Strategic Studies, 2016. *The Military Balance 2016*. London: Routledge.

Jackson, P., 2012. *Jane's All the World's Aircraft*. Surrey: Jane's Information Group.

Kane, T. M. 2002. *Chinese Grand Strategy and Maritime Power*. London: Frank Cass.

Kondapalli, S., 2001. *China's Naval Power*. New Delhi: Knowledge World.

Landler, M., 2010. Offering to Aid Talks, U.S. Challenges China on Disputed Islands. *The New York Times* [online]. Available at: www.nytimes.com/2010/07/24/world/asia/24diplo.html?_r=0 [accessed 15 August 2016].

Li, N., 2011. The Evolution of China's Naval Strategy and Capabilities: From 'Near Coast' and 'Near Seas' to 'Far Seas'. In: P. C. Saunders, C. D. Yung, M. Swaine, and A. N.

Yang, eds., *The Chinese Navy: Expanding Capabilities, Evolving Roles*. Washington, DC: National Defense University Press, pp. 109–140.

Liu, F., 2004. Nengyuan Anquan Zaoyu 'Maliujia Kunju' Zhong Ri Han Nengfou Xieshou? [Can China, Japan and Korea work hand in hand to solve the energy security issue posed by the 'Malacca Dilemma'? *People's Daily* [online]. Available at: www.people.com.cn/BIG5/guoji/14549/2570978.html [accessed 15 August 2016].

Liu, H., 2007. *Liu Huaqing Huiyilu* [Memoirs of Liu Huaqing]. Beijing: People's Liberation Army Press.

Liu, X., 2013. Dili Juli, Juli Shuijian Guilu yu Haiwai Junshi Jidi [Geographical Distance, Law of Distance Attenuation and Overseas Military Bases]. *Zhongguo Junshi Kexue*, 26(3), pp. 144–152.

Mahan, A. T. 2007. *The Influence of Sea Power Upon History*. New York: Cosimo Classics.

Majumdar, D., 2015. Exposed: China's J-15 Flying Sharks Train Onboard Carrier Liaoning. *The National Interest* [online]. Available at: http://nationalinterest.org/blog/the-buzz/exposed-chinas-j-15-flying-sharks-train-onboard-carrier-14764 [accessed 15 August 2016].

———, 2016. China's Aircraft Carriers: The Ultimate Paper Tiger? *The National Interest* [online]. Available at: http://nationalinterest.org/blog/the-buzz/chinas-aircraft-carriers-the-ultimate-paper-tiger-15415 [accessed 15 August 2016].

National Bureau of Statistics of China, 2014. *China Statistical Yearbook 2014* [online]. Available at: www.stats.gov.cn/tjsj/ndsj/2014/indexeh.htm [accessed 15 August 2016].

Office of Naval Intelligence, 2015. *The PLA Navy: New Capabilities and Missions for the 21st Century* [online]. Available at: www.oni.navy.mil/Intelligence_Community/china_media/2015_PLA_NAVY_PUB_Interactive.pdf [accessed 15 August 2016].

Organization of the Petroleum Exporting Countries, 2014. *2014 World Oil Outlook* [online]. Available at: www.opec.org/opec_web/static_files_project/media/downloads/publications/WOO_2014.pdf [accessed 15 August 2016].

O'Rourke, R. 2016. *China Naval Modernization: Implications for U.S. Navy Capabilities* [online]. Available at: www.fas.org/sgp/crs/row/RL33153.pdf [accessed 15 August 2016].

Panda, A., 2014. Obama: Senkakus Covered Under US-Japan Security Treaty. *The Diplomat* [online]. Available at: http://thediplomat.com/2014/04/obama-senkakus-covered-under-us-japan-security-treaty/ [accessed 15 August 2016].

———, 2017. The US Navy's First Trump-Era South China Sea FONOP Just Happened: First Takeaways and Analysis. *The Diplomat* [online]. Available at: http://thediplomat.com/2017/05/the-trump-administrations-first-south-china-sea-fonop-is-here-first-takeaways-and-analysis/ [accessed 12 August 2017].

Posen, B., 2003. Command of the Commons. *International Security*, 28(1), pp. 5–46.

Roy, D., 2015. China Is Playing Offense, Not Defense, in the South China Sea. *The Diplomat* [online]. Available at: http://thediplomat.com/2015/06/china-is-playing-offense-not-defense-in-the-south-china-sea/ [accessed 15 August 2016].

Storey, I. 2006. China's 'Malacca Dilemma, *China Brief* [online]. Available at: www.jamestown.org/programs/chinabrief/single/?tx_ttnews%5Btt_news%5D=31575&no_cache=1 [accessed 15 August 2016].

Tang, F., Wang, Q., and Wang, Y., 2011. Zhongguo Gongchangdang Lingdao Renmin Haijun Jianshe Fazhan Qiben Jingyan [Basic experience in building, the People's Navy led by the Communist Party of China]. *Zhongguo Junshi Kexue*, 24(3), pp. 27–37.

Tate, A., 2014a. China Adding Towed Sonars to Type 054A, Type 056 Vessels. *Jane's Defence Weekly* [online]. Available at: https://janes.ihs.com/Janes/Display/1720934 [accessed 15 August 2016].

———, 2014b. China Unveils ASW Version of Z-18 Helicopter. *IHS Jane's 360* [online]. Available at: https://janes.ihs.com/Janes/Display/1720122 [accessed 15 August 2016].

———, 2015. New PLAN Replenishment Ship Type Emerges. *IHS Jane's 360* [online]. Available at: https://janes.ihs.com/Janes/Display/1757711 [accessed 15 August 2016].

———, 2016a. PLAN Commissions 25th Type 056 Corvette. *IHS Jane's 360* [online]. Available at: www.janes.com/article/58289/plan-commissions-25th-type-056-corvette [accessed 15 August 2016].

———, 2016b. Fourth Type 052D Destroyer Joins China's South Sea Fleet. *Jane's Defence Weekly* [online]. Available at: https://janes.ihs.com/Janes/Display/1773887 [accessed 15 August 2016].

———, 2017. Assessing the Capabilities of China's Type 055 Destroyer. *Jane's Defence Weekly* [online]. Available at: https://janes.ihs.com/Janes/Display/jdw66480-jdw-2017 [accessed 12 August 2017].

Tiezzi, S., 2015. Japan: China Sent Armed Coast Guard Vessel Near Disputed Islands. *The Diplomat* [online]. Available at: http://thediplomat.com/2015/12/japan-china-sent-armed-coast-guard-vessel-near-disputed-islands/ [accessed 15 August 2016].

———, 2016. China Has 'Reached Consensus' With Djibouti on Military Base. *The Diplomat* [online]. Available at: http://thediplomat.com/2016/01/china-has-reached-consensus-with-djibouti-on-military-base/ [accessed 15 August 2016].

United Nations Conference on Trade and Development, 2015. *Review of Maritime Transport 2015* [online]. Available at: http://unctad.org/en/PublicationsLibrary/rmt2015_en.pdf [accessed 15 August 2016].

Valencia, M., 2017. US FONOPs in the South China Sea: Intent, Effectiveness, and Necessity. *The Diplomat* [online]. Available at: http://thediplomat.com/2017/07/us-fonops-in-the-south-china-sea-intent-effectiveness-and-necessity/ [accessed 12 August 2017].

Vego, M., 2003. *Naval Strategy and Operations in Narrow Seas*. London: Frank Cass.

———, 2010. The Right Submarine for Lurking in the Littorals. *US Naval Institute Proceeding* [online]. Available at www.usni.org/magazines/proceedings/2010–06/right-submarine-lurking-littorals [accessed 15 August 2016].

Wang, L., 2007. *Guojia Haishang Liyi Lun* [On National Maritime Interests]. Beijing: Guofang Daxue Chubanshe.

Wang, W., 2002. Shi Zhi Jiaotongquan? Haishi Zhi Wuliuquan? [Domination of Traffic or Domination of Flow of Materials]. *Zhongguo Junshi Kexue*, 15(3), pp. 133–134.

World Shipping Council, 2016. *Top 50 World Container Ports* [online]. Available at: www.worldshipping.org/about-the-industry/global-trade/top-50-world-container-ports [accessed 15 August 2016].

World Trade Organization, 2015. *International Trade Statistics 2015* [online]. Available at: www.wto.org/english/res_e/statis_e/its2015_e/its15_world_trade_dev_e.pdf [accessed 15 August 2016].

Xu, D., 2004. Zhongguo Shiyou Maliujia Zhi Kun: Zuida de Wexie bu shi Haidao Chanjue ['Malacca Dilemma' and Chinese oil supplies: the greatest threat is not rampant piracy]. *China Daily* [online]. Available at: www.chinadaily.com.cn/gb/focus/2004-07/23/content_351070.html [accessed 15 August 2016].

Xu, L., 2013. Zhe jiu shi Changjian-10 Xunhang Daodan Zhenrong? [So this is what the CJ-10 really looks like?]. *Huanqiu* [online]. Available at: http://mil.huanqiu.com/photo_china/2013-03/2686083.html [accessed 15 August 2016].

Yahuda, M., 2013. China's New Assertiveness in the South China Sea. *The Journal of Contemporary China*, 22(81), pp. 446–459.

Yung, C. D., 1996. *People's War at Sea: Chinese Naval Power in the Twenty-First Century* [online]. Available at: www.dtic.mil/cgi-bin/GetTRDoc?AD=ADA306680 [accessed 15 August 2016].

Zhang, J., 2005. Zhongguo Nengyuan Anquan Zhong de Maliujia Yinsu [The Malacca factor in China's energy security]. *Guoji Zhengzhi Yanjiu*, 2005(3), pp. 18–27.

Zhang, Y., Liu, S., Xia, C., 2010. Lun Xinxihua Zhanzheng de Zhanju Kongzhi Yishu [On the art of controlling war situations in informationized warfare]. *Zhongguo Junshi Kexue*, 23(2), pp. 24–31.

Zhang Y., Yu S., and Zhou X., 2006. *Zhanyi Xue* [Military Campaign Studies]. Beijing: National Defense University Press.

Zhen Z., and Liu, C., 2002. 'Zhi Jiaotongquan' Lilun Yanjiu Taohui Zongshu [Summary of the Symposium on 'Control of Communication]. *Zhongguo Junshi Kexue*, 15(1), pp. 145–148.

3 Russian maritime strategy since the Ukrainian crisis

Alexandr Burilkov

The state of Russian maritime strategy

Relations between the West and Russia have markedly deteriorated since 2014 as a result of the annexation of Crimea, the war in Ukraine, Western sanctions, Russian intervention in Syria, and perceived interference in electoral processes in the U.S. as well as a number of EU states. Despite near-constant decline in capabilities since the end of the Soviet Union, Russia remains a significant naval power, second by tonnage after the U.S. and third in number of ships after the U.S. and China, though the Navy is geographically dispersed.[1] The Russian Navy has been involved in several high-profile actions since 2014. The resupply of Russian forces in the Syrian conflict has been the most prominent example of power projection, but Russian antagonism in the North Sea and the Baltic is particularly relevant for NATO's European member states, especially the newer Eastern members.[2] The election of President Trump in 2016 has not particularly altered the Russian naval calculus, and even the first meeting between Trump and Putin, in July 2017 at the G20 in Hamburg, is unlikely to do so, despite discussion of cooperation on security issues such as cybersecurity. In practical terms, the Trump presidency has not substantively altered the course of U.S. foreign policy in the areas considered vital to Russia, such as the sanctions, the Ukrainian question, or American commitment to collective security in Europe through NATO. As the Russians are very unlikely to unilaterally commit to de-escalation, the course of Russian naval strategy will continue regardless of the transfer of power in Washington.

Nonetheless, this naval assertiveness should be put in the context of the greater Russian strategy and distinctly Russian strategic thought, whereby all assets – land, air, naval, space, cyber, political, cultural, and economic – are deployed in concord in order to achieve greater political goals.[3] Under the current Putin regime, these goals focus on the removal of the sanctions for the Crimean annexation in the short term, and in the longer term the mitigation of foreign influence in regions Russia sees as part of its sphere of influence, including parts of Eastern Europe, the Caucasus, and Central Asia. Given these goals, and the relatively pragmatic and ideology-free nature of the regime, a sober assessment of Russian strategy and foreign policy would indicate that apocalyptic assessments of massive Russian aggression – especially against NATO members – that would lead to widespread interstate war are overstated, as it would not contribute to the political goals of the regime. However, what remains highly likely is limited armed aggression against weaker, diplomatically isolated states such as Georgia and Ukraine, and political and military pressure against the current world order that seeks to exploit existing internal and international cleavages without resorting to direct armed confrontation; this strategy is significantly more difficult to deter than conventional armed conflict.[4]

Prior to 2014, Russian strategy was a changing and modernizing concept that sought to modify the old Soviet doctrine of bastion defense, focused solely on NATO as adversary, especially in the Atlantic, where the disruption of American assistance to European NATO states was essential. As this modernizing movement receded, the Soviet strategy of bastion defense is once again essential to understanding Russian strategic thought.[5] It draws on a long tradition of innovative strategies of land powers seeking to arm their navies against maritime rivals, such as Germany during both World Wars and France in the nineteenth century when faced with superior British seapower. The common element remains the struggle against a superior maritime power through the clever use of denial of command of the sea.[6]

After the end of the Cold War and the long twilight of the nineties, Russian maritime strategy sought to diversify in order to better address non-state threats and challenges such as terrorism and piracy, as well as an attendant modernization of the byzantine Soviet procurement system to a modern and Westernized system of modular and flexible shipbuilding. This was exemplified by the sought acquisition of two French *Mistral* amphibious assault ships and the development of the Western-style *Steregushchy* frigate. Concurrently the core of the navy, the ballistic missile submarines and missile-armed ships were to be modernized. As remains typical in post-Soviet Russian procurement, these plans were undermined by corruption at all levels as well as pernicious technical problems, likely the result of the severe brain drain that affected the entirety of the post-Soviet space; nothing exemplifies this better than the continued failure of the Bulava SLBM program, which performs very inconsistently in trials.[7] Ultimately, the reforms, though modest, aimed to preserve Russian seapower, still based on missile-armed surface ships, submarines, and long-range naval aviation, while expanding capabilities to that of a true blue-water fleet able to conduct the missions that compose the bulk of missions undertaken and emphasized by notable Western navies.

As a result of the breakdown of relations between Russia and the NATO members after 2014, and the severe economic strain faced by the Russian government, naval planning was forced to undergo structural changes. The *Mistral* deal with France fell through. Resources were diverted to the Strategic Rocket Forces, the "vital shield of the nation", and to the land and security forces, more adept in the hybrid warfare dreamed up – or perhaps recovered from history – by Putin's strategists and "political technologists."[8] Even as the Kremlin argued that Sevastopol was enough of a vital naval base to annex Crimea over, it quietly subordinated the Navy again to the demands of a continental strategy, much as in the Soviet years. Nonetheless, the Navy does retain a place and function in the current incarnation of the new Russia, especially if it can contribute to hybrid warfare, a strategy "that blends conventional warfare, irregular warfare and cyberwarfare, and by combining kinetic operations with subversive efforts, the aggressor intends to avoid attribution or retribution." This strategy was used to great effect in the opening stages of the conflict in Ukraine, when "little green men" appeared in Crimea, followed by a rigged referendum and the explosion of violence in the east; as propaganda is central to this strategy, the precise application of military power can have effects all out of proportion, and seapower is no exception. One may ask what differentiates hybrid warfare from the gunboat diplomacy of the nineteenth century. The key difference lies in the scope of the strategy. Whereas gunboat diplomacy, as advocated and implemented by the European Great Powers, was a highly limited and purely military affair devoid of a covert aspect and thus openly conducted by states, hybrid warfare is a strategy that is distinctly Russian in that it is a holistic approach that exploits all possible means and treats the military as an extension of the greater political and informational narrative, and furthermore, seeks to conceal and deny the involvement of the state conducting it in order to create as much uncertainty and confusion as possible.

Furthermore, domestic developments play a crucial role in determining the course of Russian strategy. As the regime slides further into autocracy, following Putin's repressive response to the 2011 protests, the pretense of "managed" or "sovereign" democracy, maintained during the boom years of the early 2000s, sloughs away, replaced by the charismatic authority and authoritarianism of Putin alone. Thus, as is the case in every autocratic regime, the primary objective of any action by the regime becomes first and foremost the survival of the regime. Every foreign and domestic input is filtered by the perception that the survival of the regime is under threat.[9]

In Russia, this is worsened by the sanctions that have hit ordinary Russians hard. In order to prevent mass mobilization against the regime, the Kremlin has deployed a hodgepodge of concepts from political technology to shore up its legitimacy. The most obvious is the promotion of militarism and the garrison state, wherein it is argued that Russia is threatened abroad by nefarious Western plots and encirclement, and at home by fifth columnists that seek to sabotage the functions of the state and to subvert ordinary Russians into color revolutionaries.[10] As a result, the regime demands loyalty to the state in exchange for militarism abroad that is perceived to restore the power of Russia and avenge the collapse of the Soviet Union; however, outright ethnic Russian nationalism is discouraged in favor of a nebulous concept that is supposed to be traditionalist and conservative. After all, ethnic nationalism would threaten the fragile relations between ethno-religious groups in multicultural Russia, especially in volatile Chechnya, but also in the government itself, where non-Russians occupy posts all the way up to Defense Minister Sergey Shoygu, a Tuvan Buddhist. As a complement, the regime has also been very successful in spreading cynicism and depoliticized apathy in the Russian population, which are more readily accepted than vague conservatism; as a result of these seemingly contradictory trends, support for Putin remains high, and is likely to continue as long as the Kremlin engages in military adventurism abroad and the domestic economic situation does not rapidly deteriorate even further.

Ultimately, Russian strategy today has two fundamental objectives. The first is the preservation of the territorial integrity of Russia; Russian documents identify NATO as the greatest threat. This is a conventional objective, and is to be achieved by the application of the bastion defense strategy, centered on submarines, aircraft, missiles, and defensive surface ships.[11] The second objective is power projection, meaning the spread of Russian influence abroad through several elements. The ideational element is the promotion of a "Russian world", a civilization apart from either East or West, and with alternative values to the liberal status quo.[12] Another element relies on basing on foreign soil and support for military missions abroad. In the Russian case, this element is rather limited, centering on maintaining its sole base in Syria and its participation in the Syrian conflict. Yet another element is military to military cooperation through naval exercises (particularly with India and China) and the export of military technology. Here Russia is very active, as it remains the second largest arms exporter globally, and is the source of choice for advanced military technology for states that do not wish to, or cannot, entirely rely on Western arms exports. The final element is the concept of hybrid warfare. Much as in the case of China's operations in the South China Sea, which are aimed at intimidating the Southeast Asian states so that they do not contest the Chinese bid for hegemony, Russian maritime hybrid warfare aims to intimidate smaller peripheral states into inaction, and to fracture Western alliance and economic systems (NATO and EU). This approach is thought to be much more cost-effective and far less risky than force projection by strength at arms, and is intimately tied to the greater narrative of a struggle against the existing world order that is promoted by government-backed Russian media at home and abroad.[13]

The sources of Russian maritime strategy

Russian maritime strategy is formalized in the *National Security Strategy* and the *Military Doctrine*, which dictates rapid increases in military spending, especially for the Strategic Rocket Forces and the Navy. These documents identify the U.S. and NATO as the primary threat to Russia, both due to perceived encirclement, which limits the capacity of Russia to operate in the former Soviet sphere of influence, and also due to political meddling in the form of the dreaded color revolutions. However, internal issues, which also include terrorism and instability in the Caucasus, are to be dealt with by the new National Guard, an organization that fuses the various internal troops of the MVD and the security services. The safeguarding of Russian territorial integrity thus falls to the military, and the Navy has the crucial role of safeguarding the maritime borders and of carrying out the vital mission of deterrence through nuclear submarines, one arm of the Russian nuclear triad.

There are however debates regarding the nature of strategy – the modernized blue-water approach vs. the traditional Soviet approach – and the purpose of strategy in the Russian elite and leadership. The purpose of strategy is particularly varied, as it touches upon broader foreign policy goals. The best way to uncover these differences is by examining the various factions active in the Kremlin, and their fortunes and stance since 2014.[14] This is the "power vertical," whereby political power was centralized under Putin, and various small elite factions compete for their particular vision of policy to be implemented at the top.[15] These factions uniformly consist of members that both function within government but also have extensive business interests, and have for the most part displaced the oligarchs that dominated the Russian economy in the 1990s. Furthermore, no faction at the Kremlin (or in the sanctioned opposition parties in the Duma) would advocate for full liberal democracy.[16]

The hardliner faction, exemplified by Defense Minister Shoygu, is the most direct descendant of the mainstream Soviet government. It draws its supporters from the security services, especially the military and the FSB. They advocate a pragmatic policy to augment Russian power and avenge the collapse of the USSR, without any particular attachment to ideologies other than state power.[17] This particular faction has always been influential at the Kremlin, and since 2011 and the growth of autocracy, its influence has only increased, as it advocates a hard line towards NATO, though it would not seek direct armed confrontation under normal circumstances. This is exemplified in their approach to the Ukrainian conflict. The rebels in the DNR and LNR have been supported just enough to survive, but nowhere near enough to bring a successful conclusion to the Novorossiya project dreamed up by Russian ethno-nationalists; in fact, the security services seem to have used the crisis as a convenient way to rid themselves of troublesome far-right groups in Russia by encouraging them to go fight in Ukraine.

The antithesis of the hardliners is the technocratic faction, nominally headed by Prime Minister Medvedev, and centered on younger businesspeople from St. Petersburg with little to no experience of Soviet times. This faction supports economic development and liberalization in the mold of the Chinese model of state capitalism; furthermore, it supported the kind of "managed democracy" that was the norm in the early 2000s, as well as cautious rapprochement with the West. However, the darker recent times have made the security services ascendant, and this faction has lost some of the limited favor it previously enjoyed. Its main interest would be to end the sanctions, as these threaten the cozy business relationships that developed between Western and Russian elites, often at the expense of ordinary Russians, but its influence is limited to formulating economic policies that would allow Russia to stay afloat despite sanctions and tough times, and the faction has very little influence on strategic matters.

A minor faction, centered on a number of very wealthy oligarchs, such as former chairman of the state railways Yakunin, may best be defined as the "Orthodox" faction. This faction combines wealth with the promotion, through both state and non-state channels, of a very conservative vision for Russian society, based on ethnic Russian nationalism and the promotion of conservative Orthodox Christianity; this faction was the most enthusiastic supporter of the Novorossiya project within the Kremlin, as it saw it as part of Russia's historical destiny to unite the

Orthodox Russian people against the moral degeneracy of the West.[18] Thus, in the chaotic period after the fall of Yanukovich, this faction enjoyed a measure of support. However, this disappeared as swiftly as it came, mostly due to the extremist position of the faction, at odds with the reality of ruling the multicultural Russian Federation, and due to the excesses of the rebel commanders it sponsored in eastern Ukraine, especially the downing of the civilian airliner MH-17. This faction supports the most aggressive incarnation of Russian foreign policy, which may even be ready to adopt direct military confrontation in order to recover lost "Russian" lands such as the Baltic, but its influence is limited, and therefore the more cautious approach of the hardliners remains the norm.[19]

Another minor but increasingly important faction is that of the loyalists, solely answerable to Putin.[20] This is comprised of younger individuals, often the offspring of regional and federal officials, or individuals in Putin's inner circle. This faction's position is the most difficult to ascertain, as it depends on Putin's position, which by design is rarely clear. However, based on the course of Russian policy since Putin took office, it is reasonable to conclude that this faction's position on Russian foreign policy and strategy is unlikely to be drastically different from that of the hardliners.

Finally, there is the Chechen faction, which is not so much a real faction within the Kremlin, as much as the strong bond between Kadyrov, Chechnya's longtime leader, and Putin. Kadyrov pacifies the restive Caucasus and contributes his paramilitaries to various Russian projects, and in return, receives vast wealth from Moscow, as well as choice postings for Chechens in a number of security agencies, most notably the Federal Protection Service (FSO), the rival of the FSB. Kadyrov's interests may be limited to running Chechnya as an Islamist fief, posting on Instagram, gathering wealth, and promoting his associates in Moscow, but the presence of these Caucasian newcomers is a constant source of tension. The hardliners, especially the FSB, do not tolerate their rival, while ethnic nationalists are aghast at this intrusion of Muslims in the "Third Rome." Therefore, the Chechen faction may not have a direct impact on strategy, but it has an indirect impact due to the friction it generates with other factions vying for Putin's approval. It is possible that these factions might contemplate independent action, even in the foreign policy sphere, in order to take the initiative and thus force Putin's support for their schemes.

In sum, factionalism within the Kremlin has evolved to a point where the hardline vision of renewed Russian power is dominant. This indicates that détente and the mitigation of tensions may be difficult, as Russian strategy is consequently formulated with confrontation in mind. Unlike the early 2000s, where the balance between the hardliners and the technocrats was more established, and therefore the debate on the strategic direction of Russia more substantial, today the greater number of factions, the rivalries between factions, and the emergence of a loyalist faction indicate that from within that small part of the Russian government that actually makes foreign policy decisions, one may expect a fairly consistent course that seeks a degree of confrontation with the current world order. This is reflected when examining developments in various regions.

Regional developments

As in the Soviet years, Russian naval strategy relies on a triad of missile-armed surface ships, submarines, and long-range naval aviation; the sole remaining carrier, the *Kuznetsov*, remains in poor shape, though it was used late in 2016 to transfer a number of aircraft from the White Sea to Russia's base in Tartus, Syria. Theoretically, its role would be highly defensive, as decreed by the strategy of bastion defense that is the cornerstone of Russian strategy. This strategy emphasizes the need to defend the coast, deny access and command of the sea far from one's coast, and offensively attack the enemy's shipping and surface assets, and it stands in direct opposition to American strategy, which seeks to keep the sea, a global commons, open to navigation, and uses carrier groups in order to gain command of the sea. The legacy of the Cold War is telling.

Though marred by corruption and inefficiency, Russian military industry is still able to produce advanced systems relevant to this strategy, including various anti-ship and anti-air missiles and capable combat aircraft; notably, the Su-33 heavy fighter is a popular export, produced under license in China as the J-15, alongside other Russian exports to the PLAN that greatly strengthen its status as a competitor to the U.S. Navy and other friendly navies in the region.[21]

The following sections describe the situation and developments regarding Russian maritime power in the various regions where it is active, either directly or indirectly.

Arctic and Atlantic

The Northern Fleet is based in Severomorsk and the greater Murmansk area. It remains the main fleet of the Navy and is responsible both for the Arctic and Atlantic, and includes the majority of nuclear-powered ships of the Navy, as the SLBM submarines are expected to cruise under the Arctic icepack and into the Atlantic.

Russian strategy identifies this region as highly important.[22] The Arctic is likely resource-rich, especially in oil and gas, though prices have dropped significantly since 2014, and this trend is unlikely to reverse soon. Furthermore, changing climate patterns gradually open the Northern Sea Route, a more permanent path through the icepack from the Atlantic to the Pacific. The significance of this development remains unclear. Traffic through this route is still unreliable, and China's ambitious plans for a new Silk Road ("One Belt, One Road") as an artery of commerce between East and West may very well render this route redundant. Nonetheless, Russian planning perceives the Arctic as its backyard, though so far disputes have been settled through the Arctic Council, and interactions in the region are remarkably free of the tensions and incursions that characterize interactions in the Atlantic, Baltic, Black Sea, and northwest Pacific. As is formulated in official Russian documents, the Kremlin perceives this state of affairs to be highly advantageous, whatever the state of relations with the West, and would prefer to remain focused on the economic exploitation of the Arctic, rather than engaging in sustained militarization of the region.

The Atlantic is a different matter. Only in the Baltic is the deterioration of relations between Russia and NATO more starkly visible.[23] Since 2014, British and Norwegian aircraft have been scrambled numerous times in order to intercept Russian aircraft, including the long-range nuclear-capable Tu-95, its navalized cousin the Tu-142, and the supersonic Tu-22M, capable of carrying three anti-ship Kh-22 missiles (range 600 km) or six Kh-15 (range 300 km); however, unlike in the Baltic, no Russian aircraft to date have violated the sovereign airspace of a NATO member in the Atlantic. These incursions, alongside Russian naval exercises, signal NATO that the Soviet naval concept of bastion defense has been conclusively revitalized, and that Russian naval forces stand to aggressively deploy it in the event of hostilities. The focus has sharpened, shedding whatever diversification occurred in the early 2000s. In many ways, the situation bears similarities to the Cold War, when Soviet activity in the Atlantic presaged the strategy of bastion defense that would be used in an open conflict, with a particular focus on penetrating or seizing the GUIK gap and NATO shipping in the open ocean beyond, whereas NATO strategy naturally focused on denying this to the Soviets, with a particular role for Norway in containing Russian naval and air forces in their transit out of the White Sea.

Baltic

The Baltic Sea Fleet is based in Kronstadt and Kaliningrad, the fortified exclave in the heart of the Baltic. Though smaller in size than other commands (ten surface ships, two submarines), it is currently the most prominent, at least from the perspective of NATO, especially the newer Eastern members. This is also due to its potential to deny access to the narrow Baltic Sea in the event of confrontation or conflict.[24] The post-Soviet transition radically altered the balance of power in the Baltic, as East Germany ceased to exist, and Poland and the Baltic states joined NATO, leaving Russia without any allies in the region; though Finland and Sweden are nominally neutral, Poland and the Baltics, spurred in part by their negative experiences as Soviet satellites, were quick to join NATO.[25]

It must be noted that the Baltics hold a special place in Russian irredentism and military adventurism.[26] Much of that ideology centers on "recovering" or at least intimidating lost imperial and Soviet lands into compliance with Russian wishes and dissociation from the West. In the most extreme form, rather than allowing the existence of independent states, the whole of *Pribaltika* should be recovered; the argument is furthered by pointing out the significant Russian populations in the region (26% in Latvia and 24% in Estonia). These populations are poorly integrated and more likely to identify with Moscow than with their home countries, the EU, or NATO. Much as was done in Ukraine, nationalists and some hardliners argue it would be possible and in fact rather simple to intimidate, partition, or even outright annex these states.

The actual strategy of the Kremlin is to engage in a campaign of intimidation through armed force without any actual exchanges of fire. Naval forces are integral. Operations include numerous airspace violations by military aircraft, intrusions by submarines, simulated attack runs against surface ships, and exercises simulating full-scale attacks, even nuclear attacks, on neutral or NATO objectives in the Baltic Sea, notably the islands of Bornholm (Denmark) and Gotland (Sweden).

With respect to the newer NATO partners, this strategy is two-pronged. On the material front, it recognizes that the limited military resources of the Baltics can be deteriorated by forcing them to constantly scramble and respond to incursions. On the psychological front, it adopts the Soviet concept of reflexive conditioning, whereby stronger states are reflexively conditioned to act against their best interests by subtle pressure from a weaker opponent. In the case of the Baltics, this occurs when inevitably these states bring up in NATO the issue of Russian incursions. As no actual shooting or conflict has occurred to date, the Russian thinking goes that the Western NATO members would eventually tire of the perceived paranoia and even warmongering of the Baltics, and thus would abandon them in the event of more significant Russian pressure that aims to truly interfere in the sovereignty of the Baltics.

With respect to Denmark, which is a founding NATO member, and Sweden, the strategy seeks to Finlandize these states. Russian strategy recognizes that the appetite for armed conflict in the populations of these particular Scandinavian states is low; the rapid defunding of their militaries after the end of the Cold War is seen as proof, alongside the inevitable assertion of moral decay which is ascribed to the member states of the EU.[27] Therefore, the thinking is that these states ought to be easily intimidated by the fear of Russian aggression in the Baltic, thus leaving Sweden neutral, and leading Denmark to oppose stronger measures against Russia both within NATO and the EU. At least in Sweden, it has resulted in a fierce debate, mirroring the early years of the Cold War, on whether Sweden should join NATO; as befits the composite nature of Russian strategy, this debate has been subsequently distorted by the injection through fringe Swedish media outlets of narratives mirroring Russian objectives, a trend which has also become visible in the discourse regarding migration in Sweden.

Therefore, Russian naval strategy in the Baltic provides the template for integrating a maritime aspect to hybrid warfare, a trend also visible with Chinese strategy in the South China Sea. It is likely a learning process is underway between the two. Already the South China Sea has seen "little blue men", suspiciously heavily armed Chinese fishermen, harking to the "little green men" of 2014 Crimea.[28] Thus, Russia's Baltic strategy merits close observation, as it not only raises tensions between Russia and NATO, but is likely to crop up in a mutated form elsewhere, and furthermore to become a template for any strategist seeking to combine military and information power in the age of social media ascendant.

Black Sea and Mediterranean

The Black Sea is unique in that access to warships is governed by the 1936 Montreux Convention, broadly limiting transit of ships into the Black Sea of non-Black Sea powers, and limiting the stay of such ships to 21 days, while allowing greater freedom to the Black Sea powers, notably the USSR, and now Russia. This peculiar piece of international law has greatly restricted the ability of NATO to support its new eastern NATO members, therefore allowing the Black Sea Fleet to remain the dominant naval power in the Black Sea.[29]

The Black Sea Fleet is based in Sevastopol, central to Russia's claim over Crimea. Despite the centrality of the claim, the fleet is deceptively small, fielding six surface ships and six submarines, though it is well-supplied.[30] Furthermore, as the regime wishes to give the impression that it is not involved directly in the conflict in eastern Ukraine,[31] the fleet has not participated in that conflict; its last action was to support Russian ground forces in the fighting in Georgia in 2008. Its main role with respect to the Ukrainian crisis is to ferry supplies from the base at Novorossiysk, on the mainland, in order to keep Crimea supplied, at least as long as the Kerch Strait Bridge is still under construction; considering that this is managed by the Rotenberg brothers, close associates of Putin with a notorious role in corrupt practices in the run-up to the Sochi Olympics, it is likely that the planned completion date of 2018 may not occur. Unlike the case of the Baltic Sea, hybrid conflict in Ukraine does not call for naval support. Though it is possible to disguise the comings and goings of tanks and troops, disguising offshore support from ships would be far more difficult, and would compromise the uncertainty that is the nature of hybrid warfare, as it would decisively indicate an overt Russian role in the conflict. Therefore, it is highly unlikely that the Navy would play a major role in the Ukrainian conflict in the near future, excepting the highly unlikely chance of the conflict escalating into a direct confrontation between Ukraine and Russia itself; in that case, the Navy would do what it did in the Georgian conflict, which is blockade and shore bombardment in support of the Army.

Aside from Crimea, Russia's chief strategic interest in the region is in three radically different NATO members, and beyond the Bosporus, in projecting maritime power in support of Moscow's broader strategy of gaining influence and supporters in the chaotic post-Arab Spring Middle East, especially in Syria, where the civil war has provided Moscow with the means to reassert its influence.

Turkey is the most salient of these NATO members, not merely because of its sizeable economy, population, and military, but also due to its crucial role as one of the powers of the Middle East, ranking alongside Iran, Israel, and Saudi Arabia in the complex tapestry of influence and rivalry that characterizes the region. Furthermore, after a relatively short spat due to the shooting down of a Russian aircraft by Turkish forces on the Turkish-Syrian border in November 2015, relations have dramatically improved, even as relations between Turkey and its fellow NATO members and the EU have become severely strained after the 2016 coup attempt, which failed to depose Erdogan and his loyalists in the AKP.

The increasingly authoritarian nature of the Turkish government has led to a degree of mutual understanding with Moscow that cannot be easily replicated by its fellow NATO members. However, this has not translated to meaningful maritime cooperation, and is unlikely to do so in the near future. The Russians, alongside Iran and its proxies, support the Assad government, whereas the Turkish government, composed of an uneasy coalition of the AKP (conservative and moderate Islamist) and the MHP (ultranationalist) supports a number of rebel groups, with the definitive exception of Kurdish groups, which it seeks to destroy and prevent from linking up with Kurdish militants within Turkey itself. This highlights the fragile nature of this coalition.

The main role of the Russian Navy in the Syrian conflict has been resupply; even the highly publicized cruise of the *Kuznetsov* to Syria was little more than publicity, as the aging carrier had to be towed most of the way from Murmansk to the Russian base at Tartus. The content of the supply is more significant than the nature, as the Russians have moved anti-ship and anti-aircraft missiles (including the extremely long range S-300 missile) into Syria, thus clearly raising the cost and difficulty of an intervention hostile to Assad's faction. Given that the fighting is deep inland and the role of Russia is to provide the firepower that Assad's forces lack, there is little place for a direct role for the Navy, and little prospect of cooperation with Turkey.

The other NATO members in the Black Sea are Romania and Bulgaria, both former satellites of the USSR. Neither has a strong maritime tradition or an especially potent navy. However, their interaction with Russia mirrors a broader trend of increased Russian interest in its former satellites. The case of Romania is more conventional, and resembles the Polish relationship to Russia due to mutual animosity, including the unresolved question of Moldova, incorporated into the USSR and now mired in a frozen conflict over Transnistria. A similar pattern emerged as in the Baltic, consisting of intrusions into Romanian airspace, as well as highly publicized threats by Russian government figures. However, unlike the Baltic states, the main tool of Russian influence is decidedly not naval, but that of linkages with Romanian oligarchs and corrupt figures from Romanian parties, especially the PSD, de facto heir of the Soviet-era Communist party. This pattern repeats in Bulgaria, though the Bulgarian population is much more sympathetic to Russia due to historical linkages and the Russian role in Bulgaria gaining independence from the Ottoman Empire, much as in neighboring Serbia and Greece. However, no discernible pan-Slavism or pan-Orthodoxy dilutes the pure pragmatism of Russian strategy. Moscow gladly cooperates with Turkey at Greece's expense, despite the strong Russophilia of the Greek far-right and far-left, and this pattern repeats itself across the Balkans and beyond.

Pacific Ocean

The Pacific Fleet is based in Vladivostok, though another important base, at least for submarines, is Petropavlovsk-Kamchatsky. This is the most isolated Russian command, but highly significant due to its location in the Pacific and proximity to Alaska, Japan, and Korea. Given the disparity of capabilities with respect to American and Japanese fleets, the Pacific Fleet fields only six surface combatants, but in response, has 23 submarines of mixed attack and missile type, and is augmented by a significant naval aviation branch. This fleet, much like the Atlantic Fleet, is designed to follow a strategy of bastion defense in the event of interstate conflict; the vast distances and sparse population of the region have made the innovations seen elsewhere, such as in the Baltic, impractical. It should be noted that beginning in 2016, the Pacific Fleet has embarked on a diplomatic showcase, ceremonially visiting ports in China, Vietnam, the Philippines, and elsewhere, in order to promote the prestige of resurgent Russian maritime power. Aside from the soft power aspect, these visits serve to highlight the sophistication of Russian military and maritime technology, and therefore function well in support of Russia's role as pre-eminent arms broker to the region.[32]

The maritime security landscape in the northern Pacific is defined by the quadrangular relationship between China, Japan, Russia, and the U.S.; the lesser regional powers, such as both Koreas, the Republic of China, the ASEAN states, and even Australia, move within this framework. The end of the Cold War lowered tensions and led to a reconfiguration whereby China and Russia cooperate on a range of issues, exemplified by their founding of the Shanghai Cooperation Organization (SCO), their mutual membership in the BRICS, and their general interest in a reconfiguration of the global order, but that relationship is far from perfect.

On the other hand, Japan remains a steadfast ally of the U.S.; the deteriorating dispute between China and Japan over sovereignty on the Senkaku/Diaoyu islands has caused Japan to consider remilitarization, and this carries over to Japan's relations with Russia, which have never been easy. The Sakhalin and Kuril Islands dispute between the two has never been conclusively settled, simmering on since the Russo-Japanese war of 1905. Much as in the Atlantic, the Russians engage in regular intrusions in northern Japanese airspace. Furthermore, this dispute is unlikely to resolve soon, due to political inertia in both countries. For the Russian government, and especially for Russian nationalists, ownership of the Kuriles as war booty is an article of faith; on the other hand, the nationalist politics that play an increasingly integral role within the ruling Liberal Democratic Party in Japan are highly unwilling to compromise, regardless of personal relationships between members of the Russian and Japanese governments.

Considering the central role of the Pacific, and the increasing tension due to Chinese ambitions and the U.S. pivot to Asia, it is worthwhile to examine potential Russian influence on four maritime flashpoints in the region. These are the Senkaku/Diaoyu islands dispute; the Korean peninsula; cross-straits relations between China and Taiwan; and finally, the South China Sea. In order to properly explore these flashpoints, this section first explores the crucial role played by Russia in enabling Chinese military modernization.

It can be argued that Russia's greatest impact on the Western Pacific is not the presence of its fleet, but its technical support for Chinese military modernization; Russian technical proficiency remains high, despite the ravages of the post-Soviet period.[33] Whereas the Russian Pacific Fleet has stagnated in size and equipment, the People's Liberation Army Navy (PLAN) has grown and modernized significantly, finally adding a functional carrier, the *Liaoning*, and continually improving its missiles, aircraft, submarines, and surface ships with new, standardized Western-style ship classes.[34] However, this modernization is still reliant on Russian technology and technical know-how, especially in specific areas such as aircraft engines;

for example, the indigenous J-15 heavy fighter that ought to be the standard aircraft for naval aviation and aircraft carriers is based almost entirely on the Su-33, which is a very successful export item of its own, especially in Asia. Ultimately, Chinese maritime strategy may have taken some steps to move towards the standard blue-water approach, but it fundamentally remains modeled on the asymmetric approach of denial practiced by the Soviets; thus cooperation between China and Russia on maritime matters is a natural fit.

It is unlikely the PLAN could have modernized as quickly without Russian support, and in the near future, the linkage between Russia and China will continue to drive Chinese militarization, which in turn drives the militarization of all states that feel threatened by a resurgent China: South Korea, Japan, India, and the smaller states of Southeast Asia. Furthermore, relations between the West and Russia have deteriorated significantly since 2014, and have led through sanctions to a partial economic international isolation of Russia, thus increasing the economic dependence of Russia on China, especially regarding the trade of hydrocarbons; this changes the dynamic of the relationship, putting Beijing in a rather more senior position than Moscow, as Beijing has taken full advantage of Moscow's troubles.[35] Therefore, the link that enables the growth of Chinese sea power is likely to deepen rather than abate, given that Xi Jinping's government has taken a more belligerent stance than his predecessor, and is keen to continue modernizing with Russian assistance. However, signs do point to a preference for eventually moving towards totally indigenous Chinese military production, independent of Russian know-how, but given enduring technical problems, it is unlikely to occur soon.

The crucial enabling role played by Russia exposes its role in the four above-mentioned maritime flashpoints. It should be noted that in none of the cases is direct Russian maritime intervention the main element.

The Senkaku/Diaoyu and cross-straits flashpoints are eerily similar in that in both cases, Russia does not have a substantial interest in actually participating directly in the conflict, but rather has the unique opportunity to ensure that a revisionist challenger – China – is better equipped to challenge a status quo military power that is ultimately dependent on the U.S.; thus Russia could potentially distract or even weaken the central pillar of NATO in the distant Pacific, at a relatively low cost to itself.

The Senkaku/Diaoyu pits China against Japan, a traditional maritime power whose navy, the JMSDF, follows a conventional blue-water strategy, and is technologically and doctrinally well-integrated with the U.S. The islands are far from Chinese or Japanese shores, which complicates China's attempts to posture; it is only through its recent military modernization that it is able to do so. Furthermore, the dispute has become particularly virulent due to strong nationalist rhetoric on both sides, justified by both as the redress of historical grievances; this greatly complicates de-escalation.[36]

Up until recent times, the cross-straits maritime balance of power favored the ROC. Its modern navy, much like Japan's, draws on American technology and concepts, and the island is an unsinkable aircraft carrier. Furthermore, a delicate informal framework exists whereby Taiwanese sovereignty is highly likely to be defended by the U.S. in the case of a Chinese attack, so long as the ROC does not declare independence as the Republic of Taiwan (the one-China principle) or attempt to develop WMDs; reciprocally, under these conditions China may choose to attempt to invade the island. Therefore, harking back to the days of Mao's "people's war at sea," the Chinese approach in wargames has been to try to deny access to the island to American reinforcements, so that Chinese forces can quickly launch an amphibious assault and reduce the island. Bolstered by advanced missiles and submarines, the PLAN is ever more likely to succeed, as demonstrated by the ROC's annual Han Kuang wargames. As Sino-Russian cooperation results in ever more advanced military hardware, the chances of a successful defense of the ROC recede.

Regarding the Korean Peninsula, gone are the days of inflexible Soviet ideological support to the DPRK. Modern Russia enjoys substantial trade and economic links to South Korea. Furthermore, its Pacific Fleet is ill-equipped to intervene in any Korean conflict. Therefore, Russia's current role is chiefly as a participant in the various multinational talks that attempt to reach a lasting peaceful status in the Korean Peninsula; Russia has also continually and positively supported the denuclearization of North Korea. However, there are two admittedly unlikely scenarios under which the Pacific Fleet would become more relevant to the Korean Peninsula. In the case of a multinational consensus of a harder line on North Korea, such as the interdiction of North Korean shipping (especially of illicit activities), it would become critical that the Pacific Fleet participates transparently and effectively. Vladivostok is remote, and notorious for smuggling and other illicit activities, and the Russian military in the farther-flung outposts remains plagued by corruption at the lower ranks.[37] This would weaken a multinational blockade of North Korea; a similar situation developed in the Balkans in 1999, when Bulgarian and Romanian organized crime, often linked to political figures, smuggled vast amounts of oil and other goods into Serbia, overwhelmingly to Serbian OC and paramilitary groups. Conversely, a sudden collapse of North Korean state authority would present many of the same problems, with the added difficulty of controlling illicit arms shipments to possible armed factions in the (former) DPRK. In either scenario, the Pacific Fleet, especially its reliability and transparency, becomes an important element.

In the South China Sea, the Russian role as supplier is substantially more varied. Here, ASEAN states are eager to acquire advanced Russian hardware – especially the fourth generation Su-30/33 heavy fighter – in order to greatly bolster their military capabilities, including in order to balance against predatory Chinese ambitions regarding the islands in the South China Sea. This has two implications. First, Russian supplies may lead to a classical scenario of the spiral of instability, whereby efforts by the Southeast Asian states to bolster their security in the face of Chinese aggression lead to an increasingly hostile and militarized Chinese response, thus damaging the likelihood of a peaceful resolution to territorial disputes. Second, it shows that in this case, Russian and Chinese policy are at cross-purposes, much as in the case of Russian policy in the Indian Ocean; this ensures that Russia does not become wholly dependent on China, and can distract its erstwhile ally from Russia's vast and empty Asian domains; a stealthy Chinese takeover of Siberia, as a far more peaceful variant of Imperial Japan's Northern Strategy, is a perennial concern of Russian ultranationalists.

Indian Ocean

Beyond its influence on the Pacific Rim militaries, Russian technical influence is also reflected in India, China's burgeoning maritime rival. Though separated by the Southeast Asian island chains and naval master of the Indian Ocean, India has had a long-running rivalry with China that has begun to escalate over to the maritime realm.[38] This is due to China's strong support for Pakistan and its strategy to construct a "string of pearls", a series of deep-water ports that can be used for military purposes across the Western Pacific, but also the Indian Ocean, most notably in Pakistan and Sri Lanka.[39] Conversely, India had enjoyed a close relationship with the Soviet Union during the Cold War, even as India was one of the leaders of the Non-Aligned Movement, and this continued with Russia in the post-Cold War period. Russian expertise has played an important role in the development of the Indian armed forces, and the navy is no exception. Naval cooperation is high, represented by the biannual INDRA wargames, and a formalized commission on military and technical cooperation. Furthermore, joint Indian-Russian projects have resulted in advanced military systems, such as the potent BrahMos anti-ship missile, the Su-30MKI program, the fifth generation HAL FGFA fighter program, and others; these projects are not merely an instance of technology transfer, as in the case of China, but complete joint research and development.

It should be noted that Russian cooperation with and supply to India has largely managed to avoid the tensions of other such bilateral attempts, most notably the long-running negotiations between France and India over the purchase of Rafale fighters for the Indian Air Force. Unlike the French, the Russians have proved to be willing to share their technology and to undertake joint R&D and production, and this is reflected not just in India, but also elsewhere in Asia, the Middle East, and Latin America.[40]

Unlike in the Western Pacific, here Russia supplies a status quo power against a revisionist one, though both India and Pakistan field similar maritime forces and follow a traditional blue/green-water strategy. Much as in Southeast Asia, Russia and China work at cross-purposes in South Asia; thus despite its economic difficulties, Russia is able to sustain a foreign policy in Asia that is independent of China. Furthermore, Russia and India share a common struggle against radical Islam; though this is not strictly a maritime issue, it does allow for an ideational framework for cooperation, one that is increasingly prominent.[41]

Russia thus occupies a unique position in supplying both India and China, ostensible rivals. Whereas the Chinese are dependent on Russia for modernizing their military, but may prefer in the future to no longer be dependent, India pursues a far more equitable relationship that is likely to thrive and endure. In any case, modernization in these great powers of the Indian Ocean and Western

Pacific is accelerating the movement to a multipolar world order, where the West, and by extension the U.S., are merely the "first amongst equals."

Lastly, the limited resurgence of piracy in the Gulf of Aden, which at its previous peak drew a vigorous and varied multinational response that included a limited Russian contingent, shows that there is space for including Russia in multinational efforts against new, non-state maritime threats and issues. Though the Russian contingent did operate autonomously, it showed that in areas that the Russian government does not consider essential to its national security or sphere of influence, there can be the opportunity to cooperate with the West, meaning NATO and the EU.[42] This should remain a valuable conduit for cooperation with Russia, which in turn may over time slightly alleviate friction on critical issues such as Russian-NATO contestation. Ultimately, and on a much grander scale than its former Eastern European satellites, which through technical assistance strongly contribute to humanitarian assistance, the Russian government retains substantial and unique capabilities for dealing with a range of security and humanitarian issues. However, this should not be taken to indicate that yielding to Russian interests on crucial issues in order to gain their cooperation would be productive. It is in relatively neutral ground – such as the Gulf of Aden – that the opportunity for cooperation should be explored.

Outlook

Russian sea power suffered greatly as a result of the collapse of the USSR, but after a period of stagnation came a degree of revitalization. The deterioration of relations with the West after 2014 led to a maritime strategy of confrontation with the status quo of NATO in the Atlantic, the Baltic, and the Black Sea, and conversely, to cooperation with rising powers dissatisfied with the status quo in Asia. After a short experiment with adopting a more blue-water approach, Russian strategy reverted to the asymmetric, denial-based approach favored during Soviet times. From the various developments in regions since 2014, two clear trends emerge. Both relate to the greater context of Russia's challenge to the established world order, which is brought about by the sanctions levied for the conflict in Ukraine. It must be noted that this challenge is likely to abate to a certain degree should sanctions ever be lifted, but for the sake of factionalism in the Kremlin, and the generation of domestic support for the Putin regime, it is highly unlikely to truly fade away; at the most, it will become less pronounced and less challenging.

The first trend is the re-emergence of hybrid warfare. This method has proven to be a useful tool for revisionist states seeking to push their claims at a low risk, and it is also useful in constructing specific narratives for domestic as well as international consumption by the use of state-sponsored media conglomerates. Furthermore, there is a process of learning underway, especially between Russia and China. However, it should be noted that this is not a simple strategy, and it is unlikely that any given revisionist power would be able to implement it so thoroughly.

The second trend is the indirect support Russia provides through its technical know-how to states that challenge the status quo. Russian weapons systems excel in a number of fields, especially missiles, and can provide capabilities not only unmatched by Western systems, but specifically designed to counter Western systems and approaches to warfare. By providing these systems to various consumers across the globe, Russia erodes the force projection capabilities of its perceived rivals in NATO, the U.S., and elsewhere.

Notes

1. Jane's, 2016.
2. Schaub Jr., 2017, 32.
3. Adamsky, 2010.
4. Lanoszka, 2016, 13. Blank, 2015a, 68.
5. Chernavin, 1982. Gorshkov, 1977.
6. Till, 2013. Gray, 1999.
7. Jane's, 2014.
8. Murray and Mansoor, 2012, 1–18. Hoffman, 2009.
9. Oliker et al., 2015, 22–23.
10. Tsygankov, 2016.
11. Herrick, 2003.
12. Tsygankov, 2016. Feklyunina, 2016.
13. Monaghan, 2015.
14. Teague, 2017.
15. Shevtsova, 2015.
16. Gill and Young, 2013, 28.
17. Maness and Valeriano, 2015, 46.
18. O'Loughlin et al., 2017, 129–131.
19. Kofman et al., 2017, 6–69.
20. Hill, 2017.
21. Blank and Levitzky, 2015, 74–75.
22. Burke, 2016.
23. Gramer, 2016. Hudson and Roberts, 2016, 83.
24. Lanoszka and Hunzeker, 2016, 15–18.
25. Kramer, 2015.
26. Maigre, 2015.
27. Braw, 2015.
28. Erickson and Kennedy, 2015.
29. Delanoe, 2014.
30. Delanoe, 2014.
31. Allison, 2014.
32. Blank and Levitzky, 2015.
33. Blank and Levitzky, 2015, 83.
34. Kirchberger, 2015.
35. Kaczmarski, 2015.
36. Hollihan, 2014.
37. Krasova and Ma, 2015, 119.
38. Agnihotri, 2011.
39. Khurana, 2008.
40. Rekha, 2017.
41. Rekha, 2017.
42. Gebhard and Smith, 2015, 124.

Bibliography

Adamsky, Dima. 2010. *The Culture of Military Innovation: The Impact of Cultural Factors on the Revolution in Military Affairs in Russia, the US, and Israel*. Stanford: Stanford University Press.

Agnihotri, Kamlesh Kumar. 2011. Modernisation of the Chinese Navy, Its Strategic Expansion into the Indian Ocean Region and Likely Impact on the Regional Stability. *Maritime Affairs: Journal of the National Maritime Foundation of India*, 7(1), pp. 48–64.

Allison, Roy. 2014. Russian 'deniable' Intervention in Ukraine: How and Why Russia Broke the Rules. *International Affairs*, 90(6), pp. 1255–1297.

Blank, Stephen J. 2015. Imperial Ambitions: Russia's Military Buildup. *World Affairs*, 178(1), pp. 67–76.

Blank, Stephen, and Edward Levitzky. 2015. Geostrategic Aims of the Russian Arms Trade in East Asia and the Middle East. *Defence Studies*, 15(1), pp. 63–80.

Braw, Elisabeth. 2015. Bully in the Baltics: The Kremlin's Provocations. *World Affairs* 177(6), pp. 31–39.

Burke, Danita Catherine. 2016. *Russia's Arctic Strategies and the Future of the Far North*. pp. 456–460.

Chernavin, V. 1982. On Naval Theory. *Morskoy Sbornik*, 1.

Delanoe, Igor. 2014. After the Crimean Crisis: Towards a Greater Russian Maritime Power in the Black Sea. *Southeast European and Black Sea Studies*, 14(3), pp. 367–382.

Erickson, Andrew S., and Conor M. Kennedy. 2015. Directing China's 'Little Blue Men': Uncovering the Maritime Militia Command Structure. *AMTI*. Available at: http://amti.csis.org/directing-chinas-little-blue-men-uncovering-the-maritime-militia-command-structure/ [accessed 6 November 2015].

Feklyunina, Valentina. 2016. Soft Power and Identity: Russia, Ukraine and the 'Russian World (s)'. *European Journal of International Relations*, 22(4), pp. 773–796.

Gebhard, Carmen, and Simon J. Smith. 2015. The Two Faces of EU–NATO Cooperation: Counter-Piracy Operations Off the Somali Coast. *Cooperation and Conflict*, 50(1), pp. 107–127.

Gill, Graeme, and James Young eds., 2013. *Routledge Handbook of Russian Politics and Society*. London: Routledge.

Gorshkov, Sergei Georgievich. 1977. *The Sea Power of the State*. pp 24–29.

Gramer, Robbie. 2016. Russia's Ambitions in the Atlantic. *Foreign Affairs*.

Gray, Colin S. 1999. *Modern Strategy*. Vol. 42. Oxford: Oxford University Press.

Herrick, Robert. 2003. *Waring. Soviet Naval Doctrine and Policy, 1956–1986*. Lewiston: Edwin Mellen Press.

Hill, Fiona. 2017. The Next Mr. Putin? The Question of Succession. *Daedalus*, 146(2), pp. 41–52.

Hoffman, Frank G. 2009. *Hybrid Warfare and Challenges*. National Defense University: Institute for National Strategic Studies.

Hollihan, T., ed. 2014. *The Dispute Over the Diaoyu/Senkaku Islands: How Media Narratives Shape Public Opinion and Challenge the Global Order*. London: Springer.

Hudson, Peter, and Peter Roberts. 2016. V. The UK and the North Atlantic: A British Military Perspective. *Whitehall Papers*, 87(1), pp. 75–91.

IHS Markit. 2014. Jane's Weapons Systems: Naval. *IHS Markit*.

———. 2016. Jane's World Navies. *IHS Markit*.

Kaczmarski, Marcin. 2015. *Russia-China Relations in the Post-Crisis International Order*. Vol. 101. London: Routledge.

Khurana, Gurpreet S. 2008. China's 'String of Pearls' in the Indian Ocean and Its Security Implications. *Strategic Analysis*, 32(1), pp. 1–39.

Kirchberger, Sarah. 2015. *Assessing China's Naval Power*. Springer Berlin Heidelberg: Imprint: Springer.

Kofman, Michael, et al. 2017. *Lessons from Russia's Operations in Crimea and Eastern Ukraine*. Santa Monica: Rand Corporation.

Kramer, Mark. 2015. The New Russian Chill in the Baltic. *Current History*, 114(770), p. 108.

Krasova, Elena Viktorovna, and Yingxin Ma. 2015. Free Port of Vladivostok: Development Conditions, Prospects, Risks. *Economic and Social Changes: Facts, Trends, Forecast*, 6, pp. 108–122.

Lanoszka, Alexander. 2016. Russian Hybrid Warfare and Extended Deterrence in Eastern Europe. *International Affairs*, 92(1), pp. 175–195.

Lanoszka, Alexander, and Michael A. Hunzeker. 2016. Confronting the Anti-Access/Area Denial and Precision Strike Challenge in the Baltic Region. *The RUSI Journal*, 161(5), pp. 12–18.

Maigre, Merle. 2015. *Nothing New in Hybrid Warfare: The Estonian Experience and Recommendations for NATO*. Policy Brief, German Marshall Fund of the United States, February. Available at: www.gmfus.org/publications/nothing-new-hybrid-warfare-estonian-experience-and-recommendations-nato [accessed 12 June 2015].

Maness, Ryan C., and Brandon Valeriano. 2015. Rivalry Persistence and the Case of the United States and Russia: From Global Rivalry to Regional Conflict. *Russia's Coercive Diplomacy*. Palgrave Macmillan, pp. 45–84.

Monaghan, Andrew. 2015. The'war'in Russia's' Hybrid Warfare. *Parameters*, 45(4), p. 65.

Murray, Williamson, and Peter R. 2012. Mansoor. *Hybrid Warfare: Fighting Complex Opponents From the Ancient World to the Present*. Cambridge: Cambridge University Press.

Oliker, Olga, et al. 2015. *Russian Foreign Policy in Historical and Current Context: A Reassessment*. No. PE-144-A. RAND Arroyo Center Santa Monica CA.

O'Loughlin, John, Gerard Toal, and Vladimir Kolosov. 2017. The Rise and Fall of "Novorossiya": Examining Support for a Separatist Geopolitical Imaginary in Southeast Ukraine. *Post-Soviet Affairs*, 33(2), pp. 124–144.

Rekha, Chandra. 2017. *India-Russia Post Cold War Relations: A New Epoch of Cooperation*. Oxford: Taylor & Francis.

Schaub Jr, Gary, Martin Murphy, and Frank G. Hoffman. 2017. Hybrid Maritime Warfare: Building Baltic Resilience. *The RUSI Journal*, 162(1), pp. 32–40.

Shevtsova, Lilia. 2015. Forward to the Past in Russia. *Journal of Democracy*, 26(2), pp. 22–36.

Teague, Elizabeth. 2017. All the Kremlin's Men: Inside the Court of Vladimir Putin. *International Affairs*, 93(1), pp. 220–221.

Till, Geoffrey. 2013. *Seapower: A Guide for the Twenty-First Century*. London: Routledge.

Tsygankov, Andrei P. 2016. *Russia's Foreign Policy: Change and Continuity in National Identity*. Rowman & Littlefield.

4 Contemporary Europe in the Indian Ocean and the Western Pacific

Douglas Carl Peifer

Europe's influence and presence in the Indo-Pacific region has shrunk dramatically since 1945. France and Britain continue to govern a number of islands in the area, but following Britain's decision to withdraw militarily from east of Suez in 1971, the European footprint in the Indian Ocean became vestigial. Britain's handover of Hong Kong in 1997 marked the final curtain call to an era when Europeans had substantial military and political influence in the region. The vast majority of Europeans now travelling to the region do so as tourists or for business reasons, with European diplomacy at the national and European level focused on commerce, investment, and development. Several European nations have responded to the problems of piracy, human trafficking, and terrorism by sending ships, aircraft, and soldiers back into the region. Yet while European ships, soldiers, and aircraft have returned to the Western Indian Ocean in a limited way since 2008, neither the European Union as a whole nor particular European nations with the possible exception of France and Great Britain have the capacity to become players in the Great Power contest developing in the Indian Ocean, the South China Sea, and the East China Sea.

The following analysis will examine the role of contemporary Europe in the Indian Ocean from three perspectives. First, it will examine the interests, objectives, and capabilities of those individual European nations that still have territories, garrisons, and national security commitments in the region. Second, it will analyze how Europe as a whole has taken up security duties in the Western Indian Ocean, reflecting the aspiration of certain European nations to strengthen the European Union's Common Foreign and Security Policy (CFSP) by supporting limited military and civilian missions outside the Euro-Atlantic region. Lastly, it will analyze how NATO concurrently has shouldered responsibility for various anti-terrorist missions around the Horn of Africa and in the Persian Gulf. In short, since 2008 various European nations have recognized that they continue to have geopolitical interests east of Suez, but have been uncertain how best to protect and advance these interests. They have pursued national and European objectives through a welter of overlapping missions, mandates, and security commitments.

National interests, objectives, and capabilities: France and Britain in the Indian Ocean

France and Britain remain the last European nations with territories, security obligations, and defense commitments in the region. Britain maintained significant military forces in Aden, the Gulf States, Malaysia, and Singapore throughout the 1950s and 1960s, but following its decision to draw down its presence east of Suez in 1971, the British footprint in the region all but disappeared. If measured in terms of territory, population, and military posture, the French presence in the Indo-Pacific region is now more significant than that of Great Britain.

Two of France's five overseas regions (Région d'outre-mer) are islands located in the southwest Indian Ocean, with La Réunion France's largest overseas region in terms of population (2015 population estimate 843,529) and Mayotte its smallest (2015 population estimate 226,915).[1] Considered integral parts of the French Republic, La Réunion and Mayotte elect representatives to the French National Assembly, Senate, and the European Parliament; use the euro as currency; and are governed by French laws and regulations. An additional 130,000 French citizens work and live elsewhere in the Asia-Pacific region, chiefly in India, China, Thailand, and Australia.[2] France claims sovereignty over various uninhabited islands off the coast of Madagascar (the Crozet Islands, the Scattered Islands) and the Southern Indian Ocean (the Kerguelen Islands, St. Paul and Amsterdam islands), along with a sliver of Antarctica (Adélie Land). These French Southern and Antarctic Territories have no permanent civilian populations, but France upholds its claims to them by military visits and scientific expeditions. France's overseas regions, collectivities, and territories, collectively termed *France d'outre-mer*, validate France's assertion that it is a global power deserving of its permanent seat on the United Nations Security Council. French territories stretch from the Indian Ocean to the Caribbean, and from Melanesia and Polynesia to the Grand Banks. While France's overseas regions and territories individually rank low as security interests, they collectively are important. Based on its overseas holdings, France claims the world's second largest maritime exclusive economic zone (EEZ). France's 11.0 million square kilometer EEZ is only slightly smaller than that of the United States in total area, and eclipses the claims of India and China.[3] France's enormous EEZ is located primarily in the Pacific (62%), with waters surrounding its holdings in the Indian Ocean making up 24% of its total claim.[4]

France maintains a permanent presence in the Indian Ocean, organized as the *Forces armées dans la zone sud de l'Océan Indien* (FAZSOI). The joint command, based in Réunion, was created in 2011, with a subordinate command located on Mayotte. A French general officer, supported by a joint staff, commands the approximately 1,600 personnel assigned to FAZSOI. All three services have forces assigned to the command, with the Second Marine Infantry Parachute Regiment (the 2[e] RPIMa), two helicopter equipped frigates, a patrol-boat, and a small aviation detachment based in Reunion, and a French Foreign Legion detachment and a patrol-boat based in Mayotte.[5] In addition, France provides opportunities for young volunteers to join the Adapted Military Service in both locales. This program provides professional skills and work experience to young volunteers. While organized and administered by the French military, the Adapted Military Service is more vocational in nature than military.

The French FAZSOI command has a variety of missions. Its presence protects the inhabited islands of Réunion and Mayotte, and perhaps more importantly, enforces French sovereignty over various uninhabited islands claimed by France off Madagascar and in the South Indian Ocean. French naval and air units conduct surveillance of France's maritime exclusive economic zone, enforce fishing regulations, intercept illegal migrants, and fight piracy and smugglers. France, with over one million French citizens resident in the Indian Ocean on Réunion and Mayotte, continues to have territorial interests in the region.

Further to the North, France maintains a military base in its former colony of Djibouti and has negotiated an agreement with the United Arab Emirates for a permanent French military presence in the Gulf. The French base in Djibouti traces back to the 1860s, with France negotiating a Defense Protocol with the Republic of Djibouti following its vote for independence in 1977. The agreement allows France to preposition French forces and equipment in Djibouti, with the provision that France will not use Djibouti as a base for armed intervention against other countries.[6] The French presence is Djibouti is significantly more robust than its military footprint in the South Indian Ocean, totaling 1,700 military personnel. In addition to the 5th joint overseas regiment and a detachment of helicopters (four Pumas, two Gazelles), the French have positioned a detachment of Mirage 2000 fighter aircraft and a special force group in Djibouti.[7] Situated at the outlet of the Red Sea and across the Bab el-Mandeb from Yemen, the French base in Djibouti functions as a critical post for monitoring the situation in Yemen and the Horn of Africa. In addition, the French military in Djibouti trains African peacekeepers as part of France's RECAMP program (Reinforcement of African Capacity to Maintain Peace). France has designated Djibouti as one of its two primary advance operational bases in Africa (the other is located in Côte d'Ivoire), with the base serving as a convenient staging area for French units participating in EU and NATO operations directed against pirates, violent extremists, and human smugglers.

In 2008, the French government signed an agreement with the United Arab Emirates establishing a permanent military presence in the UAE. French forces in the UAE are tasked with deepening military cooperation between the two nations, supporting French operational deployments in the region, and training troops in desert and urban warfare. The command numbers around 700 personnel, with a land component (the 5th Curirassier Regiment), an air component (six Rafale combat aircraft), and a naval base that can accommodate French ships up to but not including France's aircraft carrier. The French commander is responsible for all French military activities in the Indian Ocean, authorized to draw upon French forces in Djibouti and the Southern Indian Ocean as necessary.

France maintains additional troops, aircraft, and ships in New Caledonia (~ 1,800 personnel) and French Polynesia (~1,000 personnel), supplying these outposts via sea and air lanes across the Indian Ocean. In 2016, the French Ministry of Defense updated its policy paper on *France and Security in the Asia-Pacific*. Quoting from the earlier 2013 French White Paper on Defense and National Security, the update asserted that "The security of the Indian Ocean . . . is a priority for France and for Europe" since "[French] companies and citizens are present in increasing numbers in the region and its prosperity is now inseparable from that of the Asia-Pacific region."[8] Among the security interests listed in the study are international terrorism, nuclear proliferation, and the "the lawful, free, and unhampered use of all oceans and their above airspaces, in accordance with the United Nations Convention on the Law of the Sea."[9]

Since the close of the Cold War, France has preferred to operate multi-nationally and with an international mandate whenever possible. It has supported humanitarian assistance operations in Djibouti (Operation Godoria, 1991), non-combatant evacuation operations in Somalia (Operation Bérénice, 1991), the UN's Chapter VII intervention in Somalia (UNOSOM II, 1993), and various other multinational humanitarian operations. Yet France has been willing to intervene unilaterally with hard force when its interests or citizens have been threatened. France responded to coup attempts in the Comoros in 1989 and 1995 by dispatching paratroopers, frigates, and transport aircraft to protect its citizens and restore the Comorian government.[10] Given its significant capabilities, ranging from the Charles de Gaulle carrier battlegroup to minesweeper task groups to special force detachments, France can act alone when necessary. But as will be discussed later, its security strategy in the Indian Ocean envisions European, multinational, and regional responses whenever possible.

France is one of the world's top military powers, if measured in terms of expenditure, ranking number five in 2014 and coming in seventh in 2015.[11] Its military forces number over 200,000 (Army – 109,444; Air Force 42,037; Navy 35,411; Gendarmarie and misc. 16,072), with an additional 60,000 civilian personnel supporting the military force structure. Its first class navy has 72 combat and support ships, including the *Charles de Gaulle* carrier with 42 multirole Rafale jets and 3 E2C Hawkeyes, 3 amphibious assault (LHD) ships, 17 first class frigates, 4 nuclear-powered ballistic missile submarines, 4 nuclear-powered attack submarines, and assorted command, patrol, and specialized ships. The French air force consists of over 200 combat aircraft, 78 transport aircraft, and assorted support and training vehicles, along with 7 UAV systems.[12] As of October 2015, over 6,500 French soldiers, sailors, and airmen were engaged in military operations outside of metropolitan France, chiefly in the Sahel (Operation Barkhane, 3,500 personnel), in Lebanon and the Levant (Operation Daman, 900 personnel; Operation Chammal, 1,000 personnel), in Central Africa (Operation Sangaris, 350 personnel), and off the coast of West and East Africa (Operation Corymbe, 100 personnel; OEF and Operation Atalanta, 350 personnel). A further 11,000 are based in French overseas territories or in various forward operating bases located in Africa and the Middle East.[13] Ongoing counter-terrorist combat and stability operations in the Sahel and the Middle East, along with a heightened security posture in metropolitan France following November 2015 terrorist attacks in Paris, are putting considerable strain on the French military. Despite rhetoric about rebalancing the French military towards the Indo-Pacific region, supporting freedom of navigation, and promoting a rules-based international order,[14] ongoing missions and security commitments elsewhere make it unlikely that France will be able to support these goals with substantial military power.

Britain, like France, continues to have significant overseas territories, scattered in the Caribbean (British Virgin Islands), the North and South Atlantic (Bermuda, the Falklands, Saint Helena, South Georgia), the Pacific (Pitcairn Island), and the Mediterranean (Gibraltar, Cyprus sovereign base areas). British territory in the Indo-Pacific region has shrunk to a scattered collection of islands (the Chagos Islands) located south of the equator, halfway between Africa and Sumatra. Designated the British Indian Ocean Territory, the holding consists of over 1,000 islands and rocks, the most important of which is Diego Garcia measuring some 17 square miles. In 1966, the United Kingdom and the United States signed an exchange of notes authorizing the United States to construct facilities on Diego Garcia. At the request of the United States, Britain forcibly resettled the native Chagossian population, numbering between 1,000 and 1,500 people, to neighboring Mauritius or the Seychelle Islands.[15] Descended from African slaves, Indian workers, and Malay fishermen, the exiled Chagossians subsequently initiated legal proceedings in the United Kingdom demanding that they should have a right to return. By 2008, the issue had wound its way up to the Judicial Committee of the House of Lords which ruled against the Chagossians.[16] Having failed to secure their right of return via legal channels, groups supporting the Chagossians are resorting to grassroots campaigns and internet petitions to keep their cause alive. Dozens of backbenchers in the House of Commons support them, in part motivated by concern that the United States may have used Diego Garcia as a hub in its program of extraordinary renditions during the Global War on Terror.[17]

In 2010, Great Britain declared that it was designating large sections of its British Indian Ocean Territory (BIOT) as a "marine protected area" in order to preserve its rich biodiversity of corals, sharks, mantra rays, tuna, and critically endangered species such as the green turtle. Mauritius, from which Britain administered the Chagos islands prior 1965, has long sought to regain control of the islands. It perceived the British declaration as an effort to mask power politics behind the cloak of environmentalism. Mauritius appealed the matter to the Permanent Court of Arbitration. In March 2015, the Court of Arbitration ruled that the United Kingdom violated international law in setting up the Marine Protected Area. It noted that the United Kingdom had promised Mauritius special fishing, oil, and mineral rights in September 1965, and had pledged to return the Chagos Archipelago to Mauritius once Britain no longer needed them for defense purposes.[18] The court noted that the United Kingdom had not consulted Mauritius sufficiently prior to declaring the area a protected maritime zone, adding that the United Kingdom had engaged the United States much more attentively. Leaked cables between British and American officials regarding the proposed Marine Protected Area, the return of Chagossians, and potential side effects on U.S. military operations out of Diego Garcia substantiate the court's impression.[19] In June 2017, the General Assembly of the United Nations voted 94 to 15 in favor of a resolution that the International Court of Justice render an advisory opinion on the validity of the separation of the Chagos Archepelago from Mauritius.[20]

Successive British governments have resisted pressure by Mauritius, the UN, and by former Chagossians to revisit the question of sovereignty over the Chagos Islands. The United Kingdom correctly understands that Diego Garcia is prime real estate in the Indian Ocean, and that Britain's claim to a "special relationship" with the United States rests in part on what it can provide the United States in terms of intelligence, access, and global presence. Diego Garcia, located equidistant to Africa, India, and Indonesia, provides a unique asset. Its gigantic natural harbor, protected by coral reefs, is large and deep enough to accommodate a carrier task group while its two parallel runways are long and strong enough to accommodate even the heaviest bombers.[21] The initial Anglo-American agreement of 1966 has been amended and updated nine times. By agreement, the Americans have been allowed to construct a superb operating base equipped with wharfs, piers, repair shops, ammo storage facilities, oil tanks, and the like. In addition, the U.S. military and other entities have crammed the island full of radars, satellite ground stations, and communication gears, sharing much of the intelligence with the United Kingdom under the rubric of the "Five Eyes" intelligence agreement.[22] The United States has come to regard Diego Garcia as an essential operating base, with long range bombers launching from the island to support Operation Desert Storm in 1991, Operation Enduring Freedom in 2001, and Operation Iraqi Freedom in 2003. As China, Russia, and other powers build increasingly sophisticated "anti-access, area denial" systems, Diego Garcia has become an essential U.S. outpost in the Indian Ocean as it is situated beyond the range of most missiles.[23] Great Britain, at little cost to itself, contributes a great deal to the United States' ability to project and maintain Western power in the region. As Lady Anelay, Minister of State of the Foreign and Commonwealth Office put it in November 2016, the facilities at Diego Garcia are

> used by us and our allies to combat some of the most difficult problems of the 21st century including terrorism, international criminality, instability and piracy . . . the UK continues to welcome the US presence, and the agreements will continue as they stand until 30 December 2036.[24]

Britain's withdrawal "East of Suez" in the 1970s did not end its military relationship with its former colonies and dominions in the Indo-Pacific region. The Five Power Defence Arrangements (FPDA), a series of multi-lateral agreements between the United Kingdom, Australia, New Zealand, Malaysia, and Singapore, committed these Commonwealth nations to consult with one another if Malaysia or Singapore were attacked. Initially cobbled together to reassure Malaysia and Singapore that Britain was not abandoning them during a period when tensions ran high with Indonesia, the FPDA has evolved to address other concerns such as piracy, drug smuggling, and environmental issues. The Five Powers conduct annual naval exercises, with meetings and dinners providing a forum for defense chiefs from each country to exchange views.[25] While Britain's contribution to FPDA exercises tends to be small, lagging well behind that of Australia, the forum provides an opportunity to tout British defense products, discuss regional concerns, and keep a pulse on developments in the South China Seas and Western Pacific. The Royal Navy still maintains a fuel depot and a berthing wharf at Singapore's Sembawang dockyard, with a small detachment of personnel maintaining these facilities and supporting Royal Navy port calls to the Far East. Britain's latest national security strategy indicates that the United Kingdom intends to ramp up its participation in future FPDA exercises, potentially having one of the United Kingdom's new Queen Elizabeth class aircraft carriers participate in future exercises to demonstrate its interest in the region.[26]

Britain continues to nurture lively bilateral ties with Australia and New Zealand as well, consisting of officer exchanges, ministerial consultations, and joint exercises. In 2013, the United Kingdom and Australia went a step further, signing the Australia – United Kingdom Defence and Security Cooperation Treaty. The treaty formalizes bilateral military cooperation, underlines mutual interest in interoperability, and pledges that the British and Australian militaries will explore the idea of collaborative procurement.[27] Britain continues to honor other bilateral arrangements in the region as well, most notably its arrangement to protect Brunei with a battalion of Royal Gurkha Rifles. The British battalion, paid for by the government of Brunei, serves to dissuade Brunei's neighbors from annexing the oil rich but militarily weak nation. Britain benefits from the arrangement in that the Gurkha Rifles are in effect subsidized. In addition, the British Army uses the arrangement to train its soldiers in jungle warfare, operating a small Jungle Warfare Training School in Seria, Brunei.[28]

The most important shift in Britain's posture in the Indian Ocean has been a resurrected permanent presence in the Gulf. In 2012, Chief of Defence Staff (CDS) General Sir David Richards laid out plans to deploy significant British military assets to the Middle East, in particular to the six Gulf Cooperation Council (GCC) states. He noted that Britain was reorganizing its forces into a new Joint Expeditionary Force which would be capable of "projecting power with global effect and influence," and indicated that the United Kingdom anticipated rotating expeditionary forces through the Gulf region in order to reassure Britain's friends and deter their adversaries.[29] Richards elaborated that the Defence Staff envisioned prepositioning forces and equipment in the region, asserting that "After Afghanistan, the Gulf will become our main military effort."[30]

As part of this vision, the United Kingdom is massively expanding the naval facilities at Mina Salman in Bahrain where it currently homeports four minehunter vessels. The new port facility, HMS Juffair, will be able to host the Royal Navy's Type 45 destroyers as well as support port calls by Britain's new carriers once they come on line. In addition, the United Kingdom has negotiated agreements with the United Arab Emirates and Oman to operate out of Al Minhad and Musannah airbases.

Britain's 2015 Strategic Security Strategy (*A Secure and Prosperous United Kingdom*) lists three key objectives: 1) protecting the United Kingdom's people; 2) projecting the United Kingdom's global influence; and 3) promoting British prosperity. Britain's ongoing contributions to the coalition campaign against ISIL/Daesh support all three of these objectives, and Britain is prioritizing the "fight against terrorism, radicalization and extremism at home and overseas."[31] All of Britain's services are involved in Operation Shader, the British component of the coalition campaign against ISIL. As of October 2016, RAF aircraft based in Cyprus and the Gulf have conducted over 1,000 airstrikes against ISIL targets in Iraq and Syria; the British Army has deployed over 1,000 trainers, support personnel, and special forces to the Middle East; and Royal Navy has positioned destroyers and frigates in the Eastern Mediterranean and the Gulf.[32]

Britain's interest in and commitment to peace and stability in the Middle East will persist even after the military campaign against ISIL/Daesh ends. The British government envisions a military return to east of Suez, with an emphasis on strengthening its security relationship with the member states of the Gulf Cooperation Council. The Conservative government's effort to strengthen British ties with the GCC has provoked considerable criticism. The strategy aligns the United Kingdom with Arab governments that abuse human rights, repress dissent, and muzzle the press. Even supporters of the government's determination to "Return to East of Suez" concede that the strategic purpose of the realignment needs to be better explained.[33] Vague rhetoric about building relationships and tackling threats needs to be replaced with more persuasive arguments about British interests in the region.

Whether the United Kingdom has the military means to support its strategic ambitions is debatable. In 2010, the United Kingdom's new Conservative-Liberal Democrat government undertook a full spectrum review of Britain's strategic posture. The 2010 *Strategic Defence and Security Review* reduced an already austere defense budget by an additional 7.7%, gutting the Army's armored forces, cutting Royal Air Force personnel, and mothballing the Royal Navy's only carrier. Critics pointed out that the Royal Navy would have fewer warships than any period since the reign of Henry VIII.[34] The 2015 *Strategic Defence and Security Review* restored a number of programs and stabilized personnel numbers, with the government pointing out that the United Kingdom is one of the few European nations to meet NATO guidelines to spend at least 2% of national GDP on defense.[35] According to the latest review, by 2025 the United Kingdom will have a highly capable expeditionary forces of around 50,000 consisting of a maritime task group centered on a *Queen Elizabeth* class aircraft carrier equipped with F-35 aircraft; a land division with three brigades; a special forces task group, and an air group of combat, transport and surveillance aircraft.[36] Many of these capabilities, however, are only due to be delivered in 2020 or later, with the United Kingdom's power projection ability in the near term (2015–20) severely constrained. One prominent defense commentator warns that in the interim the Royal Navy "can barely patrol the United Kingdom's own waters, much less project British influence abroad.... With morale plummeting, and its few remaining ships frequently malfunctioning at Sea, the Royal Navy's suffering might be terminal."[37]

EU interests, strategy, and operations in the Indo-Pacific region

The United Kingdom and France continue to have global interests, strategies, and commitments. Each maintains an independent nuclear deterrent, and nurtures a network of bilateral and multilateral security arrangements connecting them with former colonies, dominions, and dependencies around the world. Yet both are hard-pressed to provide resources and capabilities commensurate with their status as permanent members of the United Nation's Security Council. Faced with the reality that neither can match the military power of Russia, China, and India by themselves, France and Great Britain seek to maximize their limited resources by acting in concert with others. For decades, France has promoted the idea of Europe as a world power, promoting the concept of a European Common Foreign and Security Policy (CFSP) and a European Common Security and Defence Policy (CSDP). The British Conservative Party and much of England's population never embraced these concepts, believing instead that NATO should take the lead in planning and organizing military operations within Europe and out-of-area in North Africa and the Middle East. Tony Blair's Labour government (1997–2010) went further than any previous British government in supporting CFSP/CSDP initiatives, but Britain's embrace of the idea of Europe as a political actor withered thereafter. In 2013, Prime Minister David Cameron announced that his Conservative government would ask the British public whether they wanted to stay in the European Union. Cameron did so to placate Eurosceptic backbenchers within his parties, but the political ploy backfired. In June 2016, a majority of the United Kingdom's voters cast their vote in favor of leaving the European Union. The process and mechanics of how and when Britain will leave are being negotiated, but it seems all but certain that in the future Britain will distance itself from EU operations in the Indo-Pacific region.

Britain's decision to leave the EU has dealt a sharp blow to the concept of Common (European) Foreign and Security Policy (CSFP). France, Germany, Italy, and other member states of the EU have devoted a great deal of time, effort, and treasure to the concept, arguing that only by acting together can Europe interact as a peer with the United States, China, and India. In 2015, the European Union's High Representative for Foreign Affairs and Security Policy, Federica Mogherini, was tasked with preparing a new global strategy to replace the EU's outdated 2003 *European Security Strategy*. Mogherini had the unpleasant task of presenting the new strategy, *A Global Strategy for the European Union's Foreign and Security Policy*, shortly after the Brexit referendum in June 2016. *A Global Strategy* lays out an ambitious agenda for the EU, arguing that it must develop Europe's capacity for rapid response. It pledges that the EU will contribute to global maritime security, elaborating that "In East and Southeast Asia, we will uphold freedom of navigation, stand firm on the respect for international law, including the Law of the Sea and its arbitration process, and encourage the peaceful settlement of maritime disputes."[38] Exactly how Britain's exit from the EU will affect Europe's Common Foreign and Security Policy (CFSP) and Common Security and Defence Policy (CSDP) remains to be seen. The departure of one of Europe's leading naval powers will undoubtedly limit the EU's aspiration to play a role in promoting maritime governance and the rule of law in the Indo-Pacific region.

European nations, in particular France and Germany, responded to the problem posed by pirates operating off the Horn of African and Somalia by launching the EU's first naval military operation, *Atalanta*, in December 2008. France,

Germany, Greece, Italy, the Netherlands, Portugal, Spain, and Sweden all have contributed to the EU's counter-piracy mission, with a number of these countries preferring to operate under an EU mandate rather than as elements of NATO's anti-piracy task force.[39] Headquartered at Northwood Headquarters in the United Kingdom, the EU operation has lasted over seven years, with the number of ships assigned to *Atalanta* ranging from three to four. The operation has helped reduce piracy off the Horn and in the Western Indian Ocean, serving as a demonstration for what EU civil-military operations might accomplish.[40] In addition, the mission necessitated dialogue with representatives of the China's People's Liberation Navy (PLAN), since PLAN ships were engaged in anti-piracy operations in the region. Despite hopes that EU-Chinese anti-piracy collaboration might open opportunities for more substantial naval discussions, interactions to date have been limited to mission-oriented staff talks.[41]

NATO and coalition interests, strategy, and operations in the Indo-Pacific region

At first glance, it might seem odd to address the interests, strategy, and operations of the North Atlantic Treaty Organization in the Indo-Pacific region. Yet following the September 11, 2001 attacks on the World Trade Center and the Pentagon, NATO became involved in leading the International Security Assistance Force (ISAF) in Afghanistan. The mission, initially conceived as a security, stabilization, training, and reconstruction operation, lasted over 10 years and involved thousands of European troops, aircraft, and civilians. In order to support NATO's ISAF mission in Afghanistan, various European nations negotiated transit and basing rights in the Gulf region.

The ISAF mission, officially terminated in December 2014, laid the groundwork for other NATO out-of-area operations. Since 2008, NATO has taken on various missions off the Horn of Africa, in the Gulf of Aden, and in the Western Indian Ocean. In 2008, the North Atlantic Council approved the concept of using one of NATO's Standing Maritime Groups to safeguard World Food Program shipments bound for Somalia (Operation Allied Provider). In 2009, NATO broadened this limited mandate, creating an internationally recommended transit corridor through the piracy-infested waters off the Horn of Africa. Warships from Combined Task Force 150 monitored the route, intercepting pirate vessels, and boarding suspect ships as necessary. Operation Allied Protector (March – August 2009) and its successor, Operation Ocean Shield (August 2009 – December 2016), constitute NATO's contribution to a broader, 31-nation Combined Maritime Forces enterprise. The Combined Maritime Forces command, located at the U.S. Naval Support Activity in Bahrain, coordinates and supports three different task forces with different missions: CTF 150, which addresses maritime security and counter-terrorism; CTF 151, which focuses on counter-piracy operations; and CTF 152, which promotes security and cooperation in the Gulf.[42]

The overlap between NATO's Operation Ocean Shield, the EU's Operation Atalanta, and Combined Task Force 150's anti-piracy patrols presents numerous challenges. NATO and the EU have co-located their operational headquarters at Northwood in the United Kingdom, but the missions have separate chains of command. The Royal Navy has played an important role in coordinating the distinct operations, dual-hatting various officers in Northwood and in Bahrain. In practice, these various overlapping missions have generated remarkably little friction, with cooperation generally prevailing.[43] Whether this remarkable unity of effort will persist once Britain disassociates itself from the European Union remains to be seen.

In conclusion, the Republic of France, the United Kingdom, and the European Union all agree that they have interests in the Indo-Pacific region. Each has laid out strategies for protecting and promoting these interests, with general agreement about the importance of the region to Europe's prosperity and safety. In addition, France, the United Kingdom, and the European Union agree that protecting merchant shipping, combatting violent extremism, and promoting the rule of law in the Indo-Pacific region are important goals. Yet how to pool European resources to achieve these goals remains contested. France, Germany, and a number of smaller European nations continue to push for a European Union role in foreign and security policy, arguing that Europeans need to collaborate and speak with one voice if they aim for geo-political influence commensurate with Europe's economic weight. European federalists, long irked by the United Kingdom's lukewarm support of a Common Foreign and Security Policy, have responded to the United Kingdom's decision to leave the Union by doubling down. They are pushing for more, rather than less, European military integration. A post-Brexit United Kingdom, on the other hand, will want nothing to do with ESDP operations and missions. It may also be poorer, with some questioning whether "Little England" will be able to afford the sort of military envisioned in the pre-Brexit 2015 Strategic Defence and Security Review.[44] The United Kingdom prefers to pool resources and project power via its special relationship with the United States or via coalition constructs such as the Combined Maritime Forces, the Five Power Defence Arrangement, or NATO out-of-area operations. This British preference resonates with several other European countries, in particular Norway (a European member of NATO which has not joined the European Union) and Greece, which is growing increasingly disillusioned with the European project. Europeans are deeply divided about whether the European Union should become an "ever closer union" or whether power should devolve back to its nation-states.[45] This fundamental disagreement about Europe's future means that its two strongest air and naval powers, Britain and France, are pursuing common objectives in the Indo-Pacific region but cannot agree about how to pool or coordinate their efforts. The result is strategic confusion, characterized by disconnects between the ends, ways, and means of contemporary European strategy in the Indian Ocean.

Notes

1 INSEE, www.insee.fr/fr/themes/detail.asp?ref_id=estim-pop&
2 MoD (France), 2016b, p. 6.

3 Economist Data Team, 2016.
4 MoD (France), 2016b, p. 6.
5 MoD (France), 2016c.
6 Liebl, 2008, p. 80.
7 MoD (France), 2016d.
8 MoD (France), 2016b, pp. 2, 6.
9 MoD (France), 2016b, p. 2.
10 Rey and Germain, 2016, p. 32.
11 Perlo-Freeman, Fleurant, Wezeman and Wezeman, 2016, p. 2.
12 MoD (France), 2016a, pp. 19–21.
13 MoD (France), 2016a, pp. 17–18.
14 MoD (France), 2016b, p. 2.
15 Sand, 2009, pp. 15–24.
16 Sand, 2009, pp. 63–68.
17 Harris, 2015, p. 511.
18 Permanent Court of Arbitration, 2015, Case nr. 2011–03.
19 Vine, 2010.
20 General Assembly Resolution GA/11924.
21 Erickson, 2013, pp. 22–23.
22 Sand, 2009, pp. 35–49.
23 Erickson, 2013.
24 *The Guardian*, 16 November 2016.
25 Huxley, 2012.
26 SDSR, 2015, p. 59.
27 Davies and Schreer, 2013.
28 MoD (UK), 2016b.
29 Stansfield and Kelly, 2013, p. 7.
30 Gardner, 2013.
31 SDSR, 2015, pp. 11–12.
32 MoD (UK), 2016a.
33 Stansfield and Kelly, 2013, p. 15.
34 O'Brien, 2010; SDSR 2010.
35 SDSR, 2015, p. 5.
36 SDSR, 2015, pp. 27–32.
37 Axe, 2016.
38 EU Global Strategy, 2016, pp. 38–41.
39 Nováky, 2015, p. 501.
40 Riddervold, 2011; Pejsova, 2016.
41 Barton, 2013, p. 69.
42 Combined Maritime Forces, https://combinedmaritimeforces.com/about/
43 Gebhard, C., and Smith, J.S., 2015, pp. 109.
44 Tan, 2016.
45 Pew Research Center, 2016.

References

Axe, D., 2016. What the US Should Learn From Britain's Dying Navy. *Reuters Commentary*, [online] 11 August. Available at: <www.reuters.com/article/us-uk-military-navy-commentary-idUSKCN10L1AD> [Accessed 26 October 2016].

Barton, B. 2013. The EU's Engagement of China in the Indian Ocean. *The RUSI Journal*, 158(6), pp. 66–73.

Davies, A., and Schreer, B., 2013. Australia-UK Defence Arrangements. *The Strategist*, [online]. Available at: www.aspistrategist.org.au/australia-uk-defence-arrangements [Accessed 14 September 2016].

Economist Data Team, 2016. Drops in the Ocean: France's Marine Territories. *The Economist*, [online]. 13 January. Available at: <www.economist.com/blogs/graphic detail/2016/01/daily-chart-10> [Accessed 15 October 2016].

Erickson, A., Ladwig, W., and Mikolay, J., 2013. Diego Garcia: Anchoring America's Future Presence in the Indo-Pacific. *Harvard Asia Quarterly*, 15(2), pp. 20–28.

European Union, 2016. *Shared Vision, Common Action. A Global Strategy for the European Union's Foreign and Security*, [online] Available at: http://europa.eu/globalstrategy/en [Accessed 17 October 2016].

Gardner, F., 2013. 'East of Suez': Are UK Forces Returning? *BBC News*, [online]. 29 April. Available at: www.bbc.com/news/uk-22333555 [Accessed 17 October 2016].

Gebhard, C., and Smith, J. S., 2015. The Two Faces of EU-NATO Cooperation: Counter-Piracy Operations Off the Somali Coast. *Cooperation and Conflict*, 50(1), pp. 107–127.

General Assembly of the United Nations, Plenary Seventy-First Session, 88th Meeting. 2017. Meetings Coverage and Press Releases, GA/11924. Available at: <www.un.org/press/en/2017/ga11924.doc.htm> [Accessed 5 July 2017].

Harris, P., 2015. America's Other Guantánamo: British Foreign Policy and the US Base on Diego Garcia. *The Political Quarterly*, 86(4), pp. 507–514.

Huxley, T., 2012. The Future of the Five Power Defence Arrangements. *The Strategist*, [online] Available at: <www.aspistrategist.org.au/the-future-of-the-five-power-defence-arrangements/> [Accessed 14 September 2016].

Institut national de la statistique et des études économiques (INSEE), 2015. *Estimation de la population au 1er janvier par région, département, sexe et âge de 1975 à 2015*, [online]. Available at: <www.insee.fr/fr/themes/detail.asp?ref_id=estim-pop&> [Accessed 17 October 2016].

Liebl, V., 2008. Military Policy Options to Revise the French Military Presence in the Horn of Africa. *Comparative Strategy*, 27(1), pp. 79–87.

Ministry of Defence (France), 2016a. *Defence Key Figures*, [online]. Available at: <www.defense.gouv.fr/english> [Accessed 17 October 2016].

———, 2016b. *France and Security in the Asia-Pacific*, [online] Available at: <www.gouvernement.fr/en/defence-and-security > [Accessed 17 October 2016].

———, 2016c. *Les forces armées dans la zone sud de l'Océan Indien*, [online]. Available at: <www.defense.gouv.fr/ema/forces-prepositionnees/la-reunion-mayotte/dossier/les-forces-armees-dans-la-zone-sud-de-l-ocean-indien> [Accessed 17 October 2016].

———, 2016d. *Les forces françaises prépositionnées* [online]. Available at: <www.defense.gouv.fr/ema/forces-prepositionnees> [Accessed 17 October 2016].

Ministry of Defence (UK), 2016a. *British Forces Air Strikes in Iraq and Syria: Monthly List* [online] Available at: <www.gov.uk/government/publications/british-forces-air-strikes-in-iraq-monthly-list > [Accessed 26 October 2016].

———, 2016b. *The British Army in Brunei* [online] Available at: <www.army.mod.uk/operations-deployments/22792> [Accessed 26 October 2016].

National Security Strategy and Strategic Defence and Security Review (SDSR) (UK), 2010. *Securing Britain in an Age of Uncertainty*. London: HMSO.

———, 2015. *A Secure and Prosperous*. London: HMSO.

Niblett, R., 2015. *Britain, Europe and the World: Rethinking the UK's Circles of Influence*. London: Royal Institute of International Affairs.

Nováky, N., 2015. Deploying EU Military Crisis Management Operations: A Collective Action Perspective. *European Security*, 24(4), pp. 491–508.

O'Brien, R. 2010. Is This the End of the Royal Navy. *CBS News*, [online]. 22 October. Available at: <www.cbsnews.com/news/is-this-the-end-of-the-royal-navy/> [Accessed 26 October 2016].

Pejsova, E., 2016. *Scrambling for the Indian Ocean*. Paris: European Union Institute for Security Studies (EUISS). Available at: <www.iss.europa.eu/publications/detail/article/scrambling-for-the-indian-ocean/> [Accessed 13 September 2016].

Perlo-Freeman, S., Fleurant, A., Wezeman, P., and Wezeman, S., 2016. *Trends in World Military Expenditures, 2015*. Stockholm: Stockholm International Peace Research Institute (SIPRI). Available at: <www.sipri.org/publications/2016/sipri-fact-sheets/trends-world-military-expenditure-2015> [Accessed 16 October 2016].

Permanent Court of Arbitration, 2015. *Chagos Marine Protected Area Arbitration (Mauritius v. United Kingdom), Case nr. 2011–03*, [online]. Available at: <http://pcacases.com> [Accessed 27 October 2016].

Pew Research Center, 2016. *Euroskepticism Beyond Brexit. Significant opposition in key European countries to an ever closer EU* [online]. Available at: <www.pewglobal.org/2016/06/07/euroskepticism-beyond-brexit/> [Accessed 16 October 2016].

Rey, N., and Germain, V., 2016. *50 Years of Overseas Operations in Africa (1964–2014)*. Paris: French Employment Doctrine Center (CDEF) [online]. Available at: <www.cdef.terre.defense.gouv.fr/contents-in-english/our-publications/cahier-du-retex/cahier-du-retex-research/50-years-of-overseas-operations-in-africa> [Accessed 16 October 2016].

Riddervold, M., 2011. Finally Flexing its Muscles? Atalanta-The European Union's Naval Military Operation Against Piracy. *European Security*, 20(3), pp. 385–404.

Sand, P., 2009. *United States and Britain in Diego Garcia. The Future of a Controversial Base*. New York: Palgrave Macmillan.

Stansfield, G., and Kelly, S., 2013. *A Return to East of Suez? UK Military Deployment to the Gulf*. London: RUSI Publications. Available at: <https://rusi.org/publication/briefing-papers/return-east-suez-uk-military-deployment-gulf> [Accessed 26 October 2016].

Tan, E., 2016. After Brexit, Will Britain Leave the Asia-Pacific Too? *The National Interest*, [online]. Available at: <http://nationalinterest.org/feature/after-brexit-will-britain-leave-the-asia-pacific-too-16908?page=show> [Accessed 13 September 2016].

Vine, D., 2010. WikiLeaks Cables Reveal Use of Environmentalism by US and UK as Pretext to Keep Natives From Returning to Diego Garcia. *Foreign Policy in Focus*, [online]. Available at: <http://fpif.org/wikileak_cables_reveal_use_of_environmentalism_by_us_and_uk_as_pretext_to_keep_natives_from_returning_to_diego_garcia/> [Accessed 27 October 2016].

5 Japanese maritime perspectives, interests, objectives, and policies

Takuya Shimodaira

As a peace-loving nation Japan, since the end of the Pacific War, has contributed to the peace, stability and prosperity of the Asia-Pacific region and the world for over 70 years.[1] Recently, the Japanese Defense White paper stated, "The security environment surrounding Japan has become increasingly severe with various challenges and destabilizing factors becoming more tangible and acute."[2] The current security environment around Japan has become increasingly severe and complex due to the mixing of traditional and non-traditional security threats. Japan, therefore, should play an even more proactive role within this security environment as a major global player.

No single nation can maintain its own peace and security in the current world. Japan, therefore, has contributed to the maximum extent possible to multinational efforts to maintain and restore international peace and security – for example through United Nations (U.N.) peacekeeping operations. The Government of Japan has also been making enhancements to its security policy such as the establishment of the National Security Council (NSC), the adoption of the National Security Strategy (NSS), and the National Defense Program Guidelines (NDPG) on December 2013.[3]

These efforts are made based on the belief that Japan, as a "Proactive Contributor to Peace," needs to contribute more actively to the peace and stability of the region and the international community in cooperation with its key ally, the United States. Based on the NSS, the following is the essence of the Japanese maritime perspective, interests, objectives, and policies.

Maritime perspective

The twenty-first century is witnessing a rapid change in the global balance of power and globalization. The primary driver of this change is China, which is further increasing its presence in the Asia-Pacific region and the international community. The United States remains the world's largest power as a whole and has manifested a "rebalance" policy to shift its emphasis of national security and economic policy towards the Asia-Pacific region.[4]

Global security environment and challenges

There are six elements of the global security environment and challenges that impact Japan's security: (1) a shift in the balance of power and the rapid progress of technological innovation; (2) a threat posed by the proliferation of weapons of mass destruction and other related materials; (3) the threat of international terrorism; (4) risks to the global commons; (5) challenges to human security; and (6) the risks emerging from the global economy.

Shift in the balance of power

The balance of power in the international system has been changing on an unprecedented scale, and this has substantially influenced the dynamics of international politics. In addition, while the rapid advancement of globalization and technological innovation has deepened interdependence among states, it has also invited a change in the relative influence between states and non-state actors, and brought about a complex impact on the global security environment. Sovereign states remain the principal actors in the international community, and conflict and coordination between states continue to be the most significant factors affecting global stability. However, as the cross-border flow of people, goods, capital, information and other items have been facilitated by the advancement of globalization, non-state actors are beginning to play a more important role in decision-making in the international community.

Weapons proliferation

As the only country to have ever suffered the impact of atomic bombings in war, Japan best understands the tragedy of the use of nuclear weapons and shoulders the responsibility to realize a world free of nuclear weapons. In particular, the issue of nuclear and missile development by North Korea continues to pose grave threats to peace and stability, not only in the region but also in the entire international community.

International terrorism

Terrorist attacks continue to occur around the world, and the threat of terrorism by international terrorist organizations remains serious. International terrorism has spread and become diverse in its forms. Consequently, it has underscored the increasing importance of combating terrorism through international cooperation.

Risks to the global commons

In recent years, risks that can impede the utilization of and free access to the global commons, such as the sea, outer space, and cyberspace, have been spreading and are becoming more serious. On the seas, there have been an increasing number of cases of unilateral actions in an attempt to change the status quo by coercion without paying respect to existing international law. With regard to outer space and cyberspace, applicable norms remain to be developed due to the different positions among relevant countries. It has, therefore, become even more important to promote appropriate international regulations over the global commons and to make concerted efforts by the international community to respect such rules. "Open and Stable Seas" constitute the basis for peace and prosperity throughout the international community as a whole. However, in recent years, the number of cases of conflict of interests between or among states over natural resources and the security of those respective states is increasing. As a result, there is a growing risk of incidents at sea, and of possible escalation into unexpected situations.

The sea lanes of communication are also becoming increasingly vulnerable due to regional conflicts, international terrorism in and around the coastal states, and piracy. Japan is largely dependent on these sea lanes for its natural and energy resources. Therefore, advancing efforts to address these issues is also important for securing the sea lanes.

Challenges to human security

The Millennium Development Goals (MDGs) – common goals in the development field to be achieved by the international community – are not likely to be achieved in some regions and sectors.[5] In addition, the increasing demand for energy, food and water resources due to population growth in developing countries and the expansion of economies could cause new conflicts. These challenges could have repercussions for the peace and stability of the international community; therefore, Japan needs to promote necessary measures based on the principle of human security.

The global economy and its risks

There are concerns over fiscal problems and the slowdown in the growth of emerging economies. The visible signs of protectionism as well as reluctance towards the creation of new trade rules have been observed in some emerging economies and developing countries. With the advancement of technological innovation in the energy sector, one has seen the rise of resource nationalism in resource rich countries and a growing global demand, especially in emerging economies, for energy and mineral resources. This is exacerbated by the intensified competition for the acquisition of such resources.

Security environment and challenges in the Asia-Pacific region

There are three elements of the security environment and challenges in the Asia-Pacific region that impact on Japan's maritime concern: (1) characteristics of the strategic environment of the Asia-Pacific region; (2) North Korea's military buildup and provocative actions: and (3) China's rapid rise and intensified activities in various areas.

Characteristics of the strategic environment of the Asia-Pacific region

The Asia-Pacific region is home to a host of actors, such as countries with large-scale conventional military capabilities, as well as, in some cases, nuclear capabilities. Yet a regional cooperation framework in the security realm has not been sufficiently institutionalized. Countries in the region have contrasting political, economic and social systems, and thus their security views are diverse. The Asia-Pacific region has become more prone to so-called "gray-zone" situations which are neither pure peacetime nor contingencies over territorial sovereignty and interests. There is a risk that these "gray-zone" situations could further develop into grave situations. Therefore, it is important to further promote and develop multilayered initiatives for regional stability.

North Korea's military buildup and provocative actions

North Korea continues to face serious economic difficulties without any improvement in its human rights situation, and it heavily allocates its resources to military affairs. In addition, North Korea has enhanced the capability of WMDs, including nuclear weapons and ballistic missiles. At the same time, North Korea has repeatedly taken provocative military actions in the Korean Peninsula, including the use of inflammatory rhetoric, some of which is directed at Japan, thereby increasing the tension in the region.

China's rapid rise and intensified activities in various areas

China has been rapidly advancing its military capabilities in a wide range of areas through the continued increase in its military budget without sufficient transparency. In addition, China has taken actions that can be regarded as attempts to change the status quo by coercion based on its own assertions, which are incompatible with the existing order of international law in the maritime and aerial domains, including the East China Sea and the South China Sea. In particular, China has rapidly expanded and intensified its activities in the seas and airspace around Japan, including intrusion into Japan's territorial waters and airspace around the Senkaku Islands. Moreover, China infringed upon the freedom of overflight above the high seas by establishing its own "Air Defense Identification Zone" over the East China Sea. The People's Liberation Army Navy (PLAN) is expected to strengthen its necessary capabilities in order to gain a position of advantage in conflicts over territorial sovereignty and maritime rights and interest, strengthen deterrence against the United States, and to protect and expand China's national interests overseas.[6]

Situation of the Senkaku Islands

China has rapidly expanded its maritime activities both in qualitative and quantitative ways. The continuing intrusions of Chinese government vessels into Japanese territorial waters around the Senkaku Islands are an infringement of Japan's sovereignty. There is no doubt that the Senkaku Islands are clearly an integral part of the territory of Japan, in light of historical facts and based upon international law. Indeed, the Senkaku Islands are under the valid control of Japan. There exists no issue of territorial sovereignty to be resolved concerning the Senkaku Islands. Japan continues to strive for peace and stability in the region, which is to be established through the observance of international law.[7]

Both Japan and the United States confirmed that the Senkaku Islands are under the administration of the Government of Japan and fall within the scope of Article 5 of the Japan-U.S. Treaty of Mutual Cooperation and Security at the joint statement on February 12, 2017. The two countries also confirmed that they will oppose any unilateral attempts to undermine Japan's administration of these islands.[8]

The Japan Self-Defense Force (SDF) routinely and continuously engages in surveillance activities in the waters surrounding Japan so that it can respond to various emergencies promptly and seamlessly. The Maritime Self-Defense Forces (MSDF) routinely patrol the waters surrounding Japan – including the Senkaku Islands – with the flexible use of destroyers and aircraft as required. A state of readiness is maintained for responding quickly to situations in areas surrounding Japan. In addition, the Ground Self-Defense Force (GSDF) coastal surveillance units and MSDF security posts conduct 24/7 surveillance activities in the major sea straits.

The PLAN and government ships have been increasing and expanding rapidly in waters near Japan, including the East China Sea in recent years. The Ministry of Defense (MOD) and SDF are strengthening cooperation with relevant ministries and agencies, including routine information sharing with the Japan Coast Guard (JCG), so as to ensure that there is no gap in Japan's defense and security systems. In the event that it is deemed extremely difficult or impossible for the JCG to respond to a situation, an order for "maritime security operations" will be issued in a timely manner and the SDF will respond to the situation in cooperation with the JCG.

Principles underpinning Japanese Foreign policy

Japan is a country with a rich culture and tradition and it upholds universal values, such as freedom, democracy, respect for fundamental human rights, as well as the rule of law. Japan has a wealth of highly educated human capital and high cultural standards, and is an economic power with a strong economic capacity and high technological capabilities. Japan's economy has benefitted from an open international economic system.

Surrounded by the sea on all sides and blessed with an immense exclusive economic zone and an extensive coastline, Japan as a maritime state has achieved economic growth through maritime trade and the development of marine resources, and has pursued a policy of "Open and Stable Seas."

Since the end of the Pacific War, Japan has consistently followed the path of a peace-loving nation. Japan has adhered to a basic policy of maintaining an exclusively national defense-oriented policy, not becoming a military power that poses a threat to other countries, and observing the Three Non-Nuclear Principles.[9] In addition, Japan has maintained its security, and contributed to the peace and stability of the Asia-Pacific region, by enhancing its alliance with the United States with which it shares universal values and strategic interests, as well as by deepening cooperative relationships with other countries.

Moreover, Japan has contributed to the realization of stability and prosperity in the international community through initiatives for supporting the economic growth of developing countries and by addressing global issues based on the principle of human security, as well as through trade and investment relations with other countries. In particular, Japan's cooperation contributed to realizing stability, economic growth and democratization in many countries, especially those in Asia, including the member states of the Association of Southeast Asian Nations (ASEAN).

Furthermore, as a peace-loving nation complying with the U.N. Charter, Japan has been cooperating with the U.N. and other international organizations and has actively contributed to their activities. In particular, Japan has continuously participated in U.N. peacekeeping operations, as the role of military forces diversified after the end of the Cold War. In addition, as the only country to have ever suffered atomic bombings in war, Japan has consistently engaged in disarmament and non-proliferation efforts, playing a leading role in international initiatives to realize "a world free of nuclear weapons."

Under the evolving security environment, Japan will continue to adhere to the course it has taken to date as a peace-loving nation. As a major player in world politics and the global economy, it will contribute even more proactively in securing peace, stability and prosperity of the international community, while achieving its own security as well as peace and stability in the Asia-Pacific region, as a "Proactive Contributor to Peace" based on the principle of international cooperation. This is the fundamental principle of national security that Japan will continue to hold.

National interests

The Government of Japan needs to define its national interests and national security objectives, examine them in the context of the constantly evolving security environment and mobilize all possible means. Japan's first national interest is to maintain the peace and security of Japan, to defend its territorial integrity, to ensure the safety of life, person and properties of its nationals, and to ensure its survival based on freedom and democracy and preserving its rich culture and tradition.

In addition, Japan's national interests include achieving prosperity for Japan and its nationals through economic development, thereby consolidating its peace and security. To this end, especially in the Asia-Pacific region, it is essential that Japan, as a maritime state, strengthen the free trade regime for accomplishing economic development through free trade and competition, and to realize an international environment that offers stability, transparency and predictability.

Similarly, the maintenance and protection of the international order based on rules and universal values, such as freedom, democracy, respect for fundamental human rights and the rule of law, are also in Japan's national interests.

Objectives

In order to safeguard these national interests and to fulfill its responsibility in the international community, Japan will seek to achieve the following national security objectives. Japan's first objective is to strengthen the deterrence necessary for maintaining its peace and security and ensuring its survival, thereby preventing threats from directly reaching Japan; at the same time, if by any chance a threat should reach Japan, to defeat such a threat and to minimize the damage.

The second objective is to improve the security environment of the Asia-Pacific region and prevent the emergence of and reduce direct threats to Japan, through strengthening of the Japan-U.S. Alliance, enhancing the trust and cooperative relationships between Japan and its partners within and outside the Asia-Pacific region, and promoting practical security cooperation.

The third objective is to improve the global security environment and build a peaceful, stable and prosperous international community by strengthening the international order based on universal values and rules, and by playing a leading role in the settlement of disputes, through consistent diplomatic efforts and further personnel contributions.

Policies

The core of Japan's strategic approach is to enhance its resilience in national security by reinforcing its diplomatic power, defense force, economic strengths and technological capabilities. Japan contributes to peace and stability in the Asia-Pacific region and the international community. Japan also makes effective use of its diverse resources and promotes comprehensive policies. Japan will enhance the Japan-U.S. Alliance as the cornerstone and expand and deepen cooperative relationships with other countries to overcome national security challenges and achieve national security objectives as well as to contribute to peace in cooperation with the international community. Japan will take the following six concrete strategic approaches, centering on diplomatic policy and defense policy.

Six strategic approaches

Strengthening and expanding Japan's capabilities and roles

There are ten elements for strengthening and expanding Japan's capabilities and roles: (1) strengthening diplomacy for creating a stable international environment; (2) building a comprehensive defense architecture to firmly defend Japan; (3) strengthening efforts for the protection of Japan's territorial integrity; (4) ensuring maritime security; (5) strengthening cyber security; (6) strengthening measures against international terrorism; (7) enhancing intelligence capabilities; (8) defense equipment and technology cooperation; (9) ensuring the stable use of outer space and promoting its use for security purposes; and (10) strengthening technological capabilities.

Strengthening diplomacy for creating a stable international environment

It is necessary for Japan to realize an international order and security environment that is desirable for Japan. Japan will play a more proactive role in achieving peace, stability and prosperity of the international community as a "Proactive Contributor to Peace" based on the principle of international cooperation.

Japan must have the power to take the lead in setting the international agenda and to proactively advance its national interests. It is necessary to enhance diplomatic creativity and negotiating power through highlighting Japan's attractiveness and strengthening its soft power to advance such vibrant diplomacy.

Building a comprehensive defense architecture to firmly defend Japan

Japan will steadily develop its defense force to deter and defeat any threat that reaches it. It will also efficiently develop a highly effective and joint defense force and strive to ensure operations with flexibility and readiness based on jointness. Even in peacetime, Japan will maintain and improve a comprehensive architecture for responding seamlessly to situations ranging from armed attacks to large-scale natural disasters.

Strengthening efforts for the protection of Japan's territorial integrity

Japan will enhance the law enforcement capabilities for territorial patrols and reinforce its maritime surveillance capabilities. Furthermore, Japan will strengthen coordination among relevant ministries and agencies to be able to respond seamlessly to unexpected situations.

Ensuring maritime security

Japan will play a leading role in maintaining and developing "Open and Stable Seas," which are upheld by the rule of law, ensuring freedom of navigation and overflight, and peaceful settlement of disputes are maintained through close cooperation with other countries. In doing so, Japan will promote maritime security cooperation and joint exercises with other countries and strengthen its maritime domain awareness capabilities in a comprehensive manner.

Strengthening cyber security

Japan as a whole will make concerted efforts in comprehensively promoting cross-cutting measures to defend cyberspace and strengthen the response capability against cyber-attacks to ensure the free and safe use of cyberspace.

Strengthening measures against international terrorism

Japan will strengthen its domestic measures against international terrorism and build a network for collecting and analyzing the information of international terrorism.

Enhancing intelligence capabilities

Japan will enhance its information-collecting, intelligence analysis, consolidation, sharing capabilities and counterintelligence functions throughout the Government.

Defense equipment and technology cooperation

Japan will contribute more proactively to peace and international cooperation by utilizing defense equipment and participating in the joint development and production of defense equipment and other related items.

Ensuring the stable use of outer space and promoting its use for security purposes

Japan will promote the utilization of outer space from a security perspective, such as enhancing the functions of information-gathering satellites.

Strengthening technological capabilities

Japan will encourage the further promotion of technology, including dual use technologies, and make effective use of technology in the area of security, by combining the efforts of industries, academia and the government.

SDF and MSDF Capability

Based on the results of the capability assessments conducted in relation to various potential contingencies, the SDF will prioritize the development of capacities to ensure maritime supremacy and air superiority, which is the prerequisite for effective deterrence and response in various situations, including defense posture buildup in the southwestern region.

The SDF will selectively strengthen the following functions and capabilities in particular, paying attention to enhance joint functions with interoperability with the U.S. forces such as intelligence, surveillance, and reconnaissance (ISR) capabilities, intelligence capabilities, transport capability, command and control, and information and communication capabilities, response to an attack on remote islands, response to ballistic missile attacks, response in outer space and cyberspace, responses to major disasters, and responses focused on international peace cooperation activities and other similar activities.

The MSDF will increase the number of destroyers to 54 (14 escort divisions) by using new destroyers that offer improved response capabilities for various missions and have more compact designs, and will maintain ship-based patrol helicopter units in order to secure the defense of surrounding waters and ensure the safety of maritime traffic. Furthermore, two Aegis-equipped destroyers will be added, bringing the fleet to eight. In order to effectively carry out regular information-gathering and warning and surveillance activities, as well as patrolling of surrounding waters and defense operations, the MSDF will maintain patrol aircraft units and an augmented submarine fleet. The MSDF will also: maintain current structure (65 aircraft) of P-1/3C fixed-wing patrol aircraft and 80 SH-60K/J patrol helicopters and 22 submarines in the 2013 NDPG; refit tank landing ships (operation of amphibious vehicles and tilt-rotor aircraft); consider what the role should be of a multipurpose vessel with capabilities for command and control, large-scale transportation and aircraft operations, which can be utilized in various operations such as amphibious operations; provide new destroyers with capabilities for antimine operations; and extend the life of existing vessels (destroyers) and aircraft (P-3C, SH-60J).[10]

The most powerful of Japan's surface combatants are the Kongo and Atago class Aegis-equipped destroyers. These Aegis destroyers are based on the original U.S. Navy *Arleigh Burke* with carrying SM-2MR air defense missiles and SM-3 Block IB ballistic missile interceptors, the latter soon to be replaced with the newer Block IIA version.

Another formidable Japanese ship is the Izumo class helicopter destroyer. At 27,000 tons fully loaded and more than 800 feet long, *JS Izumo* has a full-length flight deck, an island for controlling flight operations, aircraft elevators and a hangar that spans the length of the ship.

Japan's submarine force is another major component of the MSDF. The Soryu class submarines are Japan's largest submarines at 4,100 tons submerged and are equipped with Stirling air independent propulsion systems, capable of powering the submarine silently underwater. The Soryus are equipped with six 533-millimeter bow-mounted torpedo tubes, with a mix of 20 Type 89 heavy weight homing torpedoes and Sub-Harpoon missiles.

Strengthening the Japan-U.S. alliance

The Japan-U.S. Alliance has played an indispensable role for peace and security in Japan as well as peace and stability in the Asia-Pacific region for more than 60 years. The alliance is the cornerstone for Japan and the United States and is underpinned by shared common strategic interests and universal values, such as freedom, democracy, respect for fundamental human rights and the rule of law.

Japan will further elevate the effectiveness of the Japan-U.S. security arrangements and realize a more multifaceted Japan-U.S. Alliance through the following two initiatives: strengthening Japan-U.S. security and defense cooperation in a wide range of areas and ensuring a stable presence of the U.S. forces in the region.

Japan will work with the United States to revise the Guidelines for Japan-U.S. Defense Cooperation, through discussions on roles, missions and capabilities. It will strive to enhance the deterrence and response capability of the Japan-U.S. Alliance through the following efforts: advancing joint training, joint ISR activities, and joint/shared use of facilities; working closely with the United States on operational cooperation and policy coordination on issues such as response to contingencies; strengthening its security cooperation with the United States in such broad areas as BMD, maritime affairs, outer space, cyberspace and large-scale disaster response operations; and enhancing interoperability and advancing multilayered initiatives with the United States such as defense equipment and technology cooperation and personnel exchanges.

Ensuring the stable presence of U.S. forces

In order to maintain and enhance the Japan-U.S. security arrangement, it is important for Japan to cooperate proactively with the United States to realize the optimal force posture of U.S. forces in the Asia-Pacific region. Japan will, therefore, steadily implement the realignment of U.S. forces in Japan, including the relocation of the U.S. Marine Corps in Okinawa to Guam in accordance with existing bilateral agreements, and increasingly implement measures to reduce the impact on people living near the facilities and areas of the U.S. forces in Japan.

Strengthening diplomacy and security cooperation

Japan will engage itself in building trust and cooperative relations with other partners both within and outside the Asia-Pacific region through the following series of approaches:

> Japan will strengthen cooperative relations with countries with which it shares universal values and strategic interests, such as the Republic of Korea (ROK), Australia, the ASEAN countries and India. The ROK is a neighboring country of the utmost geopolitical importance for the security of Japan. The trilateral cooperation among Japan, the U.S. and the ROK is a key framework in realizing peace and stability in the Asia-Pacific region and addressing North Korean nuclear and missile issues. Australia is an important regional partner that shares not only universal values but also strategic interests with Japan. Japan will also strengthen its strategic partnership and utilize the trilateral framework among Japan, the U.S. and Australia. The ASEAN countries are located in the critical areas of sea lanes of communication of Japan. Japan will further deepen and develop cooperative relations with the ASEAN countries in all sectors. India is becoming increasingly influential and also geopolitically important for Japan in the center of sea lanes of communication. Japan will strengthen bilateral relations in a broad range of areas based on the bilateral Strategic and Global Partnership.[11]

Stable relations between Japan and China are an essential factor for peace and stability of the Asia-Pacific region. Japan will strive to construct and enhance a mutually beneficial relationship based on common strategic interests with China in all areas. In particular, Japan will continue to encourage China to play a responsible and constructive role for the sake of regional peace, stability and prosperity, to adhere to international norms of behavior, as well as to improve openness and transparency in its advancing military capabilities.

Japan will cooperate closely with relevant countries to urge North Korea to take concrete actions towards its de-nuclearization and other goals, based on the Joint

Statement of the Six-Party Talks and relevant U.N. Security Council (UNSC) Resolutions.

It is critical for Japan to advance cooperation with Russia in all areas, including security and energy in order to ensure its security.

Japan will actively utilize and engage in the further development of functional and multilayered frameworks for regional cooperation such as Asia-Pacific Economic Cooperation (APEC), the East Asia Summit (EAS), ASEAN+3, ARF, the ASEAN Defence Ministers' Meeting-Plus (ADMM-Plus) and trilateral frameworks. In addition, Japan will contribute to the creation of a more institutional security framework in the Asia-Pacific region in the future.

Japan will also cooperate with other partners of the Asia-Pacific region towards ensuring the stability of the region. These partners include Mongolia, the Central Asian countries, Southwest Asian nations, the Pacific Island Countries (PICs), New Zealand, Canada, Mexico, Colombia, Peru and Chile.

Japan will strengthen cooperative relations with countries outside the Asia-Pacific region that play an important role in ensuring the peace and stability of the international community. Europe has the influence to formulate international public opinion, the capacity to develop norms in major international frameworks and a large economy. Japan will further strengthen its relations with Europe, including cooperation with the European Union (EU), the North Atlantic Treaty Organization (NATO), and the Organization for Security and Co-operation in Europe (OSCE) in order to establish an international order based on universal values and rules.

Emerging powers such as Brazil, Mexico, Turkey, Argentina and South Africa have been increasing their presence in international politics and global economy. Japan will endeavor to further develop relations with such countries.

Stability in the Middle East is an issue that is inseparably linked to the stable supply of energy, and therefore Japan's very survival and prosperity. Japan will engage in constructing multilayered cooperative relations with the Gulf States, encompassing wide-raging economic cooperation beyond resources and energy, as well as politics and security.

Africa is a prospective economic frontier with abundant strategic natural resources and sustained economic growth. Japan will continue to contribute to the development and the consolidation of peace in Africa through various avenues.

Proactive contribution to international efforts for peace and stability

As a "Proactive Contributor to Peace" based on the principle of international cooperation, Japan will play an active role for the peace and stability of the international community. There are five elements for proactive contribution to international efforts for peace and stability of the international community:

Strengthening diplomacy at the United Nations

Japan will further engage in active efforts by the U.N. for the maintenance and restoration of international peace and security. Moreover, Japan will actively contribute to diverse U.N.-led efforts, including U.N. peacekeeping operations (PKO) and collective security measures; diplomatic efforts such as preventive diplomacy and mediation; seamless assistance efforts from the phase of post-conflict emergency humanitarian relief to recovery and reconstruction, as well as assistance through the U.N. Peacebuilding Commission.

Strengthening the rule of law

Japan will continue to comply with international law as a guardian of the rule of law. In addition, Japan will participate proactively in international rule-making from the planning stage in order to establish the rule of law in the international community with Japanese principles of fairness, transparency and reciprocity. In particular, Japan will involve itself in realizing and strengthening the rule of law relating to the sea, outer space and cyberspace. Japan will contribute proactively to the development of international rules in these areas and to the promotion of confidence-building measures among countries of mutual interest. In addition, Japan will further strengthen capacity building efforts for developing countries in these fields.

Leading international efforts on disarmament and non-proliferation

Japan, as the only country in the world to have suffered atomic bombings in war, will continue its vigorous efforts to seek "a world free of nuclear weapons." Japan will lead international efforts on disarmament and non-proliferation, steadily implement export control measures, and engage in international efforts on conventional weapons, such as small arms and light weapons, and anti-personnel mines.

Promoting international peace cooperation

Japan will further step up its cooperation with U.N. peacekeeping efforts and other forms international peace cooperation, as well endeavoring to ensure effective implementation of its operations, through coordination with other activities, including Official Development Assistance (ODA) projects. Japan will develop a system that enables assistance to potential recipient organizations that cannot receive Japan's assistance under the current schemes. Japan will consult closely with countries or organizations that have experience in the same fields, including the United States, Australia and European countries.

Promoting international cooperation against international terrorism

It is important for the international community as a whole to take a firm position against acts of terrorism. Japan will promote international counter-terrorism efforts with the international community for national security. Japan will promote consultations and exchanges of views with other countries on the situation of international terrorism and international counter-terrorism cooperation, and reinforcement of the international legal framework.

SDF overseas activities

The NSS and the NDPG state that Japan will play a leading role in maintaining and developing "Open and Stable Seas," including maritime security cooperation with other countries. As previously described, the MOD/SDF implements capacity-building assistance on maritime security for Indonesia, Vietnam and Myanmar, thereby assisting coastal states along sea lanes and others in enhancing their capabilities, and strengthening cooperation with partners that share the same strategic interests as Japan. In addition, the Basic Plan on Ocean Policy states that in order to contribute to the creation and development of order on the ocean, it will ensure international collaboration and promote international cooperation by making use of fora such as bilateral and multilateral ocean conferences to contribute to establishment of international rules and consensus. In response to this, the MOD has been working on cooperation for maritime security within the regional security dialogue such as the ADMM-Plus and the Inter-Sessional Meeting on Maritime Security (ISMMS).

The MOD/SDF is proactively undertaking international peace cooperation activities such as U.N. PKO and international disaster relief operations to respond to largescale disasters overseas, working in tandem with diplomatic initiatives, including the use of the ODA for resolving the fundamental causes of conflicts, terrorism and other problems.

In recent years, the role of advanced capabilities in military affairs has become more diverse, and opportunities for its use in humanitarian assistance and disaster relief are growing. To contribute to the advancement of international cooperation, the SDF has also engaged in international disaster relief operations proactively from the viewpoint of humanitarian contributions and improvement of the global security environment. To this end, the SDF maintains their readiness to take any necessary action based on prepared disaster relief operation plans. Based on the consultation with the Minister for Foreign Affairs, the SDF has been proactively conducting international disaster relief operations, which fully utilize their functions and capabilities, while taking into consideration specific relief requests by the governments of affected countries and disaster situations in these countries.

Responding to specific relief requests by the governments of affected countries and the scale of disaster situations in these countries, the SDF's capabilities in international disaster relief operations encompass (1) medical services, such as first-aid medical treatment and epidemic prevention; (2) transport of personnel and equipment by helicopter and other means; and (3) water supply activities using water-purifying devices. In addition, the SDF uses transport aircraft and ships to carry disaster relief personnel and equipment to the affected area.[12]

For Japan, a major maritime state, strengthening order on the seas based on such fundamental principles as the rule of law and the freedom of navigation, as well as ensuring safe maritime transport, is the foundation for its peace and prosperity, which is extremely important. The MOD/SDF engages in anti-piracy operations, as well as promoting various initiatives including assistance for capacity building in this field for those coastal states alongside the sea lanes, and making the most of various opportunities to enhance joint training and exercises in waters other than those in the immediate vicinity of Japan.

Japan has taken measures such as escort activities in accordance with the Anti-Piracy Measures Law since 2009, and it has become possible to escort not only Japan-related ships but all vessels. P-3C patrol planes carry out patrols in the skies above the Gulf of Aden. Whenever these planes detect suspicious ships, they provide information to the escort vessels, other nations' military vessels and all private merchant ships navigating the area.

Strengthening cooperation based on universal values to resolve global issues

Japan will endeavor to share universal values and reinforce an open international economic system and advance a series of measures towards the resolution of development issues and global issues.

Japan will conduct diplomacy that contributes to addressing global issues through a partnership with countries with which Japan shares universal values, such as freedom, democracy, respect for fundamental human rights including women's rights, and the rule of law.

It is necessary for Japan to address development issues that contribute to the enhancement of the global security environment. Japan will utilize its ODA in a strategic and effective manner to contribute to the realization of human security. Japan will also strengthen efforts towards the achievement of the MDGs, in areas such as poverty eradication, global health, education and water. Japan will take the lead in international cooperation on disaster management and ensure that communities around the world have a high degree of resilience to disasters.

Japan will invite a broad range of personnel from developing countries, including eminent students and administrative officials who are expected to become future leaders. Japan will make use of such opportunities to learn from their knowledge and experience, as well as provide them with opportunities to be familiarized with Japanese systems, technologies and expertise.

In addition, Japan will contribute to the growth of the global economy, which in turn, will also bring economic growth to Japan. In addition, rule-making for trade and investment in the Asia-Pacific region strengthens the vigor and prosperity in the region, and has a strategic importance of strengthening the foundation for a stable security environment in the region.

Promoting measures such as the diversification of supply sources is necessary for securing access to stable and low-cost resource supplies. Japan will actively utilize diplomatic tools to gain the understanding of countries concerned in this course. Japan will contribute to the achievement of emission reduction by the international community as a whole and to the resolution of climate change issues.

Finally, Japan considers people-to-people exchanges to be significant as they enhance mutual understanding and friendship between countries and solidify national ties. Japan will implement measures to expand two-way youth exchanges and will seek to strengthen relations with various countries into the future.

The domestic foundations of Japanese policy approaches

In order to fully ensure national security, in addition to strengthening key capabilities with diplomatic power and defense force at their core, it is vital to reinforce the domestic foundations for these capabilities to be demonstrated effectively. Considering the importance of seeking a deeper understanding for Japan's security policies both at home and abroad to ensure national security, Japan will advance the following four measures:

> In order to develop, maintain and operate defense capability steadily with limited resources in the medium- to long-term, Japan will endeavor to engage in effective and efficient acquisition of defense equipment, and will maintain and enhance its defense production and technological bases, including strengthening international competitiveness.[13]

Japan will enhance its public relations in an integrated and strategic manner through a government-wide approach. The Government as a whole will cooperate with educational institutions, key figures and think tanks. Japan will be able to gain an accurate understanding in the forum of international public opinion, and contribute to the stability of the international community.

The Government of Japan will promote the following measures: foster respect for other countries and their people as well as love for the country and region, raise awareness with regard to security on such issues as territory and sovereignty, and ensure the understanding and cooperation of residents around defense facilities. This will serve as the foundation for the activities of the SDF and the U.S. forces in Japan, through advancing measures that widen the understanding of the general public about the current status of such activities.

In order to invigorate a national discussion and debate and contribute to high-quality policy making on national security, Japan will seek to enhance and strengthen education on security-related subjects at institutions of higher education, including the dispatch of officials of relevant ministries. In addition, Japan will promote practical research on national security, and engage in deepening exchanges among the Government, higher education institutions and think tanks, thereby promoting the sharing of insight and knowledge.

Conclusion

Japan's Peace and Security Legislation authorizing limited collective self-defense passed into law on September 19, 2015. Japan's Peace and Security Legislation and the revised Guidelines for U.S-Japan Defense Cooperation will significantly increase Japan's ability to contribute to peace and security.

One of the distinctive characteristics of Japan's national security policy in recent years is the strengthening of its security relationships with Asia-Pacific countries and organizations, such as Australia, India, the ROK and the ASEAN, in addition to its traditional alliance relationship with the United States. Japan has broadened its sphere of geopolitical engagement from mainly Northeast Asia and the Asia Pacific region to an area referred to as the "Indo-Pacific" region which underlies broadening of Japan's strategic horizons.[14] The most important aspect of the incumbent Abe government's approach to the Indo-Pacific region is the strengthening of Japan's presence and partnerships in the area of maritime security through bilateral and multilateral coordination.

The Japan-U.S. alliance matters, it matters to our two great nations, it matters to the Indo-Pacific region and it matters to the world. No one should doubt the staying power of this alliance to maintain security, prosperity and peace.

Notes

1 Ministry of Foreign Affairs of Japan, 2016a.
2 Japan Ministry of Defense, 2016, p. 1.
3 Ministry of Foreign Affairs of Japan, 2016c.
4 U.S. Department of Defense, 2012.
5 http://www.mofa.go.jp/policy/oda/mdg/
6 National Institute for Defense Studies, 2016, pp. 16–18.
7 Ministry of Foreign Affairs of Japan, 2016b.
8 The White House Office of the Press Secretary, 2017.
9 Ministry of Foreign Affairs of Japan, 1967.
10 Japan Ministry of Defense, 2016, pp. 178–180.
11 Government of Japan, 2013, pp. 23–24.
12 Japan Ministry of Defense, 2016, pp. 339–345, 352.
13 Government of Japan, 2013, pp. 35–37.
14 The National Institute for Defense Studies, 2017, p. 237.

References

Government of Japan, 2013. *National Security Strategy*, December 17. Available at: www.cas.go.jp/jp/siryou/131217anzenhoshou/nss-e.pdf#search=%27national+security+strategy+japan%27

Japan Ministry of Defense. *Defense of Japan 2016*.

Ministry of Foreign Affairs of Japan, 1967. *Three Non-Nuclear Principles*. Statement by Prime Minister Eisaku Sato at the Budget Committee in the House of Representative, December 11. Available at: www.mofa.go.jp/policy/un/disarmament/nnp/

———, 2016a *Japan's Orientation as a Peace Loving Country*, March 8, Available at: www.mofa.go.jp/p_pd/pds/page22e_000691.htm

———, 2016b. *Japanese Territory*, April 13, Available at: www.mofa.go.jp/region/asia-paci/senkaku/index.html

———, 2016c. *Japan's Security/Peace & Stability of the International Community*, April 27. Available at: www.mofa.go.jp/policy/security/

The National Institute for Defense Studies, 2017. *East Asian Strategic Review 2017*, March.

National Institute for Defense Studies, Japan, 2016. *NIDS China Security Report 2016*.

U.S. Department of Defense, 2012. *Sustaining U.S. Global Leadership: Priorities for 21st Century Defense*, January.

The White House Office of the Press Secretary, 2017. *Joint Statement from President Donald J. Trump and Prime Minister Shinzo Abe*, February 10. Available at: www.whitehouse.gov/the-press-office/2017/02/10/joint-statement-president-donald-j-trump-and-prime-minister-shinzo-abe

6 The Republic of Korea navy

Capabilities, confrontations and potential outcomes

Kevin W. Madden

Introduction

Geographically, the major nations of Northeast Asia – China, Japan, the Koreas and Russia – are predisposed to be maritime powers. Geopolitically, it is logical that they also be naval powers. However, historically this has not been the case. While China has had periods of seafaring (particularly the fourteenth and fifteenth centuries, from which the People's Republic of China base their dubious claims in the South China Sea), and Japan (in the short period building up to World War II) and the Soviet Union (in the latter years of the Cold War) established themselves as naval powers for limited periods, the region's security has been largely ground-army centric with only episodic interest in naval power.

This centuries-long paradigm transmuted at the start of the twenty-first century with the advent of a Northeast Asia comprised of, for the first time, economically able states dependent on maritime security and capable of fielding substantial indigenously produced warships, with the stark exception of the Democratic People's Republic of Korea (DPRK). While some see this as a natural state of evolution for the region's security, few have recognized it for what it is – an almost complete transmogrification from unipolar dominance to a state of increasing competition.

Of these powers, the newest competitor is the Republic of Korea's (ROK) Navy. Historically absent since Admiral Yi Sun-Shin's victory (in concert with Chinese allies) over the Japanese during the *Imjin* War (1592–98), only in the wake of the Korean War (1950–53) would a nascent naval force be formed by the ROK, largely with ships transferred from the United States Navy. However, in 1995, then-Chief of Naval Operations Admiral AN Pyong-Tae outlined a plan to transform ROK naval power beyond its coastal brown-water capability into a true blue-water force.[1] Published shortly before the 1997 Asian financial crisis that stymied the ROK defense budget for almost a decade, real construction of today's modern ROK fleet did not explode until 2004–05. Between then and now no less than 30 major combatants were laid or commissioned along with the fielding of an entire new class of patrol vessels, PKX-A.

While many argue this represents the transformation of the ROK Navy from a green-water to blue-water force,[2] a more nuanced analysis reveals that the ROK

Navy is a hybrid force designed to meet the unique exigencies posed by a belligerent North Korea while providing for maritime security in a contentious region even while participating in international anti-piracy missions. In this way, the ROK Navy may very well serve as a model for second-tier navies facing multiple challenges in a budget-constrained environment. Most importantly, in a volatile neighborhood that includes an increasingly exertive PRC, hostile DPRK, former rival Japan and renascent Russia, the ROK's approach results in a navy that cannot be easily dismissed or ignored, a navy that changes operational considerations for regional actors, thereby enhancing regional security while making valuable contributions to international efforts.

Capabilities: missions and organization

The ROK Navy prepares for three key roles in peacetime and three key roles during hostilities:[3]

In Peacetime:

(1) War Deterrence: The ROK Navy will conduct show of force through various exercises and patrols to deter enemy aggression and conduct patrol operations in adjacent maritime domains to prevent enemy unconventional warfare forces from infiltrating our territory.

(2) Protection of National Sovereignty and Maritime Interests: The ROK Navy will conduct maritime patrol to protect Sea Lane of Communication (SLOC) and navigation of merchant ships, protect marine resources within economic zone, prevent terrorism-at-sea and illicit commercial activities, conduct all-weather patrol near disputed islands, and conduct surveillance and clearance activities to prevent sea contamination within economic zone.

(3) Support Foreign Policy and Elevate National Prestige: The ROK Navy will participate in Peace-Keeping Operations (PKO) as a member of the United Nations (UN), join multilateral security cooperation such as Exercise Rim of the Pacific (RIMPAC), and elevate national prestige through port-visits of ROK Navy ships.

During War:

(1) Force Projection: The ROK Navy will strike the enemy in the flank and rear coasts with a strategic landing and conduct naval gunfire, guided missile attack and special warfare on enemy key command and control facilities and military installations and key strategic targets.

(2) Sea Control: The ROK Navy will search and destroy enemy combat forces by employing surface combatants, maritime aircraft and submarines to deny enemy maritime activities and secure our maritime activities.

(3) SLOC Protection: The ROK Navy will search and destroy enemy submarines and escort shipping with ASW ships, submarines and ASW aircraft to protect SLOCs that are critical to national prosperity and clear enemy mines and open ports, utilizing surface mine countermeasures (SMCM) and airborne mine countermeasures (AMCM).

Since its origin, much of the ROK Navy's organization has been influenced by its close and continuing relationship with the U.S. Navy. To meet its diverse missions, the ROK Navy is led by a Chief of Naval Operations and his staff, co-located with the army and air force chiefs and staffs at the *Gyeryongdae* complex near *Daejon*. The Navy is further organized under the operational command of the Commander, ROK Fleet with headquarters located in *Chinhae*, who in turn leads three geographically dispersed subordinate fleets. The 1st Fleet is located on the east coast at *Donghae*, 2nd Fleet is located on the west coast at *Pyeongtaek*, and 3rd Fleet is located in the southwest at *Mokpo*. Additionally, in 2010 the ROK Navy established its two-squadron strong 7th Mobile Fleet (a.k.a. Maritime Task Flotilla Seven, MTF-7) with each squadron consisting of one KDX-III *SEJONG THE GREAT*-Class destroyer and three KDX-II *CHUNGMUGONG YI SUN-SHIN Class destroyers*.[4] In 2015 MTF-7 moved to a new naval based built on *Jeju* Island.[5]

The ROK Marine Corps (ROKMC) is also subordinate to the Commander, ROK Fleet as part of the ROK Navy. However, given its mission set in deterring the DPRK's Korean People's Army (KPA), its deployed units are under the operational control, in most cases, of ROK Army ground commands. The ROKMC fields two division with three regiments each plus additional divisional elements as well as two separate brigades. One, the 6th Marine Brigade with headquarters located on *Baengnyeong* Island,[6] along with the 90th Marine Battalion on *Yeonpyeong* Island, garrisons the "Northwest Islands," a small group of islands placed under United Nations Command by the 1953 Armistice. In March 2016 the ROKMC formed the "Spartan 3000" unit, a regimental size force billed as a special operations force consisting of 3,000 Marines capable of deploying peninsula-wide within 24 hours of notification.[7] Billed as a force designed to counter the DPRK's latest threats, the force is designed to carry out raids against enemy military facilities but is also trained to assist the ROK populace in the case of natural disasters, a seemingly wide set of mission parameters.[8] While widely publicized, the unit, stationed on the west coast at *Pohang*, does not field any unique equipment or warfighting capability and from a practical viewpoint serves mostly to underline the ROK military's readiness and resolve to respond to potential KPA incursions.

Beyond its regular organization, in 2009 the ROK Navy established its *Cheonghae* Unit (subordinate to the 7th Mobile Fleet) as part of the multinational Combined Task Force 151 consisting of ships from Australia, Pakistan, ROK, Turkey, United Kingdom and the United States to deter piracy attacks in the Gulf of Aden and off the eastern coast of Somalia.[9] The unit came to media prominence

Figure 6.1 Locations of Key ROK Navy Headquarters
Note: Base map data from Google Maps.

in January 2011 when special operators in the task force successfully rescued the South Korean crew and tanker MV *Samho Jewelry* held hostage by Somali pirates.[10]

An additional unique organization is the Northwest Islands Defense Command.[11] The command was established on June 15, 2011 in the wake of the KPA shelling of *Yeonpyeong* Island. The establishment of this command highlights a major difference in operational command and its US counterpart. In the ROK system, the Chairman of the Joint Chiefs of Staff (CJCS) is the joint operational commander at the joint level, whereas in the U.S. system the CJCS serves as an advisor with Combatant Commander's employing forces and reporting directly to the Secretary of Defense. During the rocket attack on November 23, 2010, the

ROKMC artillery on the island was criticized for responding so slowly and ineffectively – a failure attributed to a complex approval process to initiate retaliatory fires.[12] The Northwest Islands Defense Command is designed to eliminate this delay, allowing forces in the Northwest Islands to report directly to the CJCS. It should be noted that, although the islands are by Armistice placed under the direct control of the Commander, United Nations Command, that headquarters exercises limited control over the ROK forces deployed to the islands.

Critical to wartime success against the DPRK's navy, the KPN,[13] is the ROK Fleet's integration with the U.S. 7th Fleet under the U.S.-led Naval Component Command (NCC) of the Combined Forces Command. During Armistice, the Commander, 7th Fleet is embarked on the USS Blue Ridge command ship based in Yokosuka, Japan and is in command of forward-deployed ships in Japan and Guam. During hostilities on the peninsula, the NCC controls all naval forces and maritime movement in the Korea Theater of Operations (KTO).[14]

Capabilities: equipment

Surface combatants-coastal patrol

Given its peninsular geography and the constant threat of KPA special operations incursions, it is logical that the ROKN maintain a large number of coastal patrol vessels. Indeed, the foundation of the ROKN is in fact coastal patrol. For the past four decades, the workhorse of the ROKN patrol fleet has been the *CHAMSURI*-Class patrol boat. The current version is armed with a 40mm/60 Bofors, with a range of roughly 7 kilometers, and two 20mm Sea Vulcan Gatlings in turrets. With a speed of 37 knots and manned by 24 sailors, the *CHAMSURI*-Class patrol boats have proved effective in combat with DPRK adversaries and have been sold/transferred to five other nations.[15, 16, 17] While 108 of these 170-ton craft were placed in service from 1978–94, only 52 remain in active service as the ROK Navy fields substantially larger and more lethal PKX-A and PKX-B replacements.

In 2008, the ROK Navy started fielding the *GUMDOKSURI*-Class or PKX-A patrol vessel.[18] Since then, 18 of these 570 ton craft have been commissioned. Equipped with a combined diesel and gas turbine propulsion system,[19] the class also boasts three Doosan Heavy Industries waterjets. Unlike its predecessors, the PKX-A is armed with four LIG Next1 SSM-700k *Hae Sung* anti-ship subsonic speed missiles with a range in excess of 150 kilometers. Each ship also carries an indigenously produced 76mm gun and, a dual 40mm gun and *Shin-Kung* shoulder-launched surface-to-air missile.

The first hull of the ROK Navy's latest patrol boat, designated the *CHAMSURI II*-Class and known as the PKX-B, was commissioned in 2017.[20] Smaller than the PKX-A at 210 tons, 34 ships are planned for the new class.[21] With an overall length 19 meters shorter than the PKX-A version, the *CHAMSURI II*s are believed to be faster – at 40 knots – and more maneuverable than its predecessor, while still maintaining its missile and 76mm gun armaments, making it ideal for its projected role countering KPN patrol ships and incursions.[22]

Since the mid-1990s the heavy hitters of the ROK Navy's coastal defense were the 88 meter-long, 1,200 ton *POHANG*-Class corvettes. First commissioned in 1984, 24 were produced between then and 1993. Featuring a maximum speed of 32 knots with a crew of 95 sailors, two main configurations were developed: the anti-surface warfare (ASUW) version armed with two sea-skimming MM-38 Exocet missiles with a range in excess of 72 kilometers[23] and one 76mm gun, and the anti-submarine warfare (ASW) version featuring four sea-skimming missiles (or comparable indigenously produced variant, such as the C-Star, *Haeseong* I) with a range in excess of 124 kilometers,[24] two 76mm guns and two Mark 32 triple torpedo tubes with six Blue Shark torpedos, as well as depth charges.

It was a *POHANG*-Class corvette, the ROKS *Cheonan* (PCC-772) that was sunk by a DPRK CHT-02D torpedo on March 26, 2010. While some used the sinking to magnify the vulnerabilities of the class, experts pointed out the difficult challenge of submarine detection and defense in areas with the hydrography surrounding the Northwest Islands.[25]

As ROK Navy force modernization shifts towards a blue-water emphasis, the *POHANG*-Class corvettes have been slowly retired, although 16 remain in service.

Surface combatants-ocean going

The ROK Navy's original ocean-going surface combatant capability was comprised of U.S. Fletcher-Class, Allen M. Sumner-Class, and Gearing-Class destroyers transferred to the ROK from the U.S. in the 1960s and 1970s. It wasn't until 1980, as a result of President Park Chunghee's *Yulgok* Plan,[26] that the ROK Navy commissioned its first indigenously built frigate, the 2,000 ton ROKS *Ulsan* (FF 951).

Nine ships of the *ULSAN*-Class were commissioned between 1980 and 1993, with seven remaining in service as of this writing.[27] Fitted out at 2,350 tons, the current 103-meter long versions have a speed of 34 knots and range in excess of 8,000 nautical miles, crew of 186 and are armed with eight Harpoon missiles, six Blue Shark torpedoes and two 76mm guns.

After a two-decade moratorium on frigate construction, in 2013 the ROK Navy commissioned the first frigate in the 3,251 ton *INCHEON*-Class. Of the 24 planned in three batches as replacements for the *ULSAN*-Class frigates, as of 2016 the first six were in service.[28] The class is 114 meters long, a cruising range of 8,000 kilometers with a maximum speed of 30 knots and crew of 145–170 sailors. The *INCHEON*-Class realizes a significant improvement in firepower. To support amphibious operations, the frigate mounts a 5" gun. Like its predecessor, the *INCHEON*-Class also carries anti-ship missiles (eight C-Star, *Haeseong* I) and Blue Shark torpedoes. Additionally, however, it carries RIM-116 RAM short-range missiles,[29] an embarked helicopter with ASW capability and the proven Raytheon 20mm Phalanx Block 1B for missile defense. The combination of on-board sensors linked with the ASW suite of the embarked helicopter makes this class a powerful sub hunter, filling a gap its predecessors could not.[30] The newest version, initiating Batch 2, has been designated its own class (*DAEGU*-Class) with FFG 818, ROKS *Daegu* being commissioned this year.[31] This 3,600 ton version has a single turbine with all-electric propulsion and a 16-cell Korean Vertical Launch System (K-VLS) that will allow the frigates to launch medium-range air defense, anti-submarine and longer-range cruise missiles.[32] The ROK committed $186.1 million towards further construction of the *DAEGU*-Class in the 2016 defense budget, and has requested additional funding for the out years.[33] The ROK Navy also plans to retrofit the Batch 1, *INCHEON*-Class ships with the K-VLS to increase their flexibility and lethality.[34]

The centerpieces of the ROK fleet are the destroyers of the KDX-I, KDX-II and KDX-III projects – all built within the past 20 years. The KDX-I project resulted in three 3,900 ton *GWANGGAETO THE GREAT*-Class destroyers. Commissioned in 1998–2000, the project initially envisioned 12 ships, with nine being cancelled in favor of KDX-II construction. The launching of the first ship of the class, the ROKS *Gwanggaeto the Great*, was seen as the ROK Navy's true start towards a blue-water navy capable of projecting sea power outside its shores. At 135 meters long with a complement of 286 sailors, the ship is capable of 30 knots with a cruising range of 4,500 nautical miles. The class displays impressive armament, with two quadruple Harpoon missile canisters, a 5" gun, the KVLS system with Sea Sparrow missiles, two triple 324mm torpedo tubes and Mark 46 torpedoes, and two 30mm Goalkeeper close-in weapons systems. A true submarine killer, the class also carries two Super Lynx helicopters with anti-submarine sensors that work in coordination with shipboard sensors.[35]

The second project phase, KDX-II, resulted in the *CHUNGMUGONG YI SUN-SHIN*-Class, named after the famous 16th century admiral. Lengthened to 150 meters and combat loaded to 5,433 tons, this version represented another substantial increase in firepower and capability.[36] While sporting armaments similar to the KDX-I, the six KDX-IIs placed into service between 2003–08 mount a Mk 41 VLS capable of firing SM-2 Block IIIA area-air defense missiles[37] and also have a 21-round RAM inner-layer defense missile launcher to defend against cruise missiles. The SM-2 Block IIIA has improved target detection for greater probability of hit against low altitude targets.[38]

The final phase of the KDX project, the KDX-IIIs, resulted in the ROK Navy launching some of the most modern and capable warships in the world. With the class namesake ROKS *Sejong the Great* (DDG 991) being commissioned in 2008, the ROK Navy fielded its first AEGIS Combat System-equipped ship. At 165 meters and 11,000 tons combat loaded, the guided missile destroyers of the class display a sophisticated array of armaments and sensors. The AN/SPY-1 radar system integral to the AEGIS Combat System allows the ship to locate and track targets throughout a 100+ nautical mile arc. The system integrates and controls the VLS launchers and allows the ROK Navy to operate the more effective SM-2 Block IIIB[39] missile, substantially improving its capability against ballistic missiles. This sophisticated system gives the ROK Navy a Sea-Based Terminal capability around the Peninsula.[40] With the potential acquisition of SM-3 missiles, the shoot-down range could be extended to 500 kilometers, well beyond the 150 kilometer range of the land-based Terminal High-Altitude Area Defense (THAAD) system.[41] The KDX-IIIs also have an advanced ship-to-shore attack capability with the Hyunmoo-3C cruise missile, similar to the U.S. Tomahawk.[42] Beyond this impressive array the ship also carries a state-of-the-art anti-submarine suite of sensors, rockets and torpedoes. As of 2017, three of the projected six ships of the class had been commissioned – one each in 2008, 2010 and 2012. Subsequent ships of the class – the largest surface warfare ships carrying the AEGIS system – will likewise be AEGIS equipped.[43] As part of MTF-7, the KDX-III are home-ported at the *Jeju* Island Naval Base.[44]

Surface combatants-amphibious

For more than four decades of its existence, the ROKMC was largely dependent on U.S. Navy and older landing ships for amphibious lift. In 2007 the ROK Navy significantly changed this condition with the commissioning of the ROKS *Dokdo* (LPH-6111), an amphibious assault ship with helicopter carrying capacity. An 18,800 ton vessel, ROKS *Dokdo* is the first in its class. The 199 meter vessel has a speed of 23 knots with a crew of 330 sailors. Built with state-of-the-art naval architecture, the ship can carry 720 marines, ten tanks, ten trucks, seven amphibious assault vehicles (AAVs), three howitzers and two landing craft air-cushioned (LCAC) hovercraft. The LCACs and AAVs operate from a well deck.[45] The ship can also carry ten helicopters, giving the embarked marines an "over the horizon" attack capability.[46]

The second ship in the class as part of the LPX program, the ROKS *Marado* (LPH-6112), is funded and currently under construction in the Hanjin Heavy Industries (HHI) shipyard with an expected commissioning date of 2020. When launched, the ROK Navy will have the capacity to launch two blue-water amphibious task forces consisting of an LPH, Aegis-capable destroyer, a mix of other destroyers and frigates, and ocean-going submarines, providing a potent naval capacity that enhances the balance between regional naval forces.

In addition to the *DOKDO*-Class of LPHs, the ROK Navy operates eight landing ships from two classes. The four 4,300 ton LSTs of the *GO JUN BONG*-Class were all commissioned between 1994–99, while the four newer, state-of-the-art 7,000 ton *CHEON WANG BONG*-Class ships are all new, with the first being commissioned in 2014 and the fourth one just finishing construction with a planned 2018 commissioning date. Both vessels can carry a large combination of troops, tanks, AAVs and landing craft in support of amphibious operations.

Submarines

Understanding the requirement to combat a large fleet of KPAN submarines as well as the potential to defend SLOCs against a numerically superior foe, the ROKN began fielding a submarine force in the early 1990s. The first boat was built by the German firm Howaldtswerke-Deutsche Werft (HDW) based on a 1,415-ton Type 209 design with the next two being constructed by Daewoo Shipbuilding and Marine Engineering using German kits.[47] Designated as the *CHANG*

BOGO-Class (KSS-I), subsequent boats were built wholly indigenously. After the first six boats (commissioned in 1993–97), the next three (2000–01) were improved 1,450+ ton versions capable of launching Sub Harpoon missiles. All versions are capable of 21.5 knots submerged and are armed with eight 533mm torpedo tubes in the bow and carry 14 torpedoes.

Drawing on its experience in building the *CHANG BOGO* Class and working again with Germany's HDW, the ROK Navy contracted both *Hyundai* Heavy Industries (HHI) and *Daewoo* Shipbuilding and Marine Engineering (DSME) to build a new class, the *SON WONIL*-Class (KSS-II), using HDW's Type 214 as the prototypical design. The first of nine proposed (seven have been commissioned as of this writing) was commissioned in 2007. The ROK Navy has implemented spiral improvements through the series (three batches of three boats each) with the displacement increasing from 1,860 tons to 2,400+ tons. With a length of 65 meters, the KS-IIs are capable of 20 knots submerged and have a cruising range of over 19,000 kilometers. The Thales SPHINX-D Radar System provides high power pulse radar matched with an additional pulse transmitter in the top of the mast which makes the craft highly effective against submarines.[48]

The KSS-Is and KSS-IIs provide the ROK Navy not only an undersea ship-to-ship and ship-to-shore capability, but also a lethal anti-submarine capability that could neutralize the DPRK's "small sub" threat during hostilities. It should be noted that the ROK 214 design is so well regarded, despite past glitches, that Indonesia has purchased three of the class, with the first two being built by DSME and the third by an Indonesian shipbuilder under ROK license.[49, 50]

DSME is currently building what, at 3,000+ tons, will become the largest submarine in the ROK Navy inventory.[51] With a length of almost 84 meters, speed of 20 knots and cruising range of 10,000 nautical miles, the boat will match or exceed the lethality of the KS-II Class, with a capability to launch land-attack cruise missiles.[52, 53]

Missile defense

Given the DPRK's arsenal of more than a thousand varying types of short-, medium- and long-range missiles that can range the Peninsula combined with the development of increasingly lethal – including nuclear – warheads, it is understandable that perhaps no capability is more discussed in the ROK than missile defense. Unfortunately, the ROK has taken a deliberate, parsimonious approach towards gaining a genuine defense capability. Instead, they depend substantially on the U.S. Patriot/PAC-3 mobile systems[54] deployed in the ROK, the ROK operated MIM-104 Patriot/PAC 2[55] mobile systems acquired from Germany in 2008,[56] and the recently deployed and controversial[57] ground Terminal High Altitude Area Defense (THAAD) battery. Also, they have pursued development of an indigenous Korean Air and Missile Defense System (KAMD), after 11 years in the making finally gaining support in the ROK National Assembly, with almost US$1 billion committed in 2016.[58, 59]

To fill this substantial gap, and at the encouragement of the United States who sees the potential of eventually integrating ROK missile defense systems into a larger integrated regional network, the ROK Navy began acquisition of the Aegis Combat System (Baseline 7 Phase 1) combined with the AN/SPY-1D multi-function radar antennae in 2007 for fitting on its *SEJONG THE GREAT-*Class destroyers. While this version does not provide effective missile defense, the planned upgrade to Baseline 9 and additional acquisition of SM-3 missiles for the *SEJONG THE GREAT-*Class[60] and subsequent destroyers[61] will provide a capability for the ROK to effectively shoot down a number of DPRK-launched missiles and the potential to integrate with similar vessels of the U.S. Navy and Japanese Maritime Self-Defense Force. The realization of the latter will not be immediate, given the suspicion that still exists between the ROK and Japan. Until then and without substantial investment as yet unplanned and not budgeted, key facilities and population centers in the ROK will remain vulnerable to DPRK missile attack, even with the additional defense provided by U.S. systems.

Mine and countermine

Given the lessons of the Korean War where the majority of United Nations Command vessels were damaged or destroyed by DPRK-laid mines, a minesweeping capability is critical to prosecuting naval and amphibious operations against the DPRK during potential hostilities. While this has not been a point of major emphasis in current ROK Navy planning, the ROK Navy nevertheless maintains a fleet of six coastal minehunters and three minesweeper hunters. Additionally, the fleet fields two minelayer support ships, including the recently launched MLS 570 *Nampo*.

The *GANGGYEONG*-Class coastal minehunters, with six ships of the class commissioned between 1986 and 1994, comprise the bulk of the fleet's minehunting capability. At 520 tons, the ROK Navy versions are unlicensed versions of the Italian LERICI-Class minehunter design and are very-low magnetic signature ships. As their name implies, the class has a maximum speed of 14 knots and a cruising range of only 1,500 nautical miles. The more capable 880-ton *YANGYANG*-Class, with three ships commissioned between 1999 and 2004, has a variable depth sonar and a fully-integrated minehunting system. The ship is also anti-shock and anti-magnetic with minimum underwater acoustic and electromagnetic interference.

The *NAMPO*-Class minelayer support ship is the first of four projected in the class. Delivered in 2017, the 3,000 ton ship has, besides a minelaying system, a 76mm gun, 4 KVLS cells and torpedo launchers.[62] It can also support shipboard helicopter operations.

Naval aviation

The ROK Navy, as a niche navy developing a limited expeditionary capability, has a small aviation arm centered on four functional capabilities: reconnaissance, anti-submarine warfare, transport and search and rescue. The latter is small and consists of eight UH-60P[63] and eight aging UH-1H helicopters. The UH-60P Blackhawks are produced by Korean Air under license with Sikorsky Aircraft, the bulk going to the ROK Army.[64] Unlike the Blackhawks flown by the U.S. Navy, the ROK-produced version is not marinized to resist the corrosive effects of seawater, and therefore do not operate embarked on the fleets LPH. When required for operations, the helicopters deploy to the ship for short duration. Without conducting time-consuming preservation preparation, this requirement limits the ROK Navy to short duration and distance over-the-horizon operations and makes extended expeditionary operations requiring the helicopters challenging.

To blunt the DPRK's submarine challenge and improve its search and rescue capability, the ROK Navy began operating 12 of the United Kingdom's Westland Lynx Mark 99 in 1990 and added another 12 Super Lynx Mark 99A helicopters starting in 1999.[65,66] These aircraft, including the retrofits to the Mark 99s, are equipped with a Seaspray 3 radar, FLIR and dipping sonar. In consideration of the life of these aircraft, in 2013 the ROK Navy contracted to acquire the AugustaWestland Mark 159 Wildcat, initially eight aircraft for approximately US$560 million with deliveries scheduled to begin in 2015.[67] However, deliveries did not begin until 2016 due to an investigation of ROK officials and accusations of bribery surrounding the deal.[68] The aircraft have a duration of three hours and a range of 265 nautical miles. Significantly, they are equipped with an active electronically scanned array (AESA). In addition to torpedoes and depth charges, in 2014 Korea's Defense Acquisition Program Administration announced that the ROK Navy Wildcats would be the first seaborne platform to mount Israel's Spike Non-Line-of-Sight (NLOS) missiles, giving it a 25+ kilometer surface attack range.[69] The final four of the eight were deployed to aircraft capable ships[70] in July 2017.[71]

The ROK Navy fields a sophisticated fixed-wing maritime surveillance capability with 16 Lockheed Martin's P-3C/P-3CK Orion aircraft.[72] The first eight acquired are undergoing upgrade to Lot 2 standards by Korean Air and L-3 Communications with a completion date of 2018.[73,74] Upgrades include "installation of multipurpose radar to enable detection of fixed and moving targets, high-definition electro-optical/infrared cameras, digital acoustic analysis equipment and a magnetic anomaly detector."[75] The P-3s have a cruise speed of 350 knots, range of 2,380 nautical miles, endurance of 16 hours and service ceiling of 28,300 feet.[76] The aircraft is capable of carrying air-to-surface missiles, bombs, depth charges, torpedoes and mines depending on the configuration and requirement.[77] Eight each P-3s operate out of two major airports, one on the east coast at *Pohan*g Airport and south of the Peninsula on *Jeju* International Airport on *Jeju* Island.[78]

"To expand the reach of its maritime surveillance, given the limits of the outdated anti-submarine patrol aircraft currently operated by the navy,"[79] the ROK Navy looks to expand its maritime surveillance capability with potentially 20 more aircraft, with prospective aircraft as the Boeing P-8 Poseidon, Lockheed Martin SC-130J Sea Hercules and Airbus Military C295.[80] As of late 2016, the Boeing looked to be the preferred choice.[81]

Marines

From its formation in 1949, the ROMC has largely been a light infantry organization in keeping with the international norm of naval infantry. For its light infantry assault role, today's roughly 27,000 personnel ROKMC fields an entire suite of domestically produced small arms, including the K1A 5.56mm submachine gun, K2 5.56mm assault rifle, K3 5.56 light machine gun, K4 40mm automatic grenade launcher, K6 .50 caliber heavy machine gun, K14 sniper rifle, K201 40mm underbarrel grenade launcher, K11 dual-barrel airburst weapon, K5 9mm semiautomatic pistol, KM 181 60mm mortar and KM187 81mm mortar, as well an assortment of anti-tank weapons.[82] For amphibious assault, the ROKMC depends on a variant of the USMC AAV7A1, known as the KAAV7A1 Amphibious Assault Vehicle, produced by *Hanwha Techwin* (previously *Samsung Techwin*). These vehicles are armed with a K-6 12.7mm machine gun and K-4 40x53mm high-speed automatic grenade launcher allowing the gunner to engage targets out to 1,500 meters with 360 degrees of acquisition.[83]

Due to its close relationship with the USMCs and potential wartime requirements, the ROKMC has become increasingly a combined arms force, fielding two tank battalions equipped with 120mm-gunned, 53-ton K1A1 main battle tanks. The upgraded laser rangefinder allows effective targeting in excess of 7 kilometers. Indirect fire support is provided by indigenously manufactured K-9 Thunder self-propelled 155mm howitzers and KH-179 towed 155mm howitzers.

Unlike its U.S. counterparts, the ROKMC has no dedicated aviation arm and depends on the ROK Air Force (close air support, bombing and reconnaissance) and ROK Army (rotor wing support including attack and transport) to meet its aviation needs. However, towards the development of greater operational integration, the ROKMC will take delivery of 30 KAI-produced KUH-1 Surion transport helicopters in 2017–2023 to replace the ROK Army UH-1H helicopters the ROKMC usually depends on for support.[84]

Interoperability with allies

In time of war with the DPRK, under current agreements ROK military forces would operate under the Combined Forces Command (CFC) led by a U.S. general. CFC would likely be augmented by forces contributed by the United Nations Command (UNC) sending states and other states interested in supporting the ROK and/or UNC. Because the latter is a standing command operating under an existing UN Security Council Resolution, additional action would not be necessary to generate participation from UN members. As previously noted, the existence of the Naval Component Command (NCC) under the CFC has fostered a high degree of interoperability between the U.S. and ROK Navies. Frequent exercises such as combined amphibious landings, planning exchanges, combined training and daily coordination sustain this level of interoperability. However, despite these command relations and frequent combined training opportunities, the ROK Government's emphasis on indigenous production of ships, naval weapons and ammunition, and communications has reduced the level of interoperability.

Confrontations and outcomes

The ROK Navy is primarily established to defend the homeland. It should come as no surprise then that its major operational concerns and potential areas of conflict lie close to home. First and foremost, the ROK Navy is designed, working in consonance with the U.S. 7th Fleet, to deter and defeat DPRK aggression during both armistice and war. Without doubt the ROK Navy holds a qualitative advantage over the DPRK's largely antiquated fleets. However, as recent history has shown, the ROK Navy still faces DPRK provocations in the East China Sea (known to the Koreans as the "West Sea") and must maintain vigilance to prevent DPRK incursions on the east coast. A related emerging task for the ROK Navy is providing a critical capability for ballistic missile defense against the growing DPRK threat via its Aegis-equipped destroyers.

The armistice mission has largely fallen into two major categories: defending the Northern Limit Line in the "West Sea," and preventing DPRK incursions on the east coast. Despite some notable exceptions, the ROK Navy has effectively met these missions since the signing of the Armistice.

Deterring North Korea

Nowhere has the North-South rivalry played out with greater frequency and more lethality than in the Yellow Sea, known to the Koreans as the "West Sea." Gaps in the Armistice of 1953 (intended to be a temporary document pending a concluding peace treaty) created an ambiguous situation that has resulted in several small-scale deadly naval engagements (1999, 2002 and 2009) exchanges of artillery fire between the two rivals. As late as 2011 the Peninsula tilted towards hostilities in the wake of a DPRK surprise attack on the ROK Navy corvette ROKS *Cheonan* and a subsequent rocket attack against *Baengnyeong* island.

In the Armistice's "Concrete Arrangements for Cease Fire" under paragraph II.A.13.(b), five islets north of the extension *Hwanghae* and *Kyonggi* provincial boundaries – an area otherwise placed under the North's control – were placed under the military control of the Commander-in-Chief, United Nations Command. When the Armistice was put in effect in July 1953, United Nations Command naval forces controlled all the waters surrounding the entire Peninsula.

Within this post-Armistice environment, ROK Navy patrol boats ventured north and exchanged fire with DPRK shore batteries. To prevent these confrontations, the Commander, U.S. Far East Fleet unilaterally established a "Northern Limit Line" to prevent military sea craft under the control of the United Nations Command from venturing north of the Northwest Islands.[85] This graphic control measure had little impact on the DPRK until it developed a naval patrol fleet of its own and started to challenge the line – which it declared (with some legal merit) as an illegal boundary. For its part, the ROK Government has promoted the line as a de facto international boundary, without substantial legal precedence but with, in recent times, tacit approval of the United Nations Command.[86]

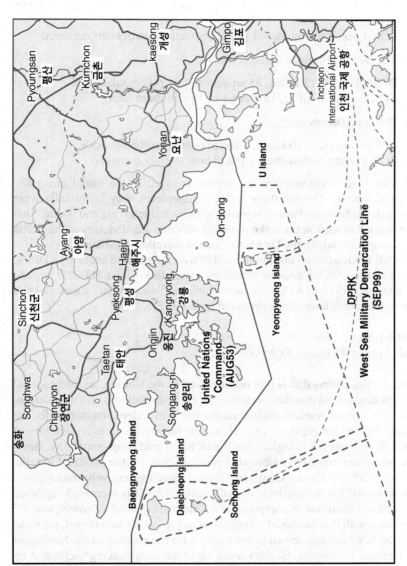

Figure 6.2 DPRK West Sea Military Demarcation Line (September 1999)

Note: Base map data from Google Maps

This line has been repeatedly tested by the DPRK, resulting in a number of high-profile and lethal (albeit small) naval engagements:

1999: The First Battle of *Yeonpyeong*[87]
- DPRK Losses: 17–30 killed, 1 torpedo boat sunk and 5 patrol boats damaged
- ROK Losses: 9 wounded, 1 patrol ship and 5 patrol boats damaged

2002: The Second Battle of *Yeonpyeong*[88]
- DPRK Losses: 13 killed, 25 wounded, 1 patrol boat damaged
- ROK Losses: 6 killed, 18 wounded, 1 patrol boat sunk

2009: Battle of *Daecheong*[89]
- DPRK Losses: 1–10 killed, 1 patrol boat severely damaged
- ROK Losses: 0 casualties, 1 patrol boat slightly damaged

In each of these confrontations the DPRK engaged in the initial direct fire against ROK vessels. Despite these lethal engagements, they historically were kept within the definition of minor skirmish with each side giving and taking. This paradigm started to shift in the wake of the ROKN one-sided victory at the Battle of *Daecheong*, after which the DPRK threatened merciless retaliation.[90]

The DPRK made good on this threat in 2010 with the surprise attack by a DPRK submarine on the ROKS *Cheonan*. Struck by a wakefollowing CHT-02D torpedo fired by either a *YONO*- or *SANGO*-Class submarine,[91] the corvette foundered and sunk about 8 minutes later with substantial loss of life.

- DPRK Losses: none
- ROK Losses: 46 killed, 1 corvette sunk

Despite DPRK claims that it was not involved in the sinking, an international commission determined that they were the culprit. Speculation is that the mission, executed by a special warfare midget submarine, was indeed retribution for the ROK Navy victory the previous year. However, faced with an excessive loss of life on the ROK vessel, it is logical that the DPRK would deny culpability. However, the attack created three unintended consequences for the DPRK. First, the ROK-U.S. Combined Forces Command started more aggressively tracking and accounting for DPRK submarines, a challenging task. This increased vigilance logically reduces the threat of a surprise DPRK submarine attack of consequence.[92] In consonance with this increased surveillance, as previously mentioned, the sinking of the *ROKS Cheonan* served as the impetus for the creation of the Northwest Islands Defense Command. Besides more rapid decision making facilitated by direct communications with the Joint Staff, the Command also significantly integrated air and sea anti-submarine operations, a critical task given the difficult hydrology surrounding the Northwest Islands. Finally, denial of its original attack on the *ROKS Cheonan* all but takes a future similar attack out of the DPRK playbook. A similar submarine attack would completely undermine the false moral outrage they have feigned for the last seven years. While this seems trivial, the importance of the regime's sense of righteousness should not be understated.

Likewise, the increased lethality of each side's patrol boats in the "West Sea" has largely made naval conflict a "lose-lose" proposition for both sides. With the majority of patrol craft, frigates, destroyers, corvettes and patrol boats missile capable and armed with up-gunned cannon, the specter of a naval engagement – even of limited nature – seems less attractive. That is not to say that the DPRK will not, as it has in the past, use such an engagement near the NLL to make a political statement if its sees value in such an act. However, within the milieu of today's North-South relations, the gain – political or military – would be minimal.

On the east coast, the ROK Navy has been challenged with a steep continental shelf that allows an enemy submarine to infiltrate close to the shore before it must surface and discharge its special operators. Some understanding of these infiltration missions was gained in 1996 and 1998 with two incidents that resulted in the ROK capturing two DPRK midget submarines. In 1996 a *SANGO*-Class submarine grounded off of *GANGNEUNG*. After making it to land, special operators executed the majority of the navy crew and attempted to exfiltrate by land to North Korea, leading tens of thousands of ROK soldiers on a 49-day running gun battle before they were all killed or captured. In 1998 a DPRK *YUGO*-Class submarine became trapped in fishing nets off of *SOKCHO*.[93] Without boarding and with the crew inside, the ROK Navy began to tow the submarine to the *DONG-HAE* Naval Base. In route, the special operators executed the sailors and then committed suicide, scuttling the boat. Just a few days later the submarine was salvaged.

In both cases, captured documents and cached equipment revealed that submarine-delivered special operators had been conducting reconnaissance missions into the ROK for years, unhindered by ROK Navy patrol operations. In light of this revelation, the ROK Navy substantially increased both the quantity and sophistication of anti-submarine patrols, integrating coastal patrol boats with more capable anti-submarine ships and P-3 reconnaissance aircraft. The end result is a tough gauntlet that has, by all estimates, halted DPK special forces' incursions on the east coast. It has also severely constrained other DPRK submarine operations, largely driving them out of ROK coastal waters.

Defeating North Korea

As discussed, the ROK Navy has three main missions during war: Force Projection, Sea Control and SLOC Protection. These manifest themselves in several specific requirements:

- sea-to-land strike
- amphibious operations
- destruction of the DRPK fleet
- deny maritime infiltration
- anti-submarine operations
- mine-clearing operations

Most strategists theorize that any general attack by the KPA on the ROK would be preceded by KPA special operations designed to disrupt the ROK Army's mobilization and preparation. These attacks would likely take form in ground infiltration, airborne insertion, agent activation and submarine and surface sea infiltration. The latter could be attempted using *NAMPO*-Class landing craft and *KONG BANG*-Class amphibious hovercraft, likely supported by the surface fleet including largely outdated frigates and torpedo missile boats. Given time distance factors involved in generating such an attack, the ROK Navy, supported by the NCC, is well-positioned and structured to at least substantially blunt if not defeat such attempts at maritime infiltration using its forward-deployed destroyers, corvettes and patrol boats. Even in the likely case of an initial "swarm-like" attack where at least some of the attacking enemy vessels would not be identified by the NCC,[94] the addition of surveillance aircraft, naval helicopters and even land-based attack helicopters and aircraft would make such an attempt on either coast costly to the point of operational failure.[95] A similar fate would likely befall any attempt at a more conventional amphibious attack. Larger and slower landing craft like the tank-carrying *HANTAE*-Class utility landing craft (LCU) would contribute little in terms of delivering significantly greater combat strength while increasing the vulnerability of the attacking force with its slower speed.

The KPN's submarine attacks would likely take two forms: special forces' infiltration using smaller submarines such as the 40+ *SANGO*-Class and attack/minelaying operations conducted by the 20 or so Type-033 ROMEO-Class diesel submarines still in surface. While it can be assumed that a number of these boats will initially find mission success, in the wake of the ROKS *Cheonan* sinking the ROK Navy has become significantly adept at track and attacking both categories of KPN boats. Substantial improvements in the ROKN antisubmarine capabilities as previously described credibly mitigate the potential wartime threat of the KPN's submarine force. The rapid (30–40 hours sailing time) arrival and integration of U.S. 7th Fleet anti-submarine ships from their bases in Japan into NCC operations would further neutralize the KPN's submarine threat, limiting its impact on CFC force generation and operations.

In the hopes of successfully prosecuting amphibious operations, the KPN would likely support such operations with the surface fleet, including major surface combatants, such as the *NAJIN*-Class frigate or *SARIWON*-Class corvettes, and recently constructed surface-effect-ships (SES). However, even with recent improvements that make several of the KPN ships credible threats to ROKN and U.S. Navy counterparts,[96] their limited numbers at best allow the KPN to maintain temporary, local parity in a place of their choosing. This would allow some amphibious craft to reach their intended landing site, but likely not enough to present an operational advantage.

The KPN, unlike the ROK Navy and United States, is also constrained by geography. ROK ownership and control of the southern half of the Korean Peninsula and contiguous waters makes coast-to-coast reinforcement an all but impossible task during conflict. In contrast, the ships of the CFC NCC can swing from coast to coast within 30 hours or less, allowing the NCC Commander to surge where needed.

Clearly, the few ships that have been modernized and recently constructed by the KPN make for a more lethal force than in the past. However, this increased lethality should not be seen as a positive gain in the balance of naval power via the ROK Navy. It cannot be forgotten that while the KPN has modernized some large ships and increased the armament of its patrol fleet with the addition or upgrade of missiles, their efforts are well behind that of the ROK Navy. In reality, the commissioning of the KSS-II submarines, KDX-series of destroyers, FFX frigates and PKX-series of patrol boats, combined with increased air attack and surveillance, gives the ROKN naval power that substantially outmatches the KPN. When this capability is added to the reinforced capability of the U.S. 7th Fleet under the banner of the NCC, the combined power is such that will likely result in the rapid destruction of the KPN above and below the surface, providing the CFC Commander with wartime maritime dominance and secure Sea Lanes of Communication to allow for the successful prosecution of the ground war.

To support this ground effort, today's ROK Navy possesses a considerable amphibious capability centered on the Landing Platform Helicopter *DOKDO*-Class. With the class's namesake active for almost a decade, the ROK Marines have trained and exercised battalion-size forced-entry, over-the-horizon expeditionary operations. This capability, particularly when linked with the Combined Marine Forces Command (CMFC) which includes the bulk of forces from U.S. Marine Forces Pacific, creates a complicated dilemma for the KPA as they try and defend against a CFC counteroffensive.

To effectively prosecute amphibious operations against the KPA, the ROK Navy requires an effective mine-clearing capability. As a historical lesson, during the Korean War the majority of ships lost by the United Nations Command were caused by KPN mines. This threat was particularly prevalent during the attempt to land at *Wonson* (where MacArthur hoped to replicate the success of the *Inchoen* landing) with several ships being sunk or damaged by KPN mines.[97] All told, during the war all five of the ships lost were sunk by mines and another six were damaged by mines.[98] During modern conflict, the quantity and effectiveness of KPN minefields would present a more difficult set of problems than encountered more than a half century ago. The six minehunters of the *GANGYEONG*-Class and four minesweepers of the *YANGYANG*-Class provide a minesweeping capability for the ROK Navy, but somewhat less than the 40+ similar craft the United Nations Command employed during the Korean War against a considerably lesser threat. This is one area where the U.S. Navy can only incrementally assist with only 11 AVENGER-Class mine countermeasures ships in the fleet, with four assigned to the U.S. 7th Fleet in Japan. Some support would likely come from the Sending States of the United Nations Command, although deployment time would be dependent on overcoming the delay of political decisions and geography. Simply put, most of these assets are half a globe away.

In sum, the ROK fleet has the core capabilities to deter the KPN and, in the case of war fighting as part of Combined Forced Command, rapidly defeat and gain maritime dominance over the KPN. The qualitative advantage the ROKN currently holds over the KPN will only continue to grow as the ROK continues to invest in a technologically advanced blue-water navy and the KPN suffers from a stagnate economy and international sanctions.

Territorial dispute with Japan

A novice looking at Northeast Asia would be baffled by the perceived level of mistrust between the ROK and Japan, the two vibrant democracies of Northeast Asia. However, a ROK strategist, cognizant of history, would be remiss if they did not consider future contention with Japan. The ROK's enduring suspicion of Japan's regional intentions plays out in a territorial dispute over the Liancourt Rocks located almost exactly equidistant from the ROK and Japan mainlands. Known to the Koreans as *Dokdo* and Japanese as *Takeshima*, each have historical claims for the small islets that consist of about 45 acres. This manifests itself in a ROK Navy that organizes and prepares for the KPN aggression but with an eye towards obtaining a level of parity with Japan's Navy to ensure that ROK rights and security are preserved with that democratic neighbor.

Used as a U.S. bombing range in the wake of World War II, both Korea and Japan claim the islets as sovereign territory. Evidence of ROK sovereignty is probably the stronger of the two, excepting one glaring point: international maritime law does not allow for islets to define either a state's continental shelf or exclusive economic zone.[99] Nevertheless, the claims for the islets remain a potential flashpoint between the two states. Presumably solved by an agreement reached between the two states in the 1965 Treaty on Basic Relations,[100] the ROK has ignored provisions in the treaty that allowed for ROK occupation and joint use but prohibited expansion of ROK police presence or facilities. On the other hand, the ROK Government has built a number of facilities on the islets while maintaining a robust police garrison supplied by the ROK Coast Guard. Additionally, it has declared the islets a nature preserve (ironic, since the ROK occupants of the islets have reportedly discharged raw sewage into the ocean creating a small environmental hazard in the surrounding waters), controlling access and limiting visits to a small number of tourists annually.

While much inflammatory rhetoric has been generated by both sides on the Liancourt Rocks issue (much of it aimed at inflaming nationalism to divert public attention from domestic policy failures), to date cooler heads have prevailed and both have sought diplomatic solutions, although the ROK Coast Guard has conducted island seizure exercises in case they must defend the current ROK presence on the rocks. That aside, from s cost-benefit analysis, a naval confrontation would substantially damage both state's international standing. For Japan, unable to escape its past, the spector of it forcibly trying to take – even if they had a right – land from an Asian neigbor would likely create a blowback that would severely restrict Japan's economic and diplomatic agenda elsewhere across the spectrum. And while Japan would likely prevail against the technically similar but outnumbered ROK Navy and Air Force in an attempt to seize the islets, the ROK defense would result in prohibitive cost to both sides.

Recognizing this, slowly but surely both sides are making efforts towards security cooperation, cognixant of the economic innervation[101] that already exists. Even though a longstanding fisheries agreement that deconflicts fishing conflicts caused by intersecting EEZs has not been renewed, both sides continue to respect the other's boundaries.[102] Joint naval operations, such as search-and-rescue exercises (particularly trilateral exercises with the United States, including an inaugural anti-submarine exercise in 2017) are on the upswing in both frequency and scope.[103, 104] In this context, the potetial for armed conflict between Japan and the ROK in the future is unikely. Despite historical animosities, both democracies understand too well that cooperaton is critical in the face of PRC's expansionist policies.

PRC expansionism

That the PRC is pursuing an expansionist policy based on "historical sovereignty" is without debate. Its actions in support of what can only be described as a dubious claim to sovereignty in the South China Sea are perhaps the most glaring example. Without any physical resistance, the PRC continues to construct islets where none existed so that it can create a claim to areas that lie in the Exclusive Economic Zones (EEZ) and territorial waters of Vietnam, Philippines, Brunei and Malaysia. However, the PRC's expansive claims of control that infringe on the sovereignty of neighbors are not limited to the South China Sea.

On November 23, 2013 the PRC announced the establishment of an "East China Sea Air Defense Identification Zone (ECSADIZ)" that would allow the PRC to "identify, monitor, control and react to aircraft entering this zone with potential air threats."[105] Part of the ADIZ overlapped about 3,000 square kilometers of South Korea's own ADIZ and included the submerged Socotra Rock (Korean: *Ieodo* and in PRC/Japan: *Suyan* Rock), long claimed by the ROK,[106] a claim contested by both Japan and the PRC.[107] While the ROK Government did not join with U.S. and Japanese protests, independently it took action.[108] On November 25 the ROK diplomatically protested the zone. Just as quickly, a spokesman for the PRC stated that the PRC "hopes to resolve the issue with South Korea through friendly consultations and negotiations, and, in an act of conciliation offered that the "ROK and China have no territorial dispute" over *Ieodo*.

To reinforce its claim over the Socotra Rock, in early December the ROK executed joint maritime operations in the vicinity of the Socotra Rocks – notable in that they did not garner any significant response from the PRC.[109] To formalize its own claims, on December 13, 2013 the ROK government announced the expansion of its own Korea Air Defense Identification Zone KADIZ to include the

Ieodo (*Suyan*) Rock as well as *Mara* and *Hong* Islands.[110] As late as August 12, 2017, PRC military aircraft entered the KADIZ without warning, overflying *Ieodo*, albeit departing the zone once they were challenged. While this has not manifested itself in a naval confrontation, the potential exists if the PRC was to try and actively enforce the declared zone as a type of boundary or if it continually ignored the KADIZ. What is notable in this aspect of the PRC-ROK relationship is how – to this point – both sides have made a genuine effort to maintain absolute diplomatic propriety.

Of greater concern to the ROK Navy is the increasing appearance of Chinese fishing boats in ROK waters – incursions that have resulted in increasing violence, particularly since the PRC has armed and trained their fishermen as naval militiamen to "defend their rights." In 2011 a Chinese fisherman stabbed and killed a ROK Coast Guardsman (described by the Chinese press as a "commando") during a boarding when the fishing boat was stopped for illegal fishing.[111] In the fall of 2016 three Chinese fishermen died during a boarding of their boat by the ROK Coast Guard.[112] A few days later a ROK Coast Guard speed boat was rammed and sunk by a Chinese fishing boat. In describing the attack, ROK National Assemblyman WON Sang-Ho described the Chinese fishermen as pirates.

To resolve incidents of Chinese illegal fishing, the PRC has been careful to be accommodating diplomatically even if not in practice, and has repeatedly promised to the ROKG, to some effect, to better control these fishing operations.[113] More than respectful concession, this "solution through diplomacy" approach more than likely represents the pragmatism of both states. For the ROK's part, its US$131 billion dollar export trade relationship[114] with the PRC is too vital to the nation's economic health. This is all too evident in the wake of PRC sanctions against the ROK in protest of the U.S deployment of THAAD to the Peninsula.[115] For the PRC, this represents a stage in its long game to wrest the ROK from the clutches of the ROK-U.S. alliance. Critical to this long-term effort is its growing naval power.

The reality is that the PRC's emergence as a regional naval power has, to date, had little impact on ROKN operations. It has, however, clearly influenced the design and development of the ROK Navy, encouraging increased capabilities in ship-to-ship missile warfare, submarine warfare, ISR, and naval special operations such as hostage rescue. While none of these are in response to any direct and present threat, a strategic review of the future might portend these threats and call for the exact capabilities being developed by the ROK Navy now – capabilities that would not necessarily play a primary role in operations against the DPRK in time of hostilities – certainly not after the first few days or weeks. For the ROK to speak of the PRC as a partner is prudent, but so is the ROK Navy's concern about a growing – in size and capability – People's Liberation Army Navy (PLAN) – a navy that is today already 3–5 times larger than the ROK. With naval warfare being a zero-sum game, the fact is that absent the U.S. 7th Fleet, the PLAN can currently dominate any one neighboring navy in an all-out conflict – a condition that underscores the importance of ROK-U.S.

naval cooperation and increasingly the efficacy of trilateral cooperation including Japan.

Support to international missions

The expanded capabilities of the ROK Navy have allowed it to increase its participation in international naval activities. Of note, the ROK Navy has participated in the bi-annual RIMPAC exercise for more than a quarter of a century. In 2016, 26 countries participated, with the ROK Navy sending one of the largest contingents, including the AEGIS destroyer ROKS *Sejong the Great*.

The ROK Navy has also earned international acclaim for its role in anti-piracy operations off the coast of Somalia since 2009. While initial participation was under the Combined Maritime Forces led by the U.S. 5th Fleet, the last three years have been as part of OPERATION Atalanta in cooperation with European Naval Forces ships.[116]

Conclusion

For the ROK Navy, the mission is today, and tomorrow is the challenge. One thing is a given: the ROK Navy operates in a tough neighborhood. Confronted with DPRK belligerence and PRC expansionism, the ROK Navy must determine how to allocate limited resources to meet the requirements posed by these challenges. Given budget constraints,[117] how does the ROK Navy build its fleet to meet the requirements of deterrence and maritime dominance against a determined DPRK while designing a force that can resist the ever-growing reaches of a hegemonic PRC? There is little doubt, as an example, that Chinese fishermen will continue to encroach on other states' EEZ as they move beyond fished-out waters to make their catch. At what point will such encroachment negatively affect the ROK people's way of life? When the PLAN is given the mission of protecting the illegal fishermen, what will be the stance of the ROK? Will this competition play itself out in the search for natural gas and oil? While the quest for resources in Northeast Asia is not yet a scramble, it is not difficult to interpolate demand with supply to realize that such a quest will be competitive rather than cooperative – with success underpinned by the strength of state's navy and air force.

For the immediate future, clearly the ROK Navy is focused on its most immediate mission: preventing DPRK incursions while maintaining readiness to defeat their adversary in case of hostilities. But as the region matures and the PRC and Japan, and even a resurging Russia, act to determine their role in the region, the ROK Navy must ensure it has the ability to balance against these forces of influence in order to maintain its own viability as a maritime trading state. This will require maintaining a deft hand, which the ROK Navy has demonstrated to date, in balancing those requirements against resources. This means that the ROK Navy will continue to develop niche capabilities directly related to its current mission, while leveraging alliances with the United States and cooperation with other partners to maintain the regional balance of naval power critical to overall regional security and prosperity.

Appendix

Table 6.1 Approximate strengths of Northeast Asia's regional navies

	\multicolumn{5}{c}{ROK (Projected thru 2018)}
	Number	Span of Commissioning	Average Age (years)	Percent Less Than 10 Years Old	Combined Tonnage
Aircraft Carriers	0	N/A	N/A	N/A	0
Submarines	18	1993–2018	12.72	44%	31920
Destroyers	12	1998–2012	12.91	33%	77820
Frigates/Destroyer Escorts	14	1985–2017	15.57	50%	39548
Corvettes	16	1986–93	27.63	0%	19200
Patrol Craft	71	1978–2017	24.87	27%	19350
Amphibious Warfare Ships	9	1994–2018	11.00	44%	64000
Mine Warfare Ships	11	1986–2017	20.81	9%	13300
	151				265,138

	\multicolumn{5}{c}{JAPAN (Projected thru 2018)}
	Number	Span of Commissioning	Average Age (years)	Percent Less Than 10 Years Old	Combined Tonnage
Aircraft Carriers	0	N/A	N/A	N/A	0
Submarines	18	2000–18	9.4	56%	73800
Destroyers	27	1986–2018	15.03	22%	188500
Frigates/Destroyer Escorts	16	1986–93	28.25	0%	62500
Corvettes	0	N/A	N/A	N/A	0
Patrol Craft	6	2002–04	15.00	0%	1440
Amphibious Warfare Ships	7	1998–2017	10.14	57%	134000
Mine Warfare Ships	24	?–?	N/A	N/A	23660
	98				483,900

PRC (Projected thru 2018)

	Number	Span of Commissioning	Average Age (years)	Percent Less Than 10 Years Old	Combined Tonnage
Aircraft Carriers	1	2012	6.00	100%	67500
Submarines (Nuclear)	14	1984–?	?	?	112500
Submarines (Conventional)	61	1990–?	?	?	184520
Destroyers	35	1982–2018	12.20	44%	193220
Frigates/ Destroyer Escorts	51	1982–2018	13.11	53%	165150
Corvettes	35	2013–17	3.26	100%	50400
Patrol Craft	220	1964–2018	26.7	0%	75546
Amphibious Warfare Ships	68	1978–2018	18.6	15%	312640
Mine Warfare Ships	31	1988–2016	19.4	10%	21900
	516				1,183,376

DPRK (Projected thru 2018) (all figures approximations)

	Number	Span of Commissioning	Average Age (years)	Percent Less Than 10 Years Old	Combined Tonnage
Aircraft Carriers	0	N/A	N/A	N/A	0
Submarines (Nuclear)	0	N/A	N/A	N/A	0
Submarines (Conventional)	70	?	?	?	?
Destroyers	0	N/A	N/A	N/A	0
Frigates/ Destroyer Escorts	3	?	?	?	6775
Corvettes	9	?	?	?	6250
Patrol Craft*	438	?	?	?	20000
Amphibious Warfare Ships	15	?	?	?	?
Mine Warfare Ships	23	?	?	?	21900

(*Total Includes patrol boats with displacement greater than 20 tons)
Information from multiple sources

Notes

1 Jo, 2000.
2 Scheer, 2013 and Pryce, 2016.
3 ROK Navy, 2017.

4   Jung, 2010.
5   Graham, 2016.
6   In 2014, the ROKN established a new naval base on Baengnyeong Island to support patrol boats.
7   RT! Question More, 2016.
8   Rothwell, 2016.
9   Commander, Combined Maritime Forces Public Affairs, 2009.
10 KIM, S., 2011.
11 KIM, T., 2011.
12 The Chosen Ilbo, 2010.
13 Commonly known as the Korean People's Army (KPN), the DPRK's navy is officially known as the *Chosun Inmingun Haegun*, or Korean People's Army's Navy.
14 Global Security, 2017.
15 Wertheim, E., 2007.
16 RP Defense, 2011.
17 Naval-Technology.Com, undated.
18 Yonhap News, 2007.
19 General Electric, 2013.
20 IHS Jane's 360, 2016.
21 General Electric, 2014.
22 Ryall, J., 2016.
23 Bolkcom, C and Pike, J., 1993.
24 Boeing, 2013.
25 Comments by multiple experts with submarine command experience to the author between April-May 2010.
26 The Yulgok Plan was an 8-year plan focused on modernizing the nation's ground, air and naval forces.
27 Yonhap News, 2015.
28 Naval Today, 2016.
29 Yonhap News, 2016.
30 Defense Industry Daily Staff, 2016.
31 The program is often referred to as KKF Ulsan Class Frigate Batch-II, confusing classing.
32 Ibid.
33 ROK National Assembly, 2015.
34 Korea Times, 2016.
35 Global Security, 2017.
36 Rahmat, 2016b.
37 NavyRecognition.Com, 2017
38 Global Security, 2017
39 United States Navy, 2017.
40 Yoon, 2016.
41 Jun, 2016.
42 Eshel, T., 2012.
43 Naval Today, 2016.
44 NavyRecognition.Com, 2016.
45 Kim, S., 2011.
46 Naval-Technology.Com, undated.
47 Military-Today.Com, 2017.
48 Mathew, A. 2017.
49 AMI International, 2009.
50 Diplomat, 2017.
51 NavyRecognition.com, 2016.
52 Rahmat, 2016a.

53 Dominguez, 2016.
54 Eight batteries of six launchers.
55 The eight batteries of six launchers owned by the ROK Air Force operate the PAC-2 GEM-T. This missile "gives the system a new fuse and systems that make its radar more sensitive to targets with small radar signatures. This allows the GEM-T to defeat more air-breathing capabilities as a complement to upgraded PAC-3 missiles within an integrated air and missile defense system."
56 Jung, 2008.
57 Missile Defense Advocacy Alliance, 2017 and Taylor, A., 2017.
58 Missile Defense Advocacy Alliance, 2017.
59 ROK National Assembly, 2015.
60 Yoon, S., 2016.
61 LaGrone, S., 2016.
62 NavalToday.Com, 2015.
63 Defense Times Korea, 2016.
64 Defense Daily, 1990
65 Lake, 1999.
66 Lake, 2000.
67 Hoyle, 2013.
68 Grisafi, 2016.
69 Eshel, 2014.
70 The Incheon-Class frigates, KDX I, II, and III destroyers and LPH ROKS Dokdo are all capable of carrying, supporting and conducting integrated operations with ship-borne helicopters.
71 Gady, 2017.
72 Perrett, 2013a.
73 Naval-Technology.Com, 2013.
74 Perrett, 2013.
75 Naval-Technology.Com, 2013.
76 Lockheed-Martin, 2017.
77 Navy.Mil, 2016.
78 NavyRecognition.Com, 2016.
79 Dominguez, 2016.
80 Perrett, 2013b.
81 Dominguez, 2016.
82 Arthur, G., 2015.
83 Army Guide, undated.
84 Waldron, 2016.
85 Joint State/Defense Message, 1973.
86 Park and Pearson, 2014.
87 Michishita, N., 2009.
88 ROK Drop, 2012.
89 Foster, P., 2009.
90 Center for Strategic & International Studies (CSIS), 2010.
91 Chosun Ilbo, 2010.
92 Rogoway, T., 2015.
93 Roblin, S., 2017.
94 Gerhardt, W. and Tilelli, J., 1998.
95 Krause, T., 1999.
96 Oliemans, J. and Mitzer, S., 2014.
97 Naval Historical Center, 1999.
98 Cagle, M. and Manson, C., 1957.
99 United Nations Convention on the Law of the Sea, 1994.
100 Treaty on Basic Relations between Japan and the Republic of Korea, 1965.

101 The Observatory of Economic Complexity, 2017.
102 Yonhap News, 2016.
103 McDonald, D., 2016.
104 Park, B., 2017.
105 Defense Spokesman Yang Yujun's Response to Questions on the Establishment of The East China Sea Air Defense Identification Zone *Ministry of National Defense of the People's Republic of China* 23 November 2013.
106 International maritime law does not allow submerged rocks to be used to establish territorial sovereignty.
107 Panda, A., 2013.
108 Voice of America, 2013.
109 Jeong Y. and Kim, S., 2013.
110 Song S, 2013.
111 Qin, Z and Zhang, Y., 2011.
112 ROKDrop, 2016.
113 Yonhap, 2015.
114 OEC, 2017.
115 Lee, 2017.
116 NavalToday.Com, 2017.
117 With US$1.199 billion allocated for naval capabilities in 2016, the ROK Navy cannot hope to compete quantitatively with a PLAN that is funded at levels well beyond that figure.

References

AMI International, Inc., 2009. *South Korea Awards Contracts for Two Trouble-Plagued Ship Programs*. Seapower International, February.

Amy Guide, undated. *KAAV*, [online] Army Guide. Available at: www.army-guide.com/eng/product4383.html [Accessed 22 June 2017].

Arthur, G., 2015. *Weapons of the Republic of Korea Marine Corps*. [online] Small Arms Defense Journal. Available at: www.sadefensejournal.com/wp/?p=3130 [Accessed 23 July 2017].

BBC News, 2010. *North Korea Scraps South Korea Military Safeguard Pact*. [online] BBC News. Available at: www.bbc.com/news/10170019 [Accessed 22 May 2017].

Bermudez, J., 2001. *The Armed Forces of North Korea*. New York: I.B. Tauris.

Blanchard, B., and Martina, M., 2017. *China is Likely to Ramp Up its Naval Abilities in Response to Trump's Unpredictability*. [online] Time. Available at: http://time.com/4683286/trump-china-navy-defense-budget/ [Accessed 30 July 2017].

Boeing Backgrounder, 2013. *Harpoon Block II* [online] Boeing. Available at: www.boeing.com/assets/pdf/defense-space/missiles/harpoon/docs/HarpoonBlockIIBackgrounder.pdf [Accessed 5 May 2017].

Bolkcom, C., and Pike, J., 1993. Chapter V – Cruise Missiles: The Other Air Breathing Threat. *Attack Aircraft Proliferation: Issues for Concern*, 1 April.

Cagle, M., and Manson, C., 1957. *The Sea War in Korea*. Annapolis: United States Naval Institute.

Center for Strategic & International Studies (CSIS), 2010. *Record of North Korea's Major Conventional Provocations Since 1960s*. [online] CSIS. Available at: https://csis-prod.s3.amazonaws.com/s3fs-public/legacy_files/files/publication/100525_North_Koreas_Provocations.pdf [Accessed 16 June 2017].

Chosun Ilbo, 2010. *S. Korea 'Unlikely' to Have Damaged N. Korean Artillery Positions*. [online] Chosen Ilbo. Available at: http://english.chosun.com/site/data/html_dir/2010/12/01/2010120101038.html [Accessed 11 July 2017].

Chosun Ilbo, 2010. *How Did N. Korea Sink the Cheonan?* [online] Chosun Ilbo. Available at: http://english.chosun.com/site/data/html_dir/2010/05/21/2010052100698.html [Assessed 28 July 2017].

CNN Wire Staff, 2011. *South Koreans Pull Off Daring Rescue of Pirated Ship.* [online] CNN U.S. Edition. Available at: http://thediplomat.com/2017/07/rok-navy-receives-new-advanced-attack-submarine/ [Accessed 23 June 2017].

Commander, Combined Maritime Forces Public Affairs, 2009. *New Counter-Piracy Task Force Established.* [online] Navy NewsStand, Available at: www.globalsecurity.org/military/library/news/2009/01/mil-090108-nns02.htm [Accessed 20 July 2017].

Defense Daily, 1990. *Korean Air/Sikorsky Announce Black Hawk production Agreement. (UH-60P military helicopters).* Available at: https://web.archive.org/web/20130929010944/www.highbeam.com/doc/1G1-9396065.html [Accessed 13 July 2017].

Defense Industry Daily Staff, 2016. *Korea's New Coastal Frigates: The FFX Incheon Class* [online] Defense Industry Daily. Available at: www.defenseindustrydaily.com/ffx-koreas-new-frigates-05239/ [Accessed 3 May 2017].

Defense Times Korea. 2016. ROK. *Military Weapons Systems* (2015–2017). Seoul.

Dominguez, G., 2016. *South Korea Mulls Purchase of Four Boeing P-8 Poseidon Aircraft, Says Report.* [online] Jane's 360. Available at: www.janes.com/article/63366/south-korea-mulls-purchase-of-four-boeing-p-8-poseidon-aircraft-says-report [Accessed 27 July 2016].

———, 2016. *South Korea Developing SLBMs for KSS-III Attack Submarines.* [online] HIS Jane's Defence Weekly. Available at: https://defcon.news/2016/06/02/south-korea-developing-slbms-for-kss-iii-attack-submarines-ihs-janes-360/ [Accessed 3 August 2017].

Eshel, T., 2012. *Hyunmoo Missiles – Seoul Going Ballistic* [online] Defense Update. Available at: http://defense-update.com/20120422_new_hyunmoo_korean_missiles.html [Accessed 22 June 2017].

———, 2014. *Seoul to Equip its New Maritime Helicopters With Israeli SPIKE Missiles.* [online] Defense Update. Available at: http://defense-update.com/20140106_seoul-equip-new-maritime-helicopters-israeli-spike-missiles.html [Accessed 19 May 2017].

Foster, P., 2009. *North and South Korea Warships Exchange Fire.* [online] The Telegraph. Available at: www.telegraph.co.uk/news/worldnews/asia/southkorea/6536557/North-and-South-Korea-warships-exchange-fire.html [Accessed 14 July 2017].

Gady, F., 2017a. *Indonesia Commissions First Attack Submarine in 34 Years.* [online] The Diplomat. Available at: http://thediplomat.com/2017/08/indonesia-commissions-first-attack-submarine-in-34-years/ [Accessed 7 August 2017].

———, 2017b. *ROK Navy Receives New Advanced Attack Submarine.* [online] The Diplomat. Available at: http://thediplomat.com/2017/07/rok-navy-receives-new-advanced-attack-submarine/ [Accessed 19 July 2017].

———, 2017c. *ROK Navy Deploys 4 More Sub-Killer Helicopters.* [online] The Diplomat. Available at: http://thediplomat.com/2017/07/rok-navy-deploys-4-more-sub-killer-helicopters/ [Accessed 13 July 2017].

General Electric, 2013. *GE LM500s Selected to Power Republic of Korea Navy's PKX-B Patrol Boat Program.* [online] General Electric. Available at: www.geaviation.com/press-release/marine-industrial-engines/ge-lm500s-selected-power-republic-korea-navy's-pkx-b-patro-0 [Accessed 13 May 2017].

———, 2014. *GE Showcases Innovative and Efficient Solutions for the Maritime Industry at SMM.* [online] General Electric. Available at: www.geaviation.com/press-release/marine-industrial-engines/ge-showcases-innovative-and-efficient-solutions-maritime [Accessed 14 May 2017].

———, 2016. *South Korea Mulls Purchase of 4 Advanced US Sub Killer Planes.* [online] The Diplomat. Available at: http://thediplomat.com/2016/09/south-korea-mulls-purchase-of-4-advanced-us-sub-killer-planes/ [Accessed 26 July 2017].

Gerhardt, William P. and Tilelli, John H., 1998. "Solving Threat SOF Challenges," [online] Military Review, Mar/Apr 98. Available at: http://www.cgsc.army.mil/MILREV/English/Mar/Apr98/tilelli.htm.

Global Security, 2017a. *KDX-I Okpo Class DDH (Destroyer Helicopter).* [online] GlobalSecurity.Org. Available at: www.globalsecurity.org/military/world/rok/kdx-1.htm [Accessed 16 June 2017].

———, 2017b. *KDX-II Chungmugong Yi Sunshin Destroyer.* [online] Global Security. Org. Available at: www.globalsecurity.org/military/world/rok/kdx-2.htm [Accessed 19 August 2017].

———, 2017c. *Seventh Fleet, Combined Naval Component Command.* [online] Global Security.Org. Available at: www.globalsecurity.org/military/agency/navy/c7f.htm [Accessed 23 August 2017].

Goertzen, S., 1993. *The Feasibility of the Over-The-Horizon Amphibious Assault for U.S. Navy and Marine Corps Forces.* Fort Leavenworth, KS: U.S. Army Command and General Staff College.

Graham, E., 2016. *A Glimpse into South Korea's New Naval Base on Jeju Island* [online] The National Interest. Available at: http://nationalinterest.org/blog/the-buzz/glimpse-south-koreas-new-naval-base-jeju-island-16415 [Accessed 14 May 2017].

Grisafi, 2016. *South Korean Navy Receives New ASW Helicopters.* [online] NK-News.Org. Available at: www.nknews.org/2016/06/south-korean-navy-receives-new-asw-helicopters/ [Accessed 6 July 2017].

Hoyle, Craig, 2013. *South Korea Picks AW159 for Maritime Helicopter Deal.* [online] Flight-Global. Available at: www.flightglobal.com/news/articles/south-korea-picks-aw159-for-maritime-helicopter-deal-381045/ [Accessed 3 June 2017]

Jane's 360, 2016. *South Korea Launches First PKX-B Missile Craft.* [online] Janes.Com. Available at: http://defensenews-alert.blogspot.com/2016/07/south-korea-launches-first-pkx-b.html [Accessed 13 May 2017].

Japan and Republic of Korea, 1965. *Treaty on Basic Relations between Japan and the Republic of Korea.*

Jeong, Y., and Kim, S., 2013. *Korean Navy Conducts Drill Close to Ieodo.* [online] Korea Joongang Daily. Available at: http://mengnews.joins.com/view.aspx?aId=2981469 [Accessed 8 June 2017].

Jo, S., 2000. *21 Segi Tongil Hangugui Daeyang Haegun Jeonryak" (21st Century Unified Korea's Oceanic Naval Strategy)* [online] Donga.com. Available at: www.donga.com/docs/magazine/new_donga/200007/nd2000070130.html [Accessed 4 June 2017].

Joint State/Defense Message, 1973. *Questions Regarding Northern Limit Line.* [online] The Origins of the Northern Limit Line Dispute, 2012. North Korea International Documentation Project, E-Dossier #6, Woodrow Wilson International Center for Scholars. Available at: www.wilsoncenter.org/sites/default/files/NKIDP_eDossier_6_Origins_of_the_Northern_Limit_Line.pdf [Accessed 16 July 2017].

Jun, J., 2016. *SM-3 Ups Speculation of Korea Joining US Missile Defense.* [online] Korea Times. Available at: www.koreatimes.co.kr/www/news/nation/2016/08/116_212298.html [Accessed 26 July 2017].

Jung, S., 2008. *Seoul Takes Over 1st Batch of German Patriot Missiles.* [online] The Korea Times. Available at: www.koreatimes.co.kr/www/news/nation/2008/11/117_35268.html [Accessed 16 May 2017].

―――, 2010. *Navy Activates 1st Strategic Mobile Fleet*. [online] Korea Times. Available at: www.koreatimes.co.kr/www/news/nation/2010/02/205_60079.html [Accessed 7 June 2017].

Kim, S., 2011a. *Cheonghae Unit's Previous Anti-Piracy Successes*. [online] The Korean Herald. Available at: www.koreaherald.com/view.php?ud=20110121000822 [Accessed 3 August 2017].

―――, 2011b. *Dokdohahmun Nalgo Sipda (The ROKS Dokdo Wants to Soar)*. [online] Bemil.Chosun.Com. Available at: http://bemil.chosun.com/nbrd/bbs/view.html?b_bbs_id=10040&pn=1&num=63808 [Accessed 7 July 2017].

Kim, T., 2011. *Northwest Islands Defense Command Inaugurated*. [online] DailyNK. Available at: www.dailynk.com/english/read.php?cataId=nk00100&num=7829 [Accessed 9 June 2017].

Korea Times, 2016. *S. Korean Navy to Arm Frigates with Tactical Ship-to-Land Missiles*. [online] Korea Times. Available at: www.koreatimes.co.kr/www/nation/2017/04/205_212354.html [Accessed 3 July 2017].

Krause, T., 1999. *Countering North Korean Special Purpose Forces*. Maxwell Air Force Base: Air Command an Staff College.

Lagrone, S., 2016. *New South Korean Destroyers to Have Ballistic Missile Defense Capability*. [online] USNI News. Available at: https://news.usni.org/2016/09/06/new-south-korean-destroyers-ballistic-missile-defense-capability [Accessed 14 July 2017].

Lake, Jon., 1999. *Westland Lynx Variant Briefing: Part 1 in World Air Power Journal*, 39, Winter. London: Aerospace Publishing, pp. 126–141.

―――, 2000. *Westland Lynx Variant Briefing: Part 2 in World Air Power Journal*, 40. Spring. London: Aerospace Publishing, pp. 112–121.

Lee, J., 2017. *The China-South Korea Trade War Must End*. [online] Japan Times. Available at: www.japantimes.co.jp/opinion/2017/03/26/commentary/world-commentary/china-south-korea-trade-war-must-end/#.WbYElK2ZP1I [Accessed 13 June 2017].

Lockheed-Martin, 2017. *P-3 Orion Specifications*. [online] Lockheed-Martin. Available at: www.lockheedmartin.com/us/products/p3/p-3-specifications.html [Accessed 11 July 2017].

Majumdar, D., 2017. *How Dangerous is North Korea's Navy?* [online] The National Interest. Available at: http://nationalinterest.org/blog/the-buzz/how-dangerous-north-koreas-navy-20258 [Accessed 17 July 2017].

Mathew, A., 2017. *South Korean Navy Receives Sixth Advanced AIP Attack Submarine*. [online] DEFPOST. Available at: https://defpost.com/south-korean-navy-receives-sixth-advanced-aip-attack-submarine/ [Accessed 21 July 2017].

McDonald, D., 2016. *South Korea and Japan Likely to Continue Improving Mutual Relations*. [online] Intelligence Observer. Available at: https://intelligenceobserver.com/2016/06/29/south-korea-and-japan-likely-to-continue-improving-mutual-relations/comment-page-1/ [Accessed 14 June 2017].

Michishita, Narushige. 2009. *North Korea's Military-Diplomatic Campaigns, 1966–2008*. London: Routledge.

Military-Today.Com, 2017. *Chang Bogo Class, Patrol Submarine*. [undated] Military-Today.Com. Available at: www.military-today.com/navy/chang_bogo_class.htm [Accessed 13 May 2017].

Missile Defense Advocacy Alliance, 2017a. *Missile Defense to Shoot Down North Korean Rockets is Ready*. [online] Missile Defense Advocacy Alliance. Available at: http://missiledefenseadvocacy.org/missile-defense-news/missile-defenses-to-shoot-down-north-korean-rockets-is-ready/ [Accessed 7 July 2017].

———, 2017b. *Patriot Missile Defense System*. [online] Missile Defense Advocacy Alliance. Available at: http://missiledefenseadvocacy.org/missile-defense-systems-2/missile-defense-systems/u-s-deployed-intercept-systems/patriot-missile-defense-system/ [Accessed 23 August 2017].

———, 2017c. *Republic of Korea*. [online] Missile Defense Advocacy Alliance. Available at: http://missiledefenseadvocacy.org/intl-cooperation/republic-of-korea/ [Accessed 23 August 2017].

Naval Historical Center, 1999. *The Wonsan Operation, October 1950-Overview and Selected Images*. [online] Naval Historical Center. Available at: www.ibiblio.org/hyperwar/OnlineLibrary/photos/events/kowar/50-unof/wonsan.htm [Accessed 14 June 2017].

Naval Today, 2015. *Korean Navy's Second Minelayer Launched*. [online] NAVALTODAY.COM. http://navaltoday.com/2015/05/27/korean-navys-second-minelayer-launched/ [Accessed 26 June 2017].

———, 2016a. *Japanese, Korean and US Destroyers to be Equipped with AEGIS Systems*. [online] NAVALTODAY.COM. Available at: http://navaltoday.com/2016/08/16/japanese-korean-and-us-destroyers-to-be-equipped-with-aegis-systems/ [Accessed 22 May 2017].

———, 2016b. *South Korea Commissions Sixth Incheon-Class Frigate ROKS Gwangju*. [online] NAVALTODAY.COM. Available at: http://navaltoday.com/2016/11/09/south-korea-commissions-sixth-incheon-class-frigate-roks-gwangju/ [Accessed 9 May 2017].

———, 2017a. *Korean Navy Destroyer Dae Jo Young Joins Counter-Piracy Operation Off Somalia*. [online] NAVALTODAY.COM. Available at: http://navaltoday.com/2017/08/25/korean-navy-destroyer-dae-jo-young-joins-counter-piracy-operation-off-somalia/ [Accessed 27 August 2017].

———, 2017b. *South Korea Starts Construction of Second Amphibious Assault Ship*. [online] NAVALTODAY.COM. Available at: http://navaltoday.com/2017/04/28/south-korea-starts-construction-of-second-amphibious-assault-ship/ [Accessed 29 April 2017].

———, 2017c. *South Korean Destroyer to Join EU Counter-Piracy Mission*. [online] NAVALTODAY.COM. Available at: http://navaltoday.com/2017/02/17/south-korean-destroyer-to-join-eu-counter-piracy-mission/ [Accessed 17 June 2017].

———, 2017d. *US, Japan, Republic of Korea Conduct Missile Warning Informational Link Exercise*. [online] NAVALTODAY.COM. Available at: http://navaltoday.com/2017/03/14/us-japan-republic-of-korea-conduct-missile-warning-informational-link-exercise/ [Accessed 23 April 2017].

———, 2017e. *US, South Korea Start Extensive Naval Drills*. [online] NAVALTODAY.COM. Available at: http://navaltoday.com/2017/03/20/us-south-korea-start-extensive-naval-drills/ [Accessed 29 April 2017].

Naval-Technology.Com, 2013. *South Korea to Procure 20 Maritime Patrol Aircraft*. [online] Naval-Technology.Com. Available at: www.naval-technology.com/news/news-south-korea-to-procure-20-maritime-patrol-aircraft [Accessed 26 June 2017].

———, Undated. *Dokdo Class Landing Platform Helicopter (LPH)*. [online] Naval-Technology.Com. Available at: www.naval-technology.com/projects/dodko-Class/ [Accessed 4 August 2017].

———, Undated. *Chamsuri Class Patrol Killer Medium Craft*. [online] Naval-Technology.Com. Available at: www.naval-technology.com/projects/chamsuriclass [Accessed 7 June 2017].

NavyRecognition.Com, 2016a. *Raytheon Restarts SM-2 Production for the Netherlands Japan Australia and South Korea*. [online] NavyRecognition.Com. www.navyrecognition.com/index.php/news/defence-news/2017/june-2017-navy-naval-forces-defense-industry-technology-maritime-security-global-news/5305-raytheon-restarts-sm-2-production-for-the-netherlands-japan-australia-and-south-korea.html [Accessed 29 June 2017].

NavyRecognition.Com, 2016b. *ROK Navy Opens New Naval Base on Jeju Island for KDX-III Aegis Destroyers*. [online] NavyRecognition.Com. Available at: www.navyrecognition.com/index.php/news/defence-news/2016/february-2016-navy-naval-forces-defense-industry-technology-maritime-security-global-news/3619-rok-navy-opens-new-naval-base-on-jeju-island-for-kdx-iii-aegis-destroyers.html [Accessed 4 May 2017].

———, 2016c. *South Korea's DAPA Selects DSME for KSS-III Batch II Heavy Submarine Design and Construction*. [online] NavyRecognition.Com. Available at: www.navyrecognition.com/index.php/news/defence-news/2016/may-2016-navy-naval-forces-defense-industry-technology-maritime-security-global-news/4025-south-koreas-dapa-selects-dsme-for-kss-iii-batch-ii-heavy-submarine-design-a-construction.html [Accessed 21 July 2017].

Observatory of Economic Complexity (OEC), 2017. *South Korea*. [online] Available at: http://atlas.media.mit.edu/en/resources/about/ [Accessed 29 July 2017].

Oliemans, J., and Mitzer, S., 2014. *KPA Navy Flag Ship Undergoing Radical Modernization*. [online] NK News.Org. Available at: www.nknews.org/2014/12/kpa-navy-flag-ship-undergoing-radical-modernization/ [Accessed 21 July 2017].

Panda, A., 2013. *The East China ADIZ and the Curious Case of South Korea*. [online] The Diplomat. Available at: http://thediplomat.com/2013/11/the-east-china-adiz-and-the-curious-case-of-south-korea/ [Accessed 11 June 2017].

Park, B., 2017. *S. Korea, US and Japan Start First Joint Antisubmarine Exercises*. [online] The Hankyoreh. Available at: http://english.hani.co.kr/arti/english_edition/e_international/789252.html [Accessed 17 June 2017].

Park, J., and Pearson, J., 2014. *The War That Never Ends Between the Koreas*. [online] Reuters. Available at: www.reuters.com/article/us-northkorea-islands-insight-idUSKBN0ES00720140617 [Accessed 23 May 2017].

Perrett, Bradley, 2013a. *South Korean Navy Pursues Anti-Sub Aviation Boost*. [online] Aviation Week Network. Available at: http://aviationweek.com/awin/south-korean-navy-pursues-anti-sub-aviation-boost [Accessed 3 May 2017].

———, 2013b. Sub-Hunting. *Aviation Week and Space Technology*, 8 July, p. 27.

Pryce, P., 2016. *The Republic of Korea Navy: Blue-Water Bound?* [online] Center for International Maritime Security. Available at: http://cimsec.org/the-republic-of-korea-navy-blue-water-bound/21490 [Accessed 13 April 2017].

Qin, Z., and Zhang, Y., 2011. *ROK Coast Guard Stabbed by Chinese Fisherman: Report*. [online] China Daily. Available at: www.chinadaily.com.cn/china/2011-12/13/content_14254771.htm [Accessed 17 July 2017].

Rahmat, R., 2016a. *DSME Lays Keel for South Korea's First KSS-III Submarine*. [online] HIS Jane's Defence Weekly. Available at: https://thaimilitaryandasianregion.wordpress.com/2016/05/20/dsme-lays-keel-for-south-koreas-first-kss-iii-submarine/ [Accessed 3 August 2017].

———, 2016b. *DSME Launches South Korea's First FFX-II Frigate*. [online] HIS Jane's Defence Weekly. Available at: www.janes.com/article/61012/dsme-launches-south-korea-s-first-ffx-ii-frigate [Accessed 7 June 2017].

Roblin, S., 2017. *How a North Korean Spy Submarine's Mechanical Meltdown End in Shocking Tragedy*. [online] The National Interest. Available at: http://nationalinterest.org/blog/the-buzz/how-north-korean-spy-submarines-mechanical-meltdown-ended-19815 [Accessed 18 June 2017].

Rogoway, T., 2015. *North Korea's Ongoing Massive Submarine Deployment is Worrisome.* [online] Foxtrotalpha. Available at: https://foxtrotalpha.jalopnik.com/north-koreas-ongoing-massive-submarine-deployment-is-wo-1726797346 [Accessed 2 August 2017].

ROK Drop, 2012. *DMZ Flashlights: The 2002 West Sea Naval Battale.* [online] ROK Drop. Available at: www.rokdrop.net/2012/06/dmz-flashpoints-the-2002-west-sea-naval-battle/ [Accessed 13 June 2017].

———, 2016a. *Illegal Chinese Fisherman Sink ROK Coast Guard Speed Boat.* [online] Korea Times. www.rokdrop.net/2016/10/illegal-chinese-fishermen-sink-rok-coast-guard-speed-boat/ [Accessed 14 July 2017].

———, 2016b. *ROK Coast Guard Kills Three During Confrontation with Illegal Chinese Fishing Boat.* [online] Reuters. www.rokdrop.net/2016/10/rok-coast-guard-kills-three-during-confrontation-with-illegal-chinese-fishing-boat/ [Accessed 14 July 2017].

ROK National Assembly, 2015. *ROK Defense Budget,* passed December.

ROK Navy, 2017. *Duty & Function.* [online] ROK Navy. Available at: www.navy.mil.kr/mbshome/mbs/eng/subview.do?id=eng_010300000000 [Accessed 19 May 2017].

Rothwell, J. 2016. *South Korea Unveils Elite "Spartan 3000" Force as KIM Jong-Un Threatens to 'Bury Our Enemies at Sea.* [online] The Telegraph. Available at: www.telegraph.co.uk/news/worldnews/asia/northkorea/12199786/South-Korea-unveils-elite-Spartan-3000-force-as-Kim-Jong-un-threatens-to-bury-our-enemies-at-sea.html [Accessed 3 August 2017].

RP Defense, 2011. *East Timor Naval Force Receives Three Patrol Vessels from South Korea.* [online] Available at: https://defense-studies.blogspot.com/2011/09/east-timor-naval-force-receives-three.html?m=1 [Accessed 26 May 2017]

RT! Question More, 2016. *S. Korea Forms Elite 'Spartan 3000' Unit to Counter North.* [online] RT! Question More. Available at: www.rt.com/news/336497-south-north-korea-spartan/ [Accessed 2 August 2017].

Ryall, J., 2016. *South Korea Orders Additional PKX-B Fast Attack Craft.* [online] Janes.Com. Available at: www.janes.com/article/64561/south-korea-orders-additional-pkx-b-fast-attack-craft [Accessed 2 August 2017].

Sanford, J., and Scobell, A., 2007. *North Korea's Military Threat Pyongyang's Conventional Forces Weapons of Mass Destruction and Ballistic Missiles.* Carlisle, Pennsylvania: Strategic Studies Institute.

Scheer, B., 2013. *South Korea's Developing Blue Water Navy.* [online] Australian Strategic Policy Institute. Available at: www.aspistrategist.org.au/south-koreas-developing-blue-water-navy/ [Accessed 4 April 2017].

Shim, E., 2017. *South Korea Military: China Hotline Wasn't Working When Bombers Deployed.* [online] United Press International. Available at: www.upi.com/Top_News/World-News/2017/01/12/South-Korea-military-China-hotline-wasnt-working-when-bombers-deployed/6071484230516/ [Accessed June 16, 2017].

Song, S., 2013. *Seoul Considers Southward Expansion of Air Defense Zone.* [online] The Korean Herald. Available at: www.koreaherald.com/view.php?ud=20131201000304 [Accessed 14 August 2017].

Taylor, A., 2017. *Why China is So Mad About THAAD, a Missile Defense System Aimed at Deterring North Korea,* [online] Washington Post. Available at: www.washingtonpost.com/news/worldviews/wp/2017/03/07/why-china-is-so-mad-about-thaad-a-missile-defense-system-aimed-at-deterring-north-korea/?utm_term=.a6ef78fcf13a [Accessed 13 June 2017].

United States Navy, 2017. *United States Navy Fact File: Standard Missile.* [online] Navy.Mil. Available at: www.navy.mil/navydata/fact_display.asp?cid=2200&tid=1200&ct=2 [Accessed 14 July 2017].

United States Navy, 2016. *P-3C Orion Long Range ASW Aircraft* [online] Navy.Mil. Available at: http://www.navy.mil/navydata/fact_display.asp?cid=1100&tid=1400&ct=1

United Nations Convention on the Law of the Sea, *Part VIII, Article 121: Regime of Islands*. United Nations Conference on the Law of the Sea (UNCLOS III), 1973–1982, In effect 1994.

Voice of America, 2013. *China Hit with Complaints Over Maritime Air Defense Zone* [online] Available at: www.voanews.com/a/china-hit-with-complaints-over-maritime-air-defense-zone/1797574.html [Accessed 23 July 2017].

Waldron, G., 2016. *LAI Secures Deal for 30 Amphibious Surions*. [online] FlightGlobal. Available at: www.flightglobal.com/news/articles/kai-secures-deal-for-30-amphibious-surions-432810/ [Accessed 25 July 2017].

Wertheim, Eric. 2007. *The Naval Institute Guide to Combat Fleets of the World*. Naval Institute Press, 2007.

Yonhap News, 2007. *Navy Launches High-Speed Patrol Boat*. [online] JoongAng Daily. Available at: http://koreajoongangdaily.joins.com/news/article/article.aspx?aid=2877409 [Accessed 7 July 2017].

———, 2015. *South Korea, China Agree to Get Tougher on Illegal Fishing*. [online] Available at: http://english.yonhapnews.co.kr/business/2015/10/30/0502000000 AEN20151030009400320.html [Accessed: 14 August 2017].

———, 2016a. *S. Korea, Japan Fail to Reach Fisheries Agreement*. [online] Available at: http://english.yonhapnews.co.kr/news/2016/06/29/15/0200000000AEN201606290055 00320F.html [Accessed 13 July 2017].

———, 2016b. *S. Korean Navy to Arm Frigates with Tactical Ship-to-Land Missiles*. [online] The Korea Times. Available at: www.koreatimes.co.kr/www/nation/2017/04/205_212354.html [Accessed 6 June 2017].

———, 2016c. *Wildcat Maritime Choppers Arrive in S. Korea*. [online] Yonhap News. Available at: http://english.yonhapnews.co.kr/national/2016/06/13/0301000000 AEN20160613007000315.html [Accessed July 2, 2017].

Yonhap News Agency, 2015. *Navy Decommissions First-Generation Indigenous Warship ROKS Seoul* [online] Available at: http://english.yonhapnews.co.kr/search1/2603000000. html?cid=AEN20151231003600315 [Accessed 16 May 2017].

Yoon, S. 2016. *Stopping North Korean Missiles: Am Alternative to THAAD*. [online] The Diplomat. Available at: http://thediplomat.com/2016/07/stopping-north-korean-missiles-an-alternative-to-thaad/ [Accessed 14 July 2017].

7 Strategic and "everyday" maritime security challenges in Southeast Asia

Maria Ortuoste

As the geographic nexus of the Indo-Pacific, Southeast Asia's political, economic and geostrategic fortunes and misfortunes have far-reaching impacts on regional security. This necessitates understanding the countries' security concerns, strategies and capabilities in the maritime realm. Southeast Asian states worry about traditional strategic issues like great power competition, but they are equally, if not more, concerned with everyday non-traditional security issues such as fisheries, smuggling, piracy and the possibility of maritime terrorism. Similar concerns, however, have not always inspired cooperation; competing national priorities, rivalries and disputes, as well as unequal maritime capabilities have also engendered some conflict. This chapter shows that while current initiatives can address maritime issues in the short-term, the long-term management of regional maritime security requires a united sense of purpose that continues to elude Southeast Asian states.

Core security concerns and Maritime challenges

Southeast Asian states are concerned with maritime security issues that fall within the timeframe of the strategic and the everyday, are a complex mix of traditional and non-traditional issues, and span domestic, regional and transnational arenas (see Table 7.1).[1] These interrelated issues are perceived by Southeast Asian leaders through the prism of consolidating their states, i.e. how geopolitics, maritime geography and marine resources play a role in maintaining national unity, in challenging territorial integrity and in ensuring regime legitimacy via economic and political performance.

Despite their long years of independence, most Southeast Asian states still grapple with maintaining national unity. Divisions within countries are as much the result of maritime geography as unresolved grievances and conflict, poor governance, and ethnic, religious and ideological schisms. Thailand and Myanmar are fighting ethnic- or religious-based insurgencies, Sabah and Sarawak want the central Malaysian government to devolve more powers, while Indonesia contends with provincial rivalries and sectarian conflict. The Philippines has been unable to end communist insurgency and Muslim secessionism or to quell the Abu Sayyaf Group's (ASG) terrorist and criminal actions.

Table 7.1 Security challenges in Southeast Asia

	Traditional	Everyday Security Challenges (Land-Based): Traditional and Non-traditional	Everyday Security Challenges (Maritime): Non-traditional
International	Great power competition Freedom of navigation	Spillovers: terrorism	Piracy Crime
Regional	Regional versus small powers Freedom of navigation Territorial/jurisdictional disputes	Spillovers: terrorism, humanitarian Transnational connections	Piracy Crime: smuggling of goods and people; armed robbery
States	Territorial integrity Sovereignty National unity	Insurgency Secessionism Political instability Terrorism	Securing resources: IUU fishing Piracy Crime: smuggling of goods and people; armed robbery; kidnappings Terrorism

Southeast Asia's maritime geography, unfortunately, tends to reinforce these divisions and even enable challengers of state authority. The sub-region has numerous "[n]arrow channels, shallow reefs and thousands of tiny islands" that are "located within or astride geographic archipelagos, inhabited [sic] with large populations with less than ideal social, political and economic conditions."[2] Crime and smuggling are not uncommon. Smuggled items include consumer goods, small arms and illegal drugs like cannabis, heroin, methamphetamine tablets, crystalline methamphetamine and ecstasy.[3] The proceeds of these illegal activities not only enrich transnational criminal organizations, but they also sustain corrupt law enforcement officials, and provide firepower to both insurgents and terrorists in the Philippines, Indonesia and, previously, Sri Lanka. In 2016, for example, Philippine police seized high-powered firearms worth $125,000 that were purportedly destined for the ASG.[4]

The most salient problem for Singapore, Malaysia, Indonesia and the Philippines is the linkages between Islamic extremist groups. The same waterways used for smuggling, especially those between Sabah and Indonesian Borneo, are used by extremists to travel to the Philippines for training or to strengthen ties with one another as was the case with *Jemaah Islamiyah* (JI), *Kumpulan Militan Malaysia* (KMM), the Moro Islamic Liberation Front (MILF) and the ASG.[5] More recently, states are worried about the inroads being made by the Islamic State (IS) in Southeast Asia. The ASG and 22 Indonesian groups have pledged allegiance to IS,[6] while Malaysian authorities arrested 100 people – former members of the defunct KMM and several military personnel – for suspected links with IS. Many governments are concerned that terrorist attacks could become more lethal either due to IS support or due to various groups vying for IS affiliation.[7]

Apart from this internal-transnational challenge to national unity, Southeast Asian states are keenly interested in maintaining their territorial integrity and sovereign rights over exclusive economic zones (EEZs) and continental shelves. Southeast Asian countries have to deal with unresolved land and maritime boundary disputes which are the results of colonialism and the coming into effect of UNCLOS in 1995. Colonialism left legacies of problematic territorial borders as evidenced by the clash between Cambodia and Thailand over Preah Vihear in 2011 and the 2013 "Lahad Datu" attacks on Sabah by members of the "Royal Sulu Army" from Mindanao.[8] The expansion of maritime zones under UNCLOS has led to claims that are "within 400 nm of each other" in Southeast Asia[9] and, eventually to confrontations such as that between Indonesia and Malaysia over Sipadan and Ligitan. The most problematic situation, however, is the South China Sea (SCS) where Brunei Darussalam, China, Malaysia, the Philippines, Vietnam and Taiwan have occupied and militarized several features, leading to minor confrontations.

The initial expansion of maritime zones coincided with economic growth in most Southeast Asian countries. Since most of their regimes stake their legitimacy on delivering prosperity, the governments had to find ways to harvest ever more living and non-living maritime resources in order to boost exports. Indonesia, Vietnam, the Philippines, Thailand and Malaysia are among the world's top 15 major producers of marine capture fisheries.[10] This industry employs around 5.4 million fishers in Southeast Asia (or 14.2% of fishers in the world) and accounts for around 1.7% to 4% of the GDPs of Indonesia, Vietnam, Thailand and the Philippines.[11] Southeast Asian waters also have reserves of oil and natural gas which have been used by states like Brunei Darussalam, Indonesia and Malaysia to drive economic expansion. Since the 1970s, Malaysia's *Petronas* and Indonesia's *PT Pertamina* have accounted for about 35% to 50% of their national revenues. Following the discovery of oil deposits after the Vietnam War, *PetroVietnam* now contributes 20% to Vietnam's GDP and 25% to 30% to the government's yearly revenues.[12] The Philippines hopes that the Malampaya gas field will satisfy some domestic demand as it currently imports 90% of its energy requirements.[13]

But dwindling fish stocks and maturing oil fields have led to resource competition. Indonesia's total production of petroleum and other liquids declined so sharply relative to domestic demand that, in 2004, it became a net importer of oil and its OPEC membership was suspended in 2009. Its crude oil reserves have similarly decreased. In contrast, oil production by Malaysia, Thailand and Vietnam have been relatively steady, and Vietnam's oil reserves increased from 0.6 to 4.4 billion barrels with the discovery of new oil fields in 2010. Current levels of production, however, may not be able to satisfy sub-regional demand which is estimated to increase by 80% from 2013 to 2035.[14] Because most coastal oil fields are now considered "mature," oil industries have been venturing farther offshore to the SCS even though there are widely varying estimates of oil reserves – from the low 2.5 billion to the high 22 billion barrels – in that area.[15] These explorations have generated some conflicts such as that between Malaysia and Indonesia over oil exploration licenses in 2005, or that between Vietnam and China over the latter's disappearing and re-appearing oil rig.[16] Indonesia also announced plans to deploy ships and aircraft to the Natunas after its run-in with Chinese ships.

Surprisingly, there have been more confrontations over illegal, unreported and unregulated (IUU) fishing which "has escalated in the past 20 years . . . [and which] takes 11–26 million tons of fish each year, for an estimated value of US$10–23 billion."[17] Indonesia claims that it loses $20 billion annually to illegal fishing.[18] The growing demand for fish has spurred countries like Vietnam and Thailand to subsidize the production of motorized fishing vessels which can venture farther to sea due to depleted fish stocks.[19] It is estimated that only 5–30% of unexploited stocks remain in Southeast Asian waters.[20] Chinese, Taiwanese and Southeast Asians constantly traverse each other's EEZs, which has led to arrests and the confiscation of boats and marine catch. Armed confrontations are also not uncommon – a Thai naval vessel fired at a Vietnamese fishing boat in July 2016 for fishing illegally in the former's EEZ.

Apart from resources, Southeast Asian waters are important thoroughfares for international trade. Twenty-five percent of the world's traded goods pass through the Straits of Malacca and Singapore (SoMS),[21] and around 25% of the world's maritime oil trade (or 15.2 million barrels per day) passed through the SoMS in 2013.[22] Annual maritime trade in the Sulu and Celebes Seas is estimated at $40 billion for approximately 55 million metric tons of goods.[23] As such, the safety of SLOCs and freedom of navigation are important for littoral and user states, as well as for the regional economy itself. Japan and Singapore, for example, are highly dependent on imports that go through the straits. Employment and revenues generated from port services are also substantial. The Port of Singapore of Authority (PSA) estimates that "the maritime industry contributes 7 per cent to Singapore's GDP" and accounts for around 10% of Singapore's services sector which, in turn, comprises 75% of Singapore's national economy.[24] Any disruption of international trade due to accidents, piracy, maritime crime or violent conflict would ultimately impact economic growth.

This high volume of maritime traffic, however, also attracts criminal elements. From the mid-1990s to 2004, Southeast Asia was the world's most piracy-prone area with most incidents occurring in the waters of Indonesia, the Philippines, Vietnam, Malaysia, the SCS and the SoMS. If left unaddressed, piracy could increase the costs for shipping companies which might look for alternative shipping routes.[25] The number of incidents declined from 2006 to 2011 but has since been steadily increasing. This is accompanied by a change in tactics – previous incidents were small-scale with perpetrators using light weapons, but some recent piracy incidents involve the hijacking of small product tankers carrying oil cargoes that were later siphoned off.[26] It is still questionable whether or not Southeast Asian states will be able to effectively respond to more sophisticated piracy tactics.

Along with transnational linkages among extremist groups, maritime terrorism has also emerged as a security concern. Although only 2% of all terrorist attacks have occurred in the seas,[27] countries like Singapore want to avoid the human, economic and ecological costs similar to those that resulted from the attacks on the USS *Cole* in Yemen (2000) and the oil tanker *Limburg* in the Gulf of Aden (2002). In the sub-region, the Philippines could have faced an energy crisis in 2016 when Indonesia prevented its ships from sailing to the Philippines because of the latter's inability to prevent the kidnapping of Indonesian crews. The Philippines imports around 70% of its coal requirements from East Kalimantan and finding new energy sources would have been too costly.[28]

There are also other reasons why the threat of maritime terrorism is treated seriously. First, terrorism itself will probably continue for the coming decades as countries like the Philippines and Indonesia have not adequately addressed the root causes of extremism, and because kidnap-for-ransom operations are lucrative. It is alleged, for example, that ASG received from $4–$8 million for four kidnapping-for-ransom operations in 2016.[29] They use their ill-gotten gains to support impoverished local communities, pay bribes or obtain better equipment for subsequent operations.

Second, many commercial ships are still relatively soft targets despite enhanced port security measures and international regulations.[30] Cargo ships and U.S. naval ships are also attractive ideological targets as they symbolize Western capitalism. But if sowing fear is the main goal, ferries are better targets. They are not only vulnerable, but they also account for 30% of annual vessel arrivals (or 36,000 ferries) in the SoMS because they are the principal means of inter-island travel.[31] The ASG has a track record of bombing ferries that have killed hundreds of civilians in the Philippines, while similar attacks on ferries have also occurred in Indonesia.[32]

Finally, Singaporean and Malaysian officials in the early 2000s had uncovered and disrupted terrorist plans to attack U.S. ships in their ports.[33] In 2016, Indonesian authorities discovered a plot by an IS-affiliated group, the *Katibah GR* or *Cell GR*, to fire a rocket into Singapore's tourist spot, Marina Bay, from Batam, Indonesia.[34]

Layered on top of these internal and intra-regional security issues is great power competition in the Indo-Pacific. While countries like the Philippines and Vietnam might claim an existential threat from Chinese military presence, the actual "threat" from great powers is in the form of interference, encroachment and disruption of trade and security. In general, many Southeast Asian states prefer minimal interference from major powers especially the United States and, lately, China. The latter's island-building and occupation of islets and reefs in the East and South China Seas have been a source of tension in the region and hasve led Southeast Asian countries to improve defense relations with the United States, Japan, Australia and South Korea. Although U.S. military presence has long been a stabilizing force in the region, Southeast Asian states are still wary about America's changing policies. The Obama administration's "rebalancing" policy has since been upturned by the Trump administration, thereby engendering more regional uncertainty. Japan's new security legislation allows it to take a more proactive stance in defense and regional security which Southeast Asian states welcome but would be worrisome for China, South Korea and North Korea. Another Chinese rival, India, has also responded by transforming its "Look East" to an "Act East" policy that involves helping Southeast Asian states develop their maritime capabilities. Finally, Russia supports China's efforts to prevent Western dominance in the region.

These factors give rise to the third concern – the potential disruption of trade and security relations. Stable politico-security relations among Southeast Asia's main trading partners are considered necessary for economic growth – escalating tensions would not only scare off foreign investors but could even force the states to choose between the long-time guarantor of regional stability (the United States) and its top trading partner (China).

Strategies and capabilities

The myriad security concerns of Southeast Asian countries are, unfortunately, not matched by enough economic resources and robust maritime capabilities except in the case of Singapore. The countries have, therefore, adopted pragmatic maritime security strategies comprised of diplomatic, legal, economic and military components that are implemented unilaterally, bilaterally and multilaterally to deal with strategic and everyday security issues.

Most territorial and jurisdictional issues are handled diplomatically. Over the years, Southeast Asian states have slowly concluded 17 bilateral agreements delimiting territorial waters, EEZs, continental shelves and historic waters. Two of the most recent agreements are between Indonesia and the Philippines over their EEZs, and between Indonesia and Singapore over Changi and Batam. Although international adjudication was not their first preference, Malaysia and Indonesia submitted their dispute over Pulau Ligitan and Sipadan to the International Court of Justice (ICJ) which ruled in favor of Malaysia. While this raised consternation in Indonesia, the two parties created a bilateral Joint Technical Committee to delimit the rest of their maritime boundaries and they have agreed to provide mutual humanitarian assistance as well as to respect their people's traditional fishing activities.

A similar approach is used in resource exploitation but with varied results. Oil-producing countries – Vietnam, Malaysia, Thailand, Brunei Darussalam and Indonesia – have been able to conclude agreements for joint exploration and development; but countries like Indonesia, Vietnam, the Philippines and Thailand have been unable to develop significant agreements in fisheries. This may be due to the their governments' assertive measures such as arresting and detaining illegal fishers, confiscating boats and catch, and even shooting at suspected poachers.

Compared to the above-mentioned issues, there are more practical cooperative activities to ensure safety of SLOCs. These activities use international conventions and regulations such as the Safety of Life at Sea (SOLAS), Maritime Search and Rescue (SAR) and the Suppression of Unlawful Acts against the Safety of Maritime Navigation (SUA) as a common starting point. The implementation of these regulations not only helps to manage maritime crime but could also be one way to restrain great power actions.

Complementing these regulations are information-sharing arrangements through the Singapore-based ReCAAP, which has 20 state members, and the Malaysia-based Piracy Reporting Center of the IMB which is a private sector initiative.[35] Both centers provide valuable real time data, warnings and trend analyses, but their institutional rivalry and their use of different metrics have been criticized as preventing the development of an "effective system of maritime domain awareness and information sharing."[36]

Littoral states have also gone beyond exchanging information. The Cooperative Mechanism (CM) for the Enhancement of Safety, Security and Environmental Protection of the SoMS is an outgrowth of a series of meetings held by the International Maritime Organization (IMO) from 2005 to 2007. Through the leadership of Indonesia, Malaysia and Singapore, several countries and organizations now participate in CM's projects to enhance safety and emergency response.[37]

Another contributor to maritime safety is the Maritime Straits Patrol (MSP) which brings together Singapore, Indonesia, Malaysia and Thailand. Its coordinated patrols, which began in 2004, reduced piracy incidents from 2006 to 2011, leading Lloyd's Joint War Risk Committee to drop the SoMS' classification as a "war-risk area."[38] With piracy incidents again on the rise, the MSP has developed the "Eyes in the Sky" program which combines maritime air patrols, real-time intelligence exchanges and joint exercises. To further hone their skills, Malaysia, Singapore and Thailand have participated in anti-piracy operations conducted by the multinational Combined Task Force 151 (CTF 151) in the Gulf of Aden.[39]

Indonesia, Malaysia and the Philippines hope to follow this example with their own agreement on maritime cooperation in the Triborder Area (TBA) signed in May 2016. They propose to mount coordinated patrols, help secure the release of ASG's hostages and hold joint navy and army exercises as well as joint air patrols. Vietnam has also undertaken bilateral coordinated patrols with Thailand, Cambodia, Malaysia and Brunei.[40]

Dealing with terrorism and incidents at sea follow the same pattern. Southeast Asian countries have expanded existing intelligence exchange arrangements to cover terrorism. Several ports in Malaysia, Singapore and Thailand are active members of the Container Security Initiative (CSI) which aims to prevent the international transport of weapons that could be used by terrorist groups. For incidents at sea, eight Southeast countries adhere to the "Code of Unplanned Encounters at Sea" adopted by the Western Pacific Naval Symposium (WPNS) and, in September 2016, ASEAN agreed with China to use CUES in their shared maritime areas. Most of the states are also parties to the Convention on the International Regulations for Preventing Collisions at Sea (COLREGS) which guides maritime activities. Bilateral initiatives complement these international measures. Singapore holds separate mine-clearance exercises with Malaysia and Indonesia, Vietnam and Thailand have developed hotlines to deal with any violations in their agreements in the Tonkin Gulf, Malaysia and Indonesia have agreed to send "rapid reaction teams" to deal with possible attacks on the western Malay peninsula, and bilateral agreements on submarine search-and-rescue are just some of these crosscutting activities.[41]

The Association of Southeast Asian Nations (ASEAN), the area's 50-year-old organization, is only recently following the lead of these bilateral and multilateral activities. The ASEAN Defense Ministers Meeting (ADMM), created in 2006, is building the foundations for joint humanitarian assistance and disaster relief (HA/DR) operations. The defense ministers also intend to establish direct communications links to improve emergency response, as well as to improve collaboration among their defense industries. Another relatively new body is the ASEAN Navy Chiefs' Meeting (ANCM) which hopes to conduct training programs and exercises to enhance interoperability in HA/DR operations.

The effectiveness of individual and cooperative defense activities, however, depends on the quantity and quality of maritime assets. The total EEZ area of Southeast Asia is more than 11 million square kilometers; Indonesia, the Philippines and Vietnam have the largest EEZs measuring 5.4, 2.3 and 1.4 million square kilometers, respectively.[42] Indonesia and the Philippines also have the second and fourth longest coastlines in the world, yet these archipelagic countries have limited and outdated equipment. It was reported that only 20% of the Indonesian navy was operational when Abdurrahman Wahid came to power in 1999,[43] while another report stated that "of the navy's 146 ships, only 83 percent of the striking force is operationally capable, over half (57 percent) of the supporting force is in decay, and only 68% of the current patrolling force is operating [by 2010]."[44]

Thus, Southeast Asian states have embarked on military modernization programs to replace or upgrade equipment. These programs account for the rise of Southeast Asia's total defense expenditures from just under $15 billion in 1988 to around $42 billion in 2015. Although the sub-region accounts for only 2.5% of the world's total defense spending, its defense spending rose by 9% from 2014–15 which is much higher than the world's spending which increased only by 1%. The most dramatic increases in spending occurred over the past five years, coinciding with greater Chinese assertiveness in the SCS. From 2014–15, defense expenditures of the Philippines and Indonesia grew by 25% and 16.5%, respectively; and from 2010–15, Indonesia's defense expenditures grew by 81.6%, followed by the Philippines and Vietnam at around 36% each, then Malaysia (26.5%), Thailand (13.2%) and Singapore (2.9%). Sub-regional defense spending rose by 35.5% from $30,891 million in 2010 to $41,842 million in 2015.[45] It is no surprise that McKinsey dubbed Southeast Asia as the world's "second largest defense import market" by TIV from 2007 to 2012.[46]

Given the complex security challenges in Southeast Asia, acquisitions are expected to focus on "multipurpose upgradeable platforms" that can be used for various missions[47] and as a step towards "more balanced portfolios."[48] The first task is to improve maritime domain awareness – Indonesia, Vietnam and Singapore have UAV programs, while the Philippines established a National Coast Watch System (with American support) in 2011 to improve coordination among various agencies. All of the countries are also procuring new, or upgrading existing, offshore patrol vessels, landing dock vessels, landing ship tanks, amphibious capabilities as well as aircraft including helicopters. Attack or assault ships are also on the list as are mine warfare ships, mine sweepers and missiles. Over the past three years, Indonesia, Malaysia, Singapore and Vietnam have been trying to procure submarines and counter-submarine platforms. Submarines are particularly useful for Southeast Asian states – first, they could be used for "surveillance, reconnaissance and intelligence gathering"[49] to prevent maritime crime; second, submarines could offset the relative weakness of small navies vis-à-vis those of China's.

Singapore has the most balanced and technologically advanced maritime capability in the sub-region – its navy has surface, sub-surface and air capabilities which can provide coastal and "seaward defense and SLOC protection."[50] These different forces are part of the Integrated Knowledge Command and Control (IKC2) designed to transform its military into a "Third Generation SAF," a "network-enabled force joining sophisticated intelligence, surveillance and reconnaissance (ISR) capabilities with advanced strike capabilities across ground, air and naval forces" by 2030.[51]

The second tier of countries – Indonesia, Malaysia, Thailand and Vietnam – are capable of "offshore territorial defense" to deal with everyday security challenges individually or collectively.[52] Among the original ASEAN members, the Philippines has the weakest navy although it has recently improved its maritime assets for coastal patrols; however, it is still a long way from being able to consistently protect the outer limits of its EEZ and the islands it occupies in the Spratlys.

Cognizant of the fact that it would be counter-productive to "catch up" with China, Japan or India, Southeast Asian countries manage strategic, traditional security issues by engaging with great and middle powers in political-diplomatic venues, by strengthening existing alliances and by establishing strategic partnerships with middle powers like Australia and Japan. In fact, Southeast Asian states have no choice but to live in this power asymmetry. Their top trading partners are China, Japan, the United States, the European Union and India and, in 2015, the region's top military suppliers were the United States, Russia and Spain. The United States has maintained its Cold War alliances with the Philippines and Thailand as well as developed special relations with Singapore, Malaysia and Indonesia. Singapore and Malaysia are also part of the Five Power Defence Arrangement (FPDA) with the UK, Australia and New Zealand.

Despite problems in the Trump administration, the United States continues to exert influence in the area. Singapore, the Philippines and Vietnam are part of the Maritime Security Initiative (MSI) which is designed to improve maritime capabilities, including domain awareness, and to expand joint exercises. The MSI will provide $425 million to Southeast Asian countries with the bulk ($79 million) going to the Philippines for the transfer of a retired coast guard cutter. Vietnam, Indonesia and Malaysia are slated to receive $40, $20 and $2.5 million, respectively.[53]

Perhaps one of the most important contributions of the United States under the Obama administration is its recognition of the concerns of Southeast Asian countries, in particular the Philippines' problems with China over the Kalayaan Island Group, Vietnam's strategy to protect its marine resources and Indonesia's stance against IUU fishing. These arrangements including the conduct of more joint exercises can be considered as some sort of "burden-sharing" as the United States will have access to Singapore's and Malaysia's ports, Philippine naval bases and, potentially, Vietnam's Cam Ranh Bay. The Enhanced Defense Cooperation Agreement (EDCA) with the Philippines similarly aims to allow access to certain locations in the country for U.S. forces for training and for pre-positioning materiel.

Despite all these activities, the United States remains coy about how it would respond to a possible attack on Philippine ships by the Chinese, or how it would respond to any access denial by the Chinese navy in the area. The tepid statement released by the United States in response to the 2016 ruling of the International Tribunal for the Law of the Sea (ITLOS), which favored the Philippines over China, also did not generate much confidence about the superpower's commitment to the sub-region especially as it has become more embroiled in the Middle East.

Because of changes in U.S. policies as well as geographic realities, Southeast Asia is not isolating China despite their suspicions. In fact, Southeast Asian states and China have several bilateral economic and military ties. Malaysian and Chinese armed forces held joint training exercises in 2015; Vietnam and China have several territorial and trade agreements; Thailand will buy three submarines from China; and Malaysia will buy four littoral mission ships. The Philippines continues to trade with China and is poised to expand defense relations. ASEAN–China partnerships in various areas, including in defense, are growing.

ASEAN, in fact, cultivated these ties since the 1990s based upon the belief that engagement, rather than confrontation, is the best way for China to become a responsible regional power. Thus, ASEAN insisted that China become a member of the ASEAN Regional Forum (ARF) in 1994 at a time when U.S.–China relations were still strained. China did become an active participant in multilateral forums but, primarily due to its continued economic and military growth, it has been able to dominate these processes. Talks to develop a binding code of conduct over the SCS have floundered over the past 20 years, and China has even been able to sow dissension among ASEAN members as seen in the Cambodia-hosted meetings when the group was not able to reach consensus on statements against China.

Given this scenario, Southeast Asian states are also developing or deepening existing strategic partnerships with middle powers such as Australia, South Korea, Japan and India. Vietnam has been the most active in this effort, concluding 15 strategic partnerships from 2001 to 2015.[54] The proximity of these middle powers is another consideration. Singapore, for example, uses designated zones in Australia to train the Singapore Armed Forces. With areas ten times the size of Singapore, Australian grounds enable 14,000 troops to get more intensive training 18 weeks in a year.[55] Australia has also conducted exercises and patrols with their neighbors. India is also strengthening relations with Southeast Asia – its agreement with Vietnam includes anti-piracy cooperation and modernization of

Vietnam's navy. The pair has also conducted joint maneuvers in the SCS since October 2000, and India plans to build a satellite tracking station in Ho Chi Minh City.[56]

But by far the most significant of these partnerships is with Japan which has strategic partnerships with Vietnam, Malaysia and the Philippines and an agreement with Indonesia on defense technology transfers. Since relaxing its ban on arms exports, Japan has provided coast guard vessels to the Philippines and Indonesia. Further, Japan's new security legislation allows the deployment of Self-Defense Forces (SDFs) for HA/DR missions and for situations that can be described as "infringement that does not amount to an armed attack." Scenarios that fall under the latter category include "an armed attack occurring against a foreign country" that, in Japan's estimation, threatens its "survival, depending on its purpose, scale and manner."[57] For countries like Vietnam and the Philippines, this could be reassuring vis-a-vis future conflicts with China; but for Malaysia and Indonesia, countries that have experienced fewer direct confrontations with China, Japan's new legislation could be a threat to regional stability itself.

Apart from these traditional approaches, ASEAN continues to insist on the relevance of the ASEAN Regional Forum (ARF). Created in 1994, the ARF's objectives were to develop confidence-building and preventive diplomacy measures as well as to move towards identifying measures for regional conflict resolution. ASEAN uses this forum to ensure that their own security needs are addressed and that they are in the forum's "driver's seat" in perpetuity. But 17 years and 27 members later, the ARF has not led to marked changes in behavior and the progress towards preventive diplomacy has been glacial. The Forum's failure to realize its potential is not only due to its cumbersome decision-making process based on consensus, but also due to the ASEAN countries' failure to coordinate and harmonize their disparate security priorities. Without a unified core leadership, the ARF became a grab bag of ideas and activities out of which participants hoped that more substantive multilateral security cooperation would emerge. Nevertheless, the 2016 ARF Ministerial Statement stated that they will promote "concrete and practical cooperation" among the countries' maritime law enforcement agencies including sharing best practices in incident management and handling of fishing vessels, and that they will develop codes of conduct and common standard operating procedures. A more promising forum is the recently established ADMM-Plus which brings together ASEAN-10 and Australia, China, India, Japan, New Zealand, South Korea, the Russian Federation and the United States. The participants are sharing information and cooperating on non-traditional security issues through exercises and skills exchanges, but it still has a long way to go.[58] These multilateral arrangements clearly are not as important as the alliances and strategic partnerships with great powers and middle powers.

Opportunities and challenges

Southeast Asian states have lately demonstrated their willingness and capability to address everyday maritime security issues either individually or with partners.

Practical cooperation has come a long way and they could possibly become stronger and more sophisticated as evidenced by the growing institutionalization of cooperation in the SoMS.

Yet sustaining military modernization programs and cooperative activities and addressing the root causes of internal conflict depend on various economic and political factors. Modernization programs are sensitive to economic crises and developing indigenous defense industries requires substantial investments. For instance, Thailand's aircraft carrier suffered from neglect as did the submarines of Indonesia.

The more important factor is domestic politics. The urgency of non-maritime problems will take precedence over maritime problems as seen in the allocation of personnel in Southeast Asian militaries – Singapore's navy is only 12.4% of its military, Thailand's is 19.4% and Vietnam's is 13.9%. The navies of archipelagic countries fare no better – the Philippine navy is only 28% of total armed forces while Indonesia's is only 16%.[59]

Political leadership and the commitment to staying the course are vital. Singapore has never veered away from its Total Defense concept largely due to the longevity of the People's Action Party (PAP). Since the 1993 decision of its Politburo, the Communist Party of Vietnam (CPV) has similarly maintained its focus on developing its maritime economy which should be protected by a modern navy and coastguard. In 2007, the Central Committee adopted a resolution on "Vietnam's Maritime Strategy Towards 2020" which is its very "first comprehensive maritime strategy."[60] Malaysia's modernization program has been criticized as rather haphazard, while the Philippines has been bedeviled by swings in foreign policy. Fidel V. Ramos and Benigno Aquino III supported these defense modernization programs and took a firm stance against China, while Gloria Macapagal-Arroyo and Rodrigo Duterte are more pro-China.

Populism and nationalism are also driving the process. Indonesia only recently enunciated a maritime concept, the *Poros Maritim Durum (PMD)*, under Widodo in 2014. Responding to criticisms that previous Indonesian presidents were more focused on foreign policy, Widodo vowed to address domestic needs, especially those of traditional fishing communities. Indonesia's problem with IUU fishing is serious, but some of the government's actions may not be conducive to reaching more amicable agreements. The government has blown up confiscated ships to demonstrate their resolve; it bolsters nationalism but can complicate foreign relations such as when Vietnam expressed concern over this practice.

Another challenge to managing maritime security is the differences in capabilities and the diverse sources of vessels and equipment used by Southeast Asian countries. Without effective interoperability among maritime forces, the full implementation of international maritime rules and regulations will not be easily realized.

Southeast Asian countries remain vulnerable to the machinations of great powers, but their own actions can affect strategic relations in the area. Will populist nationalism undermine strategic partnerships and practical cooperation? EDCA was challenged in the Philippines as was the proposed China-Philippines-Vietnam joint exploration agreement. Philippine president Duterte has threatened to scrap its defense arrangements with the United States and has stated that he will start bilateral discussions with China over the SCS and the Kalayaan Island Group, totally disregarding the Philippines' significant political victory with the ITLOS decision in 2016. Thailand's generals are also improving relations with Beijing because of negative U.S. reaction to the 2014 coup. These short-sighted and, in some cases, impetuous decisions will affect the complexion of great power relations in the near-term with China exercising a more dominant role.

Strategic partnerships with middle powers are also emerging as an important component of Southeast Asia's maritime security. On the one hand, these relationships can help improve training of naval and coast guard personnel, procure equipment and could even become the springboard for other cooperative activities. On the other hand, these partnerships with countries critical of China could also be seen by China as attempts to prevent its rise and as surrogates for an American presence.

But by far the biggest challenge of Southeast Asia is the lack of a cohesive ASEAN strategy towards regional maritime security – a strategy that could include negotiating a binding multilateral code of conduct with China, using the Tribunal's 2016 ruling as the legal framework for opening discussions on the SCS, and even taking a more proactive stance in the ARF. Internal problems and intra-regional disputes will continue to mitigate the development of such a cohesive strategy without which current unilateral and cooperative activities will only be able to solve immediate problems, leaving the sustainable management of regional maritime security subject to the whims of time and tide.

Notes

1 Thayer introduced the term "everyday security issues" to refer to domestic, land-based security challenges (2010, p. 38) which can be considered as "traditional" security issues in the sense that they challenge the territorial integrity, national unity and legitimacy of the state. This paper extends the term to cover some non-traditional security issues that occur in the maritime arena that occur on a daily basis.
2 Acharya, 2007, p. 82.
3 Heroin traffickers are using a southern maritime route from South to Southeast Asia due to better law enforcement on land. The Indian Ocean and the Andaman Sea are two of the perceived maritime routes for methamphetamine tablets, crystalline methamphetamine and ecstasy. The South China Sea is also a perceived trafficking route for ecstasy and for new psychoactive substances. Small arms go through SoMS, Makassar Straits as well as the Sulu, Celebes and Andaman Seas. See: UNODC, 2015a; UNODC Regional Office for Southeast Asia and the Pacific, 2014; UNODC, 2015b; Bateman, 2010.
4 Adamcyzk, 2016.
5 Bateman, 2010.
6 John, 2016.
7 The Star, 2016.
8 GMA News, 2013.
9 Wain, 2012, p. 53.
10 FAO, 2014, p. 10. Indonesia was ranked second, Vietnam ninth, the Philippines twelfth, Thailand fourteenth and Malaysia fifteenth. In 2013, the total value of fisheries

commodity trade and production for the five countries reached $20 billion for 15 million tons of catch. Author's calculation is based on the online database FAO Global Production Statistics, www.fao.org/fishery/topic/16140/en.
11 FAO, 2014. This number does not include the people employed in other fishing industry-related jobs like canning, preserving, transporting and selling.
12 ICG, 2016, p. 11.
13 Palma, 2012, p. 117.
14 International Energy Agency (IEA), 2013.
15 Energy Information Agency, 2013.
16 Goldrick and McCaffrie, 2013, p. 85; Do, 2016.
17 FAO, 2014, p. 84.
18 Parameswaran, 2015a.
19 FAO, 2016, pp. 15–16.
20 The most overfished areas are in the Gulf of Thailand, the Malaysian and Vietnamese coasts, and parts of Indonesia and the Philippines. See also Dupont and Baker, 2014.
21 AMTI, 2014.
22 IISS, 2015, p. 34.
23 Abuza, 2016.
24 Fabbri, 2015.
25 If ships go through the Sunda and Lombok-Makassar Straits, two to three days will be added to transit, and freight costs would increase by 20–30% (Xu and Lai, 2009, p. 187).
26 Storey, 2016, p. 6.
27 Acharya, 2007, p. 79.
28 Abuza, 2016.
29 Abuza, 2016.
30 Murphy, 2007, p. 78.
31 Based on data from STRAITREP. Available at www.mpa.gov.sg/web/portal/home/port-of-singapore/port-statistics
32 The most well-known ASG ferry bombings are *Our Lady of Mediatrix* in 2000 and the *Superferry 14* in 2004 which killed more than 200 people in the Philippines. In Indonesia, a ferry terminal (2004) and the ferry *Kalifornia* (2001) were also attacked by local extremists. See Bradford, 2005, p. 67.
33 Acharya, 2007, pp. 79–80.
34 Arshad, 2016.
35 ReCAAP stands for the Regional Cooperation Agreement on Combating Piracy and Armed Robbery against ships in Asia, while IMB refers to the International Maritime Bureau.
36 Bateman, 2015.
37 Ho, 2012, pp. 134–135.
38 Singapore Defense Ministry, 2008.
39 Koh, 2014a, p. 130.
40 Graham, 2014, p. 78.
41 Ho, 2012, p. 134; Nguyen, 2012, p. 169; Reuters, 2015.
42 Malaysia: 450,000; Thailand 305,778. Sources: CIA Worldfactbook; World Resources Institute; seaaroundus.org
43 Goldrick and McCaffrie, 2013, p. 80.
44 Taman Stevia, *Strategi Pertahanan Laut Nusantara dalam Menghadapi Provokasi Malaysia di Ambalat* [Indonesia's Sea Defense Strategy against Malaysian Provocations in Ambalat], M.A. Thesis, University of Indonesia, 2010 cited by Laksmana, 2014, p. 191.
45 These are based on 2014 US$ constant million. All figures were taken from the database of the Stockholm International Peace and Research Institute (SIPRI).
46 Dowdy et al., 2014.

47 Dowdy et al., 2014, p. 10.
48 Till and Chan, 2014, p. 4.
49 Bateman, 2007.
50 Koh, 2014b, p. 231.
51 Sullivan, 2014, p. 7.
52 Till and Chan, 2014, p. 10.
53 Simon, 2016.
54 Do, 2016.
55 Leong, 2016.
56 Goldrick and McCaffrie, 2013, p. 202; Miglani and Torode, 2016.
57 Japanese Cabinet Decision on Development of Seamless Security Legislation to Ensure Japan's Survival and Protect its People (July 1, 2014).
58 US Navy, 2016.
59 AMTI, 2014.
60 Thayer, 2016.

References

Abuza, Z., 2016. *Trilateral Maritime Patrols in the Sulu Sea: Asymmetry in Need, Capability, and Political Will*. [online] Center for International Maritime Security. Available at: <http://cimsec.org/trilateral-maritime-patrols-sulu-sea-asymmetry-need-capability-political-will/26251> [Accessed 15 July 2016].

Acharya, A., 2007. Maritime Terrorist Threat in Southeast Asia. In: K. C. Guan, and J. K. Skogan, eds., *Maritime Security in Southeast Asia*. London and New York: Routledge, pp. 78–93.

Adamcyzk, E., 2016. *Weapons destined for Abu Sayyaf group seized in Philippines*. [online] UPI. Available at: <www.upi.com/Top_News/World-News/2016/09/27/Weapons-destined-for-Abu-Sayyaf-group-seized-in-Philippines/5311474976356/> [Accessed 27 September 2016].

AMTI, 2014. *18 Maps That Explain Maritime Security in Asia*. [online] Asia Maritime Transparency Initiative. Available at: <https://amti2016.wpengine.com/atlas/> [Accessed 18 December 2016].

Arshad, A., 2016. *Marina Bay rocket attack plot from Batam 'not to be taken lightly'*. [Text] The Straits Times. Available at: <www.straitstimes.com/singapore/rocket-attack-plot-not-to-be-taken-lightly> [Accessed 18 December 2016].

Bateman, S., 2007. *Perils of the Deep: The Dangers of Submarine Operations in Asia*. IDSS Commentaries. [online] Available at: <www.rsis.edu.sg/rsis-publication/idss/895-perils-of-the-deep-the-danger/#.V3GhzTUdn-c>.

———, 2010. Regional Maritime Security: Threats and Risk Assessments. In: S. Bateman and J. Ho, eds., *Southeast Asia and the Rise of Chinese and Indian Naval Power: Between Rising Naval Powers*. London and New York: Routledge, pp. 99–113.

———, 2015. *Piracy Monitoring Wars: Responsibilities for Countering Piracy*. RSIS Commentaries.

Bradford, J. F., 2005. The Growing Prospects for Maritime Security Cooperation in Southeast Asia. *Naval War College Review*, 58(3), pp. 63–86.

Do, T. H., 2016. *Vietnam's Management of China's Maritime Assertiveness in the Post-Cold War Period*. [online] The ASAN Forum. Available at: <www.theasanforum.org/vietnams-management-of-chinas-maritime-assertiveness-in-the-post-cold-war-period1/> [Accessed 13 November 2016].

Dowdy, J., Chinn, D., Mancini, M., and Ng, J., 2014. *Southeast Asia: The Next Growth Opportunity in Defense*. McKinsey Innovation Campus Aerospace and Defense Practice. Singapore: McKinsey and Co.
Dupont, A., and Baker, C. G., 2014. East Asia's Maritime Disputes: Fishing in Troubled Waters. *The Washington Quarterly*, pp. 79–98.
Energy Information Agency, 2013. *South China Sea*. [EIA beta website] Available at: <www.eia.gov/beta/international/regions-topics.cfm?RegionTopicID=SCS> [Accessed 6 May 2016].
Fabbri, D., 2015. *How Singapore's Port Helped Change the Country's Economy*. [online] Channel NewsAsia. Available at: <www.channelnewsasia.com/news/business/singapore/how-singapore-s-port/1796336.html> [Accessed 5 September 2016].
FAO, 2014. *The State of World Fisheries and Aquaculture: Opportunities and Challenges*. Rome: Food and Agriculture Organization.
———, 2016. *2014 FAO Yearbook: Fishery and Aquaculture Statistics*. Rome: Food and Agriculture Organization.
GMA News, 2013. *Timeline of the Sabah crisis: February to March*. [online] GMA News Online. Available at: <www.gmanetwork.com/news/story/298166/news/nation/timeline-of-the-sabah-crisis-february-to-march> [Accessed 11 March 2016].
Goldrick, J., and McCaffrie, J., 2013. *Navies of South-East Asia: A Comparative Study*. Naval Policy and History. London and New York: Routledge.
Graham, E., 2014. Southeast Asian Perspectives of Regional Engagement and Power Projection. In: A. Forbes, ed., *Naval Diplomacy and Maritime Power Projection: Proceedings of the Royal Australian Navy Sea Power Conference 2013*. Australia: Sea Power CentreAustralia, pp. 73–86.
Ho, J., 2012. Singapore's Maritime Interests. In: J. Ho, and S. Bateman, eds., *Maritime Challenges and Priorities in Asia: Implications for Regional Security*. London and New York: Routledge, pp. 126–139.
ICG, 2016. *Stirring up the South China Sea (IV): Oil in Troubled Waters*. Asia Report. Brussels, Belgium: International Crisis Group.
IISS, 2015. *Asia-Pacific Regional Security Assessment 2015: Key Developments and Trends*. London: International Institute for Strategic Studies.
International Energy Agency (IEA), 2013. *Southeast Asia Energy Outlook*. World Energy Outlook Special Report. [online] Paris, France. Available at: <www.iea.org>.
John, T., 2016. Indonesia's Long Battle With Islamic Extremism. *TIME.com*. Available at: <http://time.com/4181557/jakarta-terrorist-attacks-indonesia-isis/> [Accessed 2 Nov. 2016].
Koh, S. L. C., 2014a. 'Best Little Navy in Southeast Asia': The Case of the Republic of Singapore Navy. In: M. Mulqueen, D. Sanders, and I. Speller, eds., *Small Navies: Strategy and Policy for Small Navies in War and Peace*. Farnham, England and Burlington, Vermont: Ashgate, pp. 117–131.
———, 2014b. Seeking Balance: Force Projection, Confidence-Building and the Republic of Singapore Navy. In: G. Till, and J. Chan, eds., *Naval Modernization in South-East Asia: Nature, Causes and Consequences*. London and New York: Routledge, pp. 223–241.
Laksmana, E. A., 2014. Rebalancing Indonesia's Naval Force: Trends, Nature, and Drivers. In: G. Till, and J. Chan, eds., *Naval Modernisation in South-East Asia: Nature, Causes and Consequences*. London and New York: Routledge, pp. 175–203.

Leong, J., 2016. *Singapore, Australia sign Comprehensive Strategic Partnership deals.* [online] Channel NewsAsia. Available at: <www.channelnewsasia.com/news/singapore/singapore-australia-sign-comprehensive-strategic-partnership/3201696.html> [Accessed 16 December 2016].

Miglani, S., and Torode, G., 2016. *India to Build Satellite Tracking Station in Vietnam That Offers Eye on China Reuters.* [News] Reuters. Available at: <http://in.reuters.com/article/india-vietnam-satellite-china-idINKCN0V309W> [Accessed 9 July 2016].

Murphy, M. N., 2007. *Contemporary Piracy and Maritime Terrorism: The Threat to International Security.* Adelphi Paper. London: Routledge.

Nguyen, H. T., 2012. Good Order at Sea: The Challenges and Priorities of Vietnam. In: J. Ho and S. Bateman, eds., *Maritime Challenges and Priorities in Asia: Implications for Regional Security.* London and New York: Routledge, pp. 158–178.

Palma, M. A., 2012. Maintaining Good Order at Sea: Maritime Challenges and Priorities in the Philippines. In: J. Ho and S. Bateman, eds., *Maritime Challenges and Priorities in Asia: Implications for Regional Security.* London and New York: Routledge, pp. 106–125.

Parameswaran, P., 2015a. *Explaining Indonesia's 'Sink The Vessels' Policy Under Jokowi.* [online] The Diplomat. Available at: <http://thediplomat.com/2015/01/explaining-indonesias-sink-the-vessels-policy-under-jokowi/> [Accessed 8 May 2016].

———, 2015b. *Singapore Calls for Global Action to Tackle Maritime Challenges.* [online] The Diplomat. Available at: <http://thediplomat.com/2015/05/singapore-calls-for-global-plan-to-tackle-maritime-challenges/> [Accessed 28 June 2016].

Reuters, 2015. *Malaysia, Indonesia to Deploy Rapid Response Team to Fight Soaring Piracy.* [online] Reuters. Available at: <www.reuters.com/article/shipping-attacks-asia-pac-idUSL4N11034J20150826> [Accessed 9 December 2016].

Simon, S. W. 2016. US-Southeast Asia Relations: ASEAN Centrality? *Comparative Connections: A Triannual E-Journal on East Asian Bilateral Relations*, 18(1), pp. 45–54.

Singapore Defense Ministry, 2008. *Factsheet: Milestones of Malacca Straits Patrol.* [online] Singapore Ministry of Defense. Available at: <www.mindef.gov.sg/imindef/press_room/official_releases/nr/2008/mar/28mar08_nr/28mar08_fs.html> [Accessed 9 December 2016].

The Star, 2016. *Malaysian Armed Forces Being Monitored for Alleged Links With IS.* [online] South China Morning Post. Available at: <www.scmp.com/news/asia/southeast-asia/article/2022617/malaysian-armed-forces-being-monitored-alleged-links> [Accessed 30 September 2016].

Storey, I., 2016. *Addressing the Persistent Problem of Piracy and Sea Robbery in Southeast Asia.* ISEAS Perspective. [online] Singapore: ISEAS Yusof Ishak Institute. Available at: <www.iseas.edu.sg/images/pdf/ISEAS_Perspective_2016_30.pdf>.

Sullivan, A., 2014. *Autonomous Power? Securing Singapore's Interests in the 21st Century.* Asia Strategy Series. Washington, DC: Center for a New American Security.

Thayer, C. A., 2016. *Challenges in Renewing Maritime Capabilities: Viet Nam.* [online] Available at: <www.viet-studies.net/kinhte/Thayer_VietnamMaritimesCapabilities.pdf>

Till, G. and Chan, J. eds., 2014. *Naval Modernisation in Southeast Asia: Nature, Causes and Consequences.* London and New York: Routledge.

UNODC, 2015a. *Global Maritime Crime Programme Annual Report 2015.* New York: United Nations.

———, 2015b. *The Challenge of Synthetic Drugs in East and South-East Asia and Oceania – Trends and Patterns of Amphetamine-Type Stimulants and New Psychoactive*

Substances: *A Report from the Global SMART Programme*. UN Office on Drugs and Crime.

UNODC Regional Office for Southeast Asia and the Pacific, 2014. *Drug Trafficking Trends and Border Management in South-East Asia: 'Responding to an Evolving Context of Regional Integration'*.

US Navy, 2016. *ADMM-Plus Maritime Security, Counter Terrorism FTX 2016 Underway in Brunei*. [online] US Navy. Available at: <www.navy.mil/submit/display.asp?story_id=94525> [Accessed 22 November 2016].

Wain, B., 2012. Latent Danger: Boundary Disputes and Border Issues in Southeast Asia. In: D. Singh and P. Thambipillai, eds., *Southeast Asian Affairs 2012*. Singapore: Institute of Southeast Asian Studies, pp. 38–60.

Xu, K., and Lai, H., 2009. Piracy and Energy Security in Southeast Asian Waters. In: *Asian Energy Security: The Maritime Dimension*. New York: Palgrave Macmillan, pp. 183–203.

8 Australia's maritime strategy

Alan Bloomfield and Shirley V. Scott

It is vital for Australia to have an effective maritime strategy. Australia is the largest island and the smallest continent in the world, with a 25,760 kilometres coastline, an exclusive economic zone (EEZ) of around 10 million square kilometres – the third largest in the world – and responsibility for an enormous search and rescue zone of some 53 million square kilometres. The worst-case scenarios imagined by strategists involve hostile forces operating in or even traversing the waters surrounding Australia, and as the world's twelfth largest economy[1] Australia is heavily reliant on sea-borne trade; merchandise trade contributed 33% of GDP in the 2011–14 period, 99% of which was carried by sea.[2] This chapter begins by exploring how Australia views its role in international affairs, including the contemporary debate about how Canberra should balance its relationships with China and the United States. It then examines Australian 'grand strategy' – with a particular focus on the maritime dimension of such before moving on to survey Australia's maritime capabilities, including examples of how these are operationally deployed.

Australia in a time of strategic uncertainty

Before 1942 Australia was closely tied to Great Britain; thereafter Australia became ever-more closely aligned to the United States; in the contemporary era Australia is pursuing a more complex and nuanced foreign and defence policy, debating how to maintain close relations with Washington while also coming to terms with the fact that its future prosperity, and likely its security too, is inextricably linked to the rising powers in its region.[3] Thus, maintaining close links to a so-called 'great and powerful friend'[4] has been an enduring theme in Australia's foreign policy orientation or identity for over a century, in part to ensure Australia will be assisted if threatened, and more generally, because the international order crafted and protected by its powerful 'Anglo' allies has, generally speaking, been conducive to Canberra's own interests.

This is not to say that Australia only plays a 'loyal ally' role. An enduring debate concerns whether Australia is, or should act like, a 'middle power'.[5] From the 1980s onwards, Australia's activism in multilateral forums has frequently been referred to as middle power diplomacy, although this is not to suggest Australia has directly challenged the broad global framework largely built and presided over by the United States. A second related debate concerns whether Australia is – or should be – a 'good international citizen'.[6] The term is, like that of middle power diplomacy, more associated with Labor Party figures, especially former Foreign Minister Gareth Evans, who argued in the 1990s that 'being, and being seen to be, a good international citizen' – by respecting international law and supporting the institutions which managed the international system – was one of three foreign policy priorities for Australia.[7] Conservative governments have typically been somewhat less enthusiastic about these roles. Former foreign minister Alexander Downer, for example, advised in 1996 that conservative Coalition governments would prioritise 'practical bilateralism' over multilateralism,[8] and the current foreign minister, Julie Bishop, has queried the utility of promoting Australia as a middle power.[9] Conservatives have also typically displayed somewhat more enthusiasm for the American alliance.

Nevertheless, and while the major parties continually try to wedge each other on the foreign policy issue *de jour*, this manoeuvring masks broad bipartisan agreement that Australia should generally present itself as a 'good international middle power' (to coin a phrase) for reputational purposes[10] while also advancing its traditional interests, including by working closely with Washington. Consider how recent governments have begun emphasising the importance of maintaining a 'rules-based' international order. In 2016 Malcolm Turnbull's conservative Coalition government released a defence white paper which recognised a systemic threat from mounting challenges to the legal architecture of global governance:

> The framework of the rules-based global order is under increasing pressure and has shown signs of fragility. The balance of military and economic power between countries is changing and newly powerful countries want greater influence and to challenge some of the rules in the global architecture established some 70 years ago.[11]

Previous foreign policy[12] and defence white papers[13] released by Labor governments had confirmed that Australia strongly valued this so-called rules-based order, but in the 2016 paper the phrase rated over 50 mentions and for the first time defending it was said to be a 'core interest'.[14] Michael Wesley believes this was 'largely motivated by concerns about challenges to freedom of navigation' in Asian waters[15] (see as follows).

Promoting the notion of a rules-based order enables Australia to blend its preference for projecting an image of itself as a 'responsible' actor with the pursuit of 'hard' interests, like maintaining open sea lines of communication (SLOCs). But it also reflects an understanding that Australia's region, and the global order more generally, is changing, and that Washington's regional unipolarity has been eroded by the growing investment by Asian countries in anti-access/area denial (A2/AD) weapons and by the displacement by China of the United States and Japan as the leading regional economies.[16] 'Uncertainty' and 'complexity' have become buzz-words in Australian foreign policy discourse,[17] and the greatest uncertainty concerns what effect China's rise is having, or will have, on Australia's region, its alliance with the United States, and its interests more generally.

Australia and US-China relations

In 2010 Hugh White framed the debate about how Australia should respond to China's rise as an essentially inescapable dilemma:

> There is a problem with Australia's vision of its future. On the one hand we assume China will just keep growing indefinitely, buying more and more [resources].... On the other hand, we expect America to remain the strongest power in Asia. We will have a very nice future if both these things happen. The problem is that they cannot both happen at once.[18]

He then suggested Australia may one day have to choose between security (with Washington) and prosperity (with Beijing). Official pronouncements typically avoid posing the dilemma so starkly, but they nevertheless recognise its basic contours. For example, the 2016 white paper declared that '[t]he United States will remain the pre-eminent global military power and will continue to be Australia's most important strategic partner.... Australia will seek to broaden and deepen our alliance'.[19] But it also said 'Australia welcomes China's continued economic growth and the opportunities this is bringing for Australia',[20] echoing sentiments expressed strongly in the most recent foreign policy white paper.[21]

White's thesis has generated much debate,[22] reflecting the fact that China's rise has become the single most important factor impacting Australia's perception of its national interests, including in the maritime domain. Senior figures from both sides of politics have repeatedly rejected the notion that Australia must choose,[23] but there is some evidence that policy-makers are nevertheless being forced to choose day-by-day whether to support Beijing's efforts to enhance its own influence in Asia at Washington's expense, or to whole-heartedly support Australia's traditional ally.[24] This was reflected most keenly in the debate over whether to join China's Asian Infrastructure Investment Bank; Australia did so eventually, contravening Washington's expressed preferences.[25] But the need to constantly consider how every decision will be perceived in Beijing and Washington also impacts Australia's relationships with Tokyo, New Delhi and, indeed, virtually all regional capitals.

Nick Bisley in 2014 rejected White's thesis and concluded that when Canberra invited the United States' armed forces to significantly upgrade their presence in Australia's north in 2011 this meant

> Australia communicated a clear choice about its strategic future . . . [motivated by] a sharpened sense that China's rise was generating regional instability that only the US could manage and the realisation that the economic fallout of such a move would be minimal.[26]

Consideration of recent defence white papers suggests that Bisley is essentially correct. The 2009 iteration surprised many when it announced a major military rearmament programme, bluntly stated that 'shows of force by rising powers are likely to become more common as their military capabilities grow', and pointedly noted that

> there is likely to be a question in the minds of regional states about the long-term strategic purpose of [China's] force development plans, particularly as the modernisation appears potentially to be beyond . . . [that] . . . required for a conflict over Taiwan.[27]

The 2013 white paper adopted a more balanced tone, noting that:

> The Government does not believe that Australia must choose between its longstanding Alliance with the United States and its expanding relationship with China. . . . China's defence capabilities are growing and its military is modernising, as a natural and legitimate outcome of its economic growth.[28]

But no elements of the rearmament programme announced in 2009 were abandoned. And the 2016 white paper both began implementing the rearmament programme more effectively (i.e. with more specific funding commitments)[29] and also returned to a theme from the 2009 version when it said:

> As China grows, it will continue to seek greater influence within the region. As a major power, it will be important for regional stability that China provides reassurance to its neighbours by being more transparent about its defence policies.[30]

Indeed, it went further and effectively 'called China out' in a specific context:

> Australia opposes the use of artificial structures in the South China Sea for military purposes. Australia also opposes the assertion of associated territorial claims and maritime rights which are not in accordance with international law. . . . Australia is particularly concerned by the unprecedented pace and scale of China's land reclamation activities.[31]

Events in the South China Sea have therefore become particularly concerning to Australia, both as a symbol of the broader threat of great power tensions erupting into hostilities and more directly because of the potential to block vital sea lanes; two thirds of Australia's exports and almost half its imports move through this area,[32] which explains why the 2016 white paper claimed Australia must retain 'unfettered access to trading routes . . . to support [its] economic development'.[33] Thus, how to respond to China's rise has become the single-most important debate in Australian foreign policy discourse, the maritime implications of such – especially vis-à-vis the South China Sea dispute – are becoming the focal point of this wider debate, and Australia's military capabilities and alliance-ties to Washington are steadily strengthening in response.

Australia's grand strategy and its maritime dimension

According to Wesley, Australia has traditionally done without a grand strategy, 'relying on Defence White Papers to set out a military strategy that is largely subordinate to the grand strategy of its great power ally'.[34] This is not to say that there has been no Australian grand-strategic thinking at all, just that it has typically taken place against the backdrop of a strong alliance with a great and powerful friend. Two schools of thought have traditionally vied for influence. The first, 'forward defence', required Australia to be capable of dispatching large expeditionary forces to fight alongside Australia's major allies, meaning the Australian Army received the lion's share of resources. This doctrine was only 'maritime' to the extent that Australian warships would provide 'close escort' for army units travelling to combat theatres, and it was expected that Australia's allies would provide a generally permissive maritime environment by maintaining 'sea control' over the relevant SLOCs. This tradition explains Australia's participation in the World Wars and Cold War-era conflicts like those in Korea, Malaysia and Vietnam.

Forward defence began to be eclipsed by 'continental defence' logic in the mid-1970s; the shift was precipitated by Britain's withdrawal 'East of Suez' in 1967 and US President Richard Nixon's 1969 Guam Doctrine,[35] while the emergence of a 'distinctly Australian outlook and spirit'[36] around this time also contributed. Continental defence requires the Australian Defence Force (ADF) to be capable of defeating all low- to medium-level threats without allied assistance, including being capable of 'prevent[ing] an aggressor attacking us successfully in our sea and air approaches [or] gaining a foothold on any part of our territory'. In other words, the ADF would be configured to practice 'sea denial' in the quintessentially maritime 'Air-Sea Gap' to Australia's north.

However continental defence never became as dominant as forward defence logic had been because the intention was never to achieve *full* self-reliance. Instead, 'defence self-reliance must be set firmly within the framework of our alliances',[37] meaning Australia would continue to shelter under Washington's 'nuclear umbrella', American assistance was expected if a full-scale invasion loomed, and the ADF would also be capable of dispatching 'niche' contingents to fight with American forces.[38] Accordingly, and from a maritime perspective, continental defence doctrine did not envisage Australia defending SLOCs on its own. Instead, Australia would continue to support the United States' global hegemony to keep SLOCs open: thus at least one Australian warship has been deployed to the Persian Gulf region continuously since 1990 alongside US Navy vessels and, more generally, ADF contingents continue to be regularly dispatched to support America's strategic adventures, suggesting forward defence logic remains influential. Nevertheless, the rise of continental defence has meant Australia's defence posture has shifted, with northern facilities like airfields, ports and the

Jindalee over-the-horizon radar system built or upgraded. And the force-structure emphasis has shifted from the Army to the Royal Australian Air Force (RAAF) and the Royal Australian Navy (RAN). The latter two are designed to operate in the Air-Sea Gap, making Australia's strategic posture essentially maritime in nature. Finally, in 1987 the decision was made to essentially run-down the RAN's amphibious capability, but bouts of regional instability since 1991 have led to it being slowly but steadily rebuilt.[39]

The 2016 defence white paper does not mark a major departure so much as a readjustment of Australia's strategic framework by focusing on three core interests: 'a secure, resilient Australia with secure northern approaches and proximate lines of communication', requiring the capability to 'deter, deny and defeat any attempt . . . to attack, threaten or coerce Australia'; 'a secure nearer region', requiring the capability to 'make effective military contributions to support the security of maritime South East Asia and [the South Pacific]'; and 'a stable Indo-Pacific region and a rules-based global order', requiring the capability to 'contribute military capabilities to coalition operations'.[40] The first core interest is called 'the most basic', but the lack of explicit prioritisation between the three interests (unlike previous papers, which tended to give 'highest priority to the interests and objectives closest to Australia')[41] led Peter Jennings to claim Australia's strategy is more-properly maritime than ever before because the ADF is now expected to operate effectively in the *region* – which is of course primarily maritime – rather than focusing mainly on defending the continent.[42] Lee Corder[43] also called the 2016 paper 'a significant priority shift toward maritime security' and Ross Babbage agreed (although he critiqued the change).[44]

We have focused on the military dimension of Australia's maritime strategy because it is the single-most important aspect of such. But there are other dimensions. For example, Canberra is the major foreign aid donor to Pacific states, providing 60% of the total from OECD sources. Notably, Pacific aid programmes were not reduced when the overall foreign aid budget was cut in 2015,[45] and Prime Minister Turnbull announced a new Pacific Strategy which will include greater investment initiatives. Some aid is military aid – for example, 22 patrol boats were gifted to Pacific Island nations in the 1990s, and 21 replacements will be delivered from 2018 (costing $305 million[46] over five years)[47] – but the bulk is development aid. In addition to the $280 million 'ordinary' aid dispersed in 2016–17 to Pacific states (through permanent bilateral and multilateral schemes), time-bounded, targeted multilateral programmes to foster climate change adaptation, disaster relief, sustainable fishing and to promote gender equality will provide a further $60 million annually for several years.[48] Australia also engages in bilateral and multilateral diplomacy in venues like ASEAN Regional Forum, the Pacific Islands Forum, and the Indian Ocean Rim Association (IORA). The remit of these organisations is typically wide: matters discussed at the IORA, for example, include trade and investment, fisheries management, disaster response, academic cooperation, and tourism, in addition to maritime safety and security.[49]

Finally, Australia's preferred definition of its region has changed somewhat recently. During the 1980s politicians talked of the 'Asia-Pacific', but recently the term 'Indo-Pacific' has become preferred (it appeared 70 times in the 2016 defence white paper, and Asia-Pacific was entirely absent). This matters because a regional definition 'is above all an ideological construct. Although it may be deployed in an objective, descriptive sense . . . [it is] almost invariably advanced as a political project'.[50] Official Australian policy documents claim that defining the region in this new way – implicitly including India – is meant to foster greater inclusivity and stability,[51] although others have noted the new formulation may also be aimed at facilitating collective efforts to balance against China.[52]

Australia's naval and civilian maritime capabilities

In this section we consider the capabilities Australia can deploy to advance its maritime strategy. The RAN is undoubtedly the single-most important institution but it is not solely responsible for providing maritime security, which in addition to the more-strictly military or strategic aspects requires action to prevent illegal exploitation of natural resources, marine pollution, prohibited imports/exports, illegal maritime arrivals, threats to bio-security, and piracy. Unlike in the United States, where the Coast Guard has responsibility for a wide range of tasks – maritime law enforcement, search and rescue, environmental protection, etc. – multiple Australian agencies handle these tasks. Nevertheless, the bulk of the resources which underpin Australia's maritime capabilities go to the ADF, so we discuss it first.

Australia's 2015–16 defence budget totalled $32.1 billion (US$23.5 billion), a little over 1.9 percent of GDP[53] which ranked Australia 13th in global defence spending.[54] In terms of annual operating costs the Army was allocated $6.8 billion, the RAAF $5.5 billion and the RAN $5.2 billion[55] which suggests rough-parity of resource-allocation between the services. But the capital investment figures provide a clearer picture of the relative importance of each service; currently $60 billion-worth of projects have been approved, with 39% allocated to RAN projects, 37% to RAAF projects, and 20% to Army projects.[56] Thus, spending on RAN and RAAF assets – both primarily designed for use in a maritime environment – almost quadruples spending on assets for land operations.

Specifically, the RAAF is undergoing a major renewal. The 71 'classic' F/A-18 *Hornets* will be replaced by 2023 with 72 F-35A *Lightnings*. Complementing these are 24 F/A-18 *Super Hornets*, and a further 12 EA-18G *Growlers* – 'electronic warfare' Super Hornets – will be operational by 2020. Thus, Australia currently operates 95 strike aircraft and this number will rise to 108 by 2023, supported by six *Wedgetail* 'battlespace management' aircraft and five KC-30A tankers to facilitate strikes well into maritime South East Asia. The 19 aging AP-3C *Orion* maritime patrol aircraft will also be replaced by 2025 with 15 P-8 *Poseidons* and seven MQ-4C *Triton* unmanned UAVs.[57]

The RAN is also undergoing renewal. Two recently-acquired *Canberra*-class helicopter-carriers have significantly boosted amphibious capabilities, meaning the Army can now be integrated more effectively into Australia's maritime strategy; humanitarian, stabilisation, and combat missions – including resisted-landing operations – in northern archipelagos have been facilitated by the acquisition of these two large (27,500 tonne) warships,[58] and one infantry battalion has been re-equipped for amphibious missions. Presently 10 frigates form the core of the fleet, but they will be replaced by three much larger *Hobart*-class Aegis destroyers from 2017 and nine 'future frigates' by the mid-2020s. Twenty new patrol boats will also replace the 26-strong fleet of patrol boats, minesweepers and survey vessels;[59] the new 'modular' vessels will perform varied tasks, and at 2,000 tonnes they will be significantly larger than the current 300 tonne *Armidale*-class patrol boats. But the 'big ticket item' is the Future Submarines programme. This matter spawned a veritable cottage industry of expert and media speculation, but in May 2016 the French bid beat German and Japanese tenders. This procurement programme is notable for two reasons. First, the current fleet of six *Collins*-class submarines will be replaced by 12 boats (although not for some time; the first is unlikely to enter service until the late 2020s at the earliest).[60] Second, the cost is staggering, with the media reporting the figure of $50 billion to build and $100 billion to operate.[61] While Andrew Davies[62] has noted that in 2016-dollars the cost is closer to $30 billion and $70 billion, spread over several decades, these are still very large figures.

The RAN renewal-programme, and especially its submarine component, has also become a major 'political football' because Australian manufacturing is steadily declining and South Australia has been hit especially hard with the collapse of auto-manufacturing. Naval ship-building has thus been seen as a way to 'save South Australia' (or, perhaps more accurately, to save Coalition seats there). But building in Australia rather than overseas is expected to be 30–40% more expensive.[63] Nevertheless, to both shore up Australian manufacturing (and its electoral prospects), and leave the long-standing but inefficient boom-bust cycle of naval building behind, the Turnbull Coalition government announced a 30-year 'continuous naval build' programme in April 2016.[64]

Regarding other maritime capabilities, the RAN's patrol capabilities are complemented by the Australian Border Force (ABF), which operates 8 *Cape*-class patrol boats and two larger cutters. They all carry armed personnel but the vessels are typically less-heavily armed than RAN vessels; for example, *Cape*-class vessels are essentially *Armidale*-class boats minus the 25mm Typhoon cannon. Finally, the ADF's air surveillance is contracted out to Surveillance Australia; this company currently operates 14 aircraft and it cooperates closely with the RAAF's maritime surveillance assets. The ABF's primary role at present is to intercept asylum seekers – we discuss 'Operation Sovereign Borders' below – but it is also tasked with guarding Australia's EEZ against illegal fishing, smuggling, piracy, etc.

Other more-specialised agencies also exist. For example, the Australian Fisheries Management Authority monitors small vessels and manages fisheries. The Australian Maritime Safety Authority (AMSA) performs search and rescue activities, regulates shipping, and provides navigation services; to illustrate, it implements a Department of the Environment programme whereby all ships – mainly commercial, but also foreign-military – must utilise AMSA pilots to navigate environmentally sensitive waters like the Great Barrier Reef. And the Australian Antarctic Division operates one large supply vessel, the *Aurora Australis* (to be replaced soon; just in time, given it ran aground and was damaged on 24 February 2016). Finally, the various state police services also patrol harbours and rivers. At the risk of oversimplification, readers should assume that the RAN and ABF patrol well offshore while the other agencies typically operate closer to shore and, if the latter encounter serious trouble and require support, they call in the ABF and/or the RAN.

Finally, since the 'Offshore Constitutional Settlement' of 1979, civilian responsibility for Australia's marine territory has been shared between the Commonwealth Government and the states. The aim was to govern fisheries under new arrangements that transcended the Commonwealth-state divide, although the sectoral approach to managing marine resources militated against developing an effective national approach.[65] In 1998 the release of 'Australia's Ocean Policy: Caring, Understanding, Using Wisely' was supposed to establish a system of integrated (across sectors and jurisdictions) and ecosystems-based oceans management, although while it was considered 'world leading' then it has not produced the intended shift to a truly *national* policy (i.e. oceans management remains sectoral).[66] Having said that, one initiative which did succeed was the development of marine bioregional plans and an expanded Commonwealth marine reserve system.[67] The Integrated Marine Observing System has also substantially increased the available physical, biogeochemical, and biological maritime data, which is being used to further develop Australia's 'blue economy' under the National Marine Science Plan 2015–25. It is estimated that by 2025 Australia's marine industries will contribute as much as $100 billion to the Australian economy.[68]

But fishing and tourism, etc. are not the only maritime resources which Australia must manage. The extensive offshore oil- and especially gas-extraction industries have grown rapidly: by producing 67 billion cubic metres of natural gas in 2015 Australia became the 13th biggest producer.[69] Various agencies have regulated this industry – responsibility was transferred in 2016 to the newly-formed Department of Environment and Energy – but others also operate in this space; for example, the RAN provided security to offshore rigs, while the Attorney-General's department handled the dispute with East Timor over the demarcation of the maritime border that in 2018 culminated in an agreement delimiting the first maritime border between the two countries.

Australia's contemporary maritime objectives

We now provide just a few examples of how Australia's maritime capabilities are utilised. As we noted earlier, the ADF is configured to defeat hostile invasion forces attempting to cross the northern Air-Sea Gap, but because Australia has not faced a threat comparable to this since 1942 – when the armed forces *weren't* configured to defeat that sort of threat – the ADF's operational activities are currently dominated by patrolling and exercising.

Operation Sovereign Borders (OSB) is a 'military-led, border security operation' which since September 2013 has functioned to combat people-smuggling to Australia. OSB is overseen by the Department of Immigration and Border Protection, although RAN personnel actually staff Maritime Border Command. The ADF therefore works closely with the Department's primary implementation agency, the ABF; the RAAF's Orion surveillance planes and the RAN's patrol boats (and minesweepers) are utilised regularly, and this extra strain informed the decision to accelerate the patrol boat replacement programme we discussed earlier.[70] Specifically, the Department of Immigration and Border Protection website now bluntly states that '[a]nyone who attempts to travel illegally by boat to Australia will be turned back. Settlement in Australia will never be an option for anyone who travels illegally by boat'.[71] In practice this means that RAN or ABF vessels intercept and then tow back boats which carry asylum seekers (i.e. into Indonesian waters). Further, those who arrived before then – about 2000 people in total in 2016, including several dozen children – are held in off-shore detention facilities on Manus Island (in Papua New Guinea) and on Nauru while their asylum claims are processed.

These tough border policies have been very controversial: there have been persistent reports of poor, even dangerous conditions in the camps,[72] and Australia has been accused of failing to discharge its responsibilities as a signatory to the Refugee Convention.[73] There have also been concerns at times about the RAN being politicised; the so-called 'children overboard affair', during an earlier maritime-border-control operation akin to OSB in 2001, is probably the single most controversial event.[74] Yet OSB has been successful in two senses. First, it has been highly effective in reducing the numbers of people attempting to reach Australia by boat: 20,587 tried between 1 January and 18 September 2013, (i.e. OSB began 11 days after the conservative Coalition won the 2013 federal election)[75]; but between then and 17 March 2016 only 698 attempted the journey (and all were turned back).[76] Second, OSB is popular: a mid-2014 poll showed 71% approval versus 28% disapproval,[77] and two years later support remained robust (61% versus 31%).[78] Thus, while this maritime operation prompts criticism both at home and abroad, its electoral appeal means there is effectively bipartisan support for it.

The RAAF's *Orions* also conduct regular overflights of the newly-created Chinese 'islands' in the South China Sea as part of Operation Gateway.[79] 'Nearly all' these patrols are now formally challenged by China by radio,[80] and while an RAN vessel has not yet sailed within 12-miles of one of the new 'features' the Americans – and the Opposition Labor party – have called for such to occur.[81] But this matter also illustrates how a maritime strategy is not directly equivalent to a naval strategy; while ADF operations are important and may become more so, Australia's primary response remains diplomatic. Canberra consults with the United States, ASEAN states, and other 'interested parties' – including, somewhat provocatively from China's perspective, Japan and India – and discusses the matter at regional summits. Canberra also 'engages' China bilaterally, although recently this has tended to take the form of criticism by Australia, angry rebukes by China, followed by polite but firm resolve on Canberra's part to not back down. The diplomatic spat which erupted after China declared an Air Defence Interdiction Zone over the East China Sea in 2013 is illustrative.[82] Thus, while OSB is currently the most high-profile and resource-intensive 'maritime matter', China's rise looms over Australia's maritime strategy more generally, and especially the ADF-asset-procurement decisions made recently. For example, the 2016 defence white paper noted that the decision to double the submarine fleet was prompted by the expectation that 'by 2035 around half of the world's submarines will be operating in the Indo-Pacific';[83] it left unsaid that the bulk of this increase is due to China's breakneck submarine-building programme.[84]

The RAN in particular has also begun to conduct exercises with a wider range of partners. The exemplar in this regard is India. While it is well known that India is a cautious international actor which values its 'strategic autonomy',[85] New Delhi has become somewhat more assertive vis-à-vis China recently.[86] Thus, in November 2014 the Australian and Indian governments signed a Framework for Security Cooperation which, among other things, committed them to hold 'regular bilateral maritime exercises' and, in September 2015, the first ('Ausindex') was held in the Bay of Bengal. We should not get too carried away with this development: Australia had expressed interest in joining the annual India-US *Malabar* exercise too, but New Delhi was only willing to allow Japan to become a regular participant. Nevertheless, when India's former foreign secretary Kanwal Sibal was asked whether Australia might permanently join *Malabar* he said 'I won't be surprised if at some stage we also have quadrilateral exercises'.[87]

We must stress, however, that Australia is not 'adamantly opposing' China. Instead, Canberra is walking a tightrope between maintaining close security relations with Washington without jeopardising its lucrative trade relationship with Beijing. In the maritime domain, Canberra has striven hard to signal 'good faith' by devoting considerable resources to searching for the missing Flight MH370, and its efforts have reportedly been greatly appreciated by China.[88] Nevertheless, when Wesley[89] commented on the 2016 defence white paper he observed that 'for the past twenty years, Australia has tried to . . . "socialise" China into complying with, rather than contesting regional unipolarity. This has clearly failed'. Bloomfield[90] has also argued that since 2007 Australia's hedging policy towards China has very slowly but steadily shifted towards a 'balancing' strategy (but one which falls well short of an outright 'containment' policy). Outright war between China and the United States and the latter's allies – including Australia – in the maritime regions close to Australia still remains a remote possibility. But if current trends continue, troubling scenarios of this sort are likely to steadily become somewhat less remote.

Notes

1. Australian Government, 2016, p. 45.
2. Ibid., p. 89.
3. Scott and Bloomfield, 2014.
4. Harper, 1987.
5. Ungerer, 2007; Sussex, 2011; Cotton and Ravenhill, 2011; Carr, 2014.
6. Leaver and Cox, 1997; Pert, 2014.
7. Evans and Grant, 1991, p. 33.

8 1996.
9 Conley Tyler, 2014.
10 Downie, 2016, p. 6.
11 Australian Government, 2016, p. 45
12 Australian Government, 2012, p. 72.
13 Australian Government, 2013, p. 26.
14 Australian Government, 2016, p. 68.
15 2016, p. 24.
16 Ibid., p. 25.
17 Australian Government, 2016, p. 9.
18 2010, p. 1.
19 Australian Government, 2016, p. 15.
20 Ibid., p. 44.
21 Australian Government, 2012, Chapter 1.
22 *Asia Survey*, 2014.
23 Kelly, 2013; AAP, 2013.
24 White, 2016.
25 Kelly, 2015.
26 2014, p. 403.
27 Australian Government, 2009, p. 22.
28 Australian government, 2013, p. 11.
29 Australian Government, 2016, pp. 177–184.
30 Ibid., p. 42.
31 Ibid., p. 58.
32 Griggs 2012, p. 14.
33 Australian Government, 2016, p. 70.
34 Wesley, 2016, p. 19.
35 Which signalled a reduction in US commitment to Asia (or at least to large continental deployments).
36 Clark, 1996, p. 230.
37 Australian Government, 1987, p. vii.
38 Ibid., pp. 1–9.
39 Blaxland, 2012.
40 Australian Government, 2016, p. 68.
41 Australian Government, 2000, p. 29.
42 Davies, 2016, p. 4.
43 2016, p. 103.
44 Davies, 2016, p. 6.
45 Pryke, Hayward-Jones and O'Keefe, n.d.
46 All figures in Australian dollars; at the time of writing one Australian dollar was worth 76 US cents.
47 Department of Defence, 2016b.
48 Uren, 2016; Department of Foreign Affairs and Trade, 2016a; Department of Foreign Affairs and Trade, 2016b.
49 Department of Foreign Affairs and Trade, n.d.
50 Wilkins, 2010, p. 381.
51 Australian Government, 2012, p. 3.
52 Scott, 2013, p. 426.
53 Thomson, 2015, p. vi.
54 SIPRI, 2015.
55 Thomson, 2015, p. 69.
56 The remainder is for 'civil-military traffic management' which does not directly contribute to 'war-fighting'; ibid., pp. 113–114.
57 Australian Government, 2016, pp. 94–95.

58 Blaxland, 2012, pp. 38–40.
59 Ibid., pp. 92–93.
60 Ibid., pp. 90–92.
61 Wroe, 2016c.
62 2016, pp. 11–12
63 Birkler, 2015, p. xxxvi.
64 Department of Defence, 2016a.
65 Vince et al., 2015, p. 2.
66 Ibid., p. 1.
67 Treloar et al., 2016.
68 Ibid., p. 45.
69 *Statista*, 2016.
70 Davies, 2016, pp. 8–9.
71 Department of Immigration and Border Protection, n.d.
72 Farrell, Evershed and Davidson, 2016.
73 Millar, 2015.
74 Slattery, 2003.
75 Phillips, 2014.
76 Anderson, 2016.
77 Oliver, 2014, p. 10.
78 Oliver, 2016, p. 14.
79 Ongoing since 1980: members of the Five Power Defence Pact – Australia, New Zealand, United Kingdom, Malaysia, and Singapore – jointly patrol South East Asian waters.
80 Wroe, 2016a.
81 Wroe, 2016b.
82 Murdoch, 2013.
83 Australian Government, 2016, p. 90.
84 Yoshihara, 2015, p. 65
85 Mehta, 2009.
86 Malik, 2012.
87 Parameswaran, 2015.
88 Winterbottom, 2014.
89 2016, p. 29.
90 2015.

References

AAP, 2013. No Need to Choose China or the US: Howard. *The Australian*, 6 June.
Anderson, S., 2016. *Fewer than 30 Refugees Resettled Since November as Part of 12,000 Agreed in Syria, Iraq Deal* [online]. ABC News, 17 March. Available at: www.abc.net.au/news/2016-03-17/29-refugees-resettled-under-government-12000-intake/7254784. [Accessed 28 September 2016]
Asia Survey, Special Edition: Australia's Strategic Dilemma. 54(2) (2014).
Australian Government (Department of Defence), 1987. *Defence of Australia*. Canberra.
———, 2000. *Defence 2000: Our Future Defence Force*. Canberra.
———, 2009. *Defending Australia in the Asia Pacific Century: Force 2030*. Canberra.
———, 2013. *Defence White Paper 2013*. Canberra.
———, 2016. *2016 Defence White Paper*. Canberra.
Australian Government (Department of Foreign Affairs and Trade), 2012. *Australia in the Asian Century*. Canberra.

Bateman, S., 2015. Some Thoughts on Australia and the Freedoms of Navigation. *Security Challenges*, 11(2), pp. 57–66.
Birkler, et al., 2015. *Australia's Naval Shipbuilding Enterprise*. Santa Monica: RAND Corporation.
Bisley, N. 2013. 'An Ally for All the Years to Come': Why Australia is not a Conflicted US Ally. *Australian Journal of International Affairs*, 67(4), pp. 403–418.
Blaxland, J., 2012. Game-Changer in the Pacific: Surprising Options Open Up With the New Multi-Purpose Maritime Capability. *Security Challenges*, 9(3), pp. 31–41.
Bloomfield, A., 2015. To Balance or to Bandwagon? Adjusting to China's Rise During Australia's Rudd-Gillard Era. *Pacific Review*, 29(2), pp. 259–278.
Carr, A. 2014. Is Australia a Middle Power? A Systemic Impact Approach. *Australian Journal of International Affairs*, 68(1), pp. 70–84.
Clark, M., 1996. *History of Australia*. Castle Hill: Penguin Books.
Conley-Tyler, M., 2014. Can Australia Remain a Top 20 Nation? [online]. *The Interpreter*, 23 October. Available at: www.lowyinterpreter.org/post/2014/10/23/Can-Australia-remain-a-top-20-nation.aspx?COLLCC=223762167&COLLCC=1221740 834&. [Accessed 25 September 2016]
Cordner, L., 2016. The Future of Maritime Forces in an Integrated Australian Defence Force. *Security Challenges*, 12(1), pp. 19–30.
Cotton, J., and J. Ravenhill., 2011. *Middle Power Dreaming: Australia in World Affairs 2006–2010*. Oxford: Oxford University Press.
Davies, A., 2016. Defence White Paper 2016: The Strategist Decides. *Australian Strategic Policy Institute – Strategic Insights*, 105, pp. 1–24.
Department of Defence, 2016a. *Prime Minister and Minister for Defence-Continuous Naval Shipbuilding* [online], 18 April. Available at: www.minister.defence.gov.au/2016/04/18/prime-minister-and-minister-for-defence-continuous-naval-shipbuilding/. [Accessed 2 October 2016]
———, 2016b. *Minister for Defence – Contract Signed for Replacement Pacific Patrol Boats* [online], 5 May. Available at: www.minister.defence.gov.au/2016/05/05/contract-signed-for-replacement-pacific-patrol-boats/. [Accessed 17 September 2016]
Department of Foreign Affairs and Trade, 2016a. *Overview of Australia's Pacific Regional Aid Program* [online]. Available at: http://dfat.gov.au/geo/pacific/development-assistance/pages/development-assistance-in-the-pacific.aspx. [Accessed 17 September 2016]
———, 2016b. *Pacific Regional Economic Growth: Fisheries Assistance* [online]. Available at: http://dfat.gov.au/geo/pacific/development-assistance/Pages/fisheries-assistance-pacific-regional.aspx. [Accessed 21 September 2016]
Department of Immigration and Border Protection, n.d. *Operation Sovereign Borders* [online]. Available at: www.border.gov.au/about/operation-sovereign-borders/counter-people-smuggling-communication/english/outside-australia/fact-sheet. [Accessed 20 September 2016]
Department of Foreign Affairs and Trade, n.d. *Indian Ocean Rim Association (IORA)* [online]. Available at: http://dfat.gov.au/international-relations/regional-architecture/indian-ocean/iora/pages/indian-ocean-rim-association-iora.aspx. [Accessed 14 Septembe 2016]
Downer, A, 1996. *Regional Cooperation and Security*. Speech, Australian College of Defence and Strategic Studies, Canberra, 6 December.
Downie, C., 2016. One in All In: The G20, Middle Powers, and Global Governance Reform. *Third World Quarterly*. Published online 20 September 2016, DOI: 10.1080/01436597.2016.1229564.

Evans, G., and B. Grant, 1991. *Australia's Foreign Relations: In the World of the 1990s.* Carlton: Melbourne University Press.

Farrell, P., Evershed, N., and H. Davidson, 2016. The Nauru Files: Cache of 2,000 Leaked Reports Reveal Scale of Abuse of Children in Australian Offshore Detention. *The Guardian*, 10 August.

Griggs, R. 2012. A Maritime School of Strategic Thought for Australia. In: J. Jones, ed. *A Maritime School of Strategic Thought for Australia. Perspectives.* Sea Power Centre: Canberra.

Harper, N. 1987. *A Great and Powerful Friend: A Study of Australian and American Relations Between 1900 and 1975.* St Lucia: University of Queensland Press.

Kelly, P., 2013. Julia Gillard Deserves Credit for Belated Success in Beijing, But It's Only a Start. *The Australian*, 13 April.

———, 2015. Abbott Switch on China Bank Defies US. *The Australian*, 16 March.

Leaver, R., and D. Cox., 1997. *Middling, Meddling, Muddling: Issues in Australian Foreign Policy.* St Leonards, NSW: Allen & Unwin.

Malik, M., 2012. India Balances China. *Asian Politics and Policy*, 4(3), pp. 345–376.

Mehta, P., 2009. Still Under Nehru's Shadow? The Absence of Foreign Policy Frameworks in India. *India Review*, 8(3), pp. 209–233.

Millar, L., 2015. Australia's Asylum Seeker Policies Heavily Criticised at UN Human Rights Council Review [online]. ABC News, 10 November. Available at: www.abc.net.au/news/2015-11-10/australias-asylum-policies-heavily-criticised-at-united-nations/6926032. [Accessed 22 September 2016]

Murdoch, S., 2013. Angry China Rebukes Julie Bishop Over East China Sea Dispute. *The Australian*, 7 December.

Oliver, A., 2014. The Lowy Institute Poll 2014. *Lowy Institute*, 2 June.

Oliver, A., 2016. The Lowy Institute Poll 2016. *Lowy Institute*, 21 June.

Parameswaran, P., 2015. Australia, India to Hold First Ever Naval Exercise Amid China Concerns. *The Diplomat*, 1 September.

Pert, A., 2014. *Australia as a Good International Citizen.* Annandale, NSW: Federation Press.

Phillips, J., 2014. Boat Arrivals in Australia: A Quick Guide to the Statistics. *Parliament of Australia* [online], 23 January. Available at: www.aph.gov.au/About_Parliament/Parliamentary_Departments/Parliamentary_Library/pubs/rp/rp1314/QG/BoatArrivals. [Accessed 22 September 2016]

Pryke, J., J. Hayward-Jones, and A. O'Keefe, n.d. The State of Australian Aid [online]. *The Lowy Institute.* Available at: www.lowyinstitute.org/issues/australian-foreign-aid. [Accessed 19 September 2016]

Scott, D., 2013. Australia's Embrace of the 'Indo-Pacific': New Term, New Region, New Strategy? *International Relations of the Asia-Pacific*, 13(3), pp. 433–436.

Scott, S. V., and A. Bloomfield, 2014. From the 'Tyranny of Distance' to the 'Prospects of Proximity': Australian Responses to the Rise of India and China. In: A. Mattoo and M. Joseph, eds., *Rise of China and India. Implications for the Asia Pacific.* New Delhi: Manohar Publishers, pp. 113–138.

Sheridan, G., 2016. China's Emperor at the Crossroads. *The Weekend Australian*, 16–17 July.

SIPRI (Stockholm International Peace Research Institute), 2015. *SIPRI Military Expenditure Database* [online]. Available at www.sipri.org/databases/milex. [Accessed 11 September 2016]

Slattery, K., 2003. Drowning Not Waving: The 'Children Overboard' Event and Australia's Fear of the Other. *Media International Australia*, 109(1), pp. 93–108.
Statista, 2016. *World Natural Gas Production in 2015, by Country* [online]. Available at: www.statista.com/statistics/264101/world-natural-gas-production-by-country/. [Accessed 19 September 2016]
Sussex, M. 2011. The Impotence of Being Earnest? Avoiding the Pitfalls of 'Creative Middle Power Diplomacy'. *Australian Journal of International Affairs*, 65(5), pp. 545–562.
Thomson, Mark, 2015. The Cost of Defence: ASPI Defence Budget Brief 2015–2016. Canberra, Australian Strategic Policy Institute, May.
Treloar, Gillian et al., 2016. 'The National Marine Science Plan: Informing Australia's Future Ocean Policy', *Australian Journal of Maritime & Ocean Affairs* 8(1), 43–51.
Ungerer, C. 2007. The 'Middle Power' Concept in Australian Foreign Policy. *Australian Journal of Politics and History*, 53(4), pp. 538–551.
Uren, D., 2016. PM's Pacific Climate Aid Boost. *The Weekend Australian*. 10–11 September.
Vince, J., et al. 2015. Australia's Oceans Policy: Past, Present and Future. *Marine Policy*, 57, pp. 1–8.
Wesley, M., 2016. Australia's Grand Strategy and the 2016 Defence White Paper. *Security Challenges*, 12(1), pp. 19–30.
White, H., 2010. Power Shift: Australia's Future Between Washington and Beijing. *Quarterly Essay*, 39, pp. 1–73.
———, 2016. The United States or China: 'We Don't Have to Choose'. In: Mark Beeson and Shahar Hameiri, eds., *Navigating the New International Disorder. Australia in World Affairs 2011–2015*.
Wilkins, Thomas, 2010. 'The New "Pacific Century" and the Rise of China: An International Relations Perspective', *Australian Journal of International Affairs*, 64(4) pp. 381–405.
Winterbottom, V., 2014. Australia-China Relations: Abbott Benefits From Australia's MH370 Search Role. *The Interpreter*, 11 April.
Wroe, D., 2016a. RAAF Now Being Routinely Challenged by Beijing in South China Sea. *Sydney Morning Herald*, 6 February.
———, 2016b. US Navy Commander Urges Australia to Carry Out Patrols in Disputed Islands in the South China Sea. *Sydney Morning Herald*, 22 February.
———, 2016c. Defence White Paper: New Submarine Fleet to Cost Taxpayers $150 billion. *Sydney Morning Herald*, 25 February.
Yoshihara, T., 2015. Sino-Japanese Rivalry at Sea: How Tokyo Can Go Anti-Access on China. *Orbis*, 59(1), pp. 62–75.

9 A New Zealand view

Anchored in *Oceania* – reaching out to Asia[1]

Carol Abraham

To successfully sail a course in strong or shifting winds requires the ability to both tack and jibe with purpose. This chapter outlines New Zealand's approach to maritime challenges and opportunities through an analysis of implicit grand strategy, including the influence of national identity and strategic culture, policy continuity and change since 2000, and operational choices.

Australia and New Zealand are independent sovereign nations, separated geographically by the Tasman Sea, but they are close neighbours; long-standing friends, economic partners and security allies. The nature of the relationship between Australia and New Zealand, as with that between the United States and Canada, is sometimes likened to a 'big brother – little brother' relationship of both mutual support and friendly rivalry. The two countries share commonalities of history and lineage, but their situations are distinct, and their development has been different. They have common interests, but also different responsibilities. They share common values, but their policies can differ, sometimes markedly.

Cognisant of mutually beneficial trans-Tasman relations, this paper seeks to identify some of the unique features of New Zealand's perspectives on maritime challenges, opportunities and policies in the Indian Ocean and Western Pacific. The aim in doing so is to contribute to greater understanding of nuances in New Zealand's policy and actions.

Why not an 'Australasian' view?

It is tempting for commentators and analysts based far from the South Pacific and focussed on great power geo-strategic issues to consider Australia and New Zealand as a collective entity. The two are close geographically, with an open trans-Tasman economic partnership enabled by the free flow of people, capital and goods. Both contemporary societies developed from British colonial settlements and they are in many respects like-minded politically and socially. Familial analogies as brothers or cousins are common. The Australia-New Zealand 'Anzac' bond, forged in two world wars and sustained through commitments to regional conflicts of the twentieth century, is expressed in contemporary peace support and humanitarian response operations in the South Pacific and globally, underpinned by a mutual security alliance commitment originating in the Canberra Pact of

1944.[2] Nevertheless, they have different near neighbours and people to people linkages. New Zealand's national identity and regional outlook are distinct, as are its strategic culture, policies and maritime capability choices.[3]

Twenty years ago, in the wake of the Cold War, both countries described their region as the Asia-Pacific. Analysts and leaders focussed on the opportunities and implications of rapid growth in North and South East (SE) Asian economies increasing regional trade flows, amid tensions over maritime chokepoints and conflicting maritime claims.[4] Now, China is the largest trade partner amid an expanding network of free trade agreements. Conflicting South China Sea claims are an increasing source of tension.[5] Australia's viewpoint is now that of a middle economic power with military capability superiority based on technological edge, in a much broader Indo-Pacific region. New Zealand's perspective is that of a 'smaller' state in global power terms, seeing itself first as a South Pacific nation, closely connected to Australia – its most important ally and partner – but with increasingly strong connections and inter-dependencies in Asia-Pacific.

In the absence of an overarching Foreign Policy White Paper or published National Security Strategies, comparing the two 2016 defence white papers may usefully illustrate how a New Zealand view is distinct from Australia's. At first glance much of the strategic outlook is similar. For example, three core policy drivers are sovereign control of borders and large maritime Exclusive Economic Zones; desire for stability in the region; and commitment to maintaining the global rules-based order that underpins both access to trade routes and peaceful dispute resolution. Differences include the weight of emphasis in describing the region, the scale and scope of defence force structure, and structure of international security relationships.

Australia looks first to the control of its direct maritime approaches to the North and West, including island territories and sea lines of communication; secondly to a near region that includes South Pacific Islands – particularly Melanesia – and Papua New Guinea, East Timor and Indonesia; then to a broad Indo-Pacific area of interest. Sea-freight lines of communication (SLOCs) to top trading partners underpin the Australian characterisation of Indo-Pacific as an interconnected region, dependent on freedom of navigation.[6] Geo-strategically, the Indo-Pacific concept reflects Australia's desire to deepen its relationship with India and develop Indian Ocean regional security architectures.[7] While Australia is New Zealand's closest security partner, Australia's alliance with the United States and the impact of changing great power relationships in the Indo-Pacific appear central to Australia's maritime strategy and policy. Australia's defence policy includes higher spending commitments and future force structure geared towards "capability edge and ... more complex and high tech conflicts of the future."[8] New Zealand shares the view that SLOCs create critical interdependencies across the wider region, but is more focussed on the security architectures of the South Pacific and SE Asia.

For New Zealand, the highest maritime priority is its extensive Exclusive Economic Zone (EEZ), the fourth largest in the world, closely followed in priority by the South Pacific – particularly Polynesia – and the Southern Ocean and Antarctica (Ross Dependency).[9] Responsibilities include offshore islands and constitutional obligations for foreign affairs and defence of Pacific Island states Niue, Cook Islands and Tokelau.[10] These considerations drive maritime policies and defence force structure. Security and stability of sea, air and electronic lines of communication through SE Asia are next important. New Zealand's top five trading partners are China, Australia, United States, Japan and the Republic of Korea, while the Association of South East Asian Nations (ASEAN) economies are collectively equivalent to New Zealand's fourth largest trading partner.[11] Maritime security in the broader region influences defence policy via the alliance commitment to Australia and partner expectations for credible capabilities to support the international maritime rules-based order.

Maritime resources and the Indian Ocean and Western Pacific trade routes are critical to prosperity and security for both New Zealand and Australia. Nevertheless, the regional perspective and strategic security narratives in New Zealand are subtly different.

National identity and regional perspective

Colin Gray observes "all strategic behavior is cultural behavior" and strategic culture is "a pattern of reliance upon one or several of the range of instruments of grand strategy."[12] Reflecting a strong egalitarian self-image, New Zealanders see liberal values such as justice, freedom, the rule of law, equal opportunity and human rights as key factors in creating long-term stability and security within states and the international system. Authoritarian government or unilateral control of strategic international waterways can produce stability, but not security as New Zealanders view it. There is an emerging sense of identity as what one scholar has described as a "post-modern state."[13] At the same time as traditional security relationships are maintained or renewed, the strategic culture in New Zealand has arguably moved beyond a focus on balance-of-power to a construct based on openness, pluralism, institutions, agreed norms and multilateralism.[14] A strong commitment to international institutions and the rule of law dovetails with a preference for retaining sovereign autonomy within international partnerships.

New Zealand has a long and proud identity as a maritime nation and a globally connected trading nation. The tendency to look outwards originated in marine resources for both Maori and the first European whalers, expanding to land-based food production and a British market for colonial products, with increased reliance on imported oil and manufactured goods since the mid-twentieth century. Economic and trade deregulation has gradually led to a more diverse, globally interconnected economy.[15] The core of the economy remains production of high quality protein (dairy, meat and fish) for export, complemented by added-value products – wine, fine wool textiles, services and tourism.[16] Advances in global information technology have increased opportunities for research, design and creative exports. The *Defence White Paper 2016* recognises that "economic prosperity depends upon open sea, air and electronic lines of communication."[17] Economic prosperity is thus central to New Zealanders' concept of security, supported by sovereignty and maritime resource security.

New Zealanders recognise they live in a country with modest power resources, where the population of 4.4 million is small relative to land, EEZ, neighbouring continents and other developed economies.[18] However, a large EEZ with no border disputes – pending UN delimitation of the extended continental shelf with Tonga and France – is a positive consequence of isolation and a space of great opportunity, as well as responsibility.[19] Smaller South Pacific countries also have large EEZs and face significant maritime management challenges. Despite, or likely because of, its geopolitical power position New Zealand is also globally connected and (inter)dependent on larger powers. Interdependence underpins commitment to an open market economy, an international trade system governed by the World Trade Organisation and high quality bilateral and multilateral Free Trade Agreements.[20] New Zealand's focus on economic security accords with scholarly observations of small states: border security and external defence serve economic security, and there is less focus on geophysical security.[21]

The maritime dimension of national identity is also strongly linked to being 'in and of' the relatively sparsely populated South Pacific.[22] Familial connections with Pacific Islands, and increasingly with Asia, are reinforced by contemporary migration patterns that see high annual flows. The ethnic identity mix in the population is 74.6% European, 15.6% Maori, 12.2% Asian and 7.8% South Pacific peoples, with a trend towards increasing diversity.[23] New Zealand has responsibility for the world's third largest Search and Rescue Region, extending from the equator to the South Pole. The vulnerability of people living in low-lying islands, combined with close people-people connections, creates a cultural expectation that New Zealand will provide practical assistance in preparing for and responding to major crises and natural disasters; a view recognised as having a moral foundation.[24] Pacific Island peoples are even more intimately connected to the Ocean and each other, reflected in both historical and contemporary migratory patterns of *Oceania*.[25] An influential 1993 essay identifies a local cultural perspective of *Oceania* as a "sea of islands", as distinct to a continental view of isolated "islands in a far sea".[26] New Zealanders strive to be conscious of respecting Pacific Island cultures and local perspectives. Being a good global citizen starts with being a good friend in the South Pacific.

Geo-strategically, identity and culture are influenced by a complex mix of historical ties, regional focus, alliances, arrangements and partnerships – all managed through the lens of a "steadfast commitment to making independent policy decisions."[27] The idea of independent foreign policy has long historical threads in New Zealand, originating in the process of settlements gaining autonomy and a voice within the British Empire, and is now ubiquitous across the political spectrum.[28] The relationship with Australia is today underpinned by Closer Economic Relations and Closer Defence Relations agreements.[29] The United States suspended ANZUS treaty obligations to New Zealand in response to nuclear free legislation in the mid 1980s.[30] That relationship was strained but not broken by these events, with activities such as Antarctic science and logistics continuing, and increased counter-terrorism cooperation. Policy reflected in the Wellington Declaration of 2010 and Washington Declaration of 2012 is strengthening the relationship.[31]

Likewise, New Zealand and France have moved past twentieth-century disputes over nuclear testing in the South Pacific. Other traditional security partners (the United Kingdom and Canada) also still influence strategic policy, defence capability, military doctrine and intelligence networks.

In the near region, South Pacific multilateral cooperation is encouraged through the Pacific Islands Forum, of which New Zealand is a full member. The long-standing Five Power Defence Arrangements (FPDA) between New Zealand, Malaysia, Singapore, Australia and the United Kingdom provide an evolving platform for engagement on maritime security issues. Equally, New Zealand supports new initiatives such as the ASEAN Defence Ministers Meetings + (ADMM+) and describes China as an important strategic partner.[32] Globally, New Zealand was a founding member of the United Nations and elected to a non-permanent seat on the United Nations Security Council (UNSC) for 2015/2016.[33] New Zealanders expect their government to support multilateral institutions, liberal rules-based systems and negotiated dispute resolution consistently.

New Zealanders do not see their country, nor others in the region, as merely net consumers of great-power geopolitics where "the strong do what they can, and the weak suffer what they must."[34] Alongside a proud wartime legacy, there is a cultural preference for soft power options. Small does not necessarily mean weak and small states may, in fact, have significant issue-specific power – either hard, such as economic leverage, or New Zealand's preferred mode influence on regional norms.[35] It is in every country's interests to mitigate effects on the region of international storms, tempests and tectonic power shifts.

New Zealand's grand strategy – a Maritime strategy?

Grand Strategy articulates what a nation seeks to accomplish, together with why and how it intends to act: "a purposeful and coherent set of ideas about what a nation seeks to accomplish in the world, and how it should go about doing so." It provides "form and structure" across government policy, weaving the threads of hard and soft power into a coherent fabric.[36] Grand strategy thus matters to both small and powerful countries, albeit small states may focus on a narrower range of issues or geopolitical area of interest.[37]

A scan of all-of-government policy and practice since 2000 suggests that New Zealand acts with purpose regionally, with relatively stable policy continuity across centre-left and centre-right governments. Policies reflect the interdependence of economic security and soft-power foreign policy goals, for example promoting liberal norms and rules that underpin high quality multilateral trade agreements; participating in multinational maritime security operations; or undertaking coalition military operations only with recognised international legitimacy. The latter principle is why New Zealand decided not to take part in the 2003 US-led war in Iraq.

Although New Zealand does not have declaratory grand strategic goals, practice suggests twin outcomes of a high standard of living in a secure, globally interdependent economy and an international role as a trusted partner and interlocutor.

The following sections outline first the basis of these two national goals, then illustrate implementation through four lines of effort – resilience, relationships, capacity building and regional security contributions. While the core of New Zealand's implicit Grand Strategy is not a maritime strategy *per se*, the centrality of maritime considerations to New Zealand and its region has a significant influence on policy.

The destination: strategic ends

There are clear threads of continuity in New Zealand policy since 2000, even as observers note the centre-left preference for liberal internationalist and human rights programmes giving way to more politically centre-right interests, aligned with a global trend towards defensive realist arguments.[38] In 2000, the economy was still recovering from the 1997 Asian financial crisis. No direct state-based threat was perceived then or now. Security concerns included inter-state tension fuelling an arms race in East Asia, increasing intra-state conflict and weak governments, competition for marine resources and global illegal trade.[39] While extremist terrorism now holds the spotlight, earlier challenges have not dissipated. In 2000 the Labour-led coalition government reaffirmed commitment to the nuclear-free legislation and a future nuclear-free South Pacific.[40] It is a politically popular policy and has been maintained by National-led centre right governments.

The desired future state since 2000 has included diverse trading partners and a growing, resilient economy, connected to a stable, democratic, developing South Pacific and Asia where New Zealand's support was welcome. Those aspirations were not changed by shocks to follow. The 9/11 terrorist attacks and subsequent US-led wars in the Middle East, 2004 Aceh tsunami in Indonesia, 2005 Bali Bombing, internal security crises in South Pacific states, 2008 global financial crisis, and the 2011 major earthquakes in Christchurch and Japan all affected New Zealand. These events reinforced the need for national resilience and benefits of regional cooperation. One consequence of 9/11 and the Bali bombing is a more assertive protection and risk management approach to security, driving increased resources for intelligence agencies and amendments to the legal framework for counter-terrorism and surveillance. A regionally credible defence partnership with Australia and influential relationships with major power centres of the Asia-Pacific and international institutions also remain relevant.

New Zealand's defence policy is evolving away from describing security interests in a geographic frame of reference, though the geography still matters.[41] Previously, five concentric zones ranged from "a secure New Zealand" to a global approach that "strengthens New Zealand's international economic linkages."[42] The *Defence White Paper 2016* shows broad policy continuity across more general local, regional and global frames of reference. Bilateral relations remain valued as a foundation for multilateral organisations and for cooperative dispute resolution. The 2011 policy document *New Zealand's National Security System* articulated seven national security objectives, which were restated in 2016.[43] They are: preserving sovereignty and territorial integrity; protecting lines of communication;

strengthening international order to promote security; sustaining economic prosperity; maintaining democratic institutions and national values; ensuring public safety; and protecting the natural environment.

An all-of-government approach drives many of the policy, resourcing and operational choices flowing from security objectives. New Zealand government agencies with responsibilities in the maritime domain, including Customs and the Ministry of Primary Industries, recognise the centrality of trade to as a foundation for a secure, globally interdependent economy.[44] MFAT's "NZ Inc Strategies" grow trade and investment by driving horizontal integration across government agency efforts, to create connections with a global economy.[45]

The second national goal of an international role as a trusted partner and interlocutor is visible in the ways New Zealand contributes to regional security and trade agreements. Autonomy within international partnerships is culturally significant, but New Zealanders do not see this as inconsistent with commitments to international institutions. A Minister of Defence statement after signing the Washington Declaration observes that "This high-level arrangement recognizes the significant security cooperation that exists . . . within the context of our independent foreign policy."[46] Prime Minister John Key also emphasised that "New Zealand is known for its integrity, reliability and independence." Election of New Zealand to the UNSC is an opportunity to "reaffirm our reputation as a fair-minded and constructive contributor in international affairs."[47] Highlighting small island states' views of opportunities and risks and efforts to improve UNSC functioning are examples of a constructive approach.

New Zealand's actions indicate that it is at pains to maintain a high level of trust. A global soft power report in 2012 ranked New Zealand 21st overall and 7th of 40 countries in the Government sub-index.[48] Debate on military operations always includes a legitmate mandate for action, international humanitarian law, and maintaining the respect and confidence of all parties.[49] In the South Pacific, the Regional Assistance Mission to the Solomon Islands is an example of successful regional and multi-agency security cooperation. New Zealand's political and policy discourse on geo-political competition and maritime disputes consistently emphasise peaceful resolution, multilateral confidence building, international law as the basis for a stable order and acceptable actions, and respect for claimant states both large and small.[50] New Zealand offers potential to contribute more as a future interlocutor in the resolution of maritime disputes.

Policy choices: ways and means

New Zealand pursues its national goals – a high standard of living in a secure, globally interdependent economy, and an international role as a trusted partner and interlocutor – through four lines of effort. These are: building resilience in society and the economy; developing bilateral and multilateral international relationships; capacity building in Asia-Pacific; and contributions to security, stabilisation and peacekeeping operations.

Closest to home, building Resilience in the economy relies on balancing sustainable economic development and environmental protection. Resolving tension between limited resources to both protect and maximise value from the EEZ requires domestic and international inter-agency cooperation. Resource management policies, including aquaculture, wild fisheries, offshore oil exploration and marine reserves aim to preserve biodiversity and provide sustainable economic development. To the North, New Zealand is expanding the Kermadec Marine Reserve to create an EEZ ocean sanctuary where mining and fishing are prohibited.[51] At the same time other areas are being opened – somewhat controversially – to oil and gas exploration, an opportunity that could expand export receipts from 3bn to 30bn over a decade.[52]

The need for regulatory monitoring, domain awareness, control of the border, safety at sea and prevention of criminal exploitation underpins integrated maritime surveillance. Security sector agencies in New Zealand cooperate to fill the role that larger countries meet with dedicated coast guard and search and rescue forces.[53] Using military assets to support civilian agencies security responsibilities is now recognised as an output rather than just efficient use of spare contingent military capacity.[54] To ensure transparency a National Maritime Coordination Centre (NMCC) coordinates capability and task priorities, supported by the intelligence community.[55] Thus, the NZDF, particularly the Naval fleet and the Air Force airborne surveillance force, support agencies to deliver EEZ maritime constabulary tasks.

In the near region, South Pacific countries control extensive EEZ fisheries resources, including valuable migratory species such as tuna at risk from unsustainable exploitation in adjacent high seas. South Pacific countries, including New Zealand, both need and are in tension with the major fishing fleets from distant water fishing nations. Fleet licencing and regulation is critical for safety, sustainability and economic benefit. Maritime surveillance support to the region is both bilateral and through the multilateral Pacific Islands Forum Fisheries Agency (FFA). FFA coordinates operational monitoring and fisheries development advice. It also provides a South Pacific regional approach to the Western and Central Pacific Fisheries Commission (WCPFC) tuna management system, which came into force in 2004 after a decade of negotiation.[56] Parties to the Nauru Agreement (PNA) is a forum with a similar management role in the Micronesian and Melanesian sub-regions. WCPFC is potentially a model for cooperative multilateral management of other shared maritime zone resources of the Indian Ocean and Western Pacific.

More broadly, the New Zealand capacity-building focus is on strengthening international and bilateral standards for regulating cross border flows, sensitive to the risks of terrorism, transnational crime and biosecurity.[57] For example, New Zealand is a participant in post-9/11 US-led initiatives including the Container Security Initiative (CSI) and Proliferation Security Initiative (PSI). As inter-agency expertise grows, New Zealand's ability to provide capacity-building assistance to the region is also enhanced.

Capacity building in Asia-Pacific goes hand in glove with developing international relationships. Foreign Minister McCully recently described the close relationship with the South Pacific as "the greatest comparative advantage that New Zealand offers in the international space."[58] MFAT funds NZAID programmes that aim to build prosperity, stability and resilience. Recognising challenges of imported energy dependence and climate change impacts, recent programmes have focussed on renewable energy and water systems.[59] New Zealand security sector agencies also have complementary programmes for development. A recent success is Customs work assisting Pacific Island states' to develop compliance systems for import/export certification, which aids economic development and constrains transnational crime.[60] NZDF also supports Pacific Islands with EEZ surveillance and surface patrol and provides seconded personnel to work with local agencies, complementary to Australia's Pacific Maritime Security Program provision of patrol boats. MFAT (NZAID) and NZDF conduct annual exercises to build disaster response capability and capacity in the Pacific and are often disaster first responders. These efforts are both a moral obligation to neighbours and a confidence-building mechanism.

An equally important challenge is supporting Pacific Island countries' to voice their needs and increase capacity to absorb international aid in a way that achieves good outcomes. One way is to work with outside donors on projects, such as a Cook Islands – China – New Zealand project to replace the water supply system on Rarotonga.[61] Another is to work multilaterally. Globally, this has included facilitating dialogue on small island states issues at the United Nations. Locally, a New Zealand university initiated a new conference in February 2015 titled 'China and the Pacific: The View from Oceania', held in Samoa.[62] Participants saw Chinese investment as an opportunity to be managed, with the potential for geopolitical rivalry less concerning than ensuring projects were structured to benefit whole communities, negotiating as equals, reducing the risk of debt burden from soft loans and conserving the tuna fishery.

New Zealand prioritises engagement with the Pacific Islands Forum (PIF), which includes both New Zealand and Australia as full members. An expanded PIF trade agenda now includes economic development and political governance and security.[63] While PIF is the largest and oldest regional forum, there are challenges to the stable and cooperative regional framework. Smaller overlapping organisations include the Melanesian Spearhead Group and a nascent Pacific Islands Development Forum (PIDF), the latter initiated by Fiji after PIF suspended Fiji in the wake of a 2006 coup.[64]

The regional response to the Fiji coups is a useful case study. Targeted sanctions, including cessation of military cooperation and diplomatic isolation of regime elites, were complemented by open civil society connections and dialogue with international institutions encouraging a return to democracy. New Zealand development assistance, search and rescue and disaster response continued, maintaining a commitment to human security. In September 2014 Fiji finally held democratic elections. New Zealand has since lifted sanctions and progressively resumed formal diplomatic and military ties.[65] Some tensions remain around influence and Fiji has to date chosen not to attend formal PIF meetings.[66]

MFATs *NZ Inc* strategies indicate a maturing approach from an earlier focus on overseas aid and trade development to a cross-government intent to "strengthen economic, political and security relationships." Areas selected reflect opportunity in the Indian Ocean and Western Pacific, including India, China, Australia,

ASEAN and the Gulf Cooperation Council.[67] A notable exception is the absence of a South Pacific *NZ Inc* Strategy. This likely reflects a view that economic trade growth potential for New Zealand is modest, but it may also reflect caution on local perceptions. There is potential for a South Pacific *NZ Inc* to enhance guidance to New Zealand multi-agency programmes, focusing on *regional* benefits and cognizant of Pacific Island viewpoints.

New Zealand pursues cooperative relationships with a broad range of partners, calibrating the scope of activity carefully. Overlapping Asia-Pacific regional free trade negotiations are welcomed, including both the Trans-Pacific Partnership (TPP) and Regional Comprehensive Economic Partnership (RCEP).[68] Recognising shared maritime interests, the Washington Declaration of 2012 between New Zealand and the United States focusses on enhancing cooperation in maritime security, including counter-proliferation, counter-terrorism and anti-piracy, as well as humanitarian assistance and disaster relief, peace-keeping and peace-support initiatives.[69] In SE Asia, commitment to the long-standing Five Power Defence Arrangements (FPDA) – between Australia, United Kingdom, Malaysia and Singapore – sits alongside support for regional initiatives to reduce South China Sea tensions, including a maritime code of conduct.[70]

ASEAN is at the core of a layered regional multilateral framework that New Zealand engages with, including as a member of the ASEAN Regional Forum. New Zealand Foreign Minister Murray McCully described regional organisations such as APEC and the East Asia Summit as 'vital' for regional stability and political, security and economic co-operation.[71] The scope of dialogue is slowly broadening from economic to security, for example through the ASEAN Defence Ministers Meeting (ADMM+).[72] In 2016 New Zealand and Brunei co-chaired an Expert Working Group on Maritime Security.[73] Working groups focus on practical cooperation within the constraints of consensus norms, providing an opportunity to work towards agreement on difficult issues such as codes of conduct in areas of tension, as well as counter-piracy and maritime terrorism challenges.

Globally, the maritime global rules-based order that New Zealand relies on includes United Safety of Life at Sea (SOLAS) governed by the International Maritime Organisation (IMO), and maritime law based on the United Nations Convention on the Law of the Sea (UNCLOS). Equally important are conventions underpinning cooperative work of organisations such as the World Trade Organisation and the Antarctic Treaty system, including the Commission for the Conservation of Antarctic Marine Living Resources (CCAMLR). The 2016 CCAMLR decision to create a Marine Protected Area in the Ross Sea Region, jointly proposed by New Zealand and the United States, is an achievement that required years of negotiation amid tension between fishing and environmental priorities.[74]

New Zealand policy articulates the global rules-based order as a driver of capability and operational deployment choices. Alliance commitments to Australia, the ability to operate independently in the South Pacific, interoperability with traditional partners and security cooperation arrangements in SE Asia will continue to underpin upgrades to combat capability and a focus on niche high technology solutions. There is long-standing tension between maintaining self-reliance for South Pacific defence deployments and carrying risk in combat capability due to the absence of major state-based threat. In 2001 the force-determinant focus narrowed to regional and peace support operations, disbanding the Air Combat Force (maritime strike), and refocussing maritime air and surface fleets on civilian requirements.[75] In 2010 policy rebalanced to include concurrent capacity for global peace and security contributions. The two ANZAC Frigates and Air Force airborne surveillance and response force (P3-K2 Orion) aircraft have been upgraded with modern systems, and NZDF strategy includes strengthening combat capability.[76] In 2014 Cabinet addressed a 2010 ends-means-ways mismatch with additional funds, indicating a resolve to sustain breadth of capability.[77]

Given no foreseen external state-based threat to New Zealand, one might expect even lower levels of resources for military, intelligence and border security capability than 1% of GDP.[78] It has become an article of faith in New Zealand discourse that defence policy is resource constrained. While the latter is a truism for most states, an interesting counterfactual question is what policy would apply in New Zealand if resources were more bountiful? Arguably, not a lot would change. The quality and depth of maritime military capabilities would likely increase, and dedicated civilian agency EEZ-constabulary capability would be a possibility. The underlying strategic culture and public security risk narrative suggest a high political hurdle to increasing breadth of capability, for example by regenerating a specialist air combat force, or acquisition of submarines or high-threat environment amphibious capabilities. Defence and security concerns are rarely a significant election issue.[79] Mitigating this is a commitment to ensuring that being a trusted partner includes the capability to contribute to regional security efforts and to prevent exploitation as an entry route for an attack on others.

Maritime capability upgrades will include frigate replacement from the mid-2020s and the Naval Patrol Force increasing its offshore capacity, including ice strengthening.[80] New maritime projection and sustainment vessels will bolster capacity for concurrent operations and Antarctic support. The Airborne Surveillance and Response Force will have an underwater-ISR upgrade in 2017 and full replacement in the early 2020's. The vast EEZ, Search and Rescue Region, offshore areas of responsibility to North and South, and physical challenges of access in the South West Pacific will determine air and maritime reach and endurance requirements.

Continuing to develop and exercise plug-and-play military interoperability creates resilience, keeps capabilities internationally relevant and builds partnerships that generate trust. In the last 15 years, New Zealand has contributed to several security assistance operations in the South Pacific, and policy recognises that a similar response in the next decade is likely.[81] Maritime surveillance support has increased, as has disaster response frequency. Although the Western Indian Ocean falls towards the 'global' and more discretionary end of New Zealand's priorities, contributions to maritime security coalition operations in the Indian Ocean region include Navy warships and Air Force maritime surveillance aircraft as part of Combined Task Force 151.[82] New Zealand also hosts and participates in Humanitarian Assistance and Disaster Relief exercises and military staff exchanges with a range of newer partners, including China and Vietnam.

The range of deployments highlighted is likely to continue, as they are useful in countering a range of transnational threats, valued by partners, and directly linked to New Zealand's reliance on sea, air and electronic lines of communication. The range of commitments stretches resources but is coherent in light of the interdependence of New Zealand's implicit grand strategic goals. Independent foreign policy does not preclude multilateral solidarity and (modest) burden sharing. Although New Zealand defence spending is modest, the importance of the maritime domain and regional relationships explains a forecast recovery to 1% of GDP. Maintaining interoperability with traditional security partners, capacity-building programmes to increase Pacific Island economic resilience and developing major bilateral relationships to drive open trade and multilateral cooperation are all underpinned by a commitment to the global rules-based order. New Zealand Prime Minister John Key put the case unusually plainly in a 2014 BBC interview discussion on responding to violent extremist group ISIL: "Even if the contribution is small – of course it will be proportional – there has to be some contribution . . . it is the price of the club."[83]

The policy mix in New Zealand is explained by the centrality of the economy to national security, combined with desired roles as trusted partner *and* interlocutor. When it comes to persuading more powerful states, New Zealand walks a fine line. The approach is arguably less about hedging modest national power resources against regional or global heavyweights than it is a deliberate strategy of leveraging soft power.

Looking out from Canberra, Australian policy makers see a large continental island surrounded by a complex and interconnected Indo-Pacific. From Wellington, the view is more one of islands dotted across a vast ocean in a mosaic of large maritime EEZs. New Zealand policy perspectives are thus anchored in *Oceania*, reaching out to Asia-Pacific with economic resilience and a liberal institutionalist global order in mind.

Notes

1. The views expressed are those of the author and are not the official policy or position of the New Zealand Government or the New Zealand Defence Force. This chapter draws in part on the authors unpublished Masters' research on the concept of New Zealand's national security strategy, undertaken while studying at USAF Air War College, AY15 (used with permission). The author also acknowledges the wise counsel of colleagues Rory Paddock and Rob Ayson.
2. New Zealand History, 2016. www.nzhistory.net.nz/nz-and-australia-sign-the-canberra-pact Te Ara www.teara.govt.nz/en/australia-and-new-zealand/page-3 For respective views of the alliance structure see Department of Foreign Affairs and Trade, 2016 http://dfat.gov.au/geo/new-zealand/pages/new-zealand-country-brief.aspx and Ministry of Foreign Affairs and Trade, 2016a. www.mfat.govt.nz/en/countries-and-regions/australia/.
3. For a comparison of New Zealand and Australia strategic cultures, see McCraw, D. 2011. Further analysis of the origins of Defence policy differences is available at Ayson, R. 2016.
4. Babbage, R. and Bateman, S. 1993, pp. xix–xx.
5. Jones, N, 2016, www.newstalkzb.co.nz/news/politics/brownlee-says-china-caused-south-china-sea-tension/.

6 Department of Defence, 2016, p. 70.
7 Department of Defence, 2016, p. 135.
8 Department of Defence, 2016, p. 10.
9 Te Ara, www.teara.govt.nz/en/interactive/6967/new-zealands-exclusive-economic-zone.
10 Governor General of New Zealand, 2015. http://gg.govt.nz/role/constofnz.htm.
11 Ministry of Defence, 2014, p. 42.
12 Gray, 1999, pp. 24, 29, 47, 129, 150.
13 Cooper, 2000, pp. 26, 28–29, 43. For contemporary examples of post-modern views in New Zealand, see Steff, 2016, and O'Brien, 2016.
14 The evolving discussion from traditional thinking about defence and security in New Zealand is illustrated by: Greener, 2010; and Hoadley, 2007.
15 New Zealand Treasury, 2015. www.treasury.govt.nz/economy/overview.
16 Statistics New Zealand, 2015. www.stats.govt.nz/browse_for_stats/snapshots-of-nz/nz-in-profile-2015.aspx.
17 Ministry of Defence, 2016a, p. 23.
18 Hey, 2003, p. 10; and World Bank, 2015 [online]; and Statistics New Zealand, 2005, pp. 4, 22–24, 28. A small state is described as modest population (e.g. < 1.5 million; < 10 million), or any state where the people self-identify or are perceived by others as being 'small'.
19 Land Information New Zealand, 2016. www.linz.govt.nz/about-linz/what-were-doing/projects/new-zealand-continental-shelf-project/map-continental-shelf.
20 Ministry of Foreign Affairs and Trade, 2015c. www.mfat.govt.nz/en/trade/nz-trade-policy/.
21 Hey, 2003, p. 17. See also Ayson, R. 2011, p. 13.
22 O'Brien, 2016, p. 9. See also McCully, 2016, p. 9.
23 Statistics New Zealand, 2015. www.stats.govt.nz/browse_for_stats/snapshots-of-nz/nz-in-profile-2015.aspx.
24 Ministry of Defence, 2016b.
25 Hau'ofa, 1994, pp. 154–155.
26 Hau'ofa, 1994, pp. 152–153.
27 Ministry of Defence, 2016a, p. 5.
28 McKinnon, M., 1993, pp. 7–13.
29 Ayson, R. 2016 suggests that bilateral Defence cooperation was not consistently sustained until the 1980s. Ministry of Foreign Affairs and Trade, 2016b, [online] CER came into force on 01 January 1983. www.mfat.govt.nz/en/trade/free-trade-agreements/ Under CDR "committed to ensuring that our defence forces can work together effectively in combined operations, to protect the vital security interests of both countries, our offshore territories and resources." www.defence.gov.au/minister/1tpl.cfm?CurrentId=211.
30 For a full account of the non-nuclear dispute, see Hensley G., 2013, *Friendly Fire*.
31 U.S. Department of State, 2010, [online] Wellington Declaration. www.state.gov/r/pa/prs/ps/2010/11/150401.htm [accessed 10 Dec 2016] See also: New Zealand Government, 2012, Washington Declaration [pdf] www.beehive.govt.nz/sites/all/files/WashingtonDeclaration.pdf.
32 New Zealand Government, 2016, pp. 33–34.
33 Ministry of Foreign Affairs and Trade, 2015b. http://beehive.govt.nz/release/new-zealand-takes-un-security-council-seat.
34 Strassler, R.B. Ed., 1993, p. 352; Hey, J.A.K. Ed., 2003, p. 17.
35 Neumann, I.B. and Gstohl, S., 2006, p. 8; and Nye, J.S., 2011, p. xiii and p. 21. Nye defines soft power through focussing on the way the instrument is used, not its nature. Hard power is about coercion and payment, while soft power focusses on persuasion and attraction. For a contemporary discussion of New Zealand soft power, see also O'Brien, T., 2016, "Should war define New Zealand's self-view?"
36 Brands, H., 2014, p. 3.
37 Nye, J.S., 2011, p. 9.

38 Steff, R., 2013, pp. 14–17.
39 New Zealand Government, 2000, p. 2
40 New Zealand Government, 2000, p. 4.
41 Ministry of Defence, 2015. Section two of the analysis considers strategic trends through a geographic lens.
42 New Zealand Government, 2000, p. 3.
43 New Zealand DPMC, 2011, pp. 3–4.
44 New Zealand Customs, 2009, p. 9; New Zealand Ministry of Primary Industries, 2015.
45 Ministry of Foreign Affairs and Trade, 2016c. NZ Inc alludes to the idea of New Zealand Incorporated, invoking coherent all-New Zealand effort as similar to a large corporate.
46 New Zealand Government, 2012.
47 Ministry of Foreign Affairs and Trade, 2009. New Zealand was an original member of the United Nations and last served on the UNSC in the early 1990s.
48 McClory, J., 2012. The soft power index assesses public institutions, political values and policy outcomes through "measures that include individual freedom, human development, violence in society and government effectiveness."
49 New Zealand Parliament, 2009.
50 McCully, M., 2016, p. 8. See also McCully quoted in McCutChan, A. 2016, p. 19.
51 Ministry for Environment, 2015, [online] Available at: www.mfe.govt.nz/marine/kermadec-ocean-sanctuary/about-sanctuary (accessed 06 Dec 2016).
52 Brownlie, G., press release: Unlocking New Zealand's Petroleum Potential 18 Nov 2009. www.beehive.govt.nz/release/unlocking-new-zealand039s-petroleum-potential Regarding ongoing controversy over this programme see for example: www.stuff.co.nz/business/industries/84445709/Large-area-off-Canterbury-coast-proposed-for-oil-exploration For a discussion of EEZ maritime resource potential, see Mossop, J., 2012, pp. 288–289.
53 New Zealand Government, 2010, p. 19.
54 New Zealand Government, 2014, pp. 24, 26–28.
55 New Zealand Customs Service, 2010.
56 Forum Fisheries Agency, 2016, [online] www.ffa.int/ www.ffa.int/wcpfc www.wcpfc.int/about-wcpfc.
57 New Zealand Customs, 2014, p. 24.
58 McCully, M., 2016.
59 McCully, M., 2016.
60 New Zealand Customs, 2009, p. 27.
61 Ministry of Foreign Affairs and Trade, 2016d, [online] www.mfat.govt.nz/en/countries-and-regions/north-asia/china/.
62 Powles, A. 2015, pp. 25–28. For a discussion of aid donors and South Pacific regional security, see also Rolfe, J. 2015.
63 Pacific Islands Forum: 2016. [online] www.forumsec.org/pages.cfm/about-us/
64 Webb, D. 2015. See Webb for a discussion of the evolving South Pacific regional order.
65 NZDF, 2015a. [online] www.nzdf.mil.nz/news/media-releases/2015/20150131-affffp.htm. See also Ministry of Foreign Affairs and Trade, 2015a for NZ AID program in Fiji.
66 Davison, I. 2015, [online] www.nzherald.co.nz/nz/news/article.cfm?c_id=1&objectid=11428607
67 Ministry of Foreign Affairs and Trade, 2016, [online] www.mfat.govt.nz/en/trade/nz-inc-strategies/
68 Ministry of Foreign Affairs and Trade, 2015c. For a full list of New Zealand free trade agreement status, see also www.mfat.govt.nz/Trade-and-Economic-Relations/2-Trade-Relationships-and-Agreements/index.php#negotiation.
69 New Zealand Government, 2012.
70 ASEAN, 2002. See also ASEAN, 2016. New Zealand is a dialogue partner of ASEAN.
71 McCully, M., 2016, p. 7.
72 For background on ADMM+ see [online] https://admm.asean.org/index.php/about-admm/about-admm-plus.html.

73 Ministry of Foreign Affairs and Trade, 2016, [online] www.mfat.govt.nz/en/countries-and-regions/south-east-asia/association-of-south-east-asian-nations-asean/.
74 CCAMLR, 2016 [online] www.ccamlr.org/en/news/2016/ccamlr-create-worlds-largest-marine-protected-area.
75 New Zealand Government, 2000, pp. 3–5.
76 NZDF, 2012.
77 New Zealand Government, 2013.
78 Ayson, R., 2011, p. 15.
79 Ayson, R., 2011, p. 12.
80 Ministry of Defence and New Zealand Defence Force, 2016, pp. 20 and 28–31.
81 New Zealand Government, *Defence White Paper 2016*, p. 39. For an overview of past NZDF operational deployments see: New Zealand Defence Force, 2015b.
82 NZDF, 2016 [online] www.nzdf.mil.nz/operations/combined-maritime-force/default.htm Multiple frigate deployments to the Arabian Gulf have also been undertaken since 2000. www.nzdf.mil.nz/operations/overseas-deployments/arabian-gulf/default.htm
83 Young, A., 2015.

References

ASEAN (Association of South East Asian Nations). 2002. "Declaration on the Conduct of Parties in the South China Sea" Available at: www.asean.org/asean/external-relations/china/item/declaration-on-the-conduct-of-parties-in-the-south-china-sea [accessed 29 November 2016]

―――. 2016. Joint Statement. 7 September 2016. Available at: www.asean.org/joint-statement-on-the-application-of-the-code-for-unplanned-encounters-at-sea-in-the-south-china-sea/ [accessed 29 November 2016]

Australian Government. 2012. *Government White Paper: Australia in the Asian Century*. Available at: www.asiaeducation.edu.au/verve/_resources/australia-in-the-asian-century-white-paper.pdf [accessed 3 February 2015].

Ayson, R., 2011. Force and Statecraft: Strategic Objectives and Relationships in New Zealand's 2010 Defence White Paper. *Security Challenges*, 7(1), Autumn, pp. 11–29. Available at: www.securitychallenges.org.au/ArticlePDFs/vol7no1Ayson.pdf

―――. 2016. [online] Future Proofing Australia-New Zealand Defence Relations, *Analyses* Sydney: Lowy Institute for International Policy. Available at: www.lowyinstitute.org/publications/future-proofing-australia-new-zealand-defence-relations [accessed 19 December 2016]

Babbage, R., and Bateman, S. eds., 1993. *Maritime Change: Issues for Asia*. St Leonards: Allen & Unwin.

Brands, H., 2014. *What Good is Grand Strategy: Power and Purpose in American Statecraft from Harry S. Truman to George W. Bush*. Ithaca: Cornell University Press.

Brownlie, G. 2009. Unlocking New Zealand's Petroleum Potential 18 November 2009. *Press release*. Available at: www.beehive.govt.nz/release/unlocking-new-zealand039s-petroleum-potential [accessed 6 December 2016]

CCAMLR, 2016. [online] CCAMLR to create world's largest Marine Protected Area. Media Release, 28 October. Available at: www.ccamlr.org/en/news/2016/ccamlr-create-worlds-largest-marine-protected-area

Cooper, R., 2000. *The Post-Modern State and the World Order*. London: Demos.

Davison, I. 2015. [online] Fiji wants NZ ousted from Pacific forum, or China let in *New Zealand Herald*, 7 April. Available at: www.nzherald.co.nz/nz/news/article.cfm?c_id=1&objectid=11428607

Department of Defence. 2016. *2016 Defence White Paper*. Department of Defence: Commonwealth of Australia.

Department of Foreign Affairs and Trade. 2016. [online]. *New Zealand Country Brief.* Canberra: Commonwealth of Australia. Available at http://dfat.gov.au/geo/new-zealand/pages/new-zealand-country-brief.aspx [accessed 29 November 2016]

Department of Prime Minister and Cabinet (DPMC). 2011. [online] *NZ's National Security System.* Available at: www.dpmc.govt.nz/sites/all/files/publications/national-security-system.pdf [accessed 29 November 2016]

Governor General of New Zealand. *New Zealand's Constitution.* Available at: http://gg.govt.nz/role/constofnz.htm [accessed 2 February 2015]

Gray, C. S. 1999. *Modern Strategy.* New York: Oxford University Press.

Greener, B. 2010. Security, Defence, Politics and the new White Paper. *New Zealand International Review*, 35(1), pp. 12–15.

Hau'ofa, E., 1994. Our Sea of Islands. *The Contemporary Pacific*, 6(1), pp. 147–161. First published in Naidu, N., Waddell, E., and Hua'ofa, E., *A New Oceania: Rediscovering Our Sea of Islands.* Sufa: School of Social and Economic Development, University of the South Pacific, 1993.

Hensley, G., 2013. *Friendly Fire: Nuclear Politics & the Collapse of ANZUS, 1984–1987.* Auckland: Auckland University Press.

Hey, J. A. K. ed. 2003. *Small States in World Politics: Explaining Foreign Policy Behavior.* Boulder, CO: Lynne Rienner Publishers Inc.

Hoadley, S. 2007. From Defence to Security: New Zealand's Hard Power, Soft Power, and Smart Power. *New Zealand International Review*, 32(5), pp. 18–21.

Jones, N. 2016. [online]. Brownlie addresses South China Sea tensions. *Newstalk ZB.* 25 August 2016. Available at: www.newstalkzb.co.nz/news/politics/brownlee-says-china-caused-south-china-sea-tension/

Key, J. 2014. [online]. *Prime Minister of New Zealand. Protecting National Security and Responding to ISIL.* Press Release 5 November 2014. Available at: http://beehive.govt.nz/release/protecting-national-security-and-responding-isil

Land Information New Zealand, 2016. [online] *New Zealand Continental Shelf Project.* Available at: www.linz.govt.nz/about-linz/what-were-doing/projects/new-zealand-continental-shelf-project/map-continental-shelf [accessed 29 November 2016]

McClory, J. 2012. The New Persuaders III: A 2012 Global Ranking of Soft Power *Institute for Government* [pdf] Available at: www.instituteforgovernment.org.uk/sites/default/files/publications/The%20new%20persuaders%20III_0.pdf [accessed 30 December 2016]

McCraw, D. 2011. Change and Continuity in Strategic Culture: The Cases of Australia and New Zealand. *Australian Journal of International Affairs*, 65(2), pp. 167–184.

McCully, M., 2016. Seeking Opportunities and Facing Challenges in *New Zealand International Review*, 41(3), May/June.

McCutchan, A., 2016. *Restraint in the face of China. Islands Business*, June, p. 19.

McKinnon, M., 1993. *Independence and Foreign Policy: New Zealand in the World Since 1935.* Auckland University Press. [ebook] 2013, available at Google Books.

Ministry for Culture and Heritage. 2014. [online] New Zealand and the United Nations. *New Zealand History.* Available at: www.nzhistory.net.nz/politics/new-zealand-and-the-united-nations [accessed 14 February 2015]

Ministry of Defence. 2010. *Defence White Paper 2010.* Wellington: New Zealand Government. Available at: www.nzdf.mil.nz/corporate-documents/defence-white-paper/default.htm

———. 2014. *2014–2017 Statement of Intent – New Zealand Defence Force.* Available at: www.nzdf.mil.nz/downloads/pdf/public-docs/2014/nzdf_soi_2014.pdf [accessed 14 February 2015]

———. 2015. [online] *Defence Assessment 2014.* Wellington: New Zealand Government. [pdf] Available at: www.defence.govt.nz/assets/Uploads/defence-assessment-2014-public.pdf [accessed 29 November 2016]

———. 2016a. *Defence White Paper 2016*. Wellington: New Zealand Government. Available at: www.defence.govt.nz/publications/publication/defence-white-paper-2016
———. 2016b. [online] *Defence White Paper 2016: Public Consultation Summary of Submissions*. [pdf] Available at; www.nzdf.mil.nz/downloads/pdf/public-docs/2016/dwp-summary-of-submissions-2016.pdf [accessed 29 November 2016]
Ministry of Foreign Affairs and Trade, 2009. *Briefing to the Incoming Minister*, 06 October. Available at: www.mfat.govt.nz/downloads/media-and-publications/BIM%202014%20Public.pdf [accessed 14 February 2015]
———. 2015a. [online] *New Zealand Aid Programme*. www.aid.govt.nz/where-we-work/pacific/fiji [accessed 14 February 2015]
———. 2015b. [online] Press Release: New Zealand takes UN Security Council seat. Available at: http://beehive.govt.nz/release/new-zealand-takes-un-security-council-seat [accessed 14 February 2015]
———. 2015c. [online] *Trans Pacific Partnership Negotiations*. www.mfat.govt.nz/Trade-and-Economic-Relations/2-Trade-Relationships-and-Agreements/Trans-Pacific/1-TPP-Talk/1-TPP-talk.php [accessed 14 February 2015]
———. 2016a. [online] *Countries and Regions: Australia*. Wellington: New Zealand Government. Available at: www.mfat.govt.nz/en/countries-and-regions/australia/ [accessed 29 November 2016]
———. 2016b. [online] Free Trade Agreements. Available at: www.mfat.govt.nz/en/trade/free-trade-agreements/ [accessed 29 November 2016]
———. 2016c. [online] What are NZ Inc strategies? Available at: www.mfat.govt.nz/en/trade/nz-inc-strategies/ [accessed 21 November 2016]
———. 2016d. [online] *Countries and Regions: North-Asia, China*. Available at: HYPERLINK "http://www.mfat.govt.nz/en/countries-and-regions/north-asia/china/" www.mfat.govt.nz/en/countries-and-regions/north-asia/china/ [accessed 29 November 2016]
———. 2016e. [online] *Countries and Regions: South East Asia, ASEAN*. Available at: www.mfat.govt.nz/en/countries-and-regions/south-east-asia/association-of-south-east-asian-nations-asean/ [accessed 29 November 2016]
Ministry of Defence and New Zealand Defence Force. 2016. [online] *Defence Capability Plan 2016*. www.defence.govt.nz/assets/Uploads/2016-Defence-Capability-Plan.pdf
Ministry of Primary Industries, 2015. [online] Our Strategy 2030 Available at: www.mpi.govt.nz/about-mpi/our-strategy-2030/ [accessed 11 February 2015]
Mossop, J., 2012. New Zealand's Maritime Challenges and Opportunities. In: Ho, J. H., and S. Bateman eds., *Maritime Challenges and Priorities in Asia*. Oxon: Routledge.
Neumann, I. B., and Gstohl, S., 2006. "Lilliputians in Gulliver's World?" In: C. Ingebritsen. et al. eds., *Small States in International Relations*. Seattle: University of Washington Press.
New Zealand Customs Service. 2009. [online] *Strategic Outlook to 2015*. Available at: www.customs.govt.nz/news/resources/corporate/Documents/Strategic%20outlook%20to%202015.pdf
———. 2010. [online] *New Border Protection System Unveiled*. Available at: www.customs.govt.nz/news/stories/Pages/newborderprotectionsystemunveiled19112010.aspx [accessed 13 February 2015].
———. 2014. [online] *Statement of Intent 2014–2017*, p. 24. Available at: www.customs.govt.nz/news/resources/corporate/documents/soi20142017.pdf
New Zealand Government. 2000. [online] *The Government's Defence Policy Framework*, June. Available at: www.defence.govt.nz/reports-publications/defence-policy-framework/defpol-frmwrk.html
———. 2012. [online] *Washington Declaration on Defence Cooperation* [pdf] Available at: www.beehive.govt.nz/sites/all/files/WashingtonDeclaration.pdf [accessed 29 November 2016]

———. 2013. [online] Cabinet Minute of Decision: Defence Mid-Point Rebalancing Review, *CAB Min*, (13) 38/5. Available at: www.defence.govt.nz/pdfs/reports-publications/dmrr-cab-min-13-38-5.pdf

———. 2014. [online] *Vote Defence Force 2014–15*. Available at: www.nzdf.mil.nz/corporate-documents/budget/default.htm [accessed 14 February 2015]

New Zealand History. 2016. [online] *NZ and Australia Sign the Canberra Pact*. Available at: www.nzhistory.net.nz/nz-and-australia-sign-the-canberra-pact [accessed 29 November 2016]

New Zealand Parliament, 2009. Urgent Debates – SAS – Deployment to Afghanistan, *Hansard* Vol 6656 p5587. Available at: www.parliament.nz/en-nz/pb/debates/debates/49HansD_20090818_00000720/urgent-debates-%E2%80%94-sas%E2%80%94deployment-to-afghanistan [accessed 11 February 2015]

New Zealand Treasury. 2015. "Economic Overview." Available at www.treasury.govt.nz/economy/overview [accessed 17 February 2015]

Nye, J. S., 2011. *The Future of Power*. New York: Public Affairs.

NZDF (New Zealand Defence Force). 2012. *Future35 – Our Strategy to 2035*. www.nzdf.mil.nz/corporate-documents/future-35.htm [accessed 16 February 2015]

———. 2015a. [online] *Air Force Flies First Fijian Patrol*. Available at: www.nzdf.mil.nz/news/media-releases/2015/20150131-affffp.htm [accessed 16 February 2015]

———. 2015b. [online] *Overseas Deployments*. Available at: www.nzdf.mil.nz/operations/overseas-deployments/default.htm [accessed 14 February 2015]

O'Brien, T. 2016. Should War Define New Zealand's Self View? *New Zealand International Review*, 41(1), January/February.

Powles, M. 2015. Conference Report, China and the Pacific: The View From Oceania. *New Zealand International Review*, 40(3), pp. 25–28.

Rolfe, J., 2015. T*he South Pacific: Regional Security and the Role of External Actors*, Strategic Background Paper – 24/2015, Centre for Strategic Studies New Zealand.

Statistics New Zealand. 2005. [online] *New Zealand in the OECD*. [pdf] Available at: www.stats.govt.nz/browse_for_stats/government_finance/central_government/nz-in-the-oecd.aspx

———. 2015. [online] *New Zealand in Profile 2015*. Wellington: Government of New Zealand. Available at: www.stats.govt.nz/browse_for_stats/snapshots-of-nz/nz-in-profile-2015.aspx [accessed 29 November 2016]

Steff, R. 2016. Strategic Liberalism and Kiwi Maximalism. *New Zealand International Review*, 41(2), March/April, pp. 14–15.

Strassler, R. B. ed., 1993. *The Landmark Thucydides*. New York: Free Press.

Te Ara. 2016. [online] *Story: Australia and New Zealand*. Available at: www.teara.govt.nz/en/australia-and-new-zealand/page-3 [accessed 29 November 2016]

U.S. Department of State. 2010. [online] *Wellington Declaration on a new strategic partnership between New Zealand and the United States of America*. Available at: www.state.gov/r/pa/prs/ps/2010/11/150401.htm [accessed 10 December 2016]

Webb, D., 2015. China's South Pacific Expansion and the Changing Regional Order: A Cause for Concern to the Regional Status Quo? *Indo-Pacific Strategic Digest Spring*. Canberra: Australian Defence College.

World Bank. 2015. *Small States* [online] Available at: www.worldbank.org/en/country/smallstates/overview#1 [accessed 14 January 2015]

Young, A. 2015. "Prime Minister John Key: ISIS Fight 'Price of the Club'", *New Zealand Herald*, 20 January www.nzherald.co.nz/politics/news/article.cfm?c_id=280&objectid=11389202&ref=rss [accessed 11 February 2015]

10 India's maritime strategy

Aspirations and reality

Amit Gupta

In recent years India has become the focus of US strategy in the Indo-Pacific region because Washington sees New Delhi as the lynchpin for ensuring regional security and helping to counterbalance China. This growth in external interest in India has been coupled with New Delhi's own attempts to establish a maritime presence in the Indian Ocean region and even further afield in the western Pacific. The desire to have a greater maritime role comes both from concerns about Chinese naval expansion and from India's increasingly globalized economy which requires a more robust maritime presence. Additionally, the demand for natural resources, as well as the rise of transnational challenges, has made the Indian government pursue a more purposeful policy towards its maritime spaces. What this chapter argues is that the future course of India's naval expansion, and the elaboration of its maritime strategy, will be shaped by several, at times contradictory, factors that may require a reorientation of emphasis in the current maritime strategy.

These factors are first, the contradiction between the global role Indian politicians see for the country and the conflicting pressures that all democracies face of balancing between the competing requirements of security and development (guns vs. butter). Secondly, the Indian Navy's own bureaucratic imperatives for the development of its force structure and doctrine partially shape maritime strategy. Thirdly, the desire among Indian politicians and the nation's defense science base to build weapons systems indigenously creates a set of constraints on naval weaponization and force projection. Fourthly, there is the pressure placed by external actors to have India pursue a more proactive role in the Indian Ocean region. Fifthly, the fact that India has challenges in the immediate littoral that consume its maritime energies, particularly dealing with the security challenge posed by Pakistan, and the use of Indian naval forces to counter it. Finally, the continued threat of terrorist attacks staged from the sea, as was the case with the 2008 Mumbai terror attacks means that the Indian Navy is faced with the challenge of maintaining security in the ports system as well as engaging in coastal defense.

As a consequence, while the country has compelling reasons to develop its naval force structure and to pursue a more proactive maritime strategy, particularly the fulfillment of the Navy's desire for a blue-water capability with Sea Control, the actual development of these forces and their employment are likely to occur both slowly and incrementally. Ashley Tellis used the term "creeping weaponization" to describe India's glacial progress in the creation of a nuclear force structure and one could similarly make the argument that what we have in terms of maritime strategy is a slow moving acquisition of a blue-water capability.[1]

Indian maritime strategy in a regional and global context

Indian politicians were always aware of the role of the Indian Ocean in threatening Indian security and Jawaharlal Nehru accepted the argument that the Indian Navy required aircraft carriers in order to project power into the Indian Ocean.[2] As one of India's early diplomats, K. M. Pannikar pointed out it was through their control of the oceans that the British were able to launch their ultimate conquest of India. In more recent times, this feeling of maritime insecurity was compounded in the 1971 war when the Indian leadership felt threatened by Richard Nixon's dispatch of the USS Enterprise into the Indian Ocean to engage in coercive diplomacy against India. In more recent times, the 2008 Mumbai terror attack highlighted the continued vulnerability of the Indian coastline and port system to attacks by non-state actors – a situation that still continues. Thus, maritime and coastal security remains of critical importance to India. Yet, despite such security challenges, there was a lack of concern about India's maritime environment and funding the Navy to meet these challenges.

None of India's neighbors had a naval capability that could threaten India nor were they seriously investing in a fleet to do so. Pakistan, India's main regional security challenger, built a small navy aimed at inflicting sufficient damage on the Indian Navy so as to deter it (this remains the goal of the Pakistan Navy which has not sought to compete with the Indian Navy by acquiring a range of systems that could be used for blue-water operations). For a long period of time the Chinese threat was a land-based one and only in the last 15 years has India raised alarms about a Chinese naval presence in the Indian Ocean with concerns about the so-called string of pearls strategy.

Further, until 1968, the British Navy remained as the security guarantor in the Indian Ocean and after its departure this role was taken over by the Navy of the United States. After the departure of the British, the Indian Navy saw itself as taking over the role of security guarantor in the Indian Ocean but the Indian government viewed such an expansion of the country's maritime role as having shades of imperialism. After the events of the 1971 India-Pakistan war, however, when the Nixon administration sent the USS Enterprise into the Indian Ocean to try to engage in coercive diplomacy against New Delhi, the Indian government decided to start investing in a naval capability. This led to the desire for a naval deterrent that would dissuade the superpowers but, at the same time, not create a force that was expeditionary in nature and sought to impose its will in the broader Indian Ocean region – a force structure that India began to pursue, albeit haltingly, from the 1980s onwards.

Another key reason for the lack of a maritime orientation was that the Indian economy was largely inward looking for the socialist structure of the country meant that it was not a significant actor in the international economic and financial systems. India's industrial, agricultural, and economic backwardness also led the country to invest more heavily in social investments rather than military ones (even today, as witnessed by the recent Rafale fighter deal, the Indian government will put economic objectives over national security objectives in making weapons procurement choices).[3] Given these facts, the cash-strapped Indian government, therefore, treated the Indian Navy as the service that required the least funding – a state of affairs that lasted into the 1980s. What changed the orientation of the Indian government was the liberalization of the Indian economy, particularly after 1991, that led to Indian trade and security interests becoming increasingly globalized.

With globalization, the growing integration of the Pacific and Indian Oceans has become vital to India given its links with the countries of Southwest, Southeast, and East Asia, and the large amounts of trade flowing between the two oceans. As a consequence, the Indians have been part of the anti-piracy efforts in the western Indian Ocean and New Delhi has sought to engage in the maritime sphere, amongst other things through naval exercises, with Japan, some of the Southeast Asian countries, and Australia. The creation of a maritime order in the Indo-Pacific region, therefore, has become an integral part of Indian diplomacy towards these countries.

Additionally, the emergence in 1998 of India and Pakistan as overt nuclear powers led to the need for India to develop a true sea-based nuclear capability. Indian nuclear strategy states that the country will have a no first-use policy unless it is hit first with nuclear, chemical, and biological weapons.[4] With this in mind having a sea-based nuclear deterrent gives India the luxury of not being pushed into the preemptive use of nuclear weapons and instead gives it, when eventually operational, a true second-use deterrent capability.

Thirdly, India's politicians since the times of Nehru, have been acutely aware that in the age of colonialism the world was carved up among a select group of nations and the overwhelming majority of people on the planet had little or no say in determining their destiny or how the resources of the planet were shared for the common good. Since independence, India has sought to ensure that it has a seat at the big table in future discussions on the fate of planetary and interplanetary resources. Thus, India joined the Outer Space treaty, the Antarctic Club, and the Law of the Seas Convention – the latter as a pioneer member – so that it could be included in the decision-making process in these institutions. It also sought to develop its nuclear, space, and maritime programs to ensure foreign policy autonomy and an ability to influence global affairs.

Thus, the Indians undertook a deep sea mining venture to become a pioneer member of the United Nations Law of the Seas treaty in 1973 and, surprisingly, recently agreed to abide with the judgement of the Law of the Seas tribunal that sided with Bangladesh in its claims to expand its Exclusive Economic Zone in relation to those of India and Myanmar.[5] This was a marked departure on the part of India in its dealings with its neighbors for with one exception in the case of Pakistan, in the 1960s, New Delhi has preferred the bilateral resolution of disputes with its neighbors.

Post 1991 developments

The year 1991 saw the Indian government of Prime Minister Narasimha Rao bow to international pressure and bring about a series of structural changes in the Indian economy. India, whose economy had been socialistic and largely inward looking, now became prone to shifts in global markets and increasingly dependent on global trade flows (before that the main systemic shocks from the global economy came from the rise of oil prices). Additionally, Rao decided to start improving India's nuclear capability and although he was prevented from carrying out a second series of tests, his successor, Atal Behari Vajpayee, was able to do so. India, once overtly nuclear, needed to develop a survivable nuclear capability and this added impetus to the ongoing nuclear submarine program.

Further, after the death of the Cold War, while the United States remained the major power in the Indian Ocean – a state of affairs that New Delhi could live with – one started to see the slow rise of China as a maritime power and Beijing began to increase its presence in the Indian Ocean region, a fact that was troubling to the government in New Delhi. India strategic analysts started to talk of the Chinese "string of pearls strategy" that saw Beijing develop a port presence in several countries that New Delhi worried would lead to Chinese naval basing in those countries and an attempt to bottle up India's maritime capability.[6] Faced by these threats, therefore, the Indian government has given greater emphasis to building up the navy to counter the growing threat of extra-regional maritime challenges.

Naval demands, interests, and capabilities

More than the other Indian services, the Indian Navy, because of its secondary role in the wars against Pakistan and China and given its bureaucratic need for a greater share of the Indian defense acquisition pie, has laid out a structured plan for its future requirements in terms of force acquisition. Thus, the Indian Maritime Doctrine (version 1.1) comprehensively spells out the missions of the Indian Navy:

Primary areas

India's primary areas of maritime interest include the following:

- India's coastal areas and maritime zones, including coastline, islands, internal sea waters, territorial waters, contiguous zone, EEZ, and continental shelf.
- The Arabian Sea, Bay of Bengal, Andaman Sea, and their littoral regions.
- The Persian Gulf and its littoral, which is the source of majority of our oil supplies and gas imports, and is home to an estimated 7 million expatriate Indians.
- The choke-points leading to, from, and across the Indian Ocean, including the Six-degree Channel, Eight/Nine-degree Channels, Straits of Hormuz, Bab-el-Mandeb, Malacca, Singapore, Sunda and Lombok, the Mozambique Channel, and Cape of Good Hope and their littoral regions.

- The Gulf of Oman, Gulf of Aden, Red Sea, and their littoral regions.
- South-West Indian Ocean, including IOR island nations therein and East Coast of Africa littoral regions.
- Other areas encompassing our SLOCs, and vital energy and resource interests.

Secondary areas

India's secondary areas of maritime interest include the following:

- South-East Indian Ocean, including sea routes to the Pacific Ocean and littoral regions in vicinity.
- South and East China Seas, Western Pacific Ocean, and their littoral regions.
- Southern Indian Ocean Region, including Antarctica.
- Mediterranean Sea, West Coast of Africa, and their littoral regions.
- Other areas of national interest based on considerations of Indian diaspora, overseas investments and political relations."[7]

In order to carry out these missions the Navy argues that,

> Sea control is the central concept around which the *IN* is structured, and aircraft carriers are decidedly the most substantial contributors to it. This is because they possess ordnance delivery capability of a very high order, often greater than the balance fleet units in the Task Force. This is by means of their substantial integral air power, which provides integral, ubiquitous and enhanced combat power, with extended reach and rapid response capability. An aircraft carrier is the central platform for protecting and projecting naval power at and from the sea. Aircraft carriers usually operate with a composite task force, including multi-purpose destroyers, frigates and logistics ships.[8]

In addition, the Navy sees itself as carrying out the following major military missions:

- Maritime Domain Awareness.
- Sea Control.
- Sea Denial.
- Blockade.
- Power Projection (including force projection).
- Force Protection.
- Compellance.
- Destruction and Attrition.[9]

Thus, the Indian Navy is attempting to develop a maritime capability that permits blue-water power projection, a denial of Indian maritime space to potential adversaries, and the ability, through blockades, to compel neighboring states as well as attrit their war-fighting capabilities. All this requires a comprehensive force of aircraft carriers, submarines, an integrated air arm of both carrier based and shore based aircraft, and a range of blue-water and coastal vessels.

Further, the Navy would be the service charged with delivering India's second strike capability both against Pakistan and China. With this is mind, India is pursuing an indigenous nuclear submarine program and has co-developed the Brahmos missile with Russia which is nuclear capable and can be launched both from the air and from surface vessels. The submarine program has faced lengthy delays and while there is a submarine that is undergoing trials, the INS *Arihant*, most observers feel that the boat will be a technology demonstrator and that India will have to work on several issues like reactor technology as well figuring out whether the boat will be a cruise missile carrier or actually launch submarine-launched ballistic missiles. To do the latter would involve testing missiles that India has not even developed and would also require a major redesign of the *Arihant* class vessel. This has been done with the second and third indigenously developed nuclear vessels the INS *Aridhaman* and INS *Arighat*. Each of which can carry either 24 K-15 missiles (with a range of over 700 kilometers) or 8 K-4 missiles (with a range of 3,500 kilometers which would give India a reliable second strike when they become operational capability against China).

Under normal circumstances, the country would be seeking to procure such capital intensive weapons systems from external suppliers as well as focusing its energies on producing certain systems domestically. Certainly in the past when India has faced existential threats (as was the case after the 1962 or, more recently, after the Mumbai terror attacks of November 2008), the government has sought to expeditiously procure much-needed weapons systems but the maritime threat environment is viewed as a long term challenge and, therefore, neither the urgency nor the funding is there to rapidly build up this capability.

Moreover, since the early years after independence the Indian leadership has sought to indigenously develop and produce weapons systems both to ensure national autonomy but also to use the country's military industry as one of the tools to industrialize and modernize the country.[10] This has created a national defense industry that operates as one of the actors in the defense acquisition process and demands it get a chance to develop new weaponry for its constituent service. India has, therefore, pursued a shipbuilding capability that like other parts of the defense industry has seen delays, cost overruns, and interference from the primary customer – the Indian Navy.

A report of the Indian parliament's Public Accounts Committee brings out the systemic problems associated with naval shipbuilding in the country. It states that India's shipbuilding efforts are met with delays and cost overruns because of the dependence on a large number of agencies, long gestation periods, the need to have state of the art systems of board leads to frequent mid-course changes, as well as the desire to have indigenized systems have all led to significant problems in the manufacture of ships domestically.[11]

Coupled with the problems associated with the domestic construction of naval vessels, have been the problems that India faces in making acquisitions from external suppliers, particularly from Russia. The Russian arms industry continues to be one of India's major suppliers of weaponry and in the case of the Navy it has not only supplied a large portion of the fleet but also supplied technologies and systems that other western nations have been unwilling to provide. Thus, the Russians provided India with a mid-sized aircraft carrier and agreed to lease a nuclear submarine to the Indian Navy but there were problems with both transactions as well as with other sales to the Navy.

Problems arose from delays in providing new weaponry to India, the fact that Russian weapons are not matching their stated standards, and hefty cost overruns, with the Russians playing hardball with their Indian counterparts. Thus, India refused to accept updated *Kilo* submarines because the *Klub* missile system that was added to it did not work properly.[12] Similarly, the Russians told the Indian Navy that they required an additional $1.2 billion to complete the refurbishment of the carrier *Gorshkov* (now renamed *Vikramaditya*).[13] This put India over a barrel since it had bought the supporting air wing based on the configuration of the carrier. India's naval chief publicly complained that the Russians had used Indian money to modernize their shipyard facilities and, in doing so, were now able to attract new business and push the Indian carrier project onto the back burner.[14]

What the Russians have also been doing is essentially tying the availability of certain weapons systems to the purchase of others. Thus, one of the reasons for buying the *Gorshkov* was that the Russians would subsequently sweeten the pot by offering India strategic systems like the *Akula*-class submarines) and Tu-22 Backfire bombers (the Backfire was deal subsequently scrapped but the Indian Navy has shown renewed interest in acquiring the bomber).[15] Further, when deals fall through in one area, there have been repercussions in the purchase of other weapons. When India declined to purchase Russian nuclear reactors after coming close to inking the deal, Moscow retaliated by asking for price increases on a series of weapons programs that included the *Gorshkov* and the Su-30MKI fighters.[16]

One should stress, however, that this is not the end of the India-Russia military relationship in the way that the Egypt-Soviet Union relationship ended in the early 1970s. The Indian defense minister was quick to distance his government from the remarks of the Indian navy chief about the delays and price increase with the *Gorshkov* project. Further, the Indian government has entered into an agreement with Russia to develop a fifth-generation fighter aircraft, and India is reportedly leasing an additional nuclear submarine from Russia. Further, both the Indian Air Force and the Indian Army continue to seek advanced systems from Russia. What we are likely to see, therefore, is a continued link with Russia, but at the same time, India will move towards other suppliers to reduce the critical dependence on Moscow in some fields.[17]

In the area of armaments Russia, because of its cash-strapped arms industry, will continue to share technology and scientific collaboration with India since New Delhi will be willing to fund Russian research and development efforts. While Beijing is also willing to provide such research and development subsidies, lingering suspicions about China's intentions will likely prevent the building of a similar military technology relationship with that country. The new arms production relationship that the Indians expect to provide dividends is the bourgeoning military relationship with the United States.

As former Defense Secretary Ashton Baldwin Carter commented in New Delhi in December 2016, "But I am confident that the U.S.-India relationship will be the defining partnership of the 21st Century. It's built, as you noted, on common values, significant progress our two nations have made over the last 15 years, and the momentum of two great handshakes. The first handshake between India's Act East policy and America's rebalance. Military-to-military cooperation is, as you noted, growing. Exercises that are unprecedented level, both with respect to other countries in the world and our history."[18] This visit concluded with India being named a major defense partner of the United States thus potentially facilitating the co-production and co-development of advanced weaponry.

Since the latter years of the Clinton Administration, there has been a warming of the India-U.S. relationship that led, in 2005, to the path breaking Indo-U.S. nuclear deal. The Manmohan Singh government and the current Modi administration have sought to build on this deal by increasing the purchase of weaponry from the United States leading to the acquisition of P-8 aircraft for the Navy as well as C-130J and C-17 transports for the Air Force. More recently, the United States has offered to transfer the F-16 production line to India so that it can meet its pressing need for fighter aircraft and fulfill Prime Minister Modi's desire to "Make in India" – i.e. produce modern weaponry within the country.

From a naval perspective, and given the blue-water ambitions of the Indian Navy, the most ambitious program is to seek American cooperation in building an indigenous aircraft carrier, the INS *Vishal*.[19] If such cooperation took place, the United States would assist India in developing its next generation carrier and possibly making it a nuclear-powered vessel equipped with an electromagnetic launch capability for aircraft – a capability that has only recently been introduced on U.S. carriers. Additionally, Tellis has suggested that India be allowed to purchase the Marine jump-jet version of the F-35 since it would make the most sense for the Indian carrier fleet given the configuration of Indian carriers.[20]

An arms production relationship with the United States would be particularly useful for India since it would ensure that such deals were above suspicion of corruption thanks to the Foreign Military Sales provisions; it would qualitatively enhance the technologies available to the Indian Navy and, as Tellis argues, give India a clear edge over the Chinese Navy (this, however, may be an optimistic assessment).

Such cooperation, however, is surrounded by its own set of problems that reside in enduring suspicions in India about the intent of the United States, residual desires for maintaining a posture of nonalignment that require the country maintain some distance from the major superpower, as well as India's concerns about not being identified too closely with the United States in what is a very fluid Asian political and geostrategic environment. Moreover, the Indian government, the foreign policy bureaucracy, and the military remember that the United States engaged in coercive democracy vis-à-vis India in the 1971 India-Pakistan war and they also point out that after the 1998 nuclear tests the United States cut off all military ties hurting the country's Light Combat Aircraft project. In Indian defense circles, therefore, the value of the United States as a supplier is always in question. This enduring suspicion, coupled with the glacial pace at which the Indian bureaucracy works, has led to some breakthroughs like the United States designating India a major defense partner but there has been little to show in the actual realm of defense manufactures. Defense purchases, however, have shown considerable progress in recent years with the procurement of the P-8 surveillance aircraft for the Navy, and the C-130 and the C-17 for the Air Force with the latter being particularly useful for long-range maritime power projection.

The continued residual feelings about nonalignment and the fear of getting entangled in drawn out expeditionary conflicts has led India to hedge its bets about participating in the major conflicts of the twenty-first century. Thus, India rejected the idea of sending a division to Iraq and has been clear to emphasize that the proposed quadrilateral maritime alliance of Japan, the United States, India, and Australia is not anti-Chinese in its orientation. The Indians also point out that geopolitical compulsions make it difficult to be a partner in American-led coalitions. They argue that while the United States can drop bombs and go home, India, driven by geographical compulsions, will continue to live with neighbors like Iran, Afghanistan, and Pakistan. Further, at a more general level, while the maritime doctrine and pronouncements from analysts talk about India playing a greater role in terms of power projection, the fact remains that India's actual threat environment and its ability to develop its force structure in a timely manner will dictate the actual extent to which India can emerge as a major maritime player in the Indo-Pacific.

The threat environment

While India's long-term security challenge is China, in the short to medium term it continues to be Pakistan and the maritime dimension of the threat cannot be separated from the land-based challenges that Pakistan poses to Indian security. The security challenge posed by Pakistan comes from three sources: Islamabad's nuclear, conventional, and unconventional (jihadi) capabilities.

In the nuclear realm, the two nations have achieved deterrence since both countries have the ability to level destruction on each other's major cities and that would significantly hurt both countries' political systems and economies. Unlike nuclear war between the United States and Russia, even a small exchange would be devastating for both nations. An Indian attack on the three major Pakistani cities of Lahore, Karachi, and Islamabad would destroy that country's major political, financial, and economic centers, leaving behind a country that was largely rural and impoverished.[21] Similarly, a Pakistani attack that devastated New Delhi, Mumbai, and Bangalore would set India's economy back by 50 years (and probably see investors run away from India Inc.) and impose severe centrifugal strains on the national polity as secessionist tendencies would gain encouragement from the loss of the central authority in New Delhi.[22]

At the conventional level, India has an advantage over Pakistan and this has been played out in the maritime realm where the Indian Navy is confident that it can blockade Pakistan's maritime space and thus lead to putting pressure on Islamabad in a war and force a non-nuclear resolution to the conflict. During the Kargil conflict, the Indian Navy deployed in the international waters of the Arabian Sea to put pressure on Pakistan to withdraw its troops from the Himalayan region.[23] While the actual war was resolved through diplomatic efforts – particularly the intervention by President Clinton, it led to the belief that India could use maritime coercion against Pakistan without lowering the nuclear threshold.

India's evolving maritime force structure that includes aircraft carriers, submarines (both nuclear and conventional), and the development with Russian collaboration of the Brahmos anti-shipping missile, all give India a capability to inflict significant damage on Pakistan's smaller maritime capabilities. Moreover, the increased maritime capability should permit the Indian Navy to assist the broader war effort and not just focus on countering the Pakistan Navy. The real problem for the India, however, is the challenge posed by Jihadi forces supported either directly or indirectly by the Pakistani military.

Jihadi groups have been able to wage asymmetric conflict against India in the mountain state of Kashmir and, quite spectacularly, in the 2008 attack on Mumbai city. The 2008 attack exposed the vulnerabilities of India's maritime spaces for it showed that India's coastal cities were soft targets for a sea-based terrorist assault. In 2008, 12 terrorists from Pakistan stole a fishing vessel and brought it right into Mumbai harbor and were able to walk up to the unprotected Taj Mahal Hotel. From there the terrorists spread out over downtown Mumbai and were able to paralyze the city because it took the Indian authorities nearly 48 hours to kill 11 of the terrorists and capture one of them – and this was at the cost of 166 Indian and foreign lives.

Despite the claim that Indian port security has been tightened, maritime routes for terror remain a major problem for India given the number of smaller ports that exist along the western coast with Pakistan. Further, there is the more dangerous possibility that the Pakistanis use a shipping vessel to smuggle a nuclear device into India to use to carry out a surprise attack. For the Indian Navy, the threats posed by unconventional forces from Pakistan, therefore, may be the most pressing as well as the most difficult to counter. Only now is the Indian government seeking to procure the Unmanned Aerial Vehicles (UAVs) *Defender* Drones from the United States to provide the sort of 24/7 surveillance capability that is required to secure a soft and lengthy maritime border. The broader security region is, of course, the Indian Ocean littoral, and India's interest in the region has grown both with the rising insecurity in the Gulf states as well as Indian interests further afield in Southern Africa.

The Indian Ocean region

India has used the Indian Navy, in recent years, to engage in maritime diplomacy in the broader Indian Ocean region. This has been done to protect India's vital economic interests like the free flow of oil and the prevention of attacks by pirates in the western Indian Ocean. The Indian government has also sought to build relationships with the countries of the Persian Gulf and the maritime nations of East and South Africa.

The Persian Gulf states are important to India not only as a source of oil but also because of the large Indian diaspora population, approximately 7 million workers, that remits large amounts of hard currency to India (in actual fact, Indians in the Gulf States still remit more money to India than their more prosperous counterparts in the United States). The United Arab Emirates also, for example, wants to increase bilateral trade by 60% and to eventually invest up to $75 billion in India.[24] As Kadira Pethiyagoda points out,

> The GCC states, of course, are situated in one of the most strategically important parts of the Indian Ocean, bordering shipping lanes through which energy and other goods flow between the Middle East, Europe, and Asia. Accordingly, the Indian navy increased its visits to GCC ports, arranged joint exercises with GCC navies, and institutionalized links to GCC states. Most recently, India and Saudi Arabia agreed to enhance cooperation to strengthen maritime security during Modi's 2016 visit. Beyond energy and defense, India's increase in global trade over the last decade gives it new impetus for cooperating with GCC states in areas like protecting lines of communication, deterring piracy, and preventing the trafficking of narcotics and weapons.[25]

Further, both in the first and second Gulf wars the Indian government had to deploy military and civil assets to rescue stranded workers from the region, so the welfare of the diaspora is of paramount concern to the Indian government since it has economic consequences for the country.

The Indian government has, therefore, built up a series of naval arrangements with both the Arab countries of the Gulf and Iran to enhance cooperation and training. Thus, the Indian navy is engaged in anti-piracy cooperation with the countries of the Gulf Cooperation Council and since 1993 has conducted bilateral naval exercises with the Oman Navy. While the free flow of oil, the protection of Indian citizens, and attracting FDI from the Gulf have led to an increase in Indian naval activity, it is marked by a degree of caution about getting entangled in the conflicts of the region. Hence while India is happy to engage in anti-piracy operations, it is reluctant to take sides in the Sunni-Shia conflict or to work with the anti-ISIS coalition in the Gulf.

While there are a set of naval commitments emerging in Southwest Asia that will lead to cooperative security arrangements on piracy, terrorism, and freedom of maritime passage, the long-term issue for the Indian government is becoming one of how to deal with the rise of China as the next global superpower.

China

The India-China relationship continues to be scarred by India's loss in the 1962 India-China war and the fact that the border between the two countries remains unresolved. In recent decades India-China trade has grown significantly and since 2015 China has become India's largest trading partner but broader concerns remain in New Delhi about Beijing's future ambitions in Asia and the fact that these can work to constrain India, particularly New Delhi's own rise to great power status.

The Indian government is concerned about China not supporting its bid for a permanent seat in the United Nations Security Council and views this lack of support as an attempt to prevent India from attaining its rightful status as a major global power. Further, Indian strategic planners are concerned that the Chinese grab of natural resources across the world is shutting out India and potentially hindering the latter's natural economic growth. The Chinese, for example, were able to outbid the Indians for developing oil fields in Angola and in Siberia. The Indian government also worries about the continuing support to Islamabad from Beijing, particularly the development of Pakistan's nuclear and conventional forces. The Chinese, in fact, after the Indian nuclear test of 1974, were able to achieve nuclear deterrence on the cheap against India by simply transferring nuclear weapons technology – including a nuclear bomb design – to Pakistan. Further, India has protested China's decision to build part of the One Belt One Road (OBOR) through a disputed part of Pakistani Kashmir that India claims.

Lastly, there is the fear in New Delhi that the Chinese are slowly creating a maritime ring of encirclement against India through what has been labeled the "string of pearls" strategy whereby China seeks bases across the Indian Ocean. The string of pearls strategy is operationalized, New Delhi believes, by China getting maritime port facilities – incorrectly described in some analyses as naval bases – in Myanmar, Sri Lanka, and more recently Gwadar, Pakistan. Along with the fear of Chinese encirclement, the Indian government has objected to the Chinese plans of building the OBOR.

China's OBOR project was authorized in 2015,

> with two main components: the Silk Road Economic Belt and the 21st Century Maritime Silk Road (exhibit). The Silk Road Economic Belt is envisioned as three routes connecting China to Europe (via Central Asia), the Persian Gulf, the Mediterranean (through West Asia), and the Indian Ocean (via South Asia). The 21st Century Maritime Silk Road is planned to create connections among regional waterways. More than 60 countries, with a combined GDP of $21 trillion, have expressed interest in participating in the OBOR action plan.[26]

Indian opposition to OBOR arises from two major concerns: one part of the road goes through Pakistan-occupied Kashmir that is claimed by India; and the maritime belt is seen as laying the groundwork for encircling India, something the Indians have worried about since the string of pearls strategy was first enunciated by western scholars.[27] India has, therefore, come up with its own set of trade initiatives such as the Kaladan project with Myanmar, the Chahbahar project with Iran, and talks of a North-South road and rail corridor connecting the Indian Ocean and Caspian Sea from Iran to Russia and Northern Europe.[28] Funding for the Indian projects remains a question and the fact remains that the OBOR is likely to have more resources because of the number of countries involved in the project.

The net result of these factors is the fear that China will stunt India's natural progress to great power status and the two countries may be embroiled in a maritime competition to add to the land-based conflict that has existed for the last 55 years between the two countries. The Indian response has been to start exploring its options in Southeast Asia and the Western Pacific to counterbalance China. This response was initially pursued through the Look East Policy of Prime Minister Narasimha Rao and has been made into a more proactive policy of engagement in the Western Pacific, closer to the Chinese maritime homeland and interests, by the Act East Policy of Prime Minister Narendra Modi.

Look East and Act East policies

The Look East Policy emerged in 1991–92 when India faced major economic challenges domestically and saw the world order it had favored internationally collapse almost overnight. Economically, the Indian economy was in the doldrums as the financial missteps of socialism had financially led to a major fiscal crisis for the Indian government. Left with only two weeks of hard currency reserves in 1991, the Indian government had to agree to an IMF package as well as far-reaching market reforms in the Indian economic system. Coupled with the dire economic situation was the seismic shift in the international system caused by the implosion of the Soviet Union.

The Soviet Union had been India's strategic ally from the early 1960s, providing it with political, military, and economic support. In the early 1960s the Soviet Union agreed to transfer a MiG-21 production line to India, setting the stage for a lucrative arms transfer relationship. Economically, the emergence of a Rupee-Ruble trade was one way India could overcome its chronic shortage of hard currency for making purchases and the Soviet Union also became a major supplier of oil to the country. Post-1991, therefore, India had to do a complete political, economic, and to some extent military reset in the way it looked at the world. Part of the new outlook was to orient Indian foreign policy towards India's neighbors to the east – the ASEAN countries.

The Look East Policy was to see greater interaction between India and the countries of Southeast Asia leading to increased military engagements and more importantly trade between the two regions. Thus, trade grew from about $2 billion in 1992 to $72 billion by 2012 but then stagnated with the slowing down of the global economy.[29] The Look East Policy also saw a greater willingness on the part of India to start engaging the ASEAN countries in military matters for, like New Delhi, the latter were concerned about the rise of China and were also seeking to diversify their foreign policy options in the international system.

The coming to power of an NDA government in 2014 saw India become more proactive about ASEAN and the Western Pacific as it unveiled an Act East Policy that was broader in its scope and sought to build relations with nations in, among other places, China's maritime backyard:

> The NDA government outlined the Act East Policy in November 2014, within six months of assuming power in May 2014. The policy seeks to revive and reinvigorate India's relations with ASEAN as well as expand the country's engagement beyond the region to encompass the Koreas in the North to Australia and New Zealand in the South, and from neighbouring Bangladesh to Fiji and Pacific Island countries in the Far East.[30]

The Act East Policy is based on a combination of India's maritime, economic, and geo-strategic interests because 40% of India's maritime trade flows through the Strait of Malacca; India seeks to increase its ties with the economic tigers of Northeast and Southeast Asia, and lastly because New Delhi, faced with a perceived Chinese expansion into the Indian Ocean, is seeking to expand its maritime options and alliances against China.

In order to counter China, India has sought to expand its broader relationships particularly with two nations under the Act East Policy – Vietnam and Japan. It has increased naval visits to Vietnam and given the Vietnamese government a $100 million line of credit to purchase naval patrol boats from India and it is suggested that India may even become a major weapons exporter to Vietnam. It has also agreed to engage in oil explorations in Vietnam's Exclusive Economic Zone even though this move has been met with serious protests from Beijing that does not want India working with Vietnam in waters, or near islands, that are disputed by China and Vietnam.[31] Further, India, in its joint declarations with these countries has signed off on the issue of freedom of navigation in the South China Seas, thus adhering to the international, rather than Chinese, position on the sovereignty issues in the disputed waters.

The India-Japan relationship is a mixture of both increased economic interaction as well as growing security cooperation, particularly in the maritime sphere. India-Japan trade now stands at $14.5 billion and the Japanese, between 2000 and 2015, have made $19.4 billion in foreign direct investments in India.[32] Prime Minister Modi was also able to get the Japanese to agree to building an Ahmedabad to Mumbai Shinkanzen (bullet train) in the future. But it is the perceived Chinese challenge that has drawn the two countries closer together, with Japan putting aside its traditional discomfort with nations that are developing their nuclear weapons capabilities.

The security relationship between the two countries first started growing in the first term of Prime Minister Abe with the two countries agreeing in 2008 to a Joint Declaration on Security Cooperation. When Abe returned to power he floated, in 2012, the Diamond Concept whereby the United States, Japan, Australia, and India formed a diamond shaped security perimeter that would work to ensure peace and stability in the Indo-Pacific region. Since then, the relationship has been marked by agreements to have joint naval training, trilateral naval exercises with the United States and Australia as third parties, and intelligence-sharing arrangements. Additionally, the two countries have established a 2+2 dialogue where the foreign and defense ministries of both nations meet to consult each other. There have also been agreements for Coast Guard to Coast Guard cooperation and, in 2016, there was a meeting of the two countries' air forces. Finally, the Japanese have agreed to participate regularly in exercise Malabar, which is a naval exercise held annually between the United States and India in either the Pacific or the Indian Ocean and the goal is to increase interoperability between these countries.[33]

The Japanese have also suggested that the military link be slowly strengthened by the Indian procurement of weaponry from Japan. Thus, the Japanese have offered the Shin Maywa US-2 amphibious aircraft to the Indian Navy and there is talk of India buying the highly regarded Japanese *Soryu* class submarines (India has, in fact, asked Japan to tender a request for information in its new submarine-purchase competition).

This decision to increase India's maritime security perimeter to include the Western Pacific is aimed at both securing new allies in the effort to put pressure on China but also to develop links with the countries that are most likely to help in the economic development of India – Japan, South Korea, and Taiwan. India's future economic growth will require substantial foreign direct investment and a corporate presence from the Northeast Asian countries which are viewed as prime suppliers of capital and technology for such growth. These ties are likely to only grow as the Northeast Asian countries see the value of the Indian market rise with the demographic shift taking place in India that is unleashing a large pool of young consumers into the market who have both earning power and are tech savvy. This aspect of the bourgeoning relationship is particularly easy to grow, especially if India undertakes substantial market reforms as Prime Minister Narendra Modi seeks to achieve in the next couple of years before calling for an election.

The security dimension of this relationship is more difficult to bring to fruition and may well, in the foreseeable future, be stuck in the current pattern of dialogue and exercises with neither India or the countries of ASEAN and Northeast Asia getting a mutually satisfactory security arrangement. These countries, while having substantive disputes with China, are locked to a far greater level of economic interdependence with Beijing, making it difficult for them to enter into an overt alliance or coalition against Chinese actions in the South and East China Seas.

Moreover, given India's diffidence in being more assertive in the maritime sphere, the nations of East and Southeast Asia are being more cautious in their dealings with New Delhi since the Indian government, while talking strategic partnerships and laying out the challenges posed by Chinese maritime expansion, is reluctant to put teeth to its rhetoric of preparing for the Chinese challenge in the Indian Ocean and the Western Pacific. Act East, therefore, while holding out the promise of greater trade and security partnerships, has been underwhelming in terms of what it has achieved to strengthen India's overall maritime security objectives.

Future policy?

For India, a more proactive maritime policy is necessary to increase its trade, ensure energy supplies, maintain coastal security, and to help in the long term with countering China. Yet India will proceed slowly in the development of its maritime capability and presence since it has to take care of pressing internal economic issues as well as not aggravate China to the point where there is open conflict of interest between the two countries.

As mentioned earlier, India's slow arms production capabilities have made plans for the ramping up of the navy get delayed because weapons systems have not come on line to allow for a substantive change in maritime doctrine. The nuclear submarine is a classic example of this since analysts believe that *Arihant* will be a technology demonstrator and in the short to medium term India will be unable to create a credible naval nuclear deterrent. While New Delhi has leased an *Akula* class nuclear submarine from Russia, a single boat does not translate into an effective maritime force structure. Instead, its greatest value may lie in familiarizing Indian naval personnel with the operation of a nuclear vessel.

Similarly, the Indian aircraft carrier program has envisaged the development of a four carrier fleet allowing the country to project power in both the Bay of Bengal and the Arabian Sea. Yet the carrier program has been beset with delays and the obsolete INS *Virat* soldiered on far past its utility to be finally decommissioned in 2017. The *Vikramaditya* was marred by cost overruns, squabbles with the Russians, and refurbishment delays and the Indian Navy only got the vessel in 2013 – five years after the agreed delivery schedule.[34] The indigenous aircraft carrier program has been delayed due to repeated modifications of the design, shortage of materials, and continued disagreement between the Navy and Cochin Shipyards over project timelines, and consequently the carrier that was due to enter service in 2018 is now expected to enter service around 2023.[35] The situation is further confused by the type of aircraft that will be launched from the carrier. The Comptroller and Auditor General's report stated, "MiG29K, the chosen aircraft for the carrier, continues to face operational deficiencies due to defects in engines, airframe and fly-by-wire system."[36] Yet the entire Indian carrier design is predicated on an aircraft that will take off without catapults, off a ski jump, and land with the aid of arrestor wires. This essentially limits India to purchasing either Russian aircraft, whose performance the Comptroller and Auditor General has questioned, or to buy the very expensive F-35B from the United States. Such delays in building the key components of power projection make it less likely that India can implement its ambitious plans for a greater maritime presence in the Indian Ocean and the Western Pacific.

The other major impediment to a proactive maritime policy is that it is tied to India's growth as a trading power and as an attractive destination for foreign investments. Prime Minister Modi would like to free India from the bureaucratic, nationalistic, and legal constraints that have made it difficult for other countries to invest in India.

Indian red tape makes doing business in India difficult and time consuming and leads businesses to say that they have "India fatigue." This is particularly the case in arms sales where it can take over a decade for an agreement to be reached, as was the case with the Rafale fighter and the Hawk trainer. This contrasts negatively with arms sales elsewhere, as is the case, for example, of US weapons sales to Saudi Arabia. The Saudis, keen to maintain a security relationship with the United States, agreed in 2017 to purchase $110 billion worth of weapons from the United States, thus dwarfing any other deals that American arms companies were negotiating. It certainly makes India's modest buys pale in comparison.

Indian business laws, both in land acquisition and the hiring and dismissal of personnel, make it cumbersome for foreign companies to invest and carry out operations in India. Further, Indian nationalism complicates foreign direct investment in the country. Since Nehru's times, India has sought to carry out import substitution but the record on it has been mixed at best. Import substitution has largely meant the assembly of products in India as opposed to the actual design, development, and manufacture of the goods. Import substitution also leads to a ballooning of prices since the country often does not have the trained man power or infrastructure to build modern technological products. The Indian government, for example, scrapped the idea of building the Rafale fighter in India because of the huge costs of setting up a production line and training people to construct the airplane.[37] Yet, the idea of Make in India, a cornerstone of Prime Minister Modi's plan to drive the economic and technological modernization of India, persists and makes it difficult for corporations to meet the demands of the Indian government. Given these constraints, India's plans to increase trade with Southeast and Southwest Asia remain ambitious proposals for the future and with it the need for greater maritime involvement also has to be questioned. Which then brings up the issue of China.

In a globalized world China and India share the need to have a stable maritime order in the Indo-Pacific because it facilitates the growth and security of both nations.[38] Yet the continuing disputes between the two countries and the Indian fear that China will deny New Delhi its rightful status as an emerging international power complicate the relationship. India, therefore, seeks to incrementally build up its naval capability to mount a future challenge against China. On the Indian side, however, this is a static analysis since it assumes that Beijing will sit by idly and watch India create a formidable maritime force. The fact of the matter is that China is building its own naval forces and its missile technology and sensors to the point where it may place India at a disadvantage should the two nations get into a naval conflict.[39] China already has 56 attack submarines and four ballistic-missile submarines and by 2030 it is expected that China will have 87 attack submarines and 12 ballistic-missile submarines, thus being significantly larger than the Indian force.[40] The US Office of Naval Intelligence states that four Chinese *Jin* class subs are in service, "This platform represents China's first credible, sea-based nuclear deterrent."[41] Obviously, such an analysis must be treated with caution since many of the 87 attack submarines will have to guard the Chinese maritime zones to engage in sea denial and one can also question the ability of many of these vessels to perform effectively in waters so far away from home. Similarly, the ballistic-missile submarines will be in place to provide China with a nuclear deterrent against the United States. But as the capability of Chinese missiles grow, these vessels could remain in waters closer to China, yet present India with a nuclear deterrent.

In contrast, by 2030, India's submarine program will not provide the country with a robust nuclear deterrent since both a fleet of submarines and reliable delivery systems would have to be constructed and, as mentioned previously, this is unlikely to happen at the pace that the Indian Navy requires. An alternative would be to lease more Russian missile boats, but Moscow is unlikely to give India carte blanche to use these boats in a nuclear confrontation with China. What then can a realistic Indian naval strategy in general and vis-à-vis China in particular look like?

The maritime strategy would involve three parts: protecting the homeland; developing a regional security framework in the Indian Ocean region; deterring China in a broader Asia context. Protecting India's 12 major ports and 200 minor and intermediate ports will require a naval grid of sensors and surveillance craft, particularly drones, as well as fast interdiction vessels to intercept sea-based threats posed by jihadi elements. Some of this set-up is already in place, but the surveillance aspect of it is of crucial importance and may be the bedrock of growing US-India cooperation. Ashley Tellis has written about the need to sell India electromagnetic catapults for its new set of carriers. This is an optimistic hope since the US Navy is unlikely to readily part with the technology and buying something so state-of-the-art to fit on carriers that are facing lengthy delays sounds impractical. Using US technology to strengthen India's port and coastal defenses is not and will find receptive ears in the United States Congress because of its emphasis on combatting terrorism.

In terms of regional security, India has been building up a useful set of cooperative linkages with the Gulf States, the ASEAN nations, and the countries of Southern Africa. This permits the use of multinational solutions to pressing problems in the Indian Ocean littoral like anti-piracy operations, disaster relief, checking the flow of weapons of mass destruction, and helps advance India's own goals for increased status and influence in the region. Such measures are only likely to continue since the Indian Navy is the largest littoral navy and it is in the interests of regional actors to cooperate with it for the contingencies listed earlier. The Indian Navy would actually be able to bring considerable force to bear in these situations but also not be perceived as a state pursuing hegemonic ambitions. India's leadership in maritime affairs and its willingness to abide by arbitration rulings from UNCLOS make it a reliable and safe partner in maritime operations. As for China, the policy toward that country must lie in securing India's maritime vulnerabilities, engaging China on the creation of a maritime order in Asia, and resolving the border dispute that also makes China's maritime efforts of concern to New Delhi.

While India seeks to invest in expensive aircraft carriers that are highly vulnerable to Chinese missile attacks, there are simpler and more cost-affordable solutions to deterring China. First, strengthening India's conventional submarine fleet would allow the Indian Navy to engage in Sea Denial against the Chinese Navy since Sea Control would be an expensive and long-drawn out process. India has thus put out a request for information for a new batch of submarines so that it can bring its force level up to 18 modern boats and France, Germany, Japan, Russia, Sweden, and Spain are expected to bid for constructing six of the new series of vessels.[42] Additionally, India has reportedly signed to lease a second *Akula* class boat from Russia. If the submarine competition can escape the usual Indian red tape and negotiating delays, the Indian Navy expects to get the boats in the next decade. Such a naval capability would work to deter Pakistan and ensure sea denial against Chinese boats.

The other defensive measure that India can take is to build up its land- and air-based capabilities in the Andaman and Nicobar Islands to give it the ability to interdict vessels coming out of the Strait of Malacca. Indian Navy P-8 maritime patrol aircraft combined with the Indian Air Force Sukhoi-30 MKIs would give that kind of interdiction capability to the Indian armed forces and make it more costly for the Chinese Navy to project power in the Indian Ocean region.

Diplomatically, India has to work with other Asian countries to create a new maritime order in Asia that recommends the peaceful settlement of maritime disputes. Further, there could also be negotiations on the modalities of naval activities in a country's Exclusive Economic Zone. At present India wants notification that foreign navies are entering its EEZ, while China demands that these navies seek the permission of Beijing to do so. An Asian effort to make notification rather than permission the norm may well help resolve some of the tensions over passage through the South China Seas.

Lastly, even though globalization has seen a growing economic interdependence between the Chinese and Indian economies, there continues to be distrust. The potential for future conflicts between the two countries remains because of the unresolved border dispute. The year 2017 has once again seen this dispute flare up as both sides have talked of possible military confrontation between them. If the border can be resolved, then much of the maritime tensions will also subside since it is in India and China's interests to grow their bilateral trade and India may even be more amenable to participating in the OBOR. Maritime order, it should be noted, is also needed if the China's vision of a Regional Comprehensive Economic Plan is to be implemented since it would be also based on increased volumes of maritime trade.

From an Indian perspective, the Indian and Pacific Ocean are getting increasingly conjoined as global forces make it into one economic market. But unless the two countries can resolve their broader political and military-strategic differences, such cooperation will remain a series of ambitious and unrealized proposals.

Notes

1 Tellis, 2001, p. 474.
2 Gupta, 1997, p. 44.
3 The Rafale deal was initially meant to see the purchase of 126 fighters from France, but ballooning costs led the Modi government to reduce the purchase to 36 aircraft.

4 Rajagopalan, 2016.
5 Iskander Rehman, 2017, p. 1.
6 Kaplan, 2011, p. 10 and pp. 127–129.
7 Indian Navy, Naval Strategic Publication1.1 Indian Maritime Doctrine, *Indian Maritime Doctrine* 2009, updated online version 2015 © Integrated Headquarters, Ministry of Defence (Navy) 2015, pp. 65–68.
8 Indian Maritime Doctrine 2009, p. 125.
9 Indian Maritime Doctrine 2009, p. 97.
10 Gupta, 1997, p. 31.
11 Public Accounts Committee, Sixteenth Lok Sabha Thirty-Second Report, *Indigenous Construction of Indian Naval Warships*, Lok Sabha Secretariat, New Delhi, December 2015, p. 3.
12 Bedi, 2008.
13 "No renegotiation on price of Gorshkov: Navy Chief," *Hindu*, 4 December 2007.
14 Unnithan, 2007.
15 Ibid.
16 Seema Mustafa, 2007.
17 Kanwal, 2007.
18 Remarks by Secretary Carter and Defense Minister Parrikar in New Delhi, India, December 8, 2016, available at, www.defense.gov/News/Transcripts/Transcript-View/Article/1025104/remarks-by-secretary-carter-and-defense-minister-parrikar-in-new-delhi-india, accessed on December 23, 2016.
19 Tellis, 2015, pp. 1–2.
20 Given the current configuration of Indian aircraft carriers, they require aircraft that have enough power to launch off a ski-jump and to land with the use of arrestor wires. This has necessitated the purchase of the MiG-29K for the carriers and as of now tied the Indian Navy to purchasing Soviet aircraft since the only other airplane that can generate enough thrust to launch off a carrier deck without a catapult is the Russian Su-30 (but as the Russians found out the size of the Su-30 was a constraint since the option was to put either 18 Sukhois or 28 MiGs on the carrier. Other carrier-based aircraft like the F-18 and the Rafale cannot use a ski-jump and while Saab has offered to build a navalized version of the Gripen that can do so, the latter is at present a design concept. In this context, the F-35B would be the ideal plane for the Indian Navy, although its high cost might serve to scare away the Indian Navy.
21 Gupta, November/December 2001, p. 1053.
22 Gupta, 2001, Ibid.
23 "On the Brink," The Telegraph (India), April 28, 2013.
24 Hokayem and Roy-Chaudhury, January 23, 2017, available at, www.iiss.org/en/iiss%20voices/blogsections/iiss-voices-2017-adeb/january-850b/india-and-the-uae-towards-strategic-cooperation-82af.
25 Pethiyagoda, February 2017, p. 9.
26 Jinchen, July 2016, available at, www.mckinsey.com/industries/capital-projects-and-infrastructure/our-insights/one-belt-and-one-road-connecting-china-and-the-world
27 Pant, June 22, 2017, available at, http://yaleglobal.yale.edu/content/india-challenges-chinas-intentions-one-belt-one-road-initiative.
28 Ibid.
29 Sajjanhar, May 2016, p. 2.
30 Ibid. p. 2.
31 Jennings, "Vietnam is chasing India to escape the grip of China, Forbes Online, July 10, 2017, available at, www.forbes.com/sites/ralphjennings/2017/07/10/vietnam-is-chasing-india-in-a-new-gambit-to-resist-china/#7beff0b75f59.
32 Ministry of Foreign Affairs Japan, available at, www.mofa.go.jp/region/asia-paci/india/data.html.
33 Lynch and Przystup, March 2017.

34 "After Five Year Delay Navy gets INS Vikramaditya," The Times of India, November 17, 2013, available at, http://timesofindia.indiatimes.com/india/After-5-year-delay-Navy-gets-INS-Vikramaditya/articleshow/25911949.cms.
35 "Delay in indigenous carrier to impact Indian Navy's capabilities: CAG," Hindustan Times, July 31, 2016, available at, www.hindustantimes.com/india-news/delay-in-indigenous-carrier-to-impact-indian-navy-s-capabilities-cag/story-HgXuqJyRFc7piP-0FVskzgN.html.
36 Report of the Comptroller and Auditor General of India, Union Government (Defence Services) Navy and Coast Guard Report No. 17 of 2016, New Delhi 2016, p. iv.
37 Rajat Pandit, April 14, 2015, available at, http://timesofindia.indiatimes.com/india/MMRCA-deal-India-to-scrap-20-billion-mega-project-for-126-Rafale-fighter-jets/articleshow/46910444.cms.

MMRCA deal: India to scrap $20 billion mega project for 126 Rafale fighter jetsMMRCA deal: India to scrap $20 billion mega project for 126 Rafale fighter jetsMMRCA deal: India to scrap $20 billion mega project for 126 Rafale fighter jetsMMRCA deal: India to scrap $20 billion mega project for 126 Rafale fighter jetsMMRCA deal: India to scrap $20 billion mega project for 126 Rafale fighter jetsMMRCA deal: India to scrap $20 billion mega project for 126 Rafale fighter jets.
38 China is now the largest importer of oil in world and much of its food imports come via the sea lanes. See Cheng, Dec 17, 2015, p. 2.
39 Cheng, p. 7.
40 Tweed and Leung, May 31, 2017, available at, www.bloomberg.com/news/articles/2017-05-31/china-s-growing-naval-might-challenges-u-s-supremacy-in-asia.
41 Military and Security Developments Involving the People's Republic of China, Office of Naval Intelligence, Department of Defense, Washington D.C., 2016, p. 26.
42 Rajat Pandit, July 24, 2017, available at, http://timesofindia.indiatimes.com/india/india-kick-starts-mother-of-all-underwater-defence-deals/articleshow/59730200.cms?utm_source=toimobile&utm_medium=Twitter&utm_campaign=referral.

References

After Five Year Delay Navy gets INS Vikramaditya, *The Times of India*, November 17, 2013. Available at: http://timesofindia.indiatimes.com/india/After-5-year-delay-Navy-gets-INS-Vikramaditya/articleshow/25911949.cms [Accessed July 14, 2017]

Bedi, R., 2008. Klub-S Missile Snags Delay Delivery of Indian Sub, *Jane's Defence Weekly*, 23 January.

Cheng, D., 2015. *China's Pivot to the Sea: The Modernizing PLA Navy*, The Heritage Foundation Backgrounder, No. 3084, December 17.

Delay in Indigenous Carrier to Impact Indian Navy's Capabilities: CAG. *Hindustan Times*, July 31, 2016. Available at, www.hindustantimes.com/india-news/delay-in-indigenous-carrier-to-impact-indian-navy-s-capabilities-cag/story-HgXuqJyRFc7piP0FVskzgN.html [Accessed 24 July 2017]

Department of Defense, 2016. *Remarks by Secretary Carter and Defense Minister Parrikar in New Delhi*, India. 8, December. Available at: www.defense.gov/News/Transcripts/Transcript-View/Article/1025104/remarks-by-secretary-carter-and-defense-minister-parrikar-in-new-delhi-india, [Accessed December 23, 2016].

Gupta, A., 1997. *Building an Arsenal: The Evolution of Regional Power Force Structures*. Westport, CT: Praeger.

———. 2001. India's Third Tier Nuclear State Dilemma: N plus 20? *Asian Survey*, XLI(6), November/December.

Hokayem, E., and Roy-Chaudhury, R., 2017. India and UAE: Towards Strategic Cooperation, *IISS Voices*, 23 January. Available at: www.iiss.org/en/iiss%20voices/blogsections/iiss-voices-2017-adeb/january-850b/india-and-the-uae-towards-strategic-cooperation-82af. [Accessed June 24, 2017]

Integrated Headquarters, of Ministry Defence (Navy) 2015. *Indian Navy, Naval Strategic Publication1.1*, Indian Maritime Doctrine 2009.

Jennings, R., 2017. Vietnam is chasing India to escape the grip of China. *Forbes* Online, 10 July. Available at: www.forbes.com/sites/ralphjennings/2017/07/10/vietnam-is-chasing-india-in-a-new-gambit-to-resist-china/#7beff0b75f59 [Accessed August 1, 2017]

Jinchen, T., 2016. *'One Belt and One Road': Connecting China and the World*, Mckinsey Corporation, July. Available at www.mckinsey.com/industries/capital-projects-and-infrastructure/our-insights/one-belt-and-one-road-connecting-china-and-the-world [Accessed 22 January 2017]

Kanwal, G., 2007. Indo-Russian partnership. *Deccan Herald*, 25 December.

Kaplan, Robert D., 2011. *Monsoon: The Indian Ocean and the Future of American Power*. New York: Random House.

Lynch III, Thomas F., and Przystup, James J., 2017. *India-Japan Strategic Cooperation and Implications for U.S. Strategy in the Indo-Asia-Pacific Region, Strategic Perspectives*. 24, NDU Press.

Ministry of Foreign Affairs Japan, 2016. Available at: www.mofa.go.jp/region/asia-paci/india/data.html [Accessed July 17, 2017].

Mustafa, M., 2007. Angry Russia hikes cost of deals. *Asian Age*, 19 November.

"No Renegotiation on Price of Gorshkov: Navy Chief," *Hindu*, 4 December 2007.

Office of Naval Intelligence, Department of Defense, 2016. Washington, DC. Military and Security Developments Involving the People's Republic of China.

"On the Brink," *The Telegraph (India)*, April 28, 2013.

Pandit, R., 2015. MMRCA, India to Scrap $20 Billion Mega Project for 126 Rafale Fighter Jets. *The Times of India*, April 14. Available at: http://timesofindia.indiatimes.com/india/MMRCA-deal-India-to-scrap-20-billion-mega-project-for-126-Rafale-fighter-jets/articleshow/46910444.cms [Accessed July 13, 2017]

———. 2017. India 'kick starts' Mother of all Defence Deals, *The Times of India*, 24 July. Available at: http://timesofindia.indiatimes.com/india/india-kick-starts-mother-of-all-underwater-defence deals/articleshow/59730200.cms?utm_source=toimobile&utm_medium=Twitter&utm_campaign=referral [Accessed July 27, 2017]

Pant, H. V., 2017. *India Challenges China's Intentions on One Belt, One Road Initiative, YaleGlobal* Online, 22 June. Available at: http://yaleglobal.yale.edu/content/india-challenges-chinas-intentions-one-belt-one-road-initiative [Accessed July 13, 2017]

Pethiyagoda, K., 2017. *India-GCC Relations: Delhi's Strategic Opportunity*, Brookings Doha Center Analysis Paper, Number 18.

Public Accounts Committee, Sixteenth Lok Sabha, 2015. *Thirty-Second Report*, Indigenous Construction of Indian Naval Warships, Lok Sabha Secretariat, New Delhi.

Rajagopalan, R., 2016. *India's Nuclear Doctrine Debate*, Carnegie Endowment for International Peace, 30 June. Available at: http://carnegieendowment.org/2016/06/30/india-s-nuclear-doctrine-debate-pub-63950 [Accessed July 27, 2017]

Rehman, I., 2017. *India, China and Differing Conceptions of the Maritime Order*, Brookings Institution.

Report of the Comptroller and Auditor General of India, 2016. Union Government (Defence Services) Navy and Coast Guard Report No. 17 of 2016, New Delhi.

Sajjanhar, A., 2016. *Taking Stock of India's Act East Policy*, ORF Issue Brief Number 142.
Tellis, A. J., 2001. *India's Emerging Nuclear Posture: Between Recessed Deterrent and Ready Arsenal*. Santa Monica, CA: Rand, p. 474.
———. 2015. *Making Waves: Aiding India's Next Generation Aircraft Carrier, Carnegie Endowment for International Peace*, Washington, DC.
Tweed, D., and Leung, A., 2017. How China's Naval Fleet is Shaping Global Politics, *Bloomberg Politics* Online, May 31, Available at: www.bloomberg.com/news/articles/2017-05-31/china-s-growing-naval-might-challenges-u-s-supremacy-in-asia [Accessed July 27, 2017]
Unnithan, S., 2007. Battle Over Gorshkov. *India Today*, 7 December.

11 Iran's maritime aims
Persistent strategy, changing capabilities

Nathan González Mendelejis

Introduction

There has been a significant degree of continuity in the maritime legacy of the Iranian Plateau-based states over the millennia. The Iranian state's strategy, regardless of a given regime's economic capacity or regional importance, has relied on a naval posture of minimal deterrence rather than power projection. This chapter aims to highlight Iran's continuity of maritime strategy, as exemplified in the Islamic Republic of Iran's naval doctrine. The aim of this effort is twofold. First, the chapter offers an overview of the naval strategy and capabilities of Iran today, which planners and political observers may find useful. Second, the chapter provides a case study into the manner in which geopolitics frames strategic goals and developments over time. The latter effort should be instructive in the understanding, not only of the Persian Gulf, but also of the ways in which states face institutional barriers to political and military strategy regardless of economic capacity, ideology, regime identity, and other factors that theorists may be tempted to identify as causal mechanisms for strategic behavior.

The chapter begins with a quick overview of maritime strategy of various Iranian-plateau based states. It goes on to introduce Iranian strategy and capabilities of the Islamic Republic of Iran, founded in 1979.

Iranian naval strategy over time

The Islamic Republic of Iran, like previous regimes that scholars and inhabitants have referred to as *Iran*, is associated with the following geographic features. First, it benefits from a natural geographic barrier to the west, in the form of the Alborz Mountains. Second, it covers the region of *Fars* (Persia), which includes the modern-day cities of Shiraz and Isfahan. Third, it has access to the Caspian Sea in the north and the Persian Gulf in the south. In the northeast, Iranian claims to the hinterlands of Greater Khorasan, which historically covered much of Central Asia, have expanded and contracted over time, though since the Russian-imposed Treaty of Turkmenchay in 1828 these regions have all but disappeared from Iranian aspirations.

Throughout much of the Iranian Plateau's history, threats on the eastern and northern flanks have been fewer and less intense. Much of Greater Khorasan, which includes modern-day Afghanistan, historically enjoyed limited state capacity. The same can be said of the lands along the northern edges of the Caspian Sea. Though Islamic history was highly impacted by cultural influences of peoples in the Central Asian steppes and modern-day Afghanistan, many of whom were of Turkic or Iranian cultural lineage, the power centers of Iran-based states most often tilted west, in modern-day Iraq or in Fars.

The Iranian state's most serious competitors often came from the west. During the pre-Islamic Sasanian era (221–634), Iran's chief rival was Rome. Later, centers of Islamic culture and power were largely in modern-day Egypt, Syria, and Iraq. This meant that Iranian states were likely to adopt a westward defensive posture, and much of their power was concentrated in land armies.

With the exception of Achaemenid times, when an Iranian-based state approached what we may now term superpower status,[1] naval power has never been a high priority for Iranian military planners. For Iranian pre-Islamic states, seafaring served as a means to project *economic* power in Arabia and the Indian Ocean. Given the relatively limited eastern reach by Iran's geopolitical competitor, Rome, Iranian naval ports at the time were set up largely absent of military uses.[2]

After the Arab-Islamic conquest of Iran, which started in 633, Islamic states with sovereignty over the Iranian plateau focused on military preparedness on land, and many set their sights on defense and expansion vis-à-vis Central Asia to the northeast, and states based in the west. The Safavids, who came to power in 1501, made a conscious effort not to pursue a naval strategy of power projection, focusing instead on their land-based capacity, and on the economic use of the waterways.[3] In fact, by the early eighteenth century the Safavids didn't have a single naval vessel under their command, and they were reduced to negotiating with Europeans and Arab tribesmen to use transport ships in order to combat Omani raids.[4] As Michael Axworthy notes, Nader Shah, during brief but ambitious spurts of conquest, built a relatively strong naval fleet, but this was mostly commandeered by non-Iranians, and efforts were short-lived and mostly used to lend support to allies along the Persian Gulf coast.[5]

The 1828 Treaty of Turkmenchay followed the third Russo-Persian War, and it arguably established the geographic and political scope of Iran as we recognize it today. Not only did the treaty cap Iranian aims in Central Asia, but it gave the Russian navy supremacy over the Caspian Sea. It also set Iran up for a long-term relationships with Russia, marked by interference into its government and territory.

Russia's involvement in Iran is also critical as it pertains to the Great Game. Given Iran's accessibility to Afghanistan, Russia and Britain came to use Iran as a diplomatic and financial battleground, though Britain eventually became much more firmly entrenched in the shah's court, in large part because of its loans, which allowed Great Britain to gain significant economic and political concessions. Ever since the nineteenth century, then, we can think of Iran as a client state of both Russia and the Great Britain, and this meant military power became dependent upon and subservient to foreign influences, funding, and training. For example, in the early twentieth century Iran's land army capacity was split between the Gendarme and the Russian-trained Cossak Brigades.

In the nineteenth century Britain's maritime dominance made the notion of a fully autonomous Iranian navy not only unrealistic but outright impractical. At this time, now under the Qajar dynasty, the Iranian state was preoccupied with its limited authority inside the country. Peripheral sources of legitimacy – tribal and provincial power – remained critical and continued to contest the state, draining significant military resources that may otherwise have been available for national defense and at least token power projection.[6]

This began to change somewhat in the aftermath of the 1921 coup by Reza Khan, a colonel in the Cossak Brigade who would later make himself shah and establish his own dynasty under the name Pahlavi. Reza Shah prioritized state building and conscription to create a semblance of a unitary state that for centuries had eluded Iranian leaders.

It was only after Reza Shah's son came to power in 1941, however, and especially as the United States became more embroiled in Iranian politics starting in the 1950s, that Iran realized a higher degree of bureaucratization of its armed forces. Aside from the goal of prestige through military prowess,[7] Iran had practical maritime aspirations in the Persian Gulf – namely, taking the disputed Abu Musa, Greater Tunb, and Lesser Tunb three islands that the Trucial States of Sharjah and Ras al-Khaymeh (both now part of the United Arab Emirates) also claimed.

It was in 1971, as Great Britain officially exited the region, that Iran made a move and landed troops on the islands. Iran's government had made an agreement with the Emirate of Sharjah to split control over Abu Musa. At the time, the island had fewer than 1,000 inhabitants (now it has about double that amount), most of whom were Arab. Since then, Iran has built most of the infrastructure on the island, and the governor is Iranian.[8] On the other hand, Ras al-Khaymeh never acceded to Iran's demands for joint ownership over the Tunbs, and to this day that emirate claims Iran is illegally occupying those islands.[9]

The islands, but especially Abu Musa, were instrumental for Iran, as they allowed it to extend its waters in what is a crowded and highly trafficked gulf. And although the UAE continues to claim rightful ownership over these territories, there is little sign that Iran will ever give up its presence on them.

The most action that the shah's navy ever saw, however, was after the king had been forced to flee the country at the close of the revolution. During the Iran-Iraq War (1980–88), with Ayatollah Khomeini now at the helm, Iran's navy, built during royal times, took part in the largest anti-shipping actions since the Second World War. The so-called Tanker War portion of the conflict, which began in 1981 and which by 1987 had pulled in the United States and the Soviet Union, was instrumental in informing Iran's present naval doctrine.

The tanker war began with Iraqi attacks on Iranian oil shipping. Given that Iraq had overland outlets for its oil and Iran didn't, the Iraqis gambled that this approach could significantly decrease Iranian revenues and tilt the war in their favor. Iran, however, responded with attacks on its own, which it concentrated on Kuwaiti tankers and tankers sailing to and from Kuwait, given that the country was supporting Iraq with massive loans.

The main weapon the Iraqis initially used was the Exocet anti-ship missile, though in 1984, when Iran joined the fray of anti-shipping activity, it also used heavy machine guns and rocket-propelled grenades. Most of these measures had limited success in sinking tankers, given the strength of the ships' hulls and the oil's viscosity and relative stability. But by 1986 Iran had acquired Silkworm missiles from China, and this missile was three times more powerful than the Exocet. The United States entered the war by reflagging and escorting Kuwaiti ships, which led Iran to aim much of its missile power toward Kuwaiti installations on land rather than ships.[10]

Writing shortly near the end of the war, Ronald O'Rourke described Iran's adaptability, which was in contrast to Iraq's relatively steady use of Exocet missiles:

> Iran's methods of attack, in contrast to Iraq's, showed considerable variety and change over the course of the year. When one tactic proved ineffective or was successfully countered, Iran shifted to another. In addition to speedboats, Iran began to employ surreptitiously laid mines; Chinese-made, shore-based Silkworm anti-ship cruise missiles; and traditional naval gunfire, among other weapons.[11]

The Iran-Iraq War and the involvement of the U.S. Navy in the conflict informed Iran's naval doctrine in one important way. It was during the Tanker War portion of the conflict when Iran began using "swarming" tactics to counteract U.S. naval warfare (more on this approach later). It was also at this time when the Islamic Revolutionary Guard Corps (IRGC) began carrying out speed boat attacks to make up in the capabilities deficit. As one Iranian commentator notes in a military web forum, since "all of Iran's equipment before the Revolution had been western and there were no native upgrades . . . the enemy knew all of [our] strengths and weaknesses. For this reason it was necessary for Iran to develop different, home-grown methods for confronting the enemy."[12] Back then, speed boats could carry mines, and since then the IRGC built up a naval base and began developing speed boats that could be retrofitted with a variety of weapons. Out of these experiments Iran's area denial doctrine was born.

Naval strategy of the Islamic republic

Like numerous states based on the Iranian plateau, the centerpiece of the Islamic Republic's naval strategy today is not power projection, but some minimal deterrence in the Persian Gulf, now in the form of area denial. Generally, the doctrine is understood to mean that in the event of hostilities, whether by sea, air, or land, Iran may block the Strait of Hormuz, a chokepoint for much of the world's energy supply. Iran would do this in large part by using some of the same swarming tactics it developed during the latter stages of the Iran-Iraq War. That is, small, fast boats would overwhelm larger ships and drop mines, use missiles, or even use explosives to engage in kamikaze missions.

This denial strategy offers two important benefits. First, given that around 30 percent of all seaborne crude and 30 percent of all liquefied natural gas[13] passes through the Strait of Hormuz on a given day, the mere threat of a campaign to block commercial shipping would impact global oil markets. That is, holding out the threat of disrupting the flow of oil, and with it, normal economic activity around globe, by itself offers a significant deterrent. Second, because Iran's main external threat comes in the form of U.S. military action, denial of access to the Gulf becomes a dominant strategy for blocking a foreign attack.[14] Eisenstadt and Paz write,

> For Iran, the principal threat of attack comes from the sea – in the form of U.S. carrier strike groups operating in the Persian Gulf and Gulf of Oman and U.S. bombers staging out of Diego Garcia in the Indian Ocean. Consistent with Iran's efforts to create a layered defense as part of its access-denial strategy in the Persian Gulf, the Islamic Republic has been working to enhance its ability to detect and interdict naval threats as far away as possible from the Strait of Hormuz and to counter possible U.S. "outside in" approaches using the Gulf of Oman as a springboard for operations inside the Persian Gulf.[15]

This area denial strategy is similar to that which China pursues along the Taiwan Strait and in the South China Sea. This strategy offers useful asymmetric components that limit the United States' ability to project power and intervene militarily. This is because, when pursued effectively, area denial can include, not only advanced conventional weaponry, but also guerrilla tactics (e.g., the "swarming" approach), along with political and informational "combat."[16] As such, area denial forces the United States to confront the possibility of incurring unacceptable levels of political, military, and economic costs for engaging in operations that, more often than not, would take place in the context of supporting friends and allies rather than protecting the American homeland or some other critical and immediate interest. In other words, area denial can make a war of choice less appealing.

For these reasons, the scope of Iran's deterrent power has to be assessed in the context, not only of the country's military assets, but also of the disruptive effect that any maritime confrontation between Iran and another state could have on the global economy.

Current naval capabilities

Iran's area denial strategy is supported by its maintenance of two distinct naval forces – the conventional Naval Force of the Islamic of Republic of Iran Army (*Niroo-ye Daryaee-ye Artesh-e Jomhuri-ye Eslami-ye Iran*) and the Naval Force of the Islamic Revolutionary Guard Corps (*Niroo-ye Daryaee-ye Sepah-e*

Pasdaran-e Enqelab-e Eslami). I refer to these two forces as the Iranian Navy and the IRGCN, respectively. While the Iranian Navy focuses on honing traditional maritime warfighting capacities, the IRGCN is focused on developing asymmetric capabilities in planning for potential confrontation with the United States and other actors.

This division between conventional and Islamic Revolutionary Guard Corps components mirrors the organization of Iran's military force on land. The conventional army, or *artesh*, is the conscripted force, while the Islamic Revolutionary Guard Corp (IRGC) is the all-volunteer praetorian entity tasked with guarding the regime and its ideology. Despite heavy losses during the Iran-Iraq War, the IRGC established its credibility in that period when it was responsible for some early tactical victories against Saddam Hussein's better trained military. For this reason, the land component of the IRGC has significantly more resources – though it also enjoys some self-reliance, given its significant footprint in the economy as owner of large conglomerates operating in the construction and research and development spheres.[17] The IRGC is also tasked with critical operations outside Iran's borders, from supporting the Iraqi and Syrian states against domestic insurgents and revolutionaries, to siphoning arms and cash to the Lebanese Hezbollah.

While the IRGC is clearly the elite fighting force on land, the maritime distribution of power between the two naval forces is not quite so lopsided. The Iranian Navy is considered one of the more professional fighting elements among all of the Iranian military establishments, and one that would be most effective in the context of a conventional war.[18] For this reason, research and development and overall funding is greater for the Navy than for the IRGCN. This funding gap is partly explained by doctrine, since the IRGCN's David vs. Goliath posture, including its reliance on swarming offensives by speed boats against large vessels, is by its nature less expensive.

This dual (rather than overlapping) strategic arrangement between the navy and the IRGCN followed a 2007 reorganization of the armed forces.[19] That reorganization reflected the new strategic landscape under which Iran found itself operating following the U.S. invasion of Iraq in 2003, when the United States was occupying two neighbors of Iran. Following is a brief overview of capabilities among the two forces.

IRGCN

Because the Revolutionary Guard is known, not only as a non-conscripted force, but also as a "true believer" corps, part of the IRGCN's deterrent capacity rests on the United States and other adversaries believing that suicide patrol boats and other similar, quick kamikaze style attacks would be difficult to deter or defend against. This reputation for doggedness and willingness of individuals to die in combat offers the IRGCN significant value relative to its procurement dollars.

The IRGCN's asymmetric doctrine was theoretically validated by the controversial Millennium '02 Challenge, a massive U.S. military exercise in which the red team, pretending to be a state similar to either Iran or Iraq, sank nearly an entire carrier group using surprise, boat-swarming tactics similar to those Iran is expected to use in the event of a real conflict. The exercise was later blasted by the red team commander and many others because the blue team's navy was made to miraculously resurface and the United States was essentially scripted to win the engagement. But the exercise itself proved useful in understanding how damaging relatively low-tech naval forces could be to the U.S. Navy. Michael Zenko recounts the exercise this way:

> Van Riper [the red team commander] decided that as soon as a U.S. Navy carrier battle group steamed into the Gulf, he would "preempt the preemptors" and strike first. Once U.S. forces were within range, Van Riper's forces unleashed a barrage of missiles from ground-based launchers, commercial ships, and planes flying low and without radio communications to reduce their radar signature. Simultaneously, swarms of speedboats loaded with explosives launched kamikaze attacks. The carrier battle group's Aegis radar system – which tracks and attempts to intercept incoming missiles – was quickly overwhelmed, and 19 U.S. ships were sunk, including the carrier, several cruisers, and five amphibious ships. "The whole thing was over in five, maybe ten minutes," Van Riper said.
>
> The red team had struck a devastating blow against the blue team. The impact of the OPFOR's ability to render a U.S. carrier battle group – the centerpiece of the U.S. Navy – militarily worthless stunned most of the MC '02 participants. Van Riper described the mood as "an eerie silence. Like people didn't really know what to do next." Blue team leader Bell admitted that the OPFOR had "sunk my damn navy," and had inflicted "an extremely high rate of attrition, and a disaster, from which we all learned a great lesson."[20]

The Iranian navy

While Iran's conventional navy plays an important role in Iran's Gulf-based area denial strategy, it is the force that has extended farther out beyond the Gulf and the Caspian Sea, and is engaged in amplifying Iran's blue-water presence and capabilities. Included in its domains are the Gulf of Oman, the Indian Ocean, the Arabian Sea, the Gulf of Aden, and the Red Sea, though it has ventured well beyond those waters for largely symbolic reasons, including to the Cape of Good Hope and the Pacific Ocean.

The Persian Gulf is a body of water that is vital to the world economy, and as such it is politically charged and teeming with naval power from various interested actors. This is in contrast with Iran's northern body of water, the Caspian Sea. While economically important for oil extraction and transportation, and also for caviar and other fishing, the Caspian does not carry the same hair-trigger characteristics as the Persian Gulf. This has to do in large part with the relations among the relevant states. Those with a Caspian shoreline are Iran, Azerbaijan, Russia, Kazakhstan, and Turkmenistan. Despite some disagreements with Azerbaijan over Iran's past support for Armenia, Iran has generally amicable relations with all involved, and it is not uncommon for the navies, in particular Russia, to make port calls at every state along the Caspian.[21]

Outside the Persian Gulf and the Caspian, the Iranian Navy's presence is generally limited to the Gulf of Oman, the Arabian Sea, and the Indian Ocean, as these complement a wider aperture of deterrence in support of area denial strategies. But there are uses for the Iranian Navy that go beyond area denial. Red Sea operations are a critical component of Iran's power projection efforts in the Middle East proper. In the Middle East, Iran's goals depend largely on proxy actors that are active in Iraq, Syria, and Lebanon, as well client groups in Palestine and Yemen. Iran's relationship with Hamas in Gaza, in particular, has required naval shipments, which usually pass through the Red Sea. For this Iran has used not only Sudan but increasingly also Eritrea, which has two naval bases (Massawa and Assab) where Iran has established a presence – in the case of Assaba, it's in the form of a permanent naval facility.[22] Weapons bound for Hamas can be transported to the Port of Sudan, and moved on land across Egypt and into Gaza.

Yemen is, of course, a critical component to Red Sea operations. In 2015 Houthi fighters took the island of Perim, on the Bab el-Mandeb Strait between Djibouti and Yemen.[23] As far as adopting an area denial strategy for the Red Sea by closing the Bab el-Mandeb Strait, capabilities are fewer than in the Strait of Hormuz. Beyond submarines and some mine-laying vessels, which include five minelayers and other ships that can be equipped with mines, Iran doesn't have the capability to send significant numbers of ships to the Red Sea.[24]

Balance of forces

While Iran has conducted joint naval exercises with China, along the Strait of Hormuz,[25] joint operations between Iran and China would not be expected in the event of a conflict between Iran and a regional or extra-regional state. This is in contrast to the states of the Gulf Cooperation Council (GCC), among whom at the very least Saudi Arabia and the United Arab Emirates would be expected to cooperate in any war against Iran. For this reason, it is important to compare Iran's forces to the totality of GCC militaries.

Iran's total naval forces, including the conventional navy, are listed on Table 11.1. These figures are taken from the Center for Strategic and International Studies (CSIS), which regularly publishes materials on the military balance in the Gulf.[26]

The balance of forces makes clear that Iran does not enjoy naval superiority vis-à-vis its neighbors, even if we were to discount a highly probable U.S. intervention in the event that hostilities were to break out between Iran and GCC states. The CSIS points out several limitations of Iran's military capabilities, which are relevant to understanding Iran's navy as well as its forces on land and in the air. For one, while Iran invests in research and development, many of the existing weapons in its arsenal are legacy systems dating back to the shah's era, and their reliability in combat would be questionable today. Second, international sanctions

Table 11.1 Balance of naval forces in the Persian Gulf

	Iran	GCC Combined	Saudi	Bahrain	Kuwait	Oman	Qatar	UAE
Support	50	38	21	2	2	6	2	5
Amphibious	17	2				1		1
Landing craft	11	63	16	9	4	5	1	28
Mine	5	9	7					2
Other patrol	108	182	70	6	42	42	16	6
Missile patrol	68	54	9	4	10	4	7	20
Corvettes	7	17	4	2		2		9
Frigates		8	4	1		3		
Destroyers		3	3					
Submarines	29	12				2		10

and Iran's pariah state status have led to a severe limitation of weapons imports compared to its neighbors. Iran further lacks the ability for sustained air-to-air and air-to-sea combat, which would be crucial for any naval confrontation in the Persian Gulf.

In short, Iran maintains a coherent naval doctrine of area denial, and this serves the purpose of making extra-regional powers think twice before engaging in direct military action against Iran. It would not, however, prevent a determined, combined force of GCC states and the United States from causing significant and lasting damage to Iran's naval forces in the event of a sustained conflict. For this reason, Iran depends on the lack of will on the part of both the United States and the GCC to successfully maintain its deterrent. Because the GCC is unlikely to be able to pull any unwilling state into a direct confrontation with Iran, the calculus remains this: So long as American leaders do not alter their threshold for intervention, or Iran does not engage in actions that significantly push the threat level past the existing threshold, Iran's naval deterrent will likely be sufficient to prevent military escalation.

Conclusion: Iran's capabilities at sea and beyond

Iran is not a great naval power, and like its predecessor states, it has come to rely heavily on the development of its land capabilities. It is on land where Iran-based states have staked most of their fortunes. For states based in Iran over the centuries, the "front porch" has been Iraq and the Levant, and the "back yard" has been Central Asia. While the Persian Gulf is important, maritime power has not been high on the strategic agenda for Iran-based states for at least 2,000 years. When Iran-based states have attempted to develop their naval capabilities, they have often done so in an already crowded field, especially after the rise of European expansionism since Early Modern times.

Despite its deficit of military prowess, the Islamic Republic of Iran has been relatively successful in investing in research and development projects that get the most deterrent capacity with the lowest cost. Iran's missile program, its secret and geographically dispersed nuclear program, and the development of its speed boat swarm tactics starting with the Iran-Iraq War, have all arguably inspired significant restraint on the part of both neighbors and extra-regional powers.

Iran's deterrent capability, however, does not rest fully on its armaments, which are ultimately limited in reach, quantity, and destructive power. Iran's deterrence instead leans heavily on several political and strategic considerations. One important consideration is Iran's ability to disrupt oil flow and increase oil prices significantly in the event of a war. It may be that some Gulf neighbors would reach that threshold of risk tolerance much sooner than American leaders. This plays to Iran's favor, since politically the GCC depends in large part on America's favor for weapons procurement and political support. Second, Iran "owns" much of the ground in Syria and Iraq, through its strong ties to the governments there, which will continue to depend significantly on Iranian military and financial support to counter anti-government insurgencies, not only from the Islamic State but from other Sunni groups, present and future.

Through its proxies Iran also has significant influence over Lebanon – the Iranian-backed Hezbollah group is currently the most effective and best armed fighting force in the country, and it is understood that they could successfully challenge the country's military if they so chose. These strategic realities, arguably more so than Iran's naval, land, and missile forces, form the backbone of Iran's deterrent. This is because a naval confrontation between Iran's forces and any neighbor or extra-regional power could have long-term impacts felt well outside the immediate field of operations. As such, the main source of power for the Islamic Republic remains on land, as it has for Iran-based states in decades and centuries past.

Notes

1. Catullo Stecchini, n.d.
2. Daryaee, 2016.
3. Ibid.
4. Michael Axworthy, "Nader Shah and Persian Naval Expansion in the Persian Gulf, 1700–1747," *Journal of the Royal Asiatic Society* 21/1 (2011): p. 32.
5. Ibid.
6. See Stephanie Cronin, *The Making of Modern Iran: State and Society under Riza Shah, 1921–1941* (London: Routledge, 2003).
7. Some of Iran's stated aspirations under the last shah were ambitious. A declassified CIA document from February 2, 1979 – following a year of revolutionary protests and some two weeks after the shah had already left the country – paraphrased Prime Minister Shaphour Bakhtiar claiming Iran would "no longer be the policeman of the Persian Gulf, let alone attempt to become a 'superpower.'" See "Military Weekly Review – Iran," Central Intelligence Agency, National Foreign Assessment Center (February 2, 1979): p. 2.
8. Erdbrink, 2012.
9. Mobley, 2003.
10. Zatarain, 2008.
11. O'Rourke, 1988.

12 The article is from the Iranian military forum military.ir, comprising current and former members of the Iranian armed forces. See King Kaveh, n.d.
13 U.S. Energy Information Administration, 2017.
14 For a critique on the "area denial" term, see Farley, 2016.
15 Eisenstadt and Paz, 2014.
16 For a discussion on the asymmetry and costs of area denial, see Freier, 2012.
17 Hen-Tov and Gonzalez, 2011.
18 Himes, 2011.
19 Ibid., p. 11.
20 Zenko, 2015.
21 Hamshahri Online, 2017a (12 July).
22 Fargher, 2017.
23 Ibid.
24 Ibid.
25 Hamshahri Online, 2017b (18 June).
26 Cordesman and Toukan, 2016, p. 128.

References

Axworthy, Michael. 2011. Nader Shah and Persian Naval Expansion in the Persian Gulf, 1700–1747. *Journal of the Royal Asiatic Society*, 21(1).
Catullo Stecchini, Livo. (n.d.). *The Size of the Persian Fleet*. [online] Iranian Military History: The Achaemenid Dynasty: An Analysis of Herodotus in The Persian Wars, The Circle of Ancient Iranian Studies.
Central Intelligence Agency. 1979. *Military Weekly Review – Iran*. National Foreign Assessment Center. 2 February.
Cordesman Anthony H., and Abdullah Toukan. 2016. *Iran and the Gulf Military Balance*. Center for Strategic and International Studies, Published Working Draft (Slides). 3 October 3.
Cronin, Stephanie. 2003. *The Making of Modern Iran; State and Society under Riza Shah, 1921–1941*. London: Routledge.
Daryaee, Touraj. 2016. The Sasanian 'Mare Nostrum': The Persian Gulf. *International Journal of the Society of Iranian Archeologists*, 2(3).
Eisenstadt Michael, and Alon Paz. 2014. *Iran's Evolving Military Presence*. Policy Watch, 2224. The Washington Institute for Near East Policy. 13 March.
Erdbrink, Thomas. 2012. A Tiny Island Is Where Iran Makes a Stand. *The New York Times* 30 April.
Fargher, James. 2017. *'This Presence Will Continue Forever': An Assessment of Iranian Naval Capabilities in the Red Sea*. Center for International Maritime Security. 5 April 5.
Farley, Robert. 2016. A2/AD Is Dead, Long Live A2/AD. *The Diplomat*. 11 October.
Freier, Nathan. 2012. *The Emerging Anti-Access/Area-Denial Challenge*. Center for Strategic and International Studies. 17 May.
Hamshahri Online. 2017a. *Lozm-e eqtedaar-e niroo-ye daryaee-ye keshvarhaa-ye khaashie-ye khazar bara-ye tosi'e-he amniat-e paaydaar*. (There is a need for the states on the Caspian shore to develop a security cooperation). 21 Tir, 1396 (12 July).
———. 2017b. *Tamreen-e moshtarak-e naavha-ye niroo-ye daryaee-ye artesh-e Iran va Chin aghaaz shod*. (Joint exercise of the [Iran Navy] and China began). 28 Khordad, 1396 (18 June).
Hen-Tov, Elliot, and Nathan Gonzalez. 2011. The Militarization of Post-Khomeini Iran: Praetorianism 2.0. *The Washington Quarterly*, 34(1).

Himes, Joshua., 2011. *Iran's Two Navies: A Maturing Maritime Strategy*. Middle East Security Report, 1. Institute for the Study of War.

King Kaveh. n.d. *Khalij-e Fars: Laaneh-e zanboorha-ye tondro-ye daryaee-ye Iran* (The Persian Gulf: Nest of Iran's Fast Naval Bees), Military.ir.

Mobley, Richard., 2003. Deterring Iran, 1968–81: The Royal Navy, Iran, and the Disputed Persian Gulf Islands. *Naval War College Review*, 56(4).

O'Rourke, Ronald. 1988. *The Tanker War*. Proceedings Magazine. U.S. Naval Institute, 114(5).

U.S. Energy Information Administration. 2017. *Three Important Oil Trade Chokepoints Are Located Around the Arabian Peninsula*. 4 August.

Zatarain, Lee Allen. 2008. *Tanker War: America's First Conflict with Iran, 1987–1988*. Philadelphia, Casemate.

Zenko, Michael. 2015. *Millennium Challenge: The Real Story of a Corrupted Military Exercise and Its Legacy*. War on the Rocks. 5 November.

12 The Arab Gulf States

Contemporary maritime perspectives, interests, objectives, and policies in the Gulf Cooperation Council

Joseph A. Kéchichian

Introduction

Over the centuries, and long before the discovery of oil, the Arabian Peninsula was caught in the whirlwind of permanent geo-strategic confrontations. Three chokepoints, the Strait of Hormuz that separated the peninsula from Iran, Bab el-Mandeb that isolated it from the African continent and, after it was inaugurated in 1869, the Suez Canal in Egypt that opened a waterway into the Mediterranean, effectively determined the fate of Arab nations caught in the vagaries of isolation and poverty. Overcoming serious environmental challenges, the peoples of the Peninsula survived, though observers mistakenly assumed they lacked strengths as few intruders ventured deep in the heart of the Peninsula to find out. When confronted by larger encroaching naval forces like the Portuguese, the French, and the British, coastal Arab powers retreated. To be sure, and while Arab navies suffered against superior fleets, most Arabian Peninsula tribes maintained minimum standing naval forces in the Gulf or the Red Sea though Omani sailors reached China and, in a quirk of history often overlooked by historians, provided the captain who navigated Vasco da Gama and his Portuguese ships that sailed through the Cape of Good Hope in 1498.[1] Notwithstanding such accomplishments, Arab maritime prowess was limited not because of any shortcomings in capabilities, but simply because of land trade preferences. Even conquering Ottomans were far more interested in overland commercial routes instead of developing naval capabilities, which explained their limited deployments or successes against the Portuguese.[2] Ottoman weaknesses were further demonstrated when Constantinople, then at the height of its military strength, "exposed Egypt to invasion by Napoleon in 1798," which was carefully noted by both Persian as well as Arab societies along the Red Sea, and inside the Gulf.[3]

Intruding into the area starting in the early 1800s to defend perceived interests, especially to secure land, naval and air links to the Empire's Crown Jewel, India, the British fought and occupied both shores of the Arabian/Persian Gulf. Determined to rule the seas, London expelled the Portuguese from Hormuz, consolidated Bandar Abbas as a pivotal trade center that brought Iran under its influence, fought the powerful Qawasim in 1809 ostensibly to end piracy in the Lower Gulf, and otherwise controlled the entire region to impose supremacy.[4] Although British historians coined the term "Pax Britannica" to justify imperialism – which lasted until 1971 in the Gulf region when London did not even build a hospital to look after the sick – it was the intruder that enjoyed military might and could, consequently, threaten indigenous populations with serious harm unless they submitted. Few realized that oil resources would alter every imaginable calculation that, combined with the legitimacy of the nation-state system, ushered in empires of wealth. Nevertheless, and despite unprecedented riches that transformed the peoples of the area, traditions endured, cultural attributes persisted, and significant internal development concerns were overcome. Two principal matters remained constant, as the autonomy of rulers and the presence of foreign powers persevered.

Led by Saudi Arabia, which restored its Third Monarchy in 1932, the Sultanate of Oman that regained its sovereignty in 1970, and the Shaykhoms of Kuwait (1960), Bahrain (1971), Qatar (1971) and the United Arab Emirates (1971), Arab Gulf States gradually honed in on their interests, objectives and policies. All six surmounted genuine internal, regional and international challenges and, notwithstanding foreign domination, entered into alliances that ensured socio-political survival. Over time, British regional hegemony was replaced by American suzerainty, even if Arab rulers were slow to settle differences, delineate their respective territories, and introduce national and supra-national loyalties. Regrettably, the advent of the modern nation-state, and the growing importance of clearly delineated boundaries to outline the possession of natural resources, kindled dormant territorial disputes that outsiders manipulated at will. Among the more controversial was the Buraymi dispute that allowed Britain to interfere in Arab internal affairs.

Still, and gradually, the six monarchies set most of their differences aside, acknowledged the necessity to cooperate with partners, devised short- and long-term security pacts, and otherwise empowered themselves with appropriate governance tools. Their efforts were not flawless and many opportunities for nasty confrontations lingered. In fact, few outsiders appreciated the serious consequences of the 1979 Soviet invasion and occupation of Afghanistan, followed successively by the spillover effects of the Iranian Revolution (1979), the eight-year long Iran-Iraq War (1980–88), the Iraqi invasion and occupation of Kuwait (1990), the Shaykhdom's U.N.-sanctioned and U.S.-led liberation (1991), the War for Afghanistan (2001–), the War for Iraq (2003–11), and the post-2011 Arab uprisings, all of which marked every Arab society as the conservative Arab Gulf monarchies skillfully adjusted. By 1981, the six conservative Arab monarchies mustered the political will to finally create a regional security alliance, even if the Gulf Cooperation Council (GCC) did not live up to its founders' expectations, chiefly because Gulf rulers mistrusted each other. It took nearly three decades of painstaking work to equip and train indigenous personnel, though it fell on the courageous King 'Abdallah bin 'Abdul 'Aziz (r. 2005–15) – who, in 2011, called for the transformation of the alliance into a full-fledged union – to finally break the proverbial camel's back, and cajole GCC rulers to end their bickering.[5]

What finally prompted Riyadh to assume the heavy burdens of power-politics was the rise of Iran as a regional hegemon, determined to deny Saudi Arabia a primacy in Arab and Muslim affairs by virtue of its intrinsic capabilities, leadership role among Arab populations, as well as the Custodianship of the Holy Mosques that bestowed enviable legitimacy.

Of course, and while Iran was not the sole threat to the stability of the GCC member-states, it nevertheless displaced Iraq as revolutionary leaders voiced satisfaction for their putative dominion over four Arab capitals. Even more boldly, several called directly, or indirectly through acolytes like the Lebanese Hezballah militia chief Hassan Nasrallah, for the removal of all Arab monarchs. Worse yet, Tehran associated GCC rulers with the United States along with the latter's alleged imperial controls of the monarchies, whose purported "surrender" gave Iran the right to oppose them. Unabashed, Tehran rejected Western deployments in the Gulf, and periodically clashed with the U.S. Navy, though its primary targets were GCC rulers. Under the circumstances, it was fair to ask what were the contemporary perspectives, interests, objectives and policies of the GCC States to deal with this major regional threat?

To better address this fundamental question, what follows is divided into four sections, all concentrating on maritime issues, even if demographic limitations pushed GCC States to favor air forces above both land and naval capabilities. The section first addresses past clashes and hones on key threats, before it dwells in the second part on major recent controversies, including the Iranian occupation of three strategically located UAE islands, Tehran's claims on Bahrain, and various clashes that involved both indigenous and Western navies. In the third section, the essay focuses on GCC naval capabilities and analyzes planning efforts before concluding with key strategic developments regarding coastal security, countermeasures against piracy and steps taken to deal with the Iranian threat, including the latest crisis with the State of Qatar.

Maritime clashes and key threats

Long before GCC States and Iran clashed over various regional contentious maritime disputes, a series of violent confrontations occurred between local actors, dating back to the sixteenth and seventeenth centuries. Reza Shah Pahlavi acceded to the Iranian throne in 1921, and though he was forced by the British to abdicate in favor of his son Muhammad Reza in 1941, the former Cossack soldier revived Persian claims to a number of islands in the Lower Gulf. Like his son, and revolutionary successors after the 1979 Revolution, Reza understood the strategic and economic importance of the Strait of Hormuz, and sought to control as much of the waterway as possible. Early on, he authorized the building of a naval capability that could challenge the British domination of the Gulf region, which was accomplished by 1927. A year later, he occupied the island of Hinjam, and began to antagonize inhabitants of several smaller islands.[6] Between 1929 and 1939, Tehran and London negotiated over the three strategically located Abu Musa, the Greater Tunb, and the Lesser Tunb islands, though without success. World War II, and the allied victory that followed, tamed the Shah as claims lingered.

What revived them was the 1968 British announcement to withdraw its military forces from east of Suez by the end of 1971. In a moment of hubris, Iranian ambitions surfaced in Bahrain (see as follows) as well as in Sharjah and Ras al-Khaimah, which alarmed Kuwait – itself the target of similar ambitions on the Warbah and Bubiyan islands, albeit from Iraq – and Saudi Arabia, because both feared that Iranian and Iraqi expansions, fueled by the Cold War between the Soviet Union and the United States, would engulf the area in fresh conflicts. Ironically, while the pro-Western Shah was a fellow monarch with whom Arab Gulf rulers could do business, few approved of his designation as the "policeman" of the West in the Gulf, or of the 1969 Richard Nixon/Henry Kissinger "Twin Pillar" policy to build up Iran and Saudi Arabia as local powers that could protect the region from the spread of Soviet influence.[7]

Alert to the growing dependence on oil, along with the limitations of the "Nixon Doctrine," the shah wasted no time to build-up Iran's military capabilities, including advanced naval assets that originated in the United States, most of which Washington destroyed in the last two decades of the twentieth century. As discussed below, the United States launched *Operation Praying Mantis* on 18 April 1988, attacking numerous Iranian targets in retaliation for Tehran's use of sea mines during the Iran-Iraq war, and repeatedly clashed with the Iranian Navy.[8] GCC States were often caught in the middle of these violent exchanges, though their interests dictated that they side with Washington.

Major recent controversies

The dispute over the Bubiyan and Warbah Islands was a key point of contention in the lengthy history of territorial conflicts between Iraq and Kuwait. In 1961, when the United Kingdom ended its protectorate over the Shaykhdom, then Iraqi Prime Minister General 'Abdul Karim Qasim asserted that Kuwait was an "integral part of Iraq" because it had been part of the former Ottoman province of Basrah, which returned to Iraq when the latter was created on 3 October 1932. Qasim threatened to occupy Kuwait but was deterred when London dispatched Marines that stayed for a few months before they were replaced by a League of Arab States peacekeeping force under the command of a Saudi officer. The Iraqis finally recognized Kuwaiti independence in 1963, though the Ba'ath regime never relinquished its claims, nor did it agree to settle on a common boundary between the two countries.[9]

After Kuwait rejected Iraqi debts that were accumulated during the 1980–88 Iran-Iraq War, Saddam Husayn reignited the dormant conflict over Warbah and Bubiyan Islands, which Baghdad considered vital to secure its access from the Gulf to its port on the Khawr 'Abdallah inlet. In fact, the waterway to the Gulf remained the only viable alternative to the closed Shatt Al-'Arab, cluttered with sunken ships and other debris from the previous war. It was not long before Baghdad, which was caught in the throes of a substantial postwar economic crisis, accused Kuwait and the United Arab Emirates of financial strangulation, allegedly by pumping additional oil and depressing prices that, in turn, hurt Iraq. Husayn invaded Kuwait in 1990 and was defeated in 1991. In November 1994, a weak and dependent Republic of Iraq formally accepted the U.N.-demarcated border with Kuwait, which were spelled out in three separate United National Security Council Resolutions – 687 (1991), 773 (1992), and 833 (1993) – that formally ended claims to Bubiyan and Warbah, even if subsequent regional developments raised questions about the longevity of said boundaries that were, it is worth repeating, imposed by a foreign power.[10]

Similar efforts were earlier exerted by the United Kingdom as it attempted to find common ground with Iran. Starting in the early parts of the twentieth century, and unable to resolve territorial disputes between Iran and the Arab Shaykhdoms most notably over Bahrain and key UAE islands, British authorities could only persuade the U.N. to create a commission to review and settle that particular dispute, hoping that Tehran would eventually do the right thing with Sharjah and Ras al-Khaimah. London was lucky in the first instance but unsuccessful in the second and while Iran reluctantly agreed to divest itself of Bahrain in 1970, its military actions a year later created a deep divide with the UAE, one that lingers to present times.

Tehran's claims to Bahrain

Iran believed that Bahrain was part of the Persian Empire and though it ceded the island to Portugal in the seventeenth century, it asserted that the Al Khalifah themselves confirmed their links to Tehran as they accepted Persian suzerainty. The Al Khalifah, who migrated from the Qatar promontory around 1783, sided with Persia during the last few years of the nineteenth century, even if such backing was the result of anti-British sentiments rather than pro-Iranian affinities. When Iran inaugurated its Parliament after the 1905 Revolution, it specifically allocated two seats to Bahrain, insisting that the archipelago was its "14th province."[11] What passed for British diplomacy in the late 1960s, however, lucked out as London secured Saudi assistance to intercede with Manama and Tehran, after the late King Faysal bin 'Abdul 'Aziz persuaded the Al Khalifah as well as the Shah to allow the United Nations committee to determine where sovereignty lay. Even if he cared less about what the people of Bahrain wanted, the Shah accepted the U.N. referendum proposal – which affirmed that the vast majority wanted independence – because King Faysal proposed a Gulf security conference, which he, the Shah, was resolute to lead. Ironically, and just before the conference could take place, Iranian maritime forces invaded and occupied the three islands of Abu Musa and the Greater and Lesser Tunbs on 30 November 1971.[12]

Iranian occupation of UAE Islands

Analysts concluded that after accepting Bahrain's independence a year earlier, Muhammad Reza Shah was indomitable in his quest to lead or, at least, not to emerge empty-handed from the British withdrawal from east of Suez. In the event, Abu Musa and the two Tunb islands were ruled by members of the Qawasim tribe, which also ruled on the Persian side of the Strait of Hormuz starting in the fourteenth century. In fact, this was the very basis of long-standing Iranian claims that the islands actually belonged to Iran because the Qawasim were indigenous to Persian lands and thus were part and parcel of the Persian Empire. Moreover, and though the British rebuffed Persian attempts to occupy several additional islands in 1881 and again in 1904, the larger Lingeh and Kish islands, which were once also under Qawasim control, were ceded to Tehran. By the late 1960s, however, what mattered was the possibility of oil fields in territorial waters, which was the overwhelming reason why the Shah ordered the 30 November 1971 occupation, conveniently scheduled for the day before the Lower Gulf Shaykhdoms gained their independence from Britain. Whether London knew about Muhammad Reza's actions and chose not to object is the subject of vociferous debate, though without military forces on Abu Musa to defend his territory, the ruler of Sharjah quickly signed an agreement with Iran that, ostensibly, allowed Sharjah to retain sovereignty. It was apparently agreed that while Iranian forces would be stationed at a designated location and Sharjah would receive an annual financial aid of 1.5 million pounds sterling for 9 years, the accord granted the Shaykhdom the right to fly its own flag over government buildings, support its remaining citizens living on the island, jointly explore for oil and gas and share income from all onshore as well as offshore resources.[13]

Ironically, Iran recognized the independence of the UAE, though its occupation stood as a shocking setback for ties with Saudi Arabia and, of course, the other Arab Gulf monarchies. What followed was an open arms race, as sensitive Iranian-GCC relations fueled military expansionism. Iran further exacerbated the islands dispute in 1992 when it refused entry to nonnative-born Arab residents, including teachers, health workers, and technicians, unless they first applied for and received Iranian visas. After 1981, it was worth underscoring, Abu Dhabi routinely sought, and received, GCC States' collective backing. Alliance members repeatedly reaffirmed their commitments with one of the more significant such avowals coming in early April 2012, when GCC States formally opposed Iranian President Mahmud Ahmadinajad's visit to Abu Musa. They insisted that the unauthorized trip was a violation of UAE sovereignty.[14]

Although no GCC ruler believed that Tehran would even consider requesting authorization to visit the occupied territory, the mere fact that this issue was brought up highlighted, once again, the super-sensitive nature of the matter. Final GCC Summit communiqués always referred to the UAE Islands, and called on Iran to end its occupation, which Tehran routinely ignored, while GCC rulers were not ready to respond militarily.

North Dome settlement

If the UAE Islands conquests poisoned Iranian-GCC ties, an equally troubling concern was the semi-settled border delineation with Qatar over the South Pars/ North Dome gas field that sits in the middle of the Gulf. As the world's largest gas field, estimated to hold 1,800 trillion cubic feet (or 51 trillion cubic meters) of natural gas and at least 50 billion barrels (7.9 billion cubic meters) of gas condensates and oil products, the field is coveted by both countries though 3,700 square kilometers (1,400 square miles) is in Iranian territorial waters and 6,000 square kilometers (2,300 square miles) falls in Qatari waters. Given this incredible wealth, contentions remained high as Doha accused Tehran of producing more natural gas from the giant field. According to Iranian media sources, Qatar currently produces 40 percent more natural gas from the joint field, which Doha denies.[15] It was unclear how differences between the two neighboring countries would be resolved though GCC States remained wary of Iranian intentions. Moreover, and in light of the latest crisis with Qatar (see as follows), it was unclear how Doha would react to future Iranian encroachments on its wealth, even if it does not seem to worry about such an outcome over the short-term.

GCC naval capabilities[16]

Even if they wanted to, Gulf Cooperation Council States' military capabilities were not strong enough to respond to Iranian incursions, without robust outside assistance. Relatively young countries, and suffering from manpower and equipment shortfalls, GCC military deficiencies were all too real even if gargantuan efforts were underway to rectify them. In fact, the proposal to boost the Peninsula Shield force, which is the Council's combined military arm, was excruciatingly slow to assemble. While the force could technically reach the 100,000 level before the end of 2017, the current 40,000 soldiers assigned to it experienced serious "jointness" problems, which could – at least technically – benefit from an expansion. Of course, the Shield was primarily a land force with a very powerful air arm, even if what was sorely needed were strong maritime units that could defend the long coasts along the Arabian Gulf as well as the Red Sea. It was critical to also note that the GCC force that deployed into Bahrain in the aftermath of the 2011 uprising in that kingdom, was chiefly composed of land units, even if Kuwait rushed several naval vessels to patrol Bahraini waters. At the time, the decision to expand the "Shield" was reached to counter Iran "and its subversive terrorist elements across the GCC" States, a constatation that was confirmed ever since because of the wars in Iraq, Syria and Yemen. What were GCC States' naval capabilities and were there any plans to expand them?

Royal Bahrain naval force

The Bahrain Defense Forces (BDF) are relatively limited and number less than 8,500 personnel. While its largest component, the Royal Bahraini Army (RBA), are the ground forces that stand at approximately 6,000 enlisted men and officers, followed by the Royal Bahraini Air Force (RBAF, formerly known as Bahrain Amiri Air Force) with about 1,500 personnel, the Royal Bahrain Naval Force (RBNF), the maritime branch of the BDF, is the smallest part with only 700 sailors under the command of Lieutenant Commander Yusuf al-Ma'luallah.[17]

In an effort to upgrade its defenses, Bahrain welcomed a GCC assistance package starting in 1982, when the Riyadh-based regional alliance allocated $10 billion spread over a decade to help improve Manama's defenses. Bahrain's defense spending since 1999 grew steadily and was estimated at $1.53 billion in 2015. Joint naval, air and ground exercises were conducted with allied forces to increase readiness throughout the Arabian Gulf and the RBNF, which consists of 11 combat vessels, 22 patrol craft, most of which are at the Mina Sulman Naval Base, operated a flight wing of two MBB BO-105 helicopters off its corvettes. The flagship of the RBNF is the vessel RBNS *Sabha*, an American-built Oliver Hazard Perry-class missile frigate given to the country as a gift from the United States in 1996. Bahrain and the United States signed a Defense Cooperation Agreement in October 1991, granting U.S. forces access to Bahraini facilities and ensuring the right to pre-position materiel for future crises. In 2003 Washington designated Bahrain as a major non-NATO ally of the United States and, since 2003, allocated over $100 million in Foreign Military Funding to pay for various high-profile weapons systems, including an AN/TPS-59(v)3B Early Warning Radar, Large Aircraft Counter-InfraRed Measures, Air-to-Air Missile Avoidance System for the King's plane, as well as several other equally sophisticated systems.[18]

In response to increased Soviet naval activities in the Gulf region throughout the second half of the twentieth century, Western forces, but especially the United States, increased their military presence in the area too. Although much attention was invariably focused on the small Middle East Force deployed on Bahrain, which eventually went through several permutations and grew into the 5th Fleet, ties between Manama and Washington was significantly strengthened in recent years. A long-standing American assistance program contributed directly to the U.S. Government's effort to maintain security in the Arabian Gulf, as Bahrain was the only Arab state to have led one of the Coalition Task Forces that patrolled the Gulf. It even offered to sail its flagship in support of the coalition counter-piracy mission. In turn, U.S. assistance helped Bahrain, which lacked the oil wealth of its neighbors, to obtain the equipment and training it needed to operate alongside U.S. air and naval forces.

The Kuwait naval force

Although Kuwait established its first naval base in 1975, a small Navy was created in 1961 with British assets, which were donated to the country after London pulled its forces out. The Shaykhdom purchased additional equipment, including the Hawk surface-to-air missile system before the 1990 Iraqi invasion and occupation that devastated it, though everything changed after the U.N.-sanctioned and U.S.-led 1991 war. Ironically, the Al Sabah ruling family's balancing acts between Arab commitments and Western alliances before 1990, which led many to conclude that Kuwait was the least pro-Western Arab monarchy, were royally abandoned after liberation, as the Al Sabah changed their calculations.

Interestingly, Kuwaitis were almost always aware of the inadequacy of the Shaykhdom's naval assets, as several of its islands were bombed by both Iran and

Iraq during the war. Consequently, and as soon as the GCC alliance was set-up in May 1981, joint naval exercises were conducted between Kuwait and Saudi Arabia precisely to protect northern Gulf waters where Iran and Iraq spread havoc to shipping lanes. In 1982, Kuwait acquired short-range tactical surface-to-air missiles and ordered several naval warships, aware that the Iran – Iraq War, which devastated the area during eight tense years, would inevitably spillover. In fact, the "Tanker War" that pitted antagonists and forced Kuwait to reflag its ships under the Stars and Stripes, attracted much international attention and some U.S. intervention and, as a result, Kuwait was caught in the middle of glorified gamesmanship. When Iran blocked Iraqi oil exports through the vital Shatt al-'Arab waterway that delineated the border between the two adversaries, and as the war turned against the Iraqis, Kuwait authorized the use of its ports to supply Baghdad. The Shaykhdom, along with Qatar, Saudi Arabia and the UAE, provided substantial financial aid to Iraq that, by some estimates, topped the $60 billion mark.[19] Few realized it at the time but Kuwait's substantial assistance to Baghdad proved futile, as Saddam Husayn pounced on the hapless country at the first opportunity.

Kuwait's navy was almost completely destroyed in 1990 when Iraqi forces captured and sank five Kuwaiti Lurssen TNC 45 type fast-attack missile boats, one Lurssen FPB 57 type fast-attack craft, and about 20 smaller vessels. These were replaced after liberation as several new vessels were ordered, including eight 245-tons *La Combattante*-class Missile Fast Patrol Boats, a TNC-45 along an FPB-57 missile crafts, and about 100 light patrol fighting ships. Plans for the acquisition of several landing crafts, including two 64 meters, one 42 meters and five 16 meters composite landing vessels were under way, all of which were scheduled to be built at ADSB's facilities in the Mussafah industrial area in the UAE. Notwithstanding the equipment replenishment program, in 2017, the Kuwait Naval Force consisted of approximately 2,500 officers and enlisted personnel, including 500 in the Coast Guard, which meant that it was the smallest service (an additional 15,500 men were active in the army, 2,500 in the air force and 7,100 served in paramilitary units). The Navy was under the Command of Jassim Al Ansari seconded by Commander Mansur Al Mas'ad.[20]

Royal navy of Oman

Before 1970, the Omani navy was just a wing known as the "Inshore Patrols Unit" under the *Oman Gendarmerie*, which fielded several pre-1960s made wooden boats (known in Arabic as *dhows*, the plural of *dhow*) for inshore patrol tasks alongside the Batinah coastline to stop smuggling and illegal immigration. In 2017, the RNO fielded 4,200 sailors and operated three primary surface combatants, British-built corvettes.

Notwithstanding its seafaring traditions, naval assets were rudimentary in 1960 when the Sultanate was still a British Protectorate. At the time, a royal ship was commissioned, though the *Al Sa'id* was also used for military purposes during the Dhuffar war. The Sultan of Oman Navy came into existence in 1970 and acquired its first three fast patrol boats in 1973, when the SNO moved to the Sultan bin

Ahmad Naval Base at Khawr Al-Mukallah in Muscat, though the country's naval headquarters were moved in 1988 to the Sa'id bin Sultan Naval Base (SBSNB) in Musannah. The SNO acquired two minesweepers in 1975, which underwent modifications to operate as regular patrol boats. The fleet was then supplied with three landing crafts, with a modern training center established in Sur in 1978. Starting in the early 1980s, several additional landing crafts were acquired, while modifications were made to the *Al Sa'id* that was renamed *Al Mabrukah*, to operate as an inshore patrol vessel along with an officers' training ship. Over the course of 1983 and 1984, three fast-attack missile boats joined the fleet (*Dhuffar*, *Al Sharqiyyah* and *Al Batinah*), while the Musandam Naval Base was formally inaugurated in 1986. A new Royal vessel, the *Musandam*, entered service in 1989.[21]

On 16 June 1990, Sultan Qabus bin Sa'id Al Sa'id changed the title of the navy to the Royal Navy of Oman (RNO), and introduced the fast gun-boats *Al Bushrah*, *Al Mansur* and *Al Najah* in 1995 and 1996, followed by *Qahir Al Amwaj* and *Al Mu'azar* in 1996 and 1997, respectively. On 15 January 2007, the Kharif [Autumn] project was launched to acquire three corvettes, *Al Shamikh*, *Al Rahmani* and *Al Rasikh*, which were delivered in June 2013, October 2013, and June 2014, respectively. An additional three inshore patrol vessels were ordered in 2012 along with the building of a second training vessel, the *Shabab Oman 2*, which was officially launched in April 2014 and delivered in Holland in September 2014. Interestingly, the Netherlands was approached for a vast new project, this one known as Bahr Oman [Sea of Oman], which was programmed to build two defense support ships for fast deployment and search and rescue operations. Finally, the RNO, led by Admiral 'Abdallah bin Khamis Al Rai'si (who was appointed to his post in February 2008), is working on the establishment of a new Sutlan Qabus Naval Base in the Southern Dhuffar Governorate that abuts the Indian Ocean.

Remarkably, the RON boasts a small but well-equipped force and fields a National Hydrographic Office, which serves all GCC States, and has an eye on critical environmental matters. It is the only GCC Navy that is producing navigational charts, prepares studies on depth data, takes seabed images, collects tidal and water currents, analyzes the seabed composition and type and component of seabed sediments, establishes sunken ship information, designs navigational aids and signs for distribution to interested parties, provides salinity and temperature figures, evaluates seismic, gravity and magnetic data, creates geodetic control station points, draws topographic features, delineates beach and port borders, and provides the kind of additional information that may assist civilian meteorological services to study and anticipate sea floods, tsunamis and other natural disasters. By any measure, these tasks are truly exceptional and, at least in the GCC countries, unique contributions to military sciences that also benefit society at large.[22]

Qatar Amiri navy

Admittedly, the Qatari Navy is very small, with less than 2,000 sailors, which includes an even smaller Coast Guard for a country that has a 350-mile (563 kilometer) coastline. Until very recently, the undermanned navy, including its marine police force and coastal defense artillery, were restricted to antiquated naval bases though a major decision was reached after 1990 to revamp the entire institution. Under the command of Commodore Muhammad Nasir al-Muhannadi, the Qatar Navy operated out of its Doha headquarters as well as from Halul Island, located about 62 miles (100 km) northeast of the capital city. Although Halul serves as a storage area as well as a loading terminal for oil from the surrounding offshore fields, its ideal location remains indispensable for the Navy.

The Navy's current assets are limited to 12 patrol and coastal combatants, including four Vosper patrol boats (120 tons), four armed Vosper Thornycroft Vita-class fast attack craft (480 tons, each carrying eight MM40 Exocet missiles and eight Mistral SAMs), three armed *La Combattante* III Fast Attack Craft (430 tonnes, also with eight MM40 Exocets missiles), and a single 76mm Goalkeeper. In addition, there are assorted boats for various duties, including 6 Vosper 110 ft. class PCs, 6 Damen Polycat PCs, 2 Keith Nelson type 44 ft. class PCs, 2 Fairey Marine Interceptor class PCs, 4 MV-45 class PCs, 25 Fairy Marine Spear PCs, 5 P-1500 class PCs, 4 DV-15 class PCs, 3 Helmatic M-160 class PCs, and 1 Robha class Landing craft capable of carrying three MBTs, 100 men as well as their equipment. The Qatari Special Maritime Forces operates 11 fast interceptor boats, and there are a variety of missiles available, including Exocets and Mistral SAMs. Inasmuch as these are largely inadequate for a small-size power entrusted with the defense of a long coastline in the middle of the Arabian Gulf, Doha plans for future acquisitions, including six new patrol boats and at least four corvettes from The Netherlands.[23]

In fact, the Qatar Coast Guard Services placed an order for 17 new fast patrol boats in 2012 from the Turkish company ARES Shipyard, that were slated for completion and delivery by 2015 though it was unclear whether these deliveries were completed by late-2017. Interestingly, in 2010 the government created the Nakilat Damen Shipyards Qatar (NDSQ), a joint venture company between Nakilat, the world's leading transporter of liquefied natural gas (LNG), and Damen, a Dutch global leader in shipbuilding. NDSQ is located at the port of Ras Laffan in the northeastern corner of Qatar and its primary purpose is to construct vessels at Qatar's premier shipyard. At a later stage, investors envisage to transform the company into a commercially viable stand-alone enterprise to build sophisticated state-of-the-art naval ships for export. Although no decisions were announced for the corvette program by mid-2016, the project is due in the near-term as well, though it is possible that construction may be delayed for several more years as Damen/Nakilat gains experience with the smaller 62-meter patrol boat hulls prior to moving on to the larger Sigma hulls. If the Navy opts to move the corvette program forward to an earlier date, it could start some of the hull blocks at Nakilat and/or at Damen in The Netherlands, though the transition is slated to occur sooner or later.

To meet the expectations of its booming economy, Qatar invested in its future by embarking on one of the most important infrastructure projects ever undertaken from scratch. The construction of a new port, renamed Hamad Port in 2015, which is strategically located outside the capital city of Doha, was slated to house a state-of-the-art civilian harbor as well as an equally up-to-date naval base. Hamad Port will also house the country's third Economic Zone (QEZ3), a self-contained area with industrial and residential facilities located adjacent to the harbor, to take advantage of booming tax-free trade. The advanced commercial port facility, part of the *Qatar National Vision 2030* master plan that intends to transform the promontory into a dynamic society, is grandiose. Formal operations started in 2016, with the first of three container terminals, although the eventual combined annual capacity was supposed to be in excess of 6 million containers, at a cost of 19 billion Qatari Riyals (US$ 5.2 billion). In addition to the container traffic, the harbor will also accommodate general cargo traffic, vehicle, livestock and bulk grain imports, and provide vessels a variety of offshore support. It will also house a brand new naval base to cater for Qatar's growing maritime security needs. Interestingly, the base will be built offshore of Hamad Port, providing berthing for Qatar's Navy and visiting naval vessels from around the world, along with a natural protection to the harbor. Current plans call for the base to offer technical support, comprehensive logistic services, material support accommodation and recreational amenities, which will dramatically change the existing facilities.[24]

On 5 June 2017, Bahrain, Egypt, Saudi Arabia, and the United Arab Emirates (UAE) severed their diplomatic ties with Qatar, withdrew their ambassadors from Doha and imposed strict trade and travel bans. The four countries, which became known as the Anti-Terror Quartet (ATQ), indicted Doha for "embrac[ing] various terrorist and sectarian groups aimed at destabilising the region," including the Muslim Brotherhood, al-Qaʻidah, the self-proclaimed Islamic State of Iraq and Syria (ISIS) also known by its Arabic acronym Daʻish, along with a myriad groups of temporary extremists supported by Iran. What the ATQ states complained about covered the gamut, as they decried Qatar's post-2011 strategic decision to bet on the ascendancy of Islamist parties, including the violent Muslim Brotherhood in Egypt and throughout the Arab Gulf region. Interestingly, Doha acknowledged this threat when it approved the Brotherhood's designation as a terrorist organization with all GCC member-states, though it apparently continued to provide financial assistance to some of its branches. Earlier, Bahrain, Saudi Arabia and the UAE withdrew their ambassadors from Qatar after differences came to a head, a crisis that ended in late 2014 after the Qatari ruler, Shaykh Tammim bin Hamad Al Thani, entered into an agreement with the late Saudi monarch, King ʻAbdallah bin ʻAbdul ʻAziz.[25]

The ongoing crisis hovered around Doha's pro-Iran policies, which were at odds with those of the overwhelming majority of Arabs. Justifiably, most feared a Persian onslaught within the realm, though reports that Shaykh Tammim objected to the 21 May 2017 American-GCC Riyadh Summit declarations toward Iran – which Doha considered to be "a great state that contribute[d] to regional stability" – were interpreted as an open endorsement of Tehran. News that a senior Qatari representative met with Major-General Qasem Soleimani, the Iranian commander of the Quds Force in the so-called "Army of the Guardians of the Islamic Revolution," bode ill too. Soleimani was partly responsible for the ongoing chaos as he helped Iran achieve one of its primary objectives – to drive a wedge among Arabs.

Of course, Qatar and Iran shared the offshore North Field from where the bulk of Doha's wealth emerged, but this did not mean that GCC States would accept that a founding member kowtow to Tehran. Moreover, and while Iran was and would remain a vital regional state, it was not a superpower. Naturally, Qatar along with every Arab state, were well advised to maintain the best of neighborly ties with Iran, though it was critical to repeat that such correct relations could not be at any price.[26]

Interestingly, several Qatari officials stated that all of the decisions reached by the Al Thani were a matter of national sovereignty, and that Doha was free to choose as it deemed best. This was and would always be the case because GCC leaders could not be natural enemies of the Shaykhdom given so much united them within conservative Arab societies. Moreover, logic dictated that no power was anxious to strip Qatar of its liberty to do what the Al Thani deemed to be in the best interests of the Qatari nation. Rather, the ATQ States were and would remain natural allies, even if alliances imposed various restrictions on its members. In fact, the cardinal alliance rule of any coalition was to prevent one party from adopting policies that harmed other members.[27]

Over several-months old with no end in sight, the Qatar crisis stood as a genuine existential calamity for the GCC, as the regional body moved towards a strong union under Saudi leadership, whether Iran liked it or not. Qatar was still part of that union because the promontory is attached to the Arabian Peninsula of which it could not, and ought not, be separated. Under the circumstances, one wondered whether entering into separate bilateral military accords with Turkey would help defuse existing tensions, or whether Doha might stand firm against extremists. Similarly, it was unclear whether the early August 2017 Qatari purchase of seven naval vessels from Italy in a €5 billion ($5.9 billion) deal, would ensure regional security even if these boats will take years to build.[28]

Royal Saudi naval forces

The Saudi navy remains a coastal force operating from bases along the Red Sea and the Arabian Gulf. Its potential grew with the delivery of four French guided-missile frigates in the mid-1980s with three more commissioned in the mid-1990s. The navy assisted in escort and minesweeping operations in the Gulf during the tense "tanker war" period of the 1980s and assumed new responsibilities ever since, participating in the post-2015 blockade of the Yemeni coast to deny Huthi rebels supply opportunities.

The development of the navy as a guardian force in the Arabian Gulf and Red Sea started in earnest in 1974 when the Saudi Naval Expansion Program (SNEP) was initiated with the assistance of the United States. Previously, the Royal Saudi Naval Forces (RSNF), which were created in 1960, deployed a few obsolete patrol boats, landing craft and utility boats. Inasmuch as Riyadh drew its fighters from among desert warriors, a naval capability was not a priority when the Kingdom was reconstituted in 1932, although the outlook changed under King Faysal (r. 1964–75) who, regrettably, confronted a genuine threat to the monarchy when the Yemen became mired in a civil war between republican and royalists forces, the first backed by Egypt that deployed its troops to fight the Imam and the second supported by the Al Sa'ud to preserve what was left of the monarchy. Naval movements through the Red Sea and the strategic Bab el-Mandeb in the 1960s, and the equally troubling threats to the vital Strait of Hormuz in the 1970s, persuaded Saudi authorities to invest in their nascent navy.

Naval personnel strength, which was less than 1,000 in 1974, reached 13,500 by 2016. An additional force of 3,000 marines existed that were divided into two infantry battalions tasked for amphibious roles. The two marine battalions were organized as an infantry regiment and were equipped with 140 BMR-600P armored vehicles of Spanish manufacture. It was reported that an expansion of the marine corps was contemplated and new inventory requirements were being prepared although these were not announced by late-2017.

The main naval headquarters are located at Riyadh as the RSNF is organized into the Western Fleet, with headquarters at Jiddah on the Red Sea, and the Eastern Fleet, with headquarters at Al Jubayl on the Arabian Gulf. All four French-build frigates and three destroyers are based in the Red Sea and the four U.S.-build corvettes in the Gulf. Other naval facilities are located at Yanbu, Dammam and Ras al Mishab. The port of Dammam had a large military sea terminal that proved fully adequate to handle U.S. and other cargoes during the buildup preceding the 1991 War for Kuwait. The two main bases at Jiddah and Al Jubayl were constructed under SNEP. They were similar to the military cities of the army, with hardened command centers, family housing, schools, mosques, shopping centers and recreational facilities for naval personnel and their families, in addition to maintenance, logistics and training facilities.

Between 1980 and 1983, the United States supplied four PCG-1 corvettes (870 tonnes) each armed with eight Harpoon anti-ship missiles in addition to six torpedo tubes. Nine fast-attack craft, also delivered in the early 1980s, were similarly equipped with Harpoon missiles. The principal combat ships of the navy, however, were four French F-2000 frigates (2,870 tons), since then renamed Madinah-class, which were commissioned in 1985 and 1986, each armed with a Dauphin helicopter, eight Otomat anti-ship missiles having a range of 160 kilometers, torpedo tubes, and a 100mm gun. In the same Sawari contract with France were two logistic support ships, 24 Dauphin helicopters, most armed with AS-15 anti-ship missiles, and support programs for training and maintenance. Based on their experiences with French naval assets, Saudi Arabia purchased three Lafayette-class destroyers (3,700 tons), since renamed the al-Riyadh-type, each armed with Exocet anti-ship missiles, a variety of weapons, and the capacity for two AS365N Dauphin helicopters. The latter entered into service between 1996 and 1999. There were also at least 69 patrol and coastal combatants, seven mine warfare/mine countermeasure vessels, eight amphibious landing crafts and 17 logistics and support platforms.[29]

Naval aviation received extensive attention too as the fleet deployed 34 AS365N Dauphin helicopters, and 12 Super Puma transports that could also carry Exocet missiles. In May 2015, Riyadh ordered ten Sikorsky MH-60R anti-submarine warfare helicopters from the United States, and was negotiating with Germany to purchase at least five submarines for around 2.5 billion ($3.4 billion). Equally interesting, in December 2014, Washington apparently awarded Lockheed Martin a contract for the Mark 41 Vertical Launching System (Mk 41 VLS), a ship-borne missile canister launching system that provides a rapid-fire launch capability against hostile threats. Since Saudi Arabia had no surface ships compatible with the Mk 41, and because there were no publicly known plans to acquire a land-based missile defense system, this indicated that the Kingdom was close to purchasing one or more VLS-equipped surface combatants. No announcements were made by late-2017, though Riyadh evaluated the *Arleigh Burke*-class DDG-51 destroyer and the 3,500-ton Multi-mission Combat Ship version of the *Freedom*-class littoral combat ship that could carry a VLS. Naturally, while these acquisitions dramatically improved the RSNF's capabilities, it remains to be determined whether they would catapult it into becoming a blue-water navy, able to expand its patrols through the Indian Ocean zone.[30]

The United Arab Emirates navy

The UAE Navy, formally created as a small coastal unit of the Union Defence Forces in 1971, was composed of 2,500 sailors, headquartered in Abu Dhabi. In 2016, it maintained 29 patrol and coastal combatants, including eight corvettes alongside an estimated ten SDVs (Swimmer delivery vehicles), or very small submarines. Although primarily concerned with coastal defense, the Navy was engaged in a major construction program when it placed its order for the first four corvettes in 2003, since then upgraded to eight units of what were essentially blue-water vessels. The *Baynunah* program for the 72-meters naval units built at the Abu Dhabi Ship Building (ADSB) facility allowed for a steady transfer of technology since the vessels were designed by Constructions Mecaniques de Normandie (CMN) of Cherbourg, France, that worked with ADSB, which provided combat systems for all ships under a government-to-government contract. The first corvette was built in Cherbourg as the ultra-modern ships relied on extensive on-board automation that substantially reduced the size of the crew. Abu Dhabi also purchased ships from Sweden, as shipbuilder Swede Ship Marine, which delivered four 24-meters Amphibious Troop Transport vessels and one 25-meters Fast Supply Vessel for the UAE Navy, brought the total number of amphibious ships to 29. The country maintained a small battalion-sized force called the UAE Marines equipped with armored personnel carriers.

In preparation for the coming years, the navy commissioned 12 *Ghannatha* Phase II class fast missile landing crafts in 2014, along with four *Falaj* 2-class patrol vessels as well as several smaller missile boats and ships. By 2017/2018, the Navy was scheduled to receive the two Damen Patrol Vessels based on the Sea Axe design with a helicopter capability, perhaps even in coordination with GCC countries as well.[31]

According to Rear Admiral of the UAE Naval Staff, Ibrahim Al Musharrakh, while shipping lanes in the Arabian Sea were primarily patrolled by a coalition of

European Union naval forces and the U.S. Fifth Fleet, GCC navies were poised to assume much of these duties in the near future. Al Musharrakh believed that a GCC force could achieve "significant results" by "taking the benefits of historical links, long-lasting economic relations and perfect knowledge of [the] Somali" piracy developments, if GCC states reached a consensus to create a counter-piracy force composed of naval assets and maritime patrol aircrafts. A 2010 GCC decision to establish a maritime intelligence information-sharing center in Bahrain was not fully operation 7 years later although the six navies were committed to increasing their cooperation activities at sea to deal more effectively with transnational crimes. It was unclear whether Qatar would participate though no declarations were made about intentions by late-2017. The UAE Navy proposed to add to the GCC's Peninsula Shield a sea component but this was still under study. Anwar Ishki, a former Saudi army general and head of the Middle East Centre for Strategic and Legal Studies in Jiddah, warned that vast resources would be required to turn the idea of a GCC naval force into reality: "With current available assets, it would be tough," especially since GCC States lacked satellite monitoring technology, which was essential for such tasks. Eshki did not rule out such deployments, though he acknowledged that very long coastlines essentially meant that GCC navies would have their work cut out for them. Admiral Al Musharrakh insisted, nevertheless, that GCC countries faced a conundrum because of their limited capabilities, recognizing shortcomings, but were determined to overcome them in time if the will to engage foes and defeat them was upheld.[32]

Collective GCC naval military capabilities

Notwithstanding their limited capabilities, and as described in the previous section, GCC States were engaged in full-fledged re-equipment programs even if what was asked from their navies were substantially larger than what available manpower levels and, more important, what serious training shortages, allowed. For now, the approach was to move along two parallel lines – acquisition of additional assets and sustained cooperation with allied navies – though the ultimate goal was to aim for interoperability and, in time, to function in a joint *GCC Navy*.

Towards that end, the introduction of new multipurpose platforms and rotary-wing aircrafts, as well as the modernization of existing assets, were the easier steps to take. Indeed, GCC leaders were fully persuaded that the modernization of naval forces could no longer be postponed though, and far more important, what few discussed was the mechanism necessary to move to the next level. In other words, and even if GCC civilian and military leaders were keen to create a joint maritime force that could counter the Iranian naval threat or, at least, deter Tehran from any adventurism in the Gulf region, most were unsure how to translate this "will-to-power" into the effective creation of a *GCC Navy*. This key question went beyond the acquisition of interoperable new longer-range, multipurpose naval combatants, as well as significantly improved mine countermeasure capabilities, all of which were high priorities. Observers wondered whether such a step could be reached without concrete political cooperation of the type that could presumably only exist in a union. Were all GCC leaders ready to concede some of their sovereignty prerogatives to serve the greater good?

While the smaller Arab Gulf monarchies were anxious to accept certain limitations on sacrosanct sovereignty prerogatives, the Sultanate of Oman was not ready, and even threatened to leave the GCC if such demands were inevitable.[33] The recent crisis with Qatar, which Doha explained as an infringement on its sovereignty, further muddled prospects. How Riyadh enticed Muscat to accept inevitable concessions for the greater good of the peoples of the Arabian Peninsula was at the heart of every political and military decision even if a new burden was now added to the mix. Oman, which assumed one of the greatest maritime burdens of any GCC member-State – the defense of the strategic Strait of Hormuz and the traffic channels that fell in their entirety in Sultani territorial waters as well as the defense of a 3,165 km (1,967 miles) coastline – took its responsibilities seriously and seldom yielded on such matters. Even severe financial limitations, which prevented the Sultanate from operating as a blue navy, were deemed insufficient to nudge it towards a GCC union. In time, nevertheless, and if only for survival reasons, all six GCC countries may well have little choice but to rise above national sovereignty constrains though, admittedly, such an outcome remains in the distant future, especially now that an open-ended crisis with Qatar threatened the GCC's very existence as a regional security organization that included all six conservative Arab Gulf monarchies.

Key strategic developments

In 2007, the Iranian Supreme Leader Ayatollah 'Ali Khamene'i, reiterated that his country's "regional prominence and prosperity [were] contingent on its naval expansion and development" and, towards that end, Tehran launched a naval reorganization strategy that "redefined the primary duties and operational areas for both the Islamic Republic of Iran Navy and [the] Iranian Revolutionary Guard Corps Navy."[34]

It was a foregone conclusion that GCC States, which conducted regular joint naval exercises for a few decades, would accelerate their endeavors to enhance combat preparedness and cooperation in joint naval operations. One of the better such efforts was the annual *Khalij al-Salam* (Gulf Peace) drill that brought GCC naval units together, now in its eighteenth edition. What GCC naval officers aimed to do with these regular maneuvers was to unify their operational concepts and accelerate integration activities as they implement various operations. How fast those training military exercises improved confidence levels, ostensibly to transform the separate GCC navies into a complete joint GCC Maritime Security Force that could ensure coastal security, was the key question that naval officers pondered. Progress was slow for political reasons (the sovereignty matter raised above), while more pressing counter-measures against piracy, and steps taken to deal with the Iranian threat, compelled civilian as well as military leaders to act.

Counter-measures against piracy

Piracy was not a new phenomenon but sharply increased off Somalia during the past few years with significant consequences on littoral states and, of course, ship owners who were forced to pay ransom for the liberation of kidnapped sailors. With increased frequencies that targeted vulnerable oil tankers, the number of maritime patrols in the Indian Ocean intensified as well. Several countries deployed their own warships to protect civilians and cargo vessels or, in the case of smaller navies, pooled their resources in coalitions. Three principal partnerships emerged: Atalanta (European Union), Task Force 508 (North Atlantic Treaty Organization), and Task Force 151 (Combined Maritime Forces), which recorded sharp progress over a very short period of time. China, Japan, Russia, India, Iran and Saudi Arabia were also active, though they opted to act independently before June 2009.[35]

In June 2009, eleven Arab countries from the Gulf and the Red Sea (Bahrain, Djibouti, Egypt, Jordan, Kuwait, Oman, Qatar, Saudi Arabia, Sudan, the United Arab Emirates and Yemen) region agreed to set up an all Arab Navy Task Force (ANTF), to prevent the spread of piracy to the Red Sea. ANTF was chiefly led by Riyadh and Yemeni coast guard patrols that produced limited results. The UAE, for example, opted to act on its own and in 2011, mounted a successful operation when it raided the Arrilah I, a UAE flagged merchant vessel hijacked by pirates. All hostages onboard were freed and the pirates arrested, which reinvigorated the UAE Navy. What did not occur, however, was a GCC endorsement of the effort, though every country expressed full backing to Abu Dhabi. In other words, the singular effort was universally praised, but the logical follow-up, to up-gauge learned lessons to the GCC level remained in abeyance. Of course, the UAE Navy shared its experiences with the GCC information-sharing center in Bahrain, though what was truly required was to adopt a common approach to deal more effectively with piracy and transnational crimes. For it was imperative for member-states to work in union on this front, and every GCC country was, and would remain, dependent on safe sailings along sea-lanes. Few could afford, at least in the short-term, very close cooperation against piracy, which required the creation of a GCC counter-piracy group. Why the ANTF was not fully reinforced remained a mystery. Why ANTF members preferred to operate on a more or less solo-basis was equally puzzling. Admittedly, there were genuine limitations on existing capabilities, but as Saudi Arabia and the UAE demonstrated, intrinsic competences existed that could be easily shared with other Arab Gulf States and their partners. The means were thus there though what seemed to be missing was the will to fully engage. Inasmuch as a GCC counter-piracy force – composed of naval assets and maritime patrol aircrafts that relied on the Bahrain information-sharing center – could function, and theoretically function relatively well, this meant that there were no intrinsic reasons not to do more. A whole lot more. For in the end, the defense of the Strait of Hormuz, Bab el-Mandeb, and the Suez Canal were GCC States' first responsibilities even if major powers, including the United States, assumed the burden. Under the circumstances, and notwithstanding the repercussions of the war in Yemen, it behooved GCC States to assume their fair share of that obligation, to keep traffic lanes open, fight against illegal activities and construct robust responses against piracy, though this was easier said than done when a full-blown regional war preoccupied decision-makers.

How to deal with the Iranian naval threat

The conservative Arab Gulf monarchies are ideal allies for the West because they are determined to keep alliances with leading Western powers intact, invest heavily in defense programs to ensure uninterrupted access to vital oil resources on which these same Western countries depend. It may be useful to add, even if this is a seldom acknowledged point but nonetheless true, GCC States are genuinely threatened by Iran, an aspiring regional hegemon seeking nuclear weapons. If in the past GCC states relied on the U.S. military as the "hub" of the wheel of their defense, dramatic recent transformations – the wars for Afghanistan (2001–), Iraq (2003–2011), and the post-2010/2011 Arab uprisings – changed their calculations. Conceived as a limited regional alliance, GCC leaders shed their fears of each other and, led by the Kingdom of Saudi Arabia, identified the quest for union as a worthwhile project. As discussed above, there was undeniable reticence, especially on the part of the Sultanate of Oman, and now most likely by Qatar, but then again individual GCC militaries – especially small navies – could not assume separate and collective responsibilities against a determined foe that sought nothing less than complete regional domination. Oman believed that Iran did not pose such an imminent danger, even if it took every precaution to prepare for such an eventuality, potentially to occur in the distant future. It was unclear what Qatar contemplated as its limited forces could not withstand an assault, even if current geopolitical stances created the illusion of permanent harmony.

Notwithstanding the 14 July 2015 Joint Comprehensive Plan of Action reached between the five permanent members of the United Nations Security Council (China, France, Russia, the United Kingdom, and the United States) plus Germany, ostensibly to eliminate Iran's stockpile of medium-enriched uranium, cut its stockpile of low-enriched uranium by 98% and reduced by about two-thirds the number of its gas centrifuges. Still, the much-touted nuclear deal signed with Tehran was only valid for a mere decade, which the new American administration concluded was problematic and imperative to change. Of course, and even if secret clauses that may have been attached to the accord remained unknown, GCC member-states were seriously preoccupied with potential Iranian activities on the Arabian Peninsula and throughout the Arab World, especially because Tehran launched a naval reorganization strategy to seek naval supremacy in Gulf waters and beyond. Indeed, GCC leaders could not possibly rely on Iran's goodwill to abide by its commitments under the P5+1 deal, aware that its leaders regularly boasted of their abilities to close the Strait of Hormuz to maritime traffic by sinking a ship in its navigation lanes. One of the more recent claims was uttered on 27 December 2011 when Vice President Mohammed-Reza Rahimi engaged in his bombastic claims to deny Western navies, led by the United States, such freedoms.[36] Even if Oman, through whose territorial waters all seaborne traffic passes, failed to react to those unsavory avowals, GCC States took notice. That is why they were and are on America's side in the effort to contain Iran militarily. And that is why GCC States looked at periodic maritime clashes between the U.S. Navy and elements of the Iranian Navy, with a great deal of apprehension.

Conclusion

As discussed by Michael Knights, the GCC alliance made "strides in three defensive mission areas, which the United States can continue to support and shape," including (1) internal security, civil defense and critical infrastructure protection, (2) shared early warning and integrated air and missile defense, and (3) exclusive economic zones, territorial water and harbor defense capabilities.[37] These, he argued, deserved closer Western backing without exacerbating military tensions. In fact, and beyond the kind of assistance Knights prescribed in the next phase, including regular deployments along GCC forces akin to the NATO "Reforger" exercises, what members of the regional alliance ought to consider was nothing short of a full-fledged transformation of their militaries. Given limited manpower and training problems, the eventual and inevitable creation of a "GCC Navy" may well have to concentrate on robotic warfare, "leapfrogging a whole generation of unattainable manned capabilities – like mine countermeasures (MCM) vessels – by embracing remotely operated or semiautonomous systems to perform antisubmarine warfare, surveillance, or MCM roles" – if member-states wish to protect their interests and become relevant in the region as well as the rest of the world.[38] For in the end, there were and are no alternatives to developing comprehensive GCC naval forces that can only be accomplished on a collective basis. Indeed, the means to achieve such a goal could easily be secured if GCC leaders committed their will for the purpose, though the latest crisis with Qatar muddied all prospects for years to come. In what was interpreted as a sign of bravura, the Qatari Minister of Foreign Affairs, Shaykh Muhammad bin 'Abdul Rahman Al Thani, visited most foreign capitals to seek support, announced a defense deal with his Italian counterpart, Angelino Alfano, and embarked on close associations with Iran and Turkey – all to circumvent the ATQ States' efforts to end Qatari backing of extremist groups. Of all these initiatives, the one that genuinely preoccupied conservative Arab Gulf rulers was the Qatari-Turkish defense cooperation, which reached new heights with fresh Turkish deployments at a dedicated base. Fortunately, and at least for now, neither Ankara nor Tehran deployed naval assets near the Qatar promontory. Such operations could well raise the ante and further delay the day when Arab Gulf monarchies become masters of their own destiny.

Notes

1 Severin, 1983. See also Agius, 2012, p. 130.
2 Lewis, 2002, pp. 13–14.
3 Lapidus, 1998, p. 615.
4 Lapidus, ibid., p 291. See also Onley, 2009.

5   Kéchichian, 2016.
6   Al-Aydarus, 1985, p. 77.
7   Rich, 2009. See also Kéchichian, 2008.
8   Winkler, 2007. See also Wise, 2007.
9   Khadduri and Ghareeb, 2001.
10 Rahman, 1993, pp. 292–306.
11 Parveen, 2006, pp. 60–63.
12 Gresh, 2015, pp. 91–98.
13 Mattair, 2005.
14 Salama, 2012, pp. 1, 4 and 8.
15 Associated Press, 2015.
16 This section updates sections from the author's *From Alliance to Union*, 2016.
17 International Institute for strategic Studies, 2016, pp. 322–323.
18 Kéchichian, 2016, pp. 30–56.
19 Spero and Hart, 2009, p. 367.
20 International Institute for strategic Studies, 2016, pp. 338–339. See also Kéchichian, 2016, pp. 57–86.
21 International Institute for strategic Studies, 2016, pp. 346–348.
22 Kéchichian, 2016, pp. 87–114.
23 International Institute for strategic Studies, 2016, pp. 349–350.
24 Kéchichian, 2016, pp. 115–145.
25 Hoon, 2017. See also Amidror, 2017.
26 For a useful background essay, see Kemrava, 2017, pp. 167–187. For a flavor of the ongoing dispute, see MacLean, El Gamal, and Finn, 2017.
27 Al-Shafi, 2017.
28 Associated Press, 2017.
29 International Institute for strategic Studies, 2016, pp. 350–353.
30 Kéchichian, 2016, pp. 183–182.
31 International Institute for strategic Studies, 2016, pp. 357–359.
32 Kéchichian, 2016, pp. 183–215.
33 Kéchichian, 2016, pp. 256–257.
34 "Leader Urges Stronger Navy," 2010. See also Himes, 2011.
35 NAVFOR, nd. See also Combined Task Force 151, 2015.
36 Press TV, 2010.
37 Knights, 2013.
38 Knights, ibid., p. xi.

References

Agius, D. A., 2012. *Seafaring in the Arabian Gulf and Oman: People of the Dhow*. London: Routledge.

Al-Aydarus, M. H., 1985. *'Ilaqat al-'Arabiyyah-al-lraniyyah, 1921–1971 (Arab-Iranian Relations, 1921–1971)*. Kuwait: Dar al-Salasil Publications.

Al-Shafi, K., (2017). Time to End Contradictions and Arrogance. *The Peninsula [Doha]*. Published on 1 August 2017. Available at <www.thepeninsulaqatar.com/editorInChief/01/08/2017/Time-to-end-contradictions-and-arrogance> [Accessed 8 August 2017].

Amidror, Y. (2017). *The Qatar Crisis: Signs of Weakness, Ramat Gan*, Israel: Bar-Ilan University Begin-Sadat Center for Strategic Studies, BESA Perspectives Papers No. 497. Published on 20 July 2017. Available at <https://besacenter.org/perspectives-papers/qatar-crisis-weakness/> [Accessed 8 August 2017].

Associated Press, 2015. *Iran Producing More Natural Gas from Field Shared with Qatar*. Published 17 March 2015. Available at <www.dailymail.co.uk/wires/ap/article-2998636/Iran-producing-natural-gas-field-shared-Qatar.html> [Accessed 16 August 2016].

———, 2017. *Qatar and Italy sign a nearly $6B deal for naval vessels, Stars and Stripes*. Published on 2 August 2017. Available at <www.stripes.com/news/middle-east/qatar-and-italy-sign-a-nearly-6b-deal-for-naval-vessels-1.481127#.WYm6Oa2ZMQ8> [Accessed 8 August 2017].

Combined Task Force 151, 2015. *Combined Maritime Forces Chairs the 35th SHADE Counter-Piracy Conference*. 26 April. Available at <https://combinedmaritimeforces.com/2015/04/26/combined-maritime-forces-chairs-the-35th-shade-counter-piracy-conference/> [Accessed 16 August 2016].

Gresh, G., 2015. *Gulf Security and the U.S. Military: Regime Survival and the Politics of Basing*. Stanford, CA: Stanford University Press.

Himes, J.C., 2011. *Iran's Maritime Evolution*. Gulf Analysis Paper, Washington, D.C.: Center for Strategic and International Studies, July.

Hoon, G. (2017). How to end the Gulf stand off? The West should tell Qatar to reform its foreign policy,. *New statesman*. Published on 20 July 2017. Available at <www.newstatesman.com/politics/staggers/2017/07/how-end-gulf-stand-west-should-tell-qatar-reform-its-foreign-policy> [Accessed 8 August 2017].

International Institute for strategic Studies, 2016. *The Military Balance*. London: Routledge.

Kéchichian, J. A., 2008. *Power and Succession in Arab Monarchies: A Reference Guide*. Boulder and London: Lynne Rienner Publishers.

———, 2016. *From Alliance to Union: Challenges Facing Gulf Cooperation Council States in the Twenty-First Century*. Brighton, Chicago, Toronto: Sussex Academic Press.

Kemrava, M., 2017. Iran-Qatar Relations. In: Anoushiravan Ehteshami, Neil Quilliam, Gawdat Bahgat, eds., *Security and Bilateral Issues between Iran and its Arab Neighbours*. New York: Palgrave Macmillan.

Khadduri, M., and Ghareeb, E., 2001. *War in the Gulf, 1990–91: The Iraq-Kuwait Conflict and Its Implications*. New York: Oxford University Press.

Knights, M., 2013. *Rising to Iran's Challenge: GCC Military Capability and U.S. Security Cooperation*. Policy Focus 127, Washington, DC: The Washington Institute for Near East Policy.

Lapidus, I. M., 1998. *A History of Islamic Societies*. New York: Cambridge University Press.

Lewis, B., 2002. *What Went Wrong? Western Impact and Middle Eastern Response*. New York: Oxford University Press.

MacLean, W., Rania El Gamal, and Tom Finn (2017). Arab States Issue Ultimatum to Qatar: Close Jazeera, Curb ties With Iran. *Reuters*. Published on 22 June 2017. Available at <www.reuters.com/article/us-gulf-qatar-demands-idUSKBN19E0BB> [Accessed 8 August 2017].

Mattair, T., 2005. *The Three Occupied UAE Islands: The Tunbs and Abu Musa*. Abu Dhabi: Emirates Center for Strategic Studies.

NAVFOR (European Union Navfor), Countering Piracy Off the Coast of Somalia. Available at <http://eunavfor.eu> [Accessed 16 August 2016].

Onley, J., 2009. *Britain and the Gulf Shaikhdoms, 1820–1971: The Politics of Protection*. Occasional Paper No. 4. Doha, Qatar: Center for International and Regional Studies Georgetown University School of Foreign Service in Qatar.

Parveen, T., 2006. *Iran's Policy Towards the Gulf*. Delhi, India: Concept Publishing Company.

PressTV, 2010. *Leader Urges Stronger Navy*. 28 November. Available at <www.presstv.ir/detail/153013.html> [Accessed 16 August 2016].

Rahman, H., 1993. Kuwaiti Ownership of Warba and Bubiyan Islands. *Middle Eastern Studies*, 29(2), pp. 292–306.

Rich, P. J., 2009. *Creating the Arabian Gulf: The British Raj and the Invasions of the Gulf*. Lanham, MD: Lexington Books.

Salama, S., 2012. UAE Recalls its Envoy to Iran for Consultation. *Gulf News*, 13 April, pp. 1, 4 and 8. Available at <http://gulfnews.com/news/gulf/uae/government/uae-recalls-its-envoy-to-iran-for-consultation-1.1007694> [Accessed 16 August 2016].

Severin, T., 1983. *The Sindbad Voyage*. London: Arena.

Spero, Joan Edelman, and Hart, Jeffrey A., 2009. *The Politics of International Economic Relations*. Boston, MA: Wadsworth Publishing.

Winkler, D. F., 2007. *Amirs, Admirals and Desert Sailors: Bahrain, the U.S. Navy, and the Arabian Gulf*. Annapolis, MD: Naval Institute Press.

Wise, H., 2007. *Inside the Danger Zone: The U.S. Military in the Persian Gulf, 1987–1988*. Annapolis, MD: Naval Institute Press.

13 South Africa and maritime security

Interests, objectives, policies and challenges

Theo Neethling

Introduction

> *It is this (the Cape Sea Route) route that is the Navy's ward. It is the Navy's duty to police it. . . . To watch it. . . . To care for its users – the mercantile fleets of the world. For this they work, and while doing it, the grey ships can strengthen the bonds of friendship with our neighbours, and can make new friends, and can hold all that is best in maintaining the brotherhood of the sea. Then they are doing their proper appointed peacetime task. They are the 'Grey Diplomats'.*[1]

These are the concluding words from the book *South Africa's navy – the first fifty years*, which traces the history of the South African Navy (SAN) back to April 1, 1922. According to the SAN, these words are still relevant to the contemporary challenges facing South Africa with regard to the country's maritime interests and responsibilities within the context of an ever-changing strategic environment in general and the Southern African region in particular.

South Africa's geographical profile can be described as a medium-sized coastal state. The country has a coastline of about 1,865 miles (3,000 km) and the SAN has to deal with some of the roughest seas of the world,[2] as well as a number of other challenges. First, the South African coastline is located on a strategic international maritime trade route. Second, the country has international obligations with regard to the safety of navigation and ships, ensuring freedom of the seas and security of shipping and the marine environment. Third, economically, South Africa is in essence an 'island economy' that is highly dependent on maritime transport. Fourth, the bulk of the country's gross domestic product (GDP) is dependent on and generated through trade, with as much as 90% of imports and exports being transported by sea. As such, South Africa and the SAN have an obligation to co-operate with other maritime nations and actors with a view to maintaining good order at sea as well as protecting the country's national interests.[3]

In view of the above, this chapter concentrates on the following: first, the way South Africa views its national interests, and second, the way in which the national interests translate into specific, contemporary maritime-oriented objectives within the context of the challenges and opportunities the South African government believes characterize the regional environment. The challenges relating to the role of South Africa (and that of the SAN) with regard to regional insecurity are also highlighted. Before these matters are explored, a background section introduces the reader to the post-apartheid maritime context in South Africa and the role and functions of the SAN in this regard. It should be noted that this chapter follows a state-centric approach by mainly focusing on the SAN.

Background: the post-1994 South African maritime context

South Africa is a maritime nation.[4] The country is endowed with a double geopolitical identity relating to the land and the sea. Its maritime border extends from the Orange River in the west to Punta do Ouro in the east. Geopolitically, South Africa is strategically situated along vital sea routes of the world, namely the South Atlantic, the Indian Ocean and the Southern Oceans. The strategic importance of its geopolitical position also relates to its maritime zones, marine resources, marine ecology and conservation as well as its maritime trade. All of these factors carry with them immediate national, regional and international obligations – and are of obvious importance to the SAN. South Africa's maritime zones span the territorial waters, the contiguous zone, the exclusive economic zone (EEZ), the continental shelf as well as the Marion and Prince Edward Islands.

The Prince Edward Island Group is a South African possession situated some 540 nautical miles (1,000 km) southeast of the Nelson Mandela Bay Metropolitan Municipality (Port Elizabeth). This island group has its own territorial waters, contiguous zone, EEZ and continental shelf. All of these zones fall within the country's jurisdiction with regard to monitoring, control and enforcement of state authority which, in total, comprises some 1.26 million square nautical miles of assets.

South Africa has total sovereignty in its territorial waters, which of course is counterbalanced with the right to innocent passage of foreign shipping. In the contiguous zone, South Africa is in a position to enforce specific national legislation with respect to customs, immigration, health and fiscal issues. In the EEZ – including the continental shelf – the country's rights and obligations are confined to the exploration, exploitation and protection of the marine resources.[5]

South Africa's *Defence Review 1998* – a landmark document in the post-apartheid context – states that South Africa's dominant position on a vital global trade sea-route, its dependence on sea trade and its vast maritime area makes maritime defense a matter of great importance. From a policy position, it is also stated in *Defence Review 1998*, that effective maritime defense in the South African context requires balanced surface and sub-surface capabilities, and that the neglect of any one of these elements will have a negative effect on overall maritime defense capabilities. For the SAN to have a minimum force level that can be maintained as a growth core, it must have strike craft, submarines, mine countermine vessels, corvette-size vessels and combat surface vessels.[6]

Post-apartheid SAN considers itself a 'contiguous' navy. The primary role of the SAN is pronounced as providing maritime military services to South Africa. These fall into three major categories:[7]

- maritime operations – naval and 'paranaval' missions;
- assistance operations – support to other government departments, such as search and rescue, disaster relief, fisheries protection, pollution and anti-smuggling patrols, as well as support for scientific programs; and
- hydrographic services.

Politically, it has always been difficult to design a defense force in South Africa to cater for all possible contingencies in view of substantial budgetary constraints. In the mid-1990s, post-apartheid SAN was confronted with the reality that it did not have a modernized force to speak of. The SAN had three Daphne-class submarines (after one had been permanently decommissioned) that were more than 25 years old and which had come to the end of their economical service lives. Moreover, the country had no patrol corvettes and nine ageing Minister-class missile-armed strike craft, which were almost 20 years old. From a peace support perspective, it is especially important to note that the SAN had no ships in the patrol corvette/frigate class, having lost its destroyers and frigates owing to obsolescence.[8] At the same time, it should be noted that the SAN had two combat support ships (replenishment ships) as well as a mine countermeasures flotilla, with four minehunters, four minesweepers, and a diving tender.[9]

Against this background, it needs to be noted that the SAN's share of the defense budget had been steadily shrinking from a peak of 17% in 1977 to about 7% in the mid-1990s. Still, the SAN maintained effectiveness and efficiency and an ability not normally associated with small navies.[10] Yet, militarily, this became a matter of great concern, as there was a growing diplomatic requirement for the SAN to become more integrated in continental affairs and to participate in multinational maritime operations of a non-offensive nature.[11] It thus became a challenge of mandate versus means, or ambition versus affordability.

It should also be noted that the final years of apartheid saw increasing civil disobedience and low-level guerrilla activity in South Africa's townships. Therefore, budgets were shifted to favor the army, police and counter-revolutionary social spending. Consequently, the main equipment of the SAN and the South African Air Force (SAAF) was allowed to run down, and both the SAN and the SAAF desperately needed rejuvenation by way of new equipment, as articulated by Engelbrecht:[12]

> The navy, whose task it is to patrol our long coastline, is barely functional. But the non-availability of spare parts internationally for South Africa's three ageing submarines makes keeping them serviceable so expensive that, at any one time, only one submarine is seaworthy. Moreover, two of six strike craft

and at least five mine hunters and minesweepers have either been decommissioned, placed in reserve or cannibalized for spares in recent years.

Against this background, Cabinet decided in 1998 that South Africa would procure the following military equipment for the SAN:[13]

- four patrol corvettes from a German Frigate Consortium to replace the ageing strike craft of the SAN (which had been in service since 1979); and
- three submarines from a German Submarine Consortium, to replace the ageing Daphne submarines (which had been in service since 1971).

South Africa's post-apartheid government clearly indicated its seriousness pertaining to the matter of maritime security. In 1997, former President Nelson Mandela pronounced that:

> The sea is a vital national interest, and that is why we maintain a navy. Just as we believe all people should be free, so too, as a nation, we believe in the freedom of the seas. This is a matter of national strategic interest. We are a maritime nation trading all over the world. We accept our obligations to combine with other nations to uphold the freedom of the seas and to protect our national interest through naval power.[14]

Since 1994 (the post-apartheid era), South Africa (and the SAN) was also increasingly integrated into the maritime affairs of the Southern African Development Community (SADC), a region consisting of 14 countries, six of which have sea borders (the Democratic Republic of Congo (DRC), Angola, Namibia, Mozambique, Tanzania and South Africa) and two island states in the Indian Ocean (Madagascar and Mauritius). On the one hand, the Southern African region represents perhaps one of the most stable maritime domains in the African context.[15] On the other hand, the SAN cannot escape the fact that a substantial increase in acts of maritime crime has been recorded along Africa's coastline, a phenomenon that (still) threatens the security and stability of the continent. Against this background, both the SADC Maritime Security Strategy (MSS) and the African Integrated Maritime Strategy 2050 (AIMS-2050) recognize the threat to human security associated with acts of maritime piracy and criminality. Practically, the Southern African region faces serious challenges relating to combating piracy and the smuggling of weapons, contraband, people and goods. Another challenge is the protection of maritime trade and resources, including fisheries, seabed minerals and energy resources.

Obviously, the above-mentioned maritime threats are primarily transnational and trans-oceanic and require relatively advanced capabilities for surveillance over the sea and for effecting search and seizure at sea. Many littoral states in the African context, however, lack the capacity to monitor their maritime areas[16] and this makes the SAN of particular importance in the sub-Saharan African maritime context in general and the Southern African context in particular. These matters will be further discussed in the sections which follow.

The contemporary strategic environment and vital national interests

Following *Defence Review 1998* as a comprehensive document relating to the South African military (and its structures, strategic environment, tasks, doctrine, policy, human resources and acquisition management), *Defence Review 2015* is arguably the most important and comprehensive defense policy framework produced in South Africa. This document is a huge improvement on previous policy documents and was approved by Cabinet in March 2014 after three years of extensive consultations by a team comprising, among others, several defense experts. Cilliers[17] describes this document as "as much a manual to fix the department [of defence] as it is a path towards the future". Although it does not set out alternative force design options, the document presents the costs of a preferred option and interprets a number of key conclusions and presents a number of policy considerations with a focus on the financial affordability of the expenditure targets. This followed widespread criticism by informed critics, analysts and observers that:

> [t]he Department of Defence is neither equipped, nor trained, nor oriented for its future missions. It is mired in indecision, endless transformation and an unsustainable use of its existing budget. Time has to come for a radical intervention if the country is to avoid future embarrassment.[18]

In fact, the chairperson's overview in *Defence Review 2015* openly and sincerely states:

> The Defence Force is in a critical state of decline, characterised by: force imbalance between capabilities; block obsolescence and unaffordability of many of its main operating systems; a disproportionate tooth-to-tail ratio; the inability to meet current standing defence commitments; and the lack of critical mobility. The current balance of expenditure between personnel, operating and capital is both severely disjointed and institutionally crippling. Left unchecked, and at present funding levels, this decline will severely compromise and further fragment the defence capability. It is clear that certain defence capabilities, if not addressed now, will be lost in the very near future. The longer this prevails, the greater the effort, time and cost will be to restore the Defence Force.[19]

This statement obviously extends to the current position of the SAN, which will be discussed later. As far as the strategic environment is concerned, *Defence Review 2015* clarifies the risks to both international and domestic security. It states that internationally, the security environment is faced by a range of traditional and non-traditional threats. These pertain to violent political, ethnic and religious extremism, acts of terror, proliferation of weapons of mass destruction, the involvement of non-state actors in conflict, high levels of international crime, and cyber threats. Moving to African security, it is stated that contemporary conflicts and insecurity in Africa derive from factors relating to a lack of political rights, weak and dysfunctional states, inadequate political and economic governance, the politicization of ethnicity, the marginalization of groups, inappropriate military involvement and unconstitutional changes of government. Other drivers of African insecurity relate to competition over scarce resources, poverty, underdevelopment and poor human insecurity and endemic diseases, as well as maritime insecurity.[20]

In order to address its constitutional mandate, South Africa requires a relevant, balanced and sustainable defense force. According to *Defence Review 2015*, this constitutional mandate pertains to four strategic goals: defend and protect South Africa, safeguard South Africa, promote regional peace and stability, and contribute to developmental and other ordered tasks. To this end, the South African National Defence Force (SANDF) generally and the SAN in particular should be in a position to conduct maritime operations. This requires a naval capability that is able and capable of providing an enduring presence in South Africa's areas of maritime interest. This presence should be pursued through maritime defense or deterrence and powerful intervention through surface, subsurface and air capabilities with a focus on South Africa's ports, territorial waters, trade routes and marine resources. In addition to a naval capability that is able to conduct riverine and inland water operations, it must be capable of strategic reach and joint rapid response across the spectrum of conflict, supporting the sustainment of protracted joint operations over long distances. The motivation or rationale underlying the above-mentioned strategic goals and required naval capability is South Africa's maritime-dependent economy and significant maritime interests. The country is obliged to defend and protect these through the configuration and maintenance of a versatile littoral maritime capability, as well as a credible deep ocean capability and effective maritime domain awareness.[21]

The importance of maritime security – and a functional and competent SAN – is evident from most if not all the defense responsibilities listed in *Defence Review 2015*. These responsibilities have a direct bearing on matters relating to South Africa's sovereignty, territorial integrity and national interests, and extend to the following:[22]

- defending South Africa against armed aggression and threats to the constitutional order;
- the execution of national tasks, such as border safeguarding, maritime security, cyber security and airspace defense;
- the protection of vital maritime, air and land trade routes, good order at sea and in the airspace, and the safety and security of trade and transport hubs;
- fulfilling South Africa's international treaty obligations;
- the safeguarding of South Africa's key infrastructure;
- assisting civil authorities with the enforcement of the rule of law and the maintenance of public order and security;

- assistance in disaster relief and in the event of a large-scale humanitarian crisis; and
- contributing to the social upliftment of the South African people within the context of a developmental state.

According to *Defence Review 2015*, there are several maritime threats. Threats include maritime piracy and terrorism, armed crimes and illegal activity at sea, such as unregulated and unreported fishing. It further extends to loss of marine biodiversity. A most significant threat in the maritime domain pertains to the illegal movement of people and goods. *Defence Review 2015* also makes it clear that the continued and increased illegal exploitation of South Africa's natural maritime resources will lead to increased crime and instability, which pose a risk to stability in certain coastal regions of South Africa.[23]

In order to fulfill its obligations, the SAN currently operates the following equipment:[24]

- auxiliaries: one replenishment ship (auxiliary oiler replenishment) and one hydrographic ship (Heccla class);
- submarines: three (Heroine class);
- frigates: four (Valor class);
- mine-countermeasures vessels: four (River class);
- offshore patrol vessels: three fast-attack craft (Warrior [ex-Minister] class); 26 harbor patrol boats (Namacurra class); three inshore patrol vessels (T craft class);
- tugs: five coastal and harbor tugs;
- maritime aircraft: four (Westland Super Lynx).

Politically and economically, South Africa is arguably a power of major importance in Africa, and its maritime responsibilities therefore extend well beyond the South African borders. The country's economy accounts for 24% of Africa's GDP and 33% of that of sub-Saharan Africa, and the country is therefore obliged to play a leadership role in continental affairs. It also has to co-operate with African partners, ranging from matters such as conflict prevention, conflict resolution and post-conflict reconstruction to security-sector reform. Practically, this pertains to military contributions in a multinational context as well as partnerships with other African states in the political, economic, social and security realms.[25] The following section expands on this in detail.

The SAN in the regional (African) context

Philosophically or ideologically, South Africa's post-1994 relations with the rest of the continent became heavily concerned with the African Renaissance vision, which basically revolved around views of Africa's long-awaited upliftment: spiritually, technologically, culturally, politically and otherwise. It can even be argued that the African Renaissance was "elevated to the level of the national interest of South Africa".[26] The African Renaissance notion was strongly driven and largely articulated by former President Thabo Mbeki who clearly expressed a strong responsibility for realizing the African dream. Mbeki (who played a leading role in foreign policy as deputy president since 1994), had a very influential hand in fashioning South Africa's post-1994 foreign policy concerns and was the prime architect in re-configuring South Africa's relations with the United States, Europe and developing countries – Africa in particular.[27] Key elements of the African Renaissance included inter alia the economic recovery and development of the African continent, the termination of neo-colonial relations between Africa and developed countries, and the mobilization of African people to assume greater responsibility for their own destiny.[28]

The notion of an African Renaissance eventually became the philosophical foundation or platform for what later formally emerged at the level of Africa's top leadership as the New Partnership for Africa's Development Plan (NEPAD), a policy or blueprint for Africa's future development. In this regard, Mbeki partnered with Nigeria's Olusegun Obasanjo together with Senegal's Abdoulaye Wade in developing NEPAD and the reconstruction of Africa's institutional architecture. Mbeki also played a leading role with his fellow heads of state in establishing the African Union as a (newly designed) continental organization.[29]

From a sentimental point of view, South Africa's relations with the rest of Africa seemed to arise from a genuine concern with the future of the continent and its people. According to a 1997 foreign policy discussion document of the ANC (as South Africa's governing party), South Africa's approach to the rest of the continent was based on the following considerations:

- the fact that South Africa is part of the African continent, and that its economic development is linked to what happens on the continent as a whole;
- the fact that South Africa has an important role to play in the economic and political revival of the continent; and
- the fact that the economic development of the African continent as a whole will be a significant step in overcoming the north–south divide.[30]

Against this background, it is hardly surprising that South Africa's security interests gradually became strongly attached to those of the rest of the continent and that the country's armed forces had been committed to participation in peace missions on African soil since Thabo Mbeki became South Africa's head of state in 1999. South Africa's *White Paper on South African Participation in International Peace Missions* (1999) clearly expressed that "although South Africa acknowledges its global responsibilities, the prioritisation afforded to Africa in South African foreign policy makes Africa the prime focus for future engagements."[31] This state of affairs was no coincidence since Africa gradually became one of post-apartheid South Africa's most important markets, particularly Southern Africa. Other than tourism and trade in minerals and niche agriculture (wine and fruit) with the North, it is in Africa that South Africa developed its strongest competitive advantages.[32] Quantitatively, Africa received more than 17% of South Africa's total trade with the international community since 2012.[33]

Apart from its economic interest in Africa, South Africa also became strongly concerned with Africa's well-being and future. Analysts often point out that state collapse and wars in the regional context affected South Africa and its future: "Without an end to these wars and the establishment of an effective state in countries such as the DRC and Angola, there cannot be stability or democracy, and therefore no sustainable development."[34] This view was also underscored by senior government functionaries.[35]

The above-mentioned are obviously of relevance to maritime affairs. On the basis of South Africa being the "major economic power of Sub-Saharan Africa," Heitman[36] maintains that the country – and the SAN in particular – have a responsibility to assist and support other African states in the field of regional security. At the same time, this is also a matter of self-interest, as South Africa needs a stable environment in which to develop its own economy.

Heitman[37] further maintains that the SAN should be regarded as a sub-Saharan asset in the field of peace support, stabilization, intervention, constabulary and humanitarian operations. This coincides with the view expressed by a former chief of the Kenyan navy when he referred to South Africa's submarines in the following way: "They are not your submarines . . . they are our submarines." This does not mean that the SAN should be expected to do everything for everyone as this would not be acceptable to the South African taxpayer, and there are limitations to the role and function of the SAN. At the same time, the SAN needs to be visible in the regional context and its role should not fall short of regional maritime security. To this end, Heitman suggests that, as a regional asset, the SAN could complement navies from other African states by providing capabilities they cannot. Practically this means the following:

- Submarines could conduct surveillance and reconnaissance operations before and during an operation. They could further provide a screen to warn of potential interference by other naval elements.
- Frigates could conduct extended duration or long-range patrols. They could also serve as flagships for small squadrons or serve as command and support ships for small craft during operations.
- The combat support ship could serve as underway replenishment ship or as a depot ship for smaller vessels conducting operations, or render logistical support and even serve as a flagship.
- Mine-countermeasure vessels and off-board systems could be deployed to conduct routine bottom surveys and respond to mine threats.

The SAN also has a role to play in peace support operations. The required role would depend on the nature of a particular mission. This could include support across the full spectrum of naval operations, such as surveillance and reconnaissance, maritime security patrols, blockades, naval gunfire support, amphibious operations, sealift operations and many more.[38]

The previous list implies an ambitious role for the SAN. It also implies a point of departure that South Africa is a regional power and that the country should exercise the security responsibilities that come with that status. It requires that the SAN should regard itself as a regional navy, and that it should develop the force design and doctrine required by that role accordingly, as well as securing the funding that it needs for its role.

Moreover, in recent years, the maritime security debate in South Africa has provoked considerable public and media attention. This could be ascribed to events and a lack of maritime security around the Horn of Africa and in the Gulf of Guinea. In short, acts of piracy have put the focus on the possibility of South African naval participation in multinational efforts to limit piracy. The general message has further been that more should be done from the side of South Africa, and that greater cooperation among African role-players is needed.[39] Thus, much is expected of South Africa and the SAN, but the current fleet is "extremely modest" and the SAN is in need of more funding and equipment if it is to fulfill a meaningful role and help shape events in a regional context with African partners.[40] This will be further discussed in the section which follows.

The South African naval dilemma: guns versus butter

> We could be part of an African solution to African issues. It is much better for South Africa to play a meaningful role in our continent than to leave that open to people from outside the continent because we don't have the capability.

These are the words of Rear Admiral Robert (Rusty) Higgs, Chief of Naval Staff, before the Seriti Commission of Inquiry in August 2013. This commission of inquiry was appointed by the South African government in October 2011 to investigate allegations of fraud, corruption, impropriety or irregularity (mainly at a political level) in the Strategic Defence Procurement Packages of 1999, commonly referred to as 'the Arms Deal', which included the purchasing of four patrol corvettes and three submarines.[41]

What should be understood from the above is that the defense – economic relationship in South Africa – and related political debates on defense equipment – was slowed down by controversy around allegations that there were deviations from traditional acquisition procedures in the process of purchasing of new defense equipment for the SAN and the SAAF. Another controversy played out around the so-called 'guns versus butter discourse', and both the above-mentioned matters impacted heavily on the role and functionality of the SAN. Regarding the guns or butter discourse, Abrahams[42] rightly states that post-apartheid activists expected that the new post-1994 government would focus more on human development as a priority than on the military, and thus move away from the highly militarized pre-1994 history of the country.

In view of the above, critics felt that post-apartheid South Africa continued to be too militarized. In the scholarly community, the writings of Professor Geoff Harris[43] are a typical example of this school of thought. Harris[44] offered two explanations for the rationale or drive behind, what he called, "South Africa's milex decisions, given the lack of any international security risk." The first was the existence of a strong military pressure group in South Africa, including the state-owned arms industry (Armscor). The success of the arms industry, he argued, rested on two almost universally accepted beliefs, namely that a strong military is necessary to promote security, and that a strong military is necessary for national pride and status – both of which, he insisted, are flawed beliefs. Outside scholarly circles, anti-militarists from civil society were also vocal, of which the following statement is a typical example:

> [t]here is growing anger that the ANC government has failed to deliver any improvement to the lives of most of its constituents. The wealth gulf between rich and poor is even wider than it was during the apartheid era. Unemployment is 42%, and the number of people living in shacks continues to increase. . . . To the electorate however, the arms deal has become symbolic of an appalling waste of energy and resources that could go to social improvement. The credibility of our constitutional democracy is at risk.[45]

The beliefs and efforts of pressure groups could be viewed in the broader context of international initiatives to exert pressure on developing states to cut back on military spending and inventories. These beliefs and efforts also form part of post-Cold War initiatives and activism in the international community to encourage progress in the demilitarization of global politics. For many activists – also in South Africa – there was hope for peace, stability and a stronger focus on human development rather than on military power. The concept of defense conversion accordingly became a prominent issue on the agenda with the idea that the redundant military resources could now be converted for civilian use.[46]

More recently, the evidence leader of the Seriti Commission, Advocate Simmy Lebala, practically continued the guns versus butter discourse when he articulated the views of many defense sceptics in his questioning of Rear Admiral Higgs on whether other African countries are operating submarines and frigates. In the words of Lebala:

> Why do we have to behave like superpowers, given our limitations. The history of our country, socio-economic factors, surroundings, and the background inform us that our priorities are health, houses, feeding the poor, HIV and Aids. . . . Still you want us to employ the military resources that we have on equating us to superpowers. Why can't we be superpowers in our own right by focusing on economic issues?[47]

Against this background, an old truth regarding naval affairs in South Africa seems to continue as a threat running through South Africa's naval history, namely that the South African existence became embroiled with local political, economic and societal issues, rather than issues of international trade and maritime power.[48] It also seems that the required will and support from the political level is lacking. Frustrations in this regard urged Mr. David Manyier, a former combat officer in the SAN and now Member of Parliament and spokesperson on finance of the official opposition party, the Democratic Alliance, to state that "the Defence Force is being held hostage by lazy and disinterested Members of Parliament serving on the Joint Standing Committee on Defence."[49]

Still, it needs to be said to the credit of South African naval officers that the SAN has been playing an important role in recent years in the protection and patrolling of the country's borders in accordance with a 'back to the borders' policy adopted by the South African military. Furthermore, the SAN's frigates, supported by its offshore vessels (converted strikecraft) have been deployed to the Mozambique Channel when Mozambique was unable to meet the threat of piracy on its own. South African frigates have been deployed on a rotational basis and managed to maintain an almost permanent presence in the northern Mozambique Channel from August 2011 until December 2015. This followed the hijacking of the Vega 5, a fishing vessel owned by a Spanish-Mozambican company, by Somali pirates in the Mozambique Channel. Officers of the Mozambican Navy have also embarked on the South African patrolling frigates. Additionally, the SAN has also used its submarines to gather intelligence and reinforce the deterrent effect of the surface and air patrols. The SAN views these operations as successful: pirates are no longer attacking targets, the sea lanes are open, the fishing fleets are active at sea and tourism is flourishing.[50]

However, these operations mean increased wear and tear on the frigates. The requirements for protecting the country's maritime frontiers and maintaining an anti-piracy patrol in the Mozambique Channel have also impacted severely on the SAN's ageing secondary warships. The SAN's three offshore patrol vessels are close to 30 years old and were not designed to operate in the rough oceans surrounding South Africa. They need to be replaced. The four mine-countermeasures vessels also have to be replaced.[51] The challenges currently facing the SAN are further exacerbated by increased personnel spending, which necessitates a reallocation of critical maintenance and repair funds.[52]

What is more is that several Chinese fishing trawlers were spotted in South African waters in May 2016 – a matter that attracted considerable media attention. The movements of the foreign vessels led to a formal intergovernmental call for assistance from the Department of Agriculture, Forestry and Fisheries (DAFF) to the SAN with regard to the monitoring and inspecting of the Chinese trawlers for suspected illegal fishing in South African waters. It should be noted that the DAFF has the civilian-political responsibility and jurisdiction to act in cases of suspected illegal fishing, but the SAN has to render the needed intergovernmental support. To this end, the Valor Class frigate, SAS Amatola, was the first warship deployed following the DAFF appeal for support to the civilian authorities. This was followed by the further deployment of the SAN's replenishment vessel, the SAS Drakensberg. Eventually, four Chinese fishing trawlers were approached by the SAN and a few DAFF vessels and escorted to East London and Cape Town harbors for further action.[53]

In view of this event, naval officers need to plan for the future and came up with a new plan to cater for the future needs of the SAN, called Project Biro. In brief, Project Biro retains both offshore patrol vessels and inshore patrol vessels, with the latter deployed at all the main ports around the South African coast. The idea is that new vessels would participate in border security missions and be ready to undertake mine-countermeasures and related tasks, such as seabed search. All of this, however, will be subject to public and political scrutiny, and have to be approved by Parliament.[54] At the same time, defence analyst Helmoed-Römer Heitman rightly warns that it won't be helpful to "add new ships to a fleet lacking the funding to look after what it has"; meaning that the SAN should have budget to carry the required operational costs as well as refits on the frigates and submarines.[55]

Conclusion

South Africa's network of ports is considered the largest, best equipped and most efficient in the African maritime context. South Africa's ports handle about 80–90% of South Africa's trade, which makes the security of shipping, sea lanes of communication, maritime resources and harbors of major importance. This matter is also recognized by other states in the region, even those land-locked states with no direct access to the sea.[56]

There is no doubt that the geo-strategic position of Southern Africa places it centrally beside major trade routes to the East and the West – a point that has been emphasized over the years by South Africa's political leadership as well as the top commanding echelons of the SAN. Furthermore, there is general agreement among South Africa's political leaders and naval commanders that good ocean governance is important for regional security. There is also a firm commitment on the part of all actors that the SAN has to attend to the protection of offshore areas and resources, which relates to both national areas of maritime jurisdiction and the high seas. As far as the latter is concerned, the SAN has declared itself committed to anti-piracy operations as part of its international obligations in addition to its primary war-fighting missions.[57]

Currently, the SAN is playing an important role in operations against the threats and challenges it encounters in its maritime domain. At the same time, the SAN needs Project Biro to be implemented in order to find itself in a position to better police its huge maritime domain. Claiming sovereignty over such a large area puts South Africa in a position where it has to exercise substantial international duties and obligations. The question is sometimes asked why it is taking so long to implement Project Biro. This is because the Department of Defense and the SAN have been in the process of reviewing the budget before they finalize the contracting process,[58] but Walker[59] also rightly argues that this can be attributed largely to the legacy of the 1999 Arms Deal. The controversy over this deal made additional military purchases economically impossible and politically difficult to justify. These matters have effectively put the SAN in an almost impossible position to purchase the new vessels it needs to ensure maritime security in the medium and longer term.

In the final analysis, the authors of *Defence Review 2015* explicitly acknowledge the fact that the SAN experiences severe pressure on its operating budget. More specifically, there is clear acknowledgement of the increased sustainment costs resulting from the increased operational work done by its frigates as well as the need to keep the obsolete offshore patrol vessels operating. In view of this, *Defence Review 2015* makes it clear that the SAN's vessels can no longer be made ready to execute the full range of operations for which they were designed[60] – all of which impact directly and heavily on South Africa's commitment to maintain good order at sea and to protect the country's national maritime interests.

Acknowledgements

The author wishes to note that this article is based upon work supported financially by the National Research Foundation of South Africa. Any opinion, findings and conclusions or recommendations expressed in this material are those of the author and therefore the NRF does not accept any liability in regard thereto.

Notes

1. SA Navy, 2015b.
2. Heitman, 1995, p. 38.
3. Defence Review Committee, 2015, p. 2/10.
4. SA Navy, 2015b.
5. SA Navy, 2015c.
6. Department of Defence, 1998.
7. SA Navy, 1997.
8. Cilliers, 1998, p. 9, p. 11; Heitman, 1995, p. 39.
9. Heitman, 1995, p. 39; SA Navy, 1997, p. 29.
10. Heitman, 1995, p. 39; SAN, 1997, p. 29.
11. Mare, 1997, p. 29.
12. Engelbrecht, 2001, p. 2, p. 5.
13. Department of Defence, 1999, p. 1.
14. Quoted by Potgieter and Pommerin, 2009, p. v.
15. Vreÿ and Mandrup, 2015, p. 10.
16. Defence Review, 2015, p. 2/9.
17. Cilliers, 2014, p. 1.
18. Cilliers, 2014, p. 1.
19. Defence Review Committee, 2015, p. vii.
20. Defence Review Committee, 2015, p. iv.
21. Defence Review Committee, 2015, pp. 9/9 – 9/12.
22. Defence Review Committee, 2015, pp. 9/9 – 9/12.
23. Defence Review Committee, 2015, p. 2/27.
24. Campbell, 2012; SA Navy, 2015a.
25. Defence Review Committee, 2015, p. 3/9.
26. Du Plessis, 2003, p. 90.
27. Le Pere and Van Nieuwkerk, 2006, p. 286.

28 Du Plessis, 2003, p. 91.
29 Habib, 2009, p. 148.
30 Botha, 2000, pp. 3−4.
31 Department of Foreign Affairs, 1999, p. 20.
32 Ahwireng-Obeng and McGowan, 1998, p. 11.
33 Freemantle and Stevens, 2012, p. 1.
34 Cilliers, 1999, p. 1.
35 See Selebi, 1999, pp. 7−8, p. 130.
36 Heitman, 2009, p. 51.
37 Heitman, 2009, p. 52.
38 Heitman, 2009, pp. 54−55.
39 Potgieter and Pommerin, 2009, p. v.
40 News24, 2013.
41 News24, 2013.
42 Abrahams, 2001.
43 Harris, 2001, pp. 67−74.
44 Harris, 2001, pp. 67−68.
45 Crawford-Browne, 2003.
46 Abrahams, 2001, p. 1.
47 As quoted by News24, 2013.
48 Potgieter and Pommerin, 2009, p. v.
49 Maynier, 2015.
50 Campbell, 2012; Walker, 2015; Helfrich, 2016a; Helfrich, 2016b.
51 Campbell, 2012; Walker, 2015.
52 Defence Review Committee, 2015, p. 9/5.
53 DefenceWeb, 2016.
54 Campbell, 2012; Walker, 2015.
55 Helfrich, 2016.
56 Potgieter and Pommerin, 2009, p. v.
57 See for instance Mudimu, 2009, p. 3.
58 Helfrich, 2016.
59 Walker, 2015.
60 Defence Review Committee, 2015, p. 9/5.

References

Abrahams, D., 2001. *Defence Conversion in South Africa: A Faded Ideal?* ISS Occasional Paper, 51, 29 March. Available at: <www.issafrica.org/Pubs/Papers/51/Paper51.html> [Accessed 8 January 2016].

Ahwireng-Obeng, F., and McGowan, P. 1998. Partner or Hegemon? South Africa in Africa (part 1). *Journal of Contemporary African Studies*, 16(1), pp. 5–38.

Botha, P., 2000. An African Renaissance in the 21st Century? *Strategic Review for Southern Africa*, XXII(1), pp. 1–26.

Campbell, K., 2012. SA Navy Reviews Fleet Needs as Antipiracy Patrol Highlights Capacity Constraints. *Engineering News*, 23 March. Available at: <www.engineeringnews.co.za/article/sa-navy-reviews-fleet-needs-as-antipiracy-patrol-highlights-capacity-constraints-2012–03–23> [Accessed 9 November 2015].

Cilliers, J,. 1998. *Defence Acquisitions – Unpacking the Package Deals*. ISS Occasional Paper, 29, 1 March. Available at: <www.issafrica.org/publications/papers/defence-acquisitions-unpacking-the-package-deals> [Accessed 12 November 2015].

———, 1999. *An Emerging South African Foreign Policy Identity*. ISS Occasional Paper, 39, 2 April. Available at: <www.issafrica.org/publications/papers/an-emerging-south-african-foreign-policy-indentity> [Accessed 9 November 2015].

———, 2014. *The 2014 South African Defence Review: Rebuilding After Years of Abuse, Neglect and Decay*. ISS Policy Brief, 56, June, pp. 1–8.

Crawford-Browne, T., 2003. ECAAR-South Africa Continues Legal Action to Block Imports. *Economists for Peace and Security*, November. Available at: <www.epsusa.org/publications/newsletter/2003/nov2003/crawford.pdf> [Accessed 12 November 2015].

Defence Review Committee. 2015. *South African Defence Review 2015*. Pretoria.

DefenceWeb. 2016. *Another Three Fishing Trawlers Escorted into a SA Port*. 23 May 2016. Available at: <www.algoafm.co.za/article/local/77817/illegal-chinese-fishing-vessels-impounded-in-east-london> [Accessed 6 June 2016].

Department of Defence, 1998. *South African Defence Review: As Approved by Parliament*, Cape Town, April.

———, 1999. Cabinet Decision on Strategic Defence Procurement. *Bulletin*, 63/99, 17 September.

Department of Foreign Affairs, 1999. White Paper on South African Participation in International Peace Missions. *Government Gazette*, 4 October, Notice 2216 of 1999.

Du Plessis, A., 2003. The Military Instrument in South African Foreign Policy: A Preliminary Exploration. *Strategic Review for Southern Africa*, XXV(2), pp. 106–137.

Engelbrecht, L., 2001. South Africa's Multi-Billion Arms Programme Revisited. *Defence Systems Daily*, 15 October. Available at: <www.armsdeal-vpo.co.za/articles03/revisited_one.html> [Accessed 2 December 2015].

Freemantle, S., and Stevens, J., 2012. EM10 and Africa: South Africa in Africa – a Steady, Yet Narrow, Ascent. *Africa Macro: Insight and Strategy*, 12 June 2012.

Habib, A. 2009. South Africa's Foreign Policy: Hegemonic Aspirations, Neoliberal Orientations and Global Transformation. *South Africa Journal of International Affairs*, 16(2), pp. 143–159.

Harris, G. 2001. The Incompatibility of Peacemaking and Military Power. *South African Journal of International Affairs*, 8(1), pp. 67–74.

Heitman, H-R., 1995. Born of Necessity. *Jane's Navy International*, 100(5), September/October, pp. 38–42.

———, 2009. African Navies and Peacekeeping: A Role for the South African Navy. In: T. Potgieter and R. Pommerin, eds., *Maritime Security in Southern African Waters*. Stellenbosch: Sun Press, pp. 43–65.

Helfrich, K., 2016. New Navy Patrol Vessels Can Wait, But the Fleet Must Have an Operational Budget – Heitman. *Defenceweb*, 19 October 2016. Available at: <www.defenceweb.co.za/index.php?option=com_content&view=article&id=45601:new-navy-patrol-vessels-can-wait-but-the-fleet-must-have-an-operational-budget—heitman&catid=111:sa-defence&Itemid=242> [Accessed 23 January 2017].

Le Pere, G., and Van Nieuwkerk, A., 2006. South Africa and Crafting Foreign Policy in a Complex Global Order: Change and Continuity. In: P. McGowan, S. Cornelissen and P. Nel, eds. *Power, Wealth and Global Equity: An International Relations Textbook for Africa*. Cape Town: UCT Press, pp. 283–300.

Manyier, D., 2015. *South Africa: Dysfunctional Joint Standing Committee on Defence Delaying the Defence Review*. Democratic Alliance Press release, Cape Town, 27 January.

Mare, L., 1997. Reinforcing the Great Revival: The People of Africa are Hungry for Change and a Chance to Silence African Pessimists Once and for All. *Salut*, 4(12), December, pp. 27–30.

Mudimu, J., 2009. Keynote Address. In: T. Potgieter and R. Pommerin, eds., *Maritime Security in Southern African Waters*. Stellenbosch: Sun Press, pp. iii–vi.

News24. 2013. *SA Navy Short of Ships*. 22 August 2013. Available at: <www.news24.com/SouthAfrica/Politics/Navy-short-of-ships-20130822> [Accessed 5 December 2015].

Potgieter, T., and Pommerin, R., 2009. Foreword. In: T. Potgieter and R. Pommerin, eds., *Maritime Security in Southern African Waters*. Stellenbosch: Sun Press, pp. iii–vi.

SA Navy. 1997. *Charting a Course into New Waters*. The official souvenir catalogue, Maritime Expo 97 (in association with Jane's Navy international). Pretoria.

———, 2015a. *Equipment*. Available at: <www.navy.mil.za/equipment/index.htm> [Accessed 2 December 2015].

———, 2015b. *Role of the SA Navy*. Available at: <www.navy.mil.za/aboutus/role/index.htm> [Accessed 7 December 2015].

———, 2015c. *SA Navy: Mission and Vision*. Available at: <www.navy.mil.za/aboutus/visionmission.htm> [Accessed 7 December 2015].

Selebi, J., 1999. *The Role of the Department of Defence in the Promotion of South Africa's Foreign Policy, Especially in Africa*. Presentation to the South African National Defence College, 10 March, pp. 1–21.

Vreÿ, F., and Mandrup, T., 2015. Introduction. In: F. Vreÿ and T. Mandrup, eds., *Towards Good Order at Sea: African Experiences*. Stellenbosch: Sun Press, pp. 5–18.

Walker, T., 2015. Can Project Biro help Africa to overcome its maritime security challenges? *ISS Today*, 4 May 2015. Available at: <www.issafrica.org/iss-today/can-project-biro-help-africa-to-overcome-its-maritime-security-challenges> [Accessed 11 January 2015].

Conclusion[1]

Howard M. Hensel

Contemporary scholars, statesmen, and military planners have become increasingly aware of the compelling relevance of the interrelationship between the Indian Ocean and the Western Pacific. Indeed, there is broad recognition that the maritime security of the Indian Ocean and the Western Pacific is absolutely essential to sustain the interdependent, industrialized, contemporary global economy, as well as, more broadly, to support the global community in the twenty-first century. Consequently, while recognizing the continuing significance and interrelationships between the various sub-regions subsumed within the broader Indian Ocean basin and the Western Pacific region, it is now more important than ever before in history to view and predicate policies based upon the fact that the Indian Ocean and the Western Pacific constitute an integrated, geo-strategic whole.

Many of the chapters in this volume, and especially those in its companion volume, *Maritime Security in the Indian Ocean and the Western Pacific*, emphasize the critical role of goods and raw materials, especially oil and liquefied natural gas, which transit through the Indian Ocean basin and the Western Pacific region. As a result, these various chapters have concluded that it is absolutely vital for global security to maintain stability in the troubled waters of the Red Sea, the Persian Gulf, the South China Sea, and the East China Sea, as well as throughout the broader expanse of the Indian Ocean and the Western Pacific. Indeed, it is especially important to ensure the security of the maritime chokepoints in these regions, such as the Suez Canal, the Bab el-Mandeb, the Strait of Hormuz, the Strait of Malacca.

As discussed in this volume, as well as in its aforementioned companion volume, a variety of contemporary challenges threaten the security of these vital maritime transit routes. Many of these challenges emanate from non-state actors and are ubiquitous throughout the entire area east of Suez. These include threats posed by: piracy; terrorism; the smuggling of arms, drugs, and other illicit goods; human trafficking; illicit fishing; and other criminal activities. Moreover, the challenges posed by environmental pollution and climate change, combined with the threat of the spread of disease and the potential of pandemics, are also ubiquitous throughout the area east of Suez. Finally, the proliferation of weapons of mass destruction and the accompanying ballistic missile systems pose a threat to both the regional powers, as well as to the broader global community.

In addition, there are a variety of other persistent challenges within the various sub-regions of the Indian Ocean and the Western Pacific. Some of these challenges emanate from non-state actors. For example, political instability caused by insurgencies and secessionist movements constitute a threat to regional security. In addition, other regional challenges involving clashing interests and objectives pursued by the various powers pose a threat to peace and stability in the Indian Ocean basin and the Western Pacific, as well as to the security of the larger international community. For example, the perceptions held by the People's Republic of China of itself within the regional and global context, its interests, its objectives, and its policies, especially in the South China Sea and the East China Sea, have sharply conflicted with the interests and objectives of other regional powers in East and Southeast Asia. In addition, Chinese initiatives have also challenged the interests, objectives, and commitments of the United States, thereby creating a dangerous situation that could potentially escalate into a regional confrontation involving the United States and possibly other global powers. Similarly, relations between the People's Republic of China and Taiwan have the potential of deteriorating into confrontation. Moreover, North Korea's nuclear weapons and accompanying ballistic missile development programs pose an extremely serious threat to regional and international peace and security. Iran also presents a significant, ongoing challenge to stability in the oil-rich Persian Gulf, a sub-region that is absolutely vital to the global economy. Finally, the national interests, objectives, and policies of many of the other regional powers often conflict, thereby leading to tensions and potential regional instability.

Despite these examples of challenges to stability in the Indian Ocean and the Western Pacific emanating from various regional and global powers, however, the national interests of the regional states, as well as those of the non-littoral great powers, are quite similar in many respects. For example, all of the states that are active in the Indian Ocean basin and the Western Pacific are absolutely committed to the preservation of their respective regimes and systems of government. Moreover, the various powers all claim to seek a stable international environment, predicated upon a rule-based international order, as governed by the Charter of the United Nations. Similarly, they all maintain that they are committed to the principle of freedom of navigation through international waters, while, simultaneously, emphasizing their commitment to defend their sovereignty, territorial integrity, and their rights within their respective exclusive economic zones. All the powers seek to promote a prosperous and growing state and global economy, with reliable access to global markets and resources, especially access to oil and natural gas. In addition, they all express their commitment to combat terrorism, illicit fishing, and other criminal activities in the regions. The various powers also express their commitment to protect their citizens, their willingness to actively support humanitarian relief efforts, and their commitment to environmental protection. While many of the regional powers, as well as the great powers, often adhere to different and, in some cases, clashing interpretations concerning the definitions and principles underpinning these concepts, the fact that there is, at least in principle, broad agreement concerning the desirability of maintaining such concepts, serves as a basis for negotiations concerning the details involving their implementation. Finally, most certainly, it is not in the interest of any regional or global power to allow rivalry and confrontation to escalate to the level of military hostilities.

Given these considerations, as suggested in several chapters, the way forward is for all the littoral states and non-littoral great powers to build upon areas of shared interests, predicated upon the principles of mutual recognition and respect for the national interests of the various powers, the peaceful resolution of disputes, respect for the territorial integrity and the internationally recognized exclusive economic zones of the various states, unfettered access to global markets, and freedom of navigation in international waters. Therefore, common threats that are ubiquitous throughout the Indian Ocean basin and the Western Pacific, such as those posed by piracy, terrorists, and other illicit activities, can be, and, indeed, have often been addressed through mutual agreements and collective or coordinated actions. Similarly, environmental challenges, as well as the challenges posed by natural and man-made disasters, can be, and have also been addressed through similar actions. In addition, on many occasions, disputes between the various Indian Ocean and Western Pacific littoral powers have been resolved peacefully or, at least, effectively managed through formal or informal diplomatic negotiations, yielding solutions based upon a mutual spirit of compromise and consensus that recognizes and respects the national interests of the various parties. Often international bodies have helped to facilitate collective or coordinated actions in response to common challenges. Similarly, international bodies have also helped to facilitate the peaceful resolution or management of regional disputes among the states of the Indian Ocean and the Western Pacific. Indeed, international cooperation in response to common challenges and the peaceful resolution or management of conflicts helps to establish a normative pattern of state cooperation that, in turn, encourages the further resolution, or at least, the effective management of more difficult challenges involving the central national interests of the various powers.

As suggested in several chapters in this volume, a synergistic mixture of policy instruments will undoubtedly be required in dealing with especially difficult challenges involving fundamental clashes of interests between the various powers, such as those involving Chinese policies in the South China Sea and the East China Sea, as well as those involving North Korea's and Iran's nuclear and missile programs. Diplomacy alone, even when reinforced by the use of informational instruments of policy, but unsupported by the application of economic instruments and not reinforced by the credible and robust presence of military power, may not be sufficient to dissuade China, North Korea, or Iran from continuing to pursue their destabilizing policies. Conversely, neither economic sanctions alone, nor economic incentives alone, without the support of diplomatic, informational, and military power will prove sufficient. Similarly, unilateral or multilateral military demonstrations that implicitly or explicitly threaten the use of military power alone, if unsupported by the use of diplomatic and economic instruments, will probably also prove to be ineffective. Indeed, they may even prove to be counterproductive in ameliorating tensions if they are perceived by the adversary as an armed provocation. Signaling is an important method by which statesmen can transmit their intentions and resolve. Care must be taken, however, to ensure that the right message and tone is transmitted and that the intended message is not misinterpreted by the adversary or the international community.

Certainly, history has shown that there have often been occasions when the threatened or actual application of military force is appropriate in defense of a state's national interests and the broader international order. In situations where military hostilities are unavoidable, however, statesmen must use military force with precision in conjunction with clearly defined objectives based upon the principle of proportionality, optimally with international authorization and broad multilateral support, and then, only as a last resort, after all other methods have failed to yield results. Moreover, with respect to the actual application of military force, military strategy and its supporting operations must be governed by the principle of distinction between combatants and non-combatants, with the principle of military necessity regulated by the principles of proportionality and humanity, in accord with the tenets of customary and conventional international humanitarian law.

Not only must all the instruments of policy be synergistically employed, the degree of emphasis placed on each of the individual instruments will situationally vary. The application of a particular mix of instruments and the degree of emphasis placed on any one or group of instruments of policy that yields results in one situational context at a particular time will probably not be generalizable in all situational contexts. Instead, the policies and the instruments utilized must be individually and synergistically tailored to the time, the context, and the nature of the adversary involved in the dispute. In short, there is no "one pattern fits all" formula that can be universally applied in all situations.

Many of the chapters in this volume have observed that, since the conclusion of World War II, a large number of the regional powers have relied upon the United States to serve as the guarantor of security in the Western Pacific, as well as, especially since 1980, in the Persian Gulf sub-region and the larger Indian Ocean basin. Consequently, in responding to vexing regional challenges, it is incumbent upon the United States to provide the leadership necessary to facilitate the delineation of common objectives and the adoption of common, collective policies that are effectively coordinated between itself and its regional allies and partners, and one that synergistically utilizes all the various instruments of policy, in order to deal with shared challenges, such as those posed by Chinese actions in the South China Sea and the East China Sea, the North Korean nuclear and missile programs, and Iranian activities in the Persian Gulf. It is important to point out, however, that, while Chinese activities present a challenge to the international maritime order in the South China Sea and the East China Sea, simultaneously, in other contexts, China can serve as an important partner in collective efforts to curb the North Korean and Iranian nuclear and missile programs.

In short, the global community confronts many challenges that are common to both the Indian Ocean and the Western Pacific and these call for a collective response involving all the littoral and non-littoral powers. Even with respect to especially difficult challenges that are unique to particular sub-regions, such as those posed by the Chinese, the North Koreans, and the Iranians, a collective effort by the regional states, facilitated by American leadership, is necessary in order to preserve peace and stability throughout the Indian Ocean and the Western Pacific.

As pointed out in several chapters, the United States must accurately assess the economic and strategic regional power configuration in its efforts to coalesce the various regional powers in order to address common challenges, as well as to promote collective efforts designed to respond to difficult regional challenges, such as those posed by China's actions in the South China Sea and the East China Sea. For example, while many regional powers in East and Southeast Asia are quite concerned about China's assertive maritime policies, at the same time, in varying degrees, these regional powers also have important economic ties with China. In addition, while it is not in the United States' interest to permit China to become the regional hegemon in the Western Pacific, similarly, it is important to recognize that it is not in Beijing's interest to acquiesce to U.S. maritime hegemony in that same region. Moreover, it is important to recognize and be sensitive to the complex and dynamic forces operating domestically within the Chinese, Iranian, and North Korean political systems. Actions taken by the United States and its partners have the potential to strengthen or, alternatively, weaken those elements within the ruling elite that are willing to moderate policy, peacefully manage or resolve differences, and, thereby, successfully ameliorate tensions. In short, given the contemporary regional power configuration in the Indian Ocean basin and the Western Pacific, as well as the internal dynamics of the various states of these regions, the United States and its partners should recognize the multilateral maritime character and complex economic, political, and strategic order in the Indian Ocean and the Western Pacific.

Naval power is a central and necessary component of the larger national military strategies of the states examined in this volume. Hence, the various chapters have analyzed and assessed the contemporary maritime goals and capabilities of the respective littoral and non-littoral powers in the Indian Ocean basin and the Western Pacific. In addition, they have examined and evaluated the maritime policies and naval deployment patterns of the various powers, as these states seek to advance their respective maritime-oriented objectives and, thereby, promote their broader national interests.

For example, as analyzed and assessed in the chapter dealing with the Chinese Navy, in recent years, Beijing has actively dedicated significant resources toward the acquisition of an effective, balanced naval capability that will contribute to its goal of establishing greater Chinese influence in the Western Pacific and beyond. As a result, the Chinese Navy has increasingly acquired the capability, should military hostilities erupt, to degrade any potential adversary's naval assets before the adversary can effectively deploy its battle fleet in the Western Pacific. In addition, this enhanced capability permits the Chinese to defend its vital sea lines of communication, as well as allows it to collectively or unilaterally engage in humanitarian operations and other operations directed against common threats within the global maritime commons. Toward that end, the Chinese have secured access to a number of port facilities throughout the Indian Ocean basin. Meanwhile, as reviewed in the chapter focusing on Russian naval policy, while the Russian Navy has continued to pursue a sea-denial/bastion-oriented naval strategy, the Russian Navy has resumed more distant naval operations in the Western Pacific and elsewhere. Similarly, as noted in the chapter dedicated to Iranian maritime policy, the Iranian Navy seeks to maintain a deterrence capability directed against potential adversaries through a maritime area-denial strategy similar to that pursued by China and Russia, while, simultaneously, engaging in very limited naval operations beyond the Persian Gulf.

As observed in several other chapters in this volume, naval capabilities also serve as force multipliers for the Japanese, the South Koreans, the Indians, the Australians, the New Zealanders, the Arab states of the Gulf, and the South Africans, as well as for the states of Southeast Asia, as they pursue the maritime dimensions of their respective defense policies. Naval capabilities among these states, however, remain uneven. For example, as noted in the chapter on Southeast Asian maritime policies, the various members of ASEAN have unequal maritime capabilities, with Singapore maintaining the most capable and balanced force, followed by the second tier naval capabilities of Indonesia, Malaysia, Thailand, and Vietnam. Finally, as discussed in the chapter dedicated to the European naval presence in the Indian Ocean and the Western Pacific, both Great Britain and France have continuously maintained a naval presence in these regions capable of defending their respective national interests, as well as participating in multilateral maritime operations.

While the various regional powers have important roles to play in the maritime balance of power in the Indian Ocean and the Western Pacific, it is important for the United States to assume a disproportionate share of the naval deployments, as well as to play a vital leadership role in assisting it allies and partners in enhancing their respective naval assets and in best deploying those assets in support of common policies and objectives. Moreover, given the nature of the contemporary maritime challenges confronting the United States and its allies and partners in the Indian Ocean and the Western Pacific, the United States must maintain and even expand its own naval presence in these regions. In doing so, however, the United States must avoid the appearance of military provocation.

Finally, as the United States and its regional partners develop their maritime strategies in response to the challenges that they commonly confront in the Western Pacific and the Indian Ocean basin, as well as their policies in response to challenges and threats that are unique to specific sub-regions, such as the Persian Gulf, the South China Sea, or the East China Sea, it is important not only to emphasize policy approaches that are specifically tailored to these sub-regions, but also for the United States and its partners to recognize and formulate policies that are predicated on the fact that, now more than ever before, the Indian Ocean and the Western Pacific constitute an integrated economic and geo-strategic whole and that the interconnected security of these regions is absolutely essential for the survival of the global economy and the peace and security of the international community.

Note

1 The opinions, conclusions and/or recommendations expressed or implied within this concluding chapter are solely those of the author and should not be interpreted as representing the views of the Air War College, the Air University, the United States Air Force, the U.S. Department of Defense, or any other U.S. Government agency.

Index

Note: Page numbers in italic indicate a figure and page numbers in bold indicate a table on the corresponding page

Abe, Shinzo 2, 185
ABF (Australian Border Force) 145
"Act East" policy 184–186
"active defense, near-seas operations" 22–23
Adapted Military Service 56
ADMM-Plus (ASEAN Defense Ministers' Meeting-Plus) 80, 82
Aegis BMD system 8
AEGIS Combat System 92, 95
AESA (active electronically scanned array) 96
Afghanistan, Soviet invasion of 208
Africa: Djibouti, French military presence in 57; SAN in African context 236–239
African Renaissance 236–237
agreements: Closer Economic Relations and Closer Defence Relations agreements 157; Defense Framework Agreement 7; EDCA 5; FPA 5; FPDA 60–61; France-UAE agreement 57; Nauru Agreement 161
Air Defense Identification Zone 72
air defense, of PLAN 28
aircraft carriers: *Charles de Gaulle* 58; India's carrier program 187, 191n20; *Kuznetsov* 42; *Liaoning* 27; *USS John Stennis* 18n46; *Vikramaditya* 178
AMCM (airborne mine countermeasures) 88
amphibious assault vehicles, KAAV7A1 97
AMSA (Australian Maritime Safety Authority) 145
ANCM (ASEAN Navy Chief's Meeting) 127
Antarctica, CCAMLR 163
anti-access naval doctrine of China 24–25

APEC (Asia-Pacific Economic Cooperation) 80
approximate strengths of northeast Asia's regional navies: China **109**; Japan **108**; North Korea **109**; ROK **108**
Arab Gulf states: anti-piracy efforts 224–225; chokepoints 207; GCC 208, 209; Iranian naval threat 225–226; Iranian occupation of UAE Islands 211–212; Kuwait naval force 214–215; maritime clashes 209–210; *Operation Praying Mantis* 210; "Pax Britannica" 207–208; Qatar Amiri Navy 216–219; recent controversies 210–211; Royal Navy of Oman 215–216; Royal Saudi naval forces 219–221; security pacts 208; Tehran's claim to Bahrain 211; UAE Navy 221–222; U.S. relations with 6–7
"arc of ascendance" 4
Arctic Council 42
the Arctic, Russia's strategy in 42–43
area-denial doctrine of China's navy 25
ARF (ASEAN Regional Forum) 130
Armistice of 1953 98
artesh 200
ASEAN (Association of Southeast Asian Nations) 74, 127, 156; ANCM 127; ARF 130
ASEAN+3 80
ASG (Abu Sayyaf Group) 120
Asia, U.S. "pivot" towards 4–5
Asia-Pacific region, security challenges in 71–72; characteristics of the strategic environment 72; China's military advancements 72; North Korea,

provocative actions of 72; Senkaku Islands situation 72–73
ASMs (anti-ship missiles) 25; DF-21D 25
Atago-class destroyers 78
Atalanta 63–64
Atlantic Ocean, Russia's strategy in 42–43
Aurora Australis 145
Australia: 2016 white paper 140–141, 143; ABF 145; Australian Fisheries Management Authority 145; 'blue economy' 146; border policies 146–147; Canberra Pact of 1944 154–155; Closer Economic Relations and Closer Defence Relations agreements 157; contemporary maritime objectives 146–148; continental defence 142; defence budget 145; dimensions of maritime strategy 143–144; diplomacy 143; FPA 5; FPDA 60–61; Framework for Security Cooperation 148; grand strategy of 142–144; 'Indo-Pacific' region 144; as middle power 138–139; naval capabilities 145–147; New Zealand, relationship to 154–156; 'Offshore Constitutional Settlement' 146; OSB 146–148; rules-based order 139–140; SLOCs 142; strategic outlook 155–156; and U.S.-China relations 140–142
Australian Fisheries Management Authority 145
aviation: RAAF 145; ROK naval aviation 95–96
Axworthy, Michael 197

Bab el-Mandeb 207
Bahrain: British naval presence in 61; Combined Maritime Forces Command 64
balance of naval forces in the Persian Gulf **203**
balance of power, shift in as challenge to Japan's security 70
Baltic Sea, Russian maritime strategy 43–44
Basic Plan on Ocean Policy 82
bastion defense 37
Battle of *Daecheong* 100
BDF (Bahrain Defense Forces) 213–214
BIOT (British Indian Ocean Territory) 59
Bisley, Nick 140–141
Black Sea, Russian maritime strategy 44–46

Blair, Tony 63
blue-water navies 28; China's development of 14; ROK 86–87
BMD (ballistic missile defense) systems, Aegis 8; *see also* AEGIS Combat System
"boomers" 6
border policies, Australian 146–148
BrahMos anti-ship missile 50
Brexit 63
Britain: Bahrain, naval presence in 61; bilateral ties with Australia and New Zealand 61; Brexit 63; fight against ISIL 61–62; interests, objectives, and capabilities in the Indian Ocean 59–62; national security strategy 61; "Pax Britannica" 207–208; Royal Navy 61–62; *A Secure and Prosperous United Kingdom* 61–62; *Strategic Defence and Security Review* 62
Brunei: Royal Gurkha Rifles 61; *see also* Southeast Asia
Bubiyan Islands dispute 210–211

Cameron, David 63
Camp Lemonnier 7, 19n62
Campbell, Kurt 4, 9
Canberra Pact of 1944 154–155
capacity-building focus of New Zealand 161–162
Carter, Ashton 179
CCAMLR (Commission for the Conservation of Antarctic Marine Living Resources) 163
CENTCOM (U.S. Central Command) 6
CFSP (Common Foreign and Security Policy) 55, 63; and Brexit 63
Chagossians, resettlement of 59–60
challenges to Japan's security: human security 71; international terrorism 70; risks to the global commons 70–71; shift in balance of power 70
CHAMSURI II-class patrol boats 90
CHAMSURI-class patrol boats 90
CHANG BOGO-class submarines 94
characteristics of strategic environment of the Asia-Pacific region 72
Charles de Gaulle 58
Chechen faction in Russia's Kremlin 41
CHEON WANG BONG-class landing ships 93
China: "active defense, near-seas operations" 22–23; air defense 28; Air Defense Identification Zone 72;

256   Index

approximate naval strength **109**; area-denial doctrine 25; carrier operations 27–28; cross-straits maritime balance of power 48–49; dependence on foreign oil 26; Diaoyu Islands, U.S. rejection of Chinese administration 8–9; expansionism of 105–107; India, relationship with 182–184; *Jin*-class submarines 188–189; jurisdictional disputes in South China Sea 11–13; Kalayaan Island Group dispute 128–129; "Malacca dilemma" 27; naval posture in Indian Ocean 25–29; naval posture in Western Pacific 22–25; "One Belt, One Road" 42, 183–184; "One China Policy" 10; Permanent Court of Arbitration report 18n44; PLAN 13–16; rivalry with India 50–51; Russian support for military modernization 47–48; supply ships 28; Taiwan, military threats towards 10; territorial disputes in South China Sea 11–13; U.S. maritime policy towards 13–16; U.S maritime strategy for. *See* China; U.S. naval superiority over 18n42; weapons, informationization of 23–24; Western Pacific, anti-access naval doctrine 24–25

China Military Science 27
chokepoints in the Arabian Peninsula 207
Chosun Inmingun Haegun 110n13
Chunghee, Park 91
CHUNGMUGONG YI SUNSHIN-class destroyers 92
CJCS (Chairman of the Joint Chiefs of Staff), ROK 89
Clinton, Bill 10
Clinton, Hillary 24
Closer Economic Relations and Closer Defence Relations agreements 157
CMFC (Combined Marine Forces Command) 103
coastal minehunters, *GANGGYEONG*-class 95
"Code of Unplanned Encounters at Sea" 126
Collins-class submarines 145
COLREGS (Convention on the International Regulations for Preventing Collisions at Sea) 126
Combined Maritime Forces Command 64
Combined Task Force 150 64–65
contemporary threats to maritime transit routes 247–248

continental defence 142
Cooperative Mechanism for the Enhancement of Safety, Security and Environmental Protection of the SoMS 126
Corder, Lee 143
core security concerns of Southeast Asia 120–125, **121**; ASEAN 127; China 129; COLREGS 126; cooperative defense activities 127; CSI 126; economic growth 122; EEZs 122; maritime capabilities 128; maritime safety 126; maritime terrorism 124; military modernization 127–128; piracy 123; power competition 124–125; resource competition 122–123; terrorism 121–122; unregulated fishing 123; *see also* Southeast Asia
corvettes, *POHANG*-class 91
CPV (Communist Party of Vietnam) 131
Crimea, Russian annexation 37–38, 45
cross-straits maritime balance of power 48–49
cruise missiles, Hyunmoo-3C 93
cruisers, *Ticonderoga*-class 8
CSDP (Common Security and Defence Policy) 63
CSI (Container Security Initiative) 126, 161
CUES (Conduct for Unplanned Encounters at Sea) protocol 4
cyber security, Japan's policy for strengthening 76

DAEGU-class frigates 91–92
Davies, Andrew 145
Defence Review 1998 231
Defence Review 2015 234–235
Defence White Paper 2016 156, 159–160
Defense Framework Agreement 7
Deng, Xiaoping 23
destroyers: *Arleigh Burke*-class 8; *Atago*-class 78; *CHUNGMUGONG YI SUNSHIN*-class 92; *Izumo*-class helicopter destroyer 78; KDX-I 92; KDX-II 92; *KDX-II CHUNGMUGONG YI SUN-SHIN*-class 88; KDX-III 92–93; *KDX-III SEJONG THE GREAT*-class 88; *Kongo*-class 78; Luyang I 28; in MSDF 77–78; *Sejong the Great* 107; *USS Curtis Wilbur* 12; *USS Decatur* 12; *USS Lassen* 12; *Zumwalt*-class 6
deterrence of North Korea 98–101, *99*

DF-21D anti-ship ballistic missile 25
DF-26 anti-ship ballistic missile 25
Diaoyu Islands: as maritime flashpoint 48–49; U.S. rejection of Chinese administration 8–9
Diego Garcia 6; resettlement of native Chagossians 59–60
diesel attack submarines 24–25
diplomacy: Australian 143; Japan's proactive approach to 76, 79–80, 80–81; middle power 138–139
disarmament, Japan's efforts in 81
Djibouti, French military presence in 57
Doha's pro-Iran policies 218–219
DOKDO-class LPH 103
domestic foundations of Japanese policy approaches 84
domestic politics as challenge for Southeast Asian states 131
Downer, Alexander 139
Duterte, Rodrigo 131–132

EAS (East Asia Summit) 80
"East of Suez" British withdrawal 60–61, 62
economic growth of Southeast Asian states 122
ECSADIZ (East China Sea Air Defense Identification Zone) 105
EDCA (Enhanced Defense Cooperation Agreement) 5
EEZs (exclusive economic zones) 11; of France 56; of India 190; of New Zealand 155–156, 161; of Qatar 218; of South Africa 231; of Southeast Asian states 122
ethnic identity mix of New Zealand 157
EU (European Union): *Atalanta* 63–64; CFSP 55; CSDP 63; *A Global Strategy for the European Union's Foreign and Security Policy* 63; interests, strategy, and operations in the Indo-Pacific region 62–64; moral decay of 44; *see also* CFSP (Common Foreign and Security Policy); France
Evans, Gareth 139
"everday security concerns" 132n1
expansionism of China 105–107

factions in the Kremlin 40–41
Fars 198
FAZSOI (*Forces armées dans la zone sud de l'Océan Indien*) 56–57

Fiji coups, New Zealand's regional response to 162
FONOPS (freedom of navigation operations) 12
force projection 101–102
foreign policy: Japan's foreign policy objectives 75; Japan's strategic policies 75; "Look East" policy 184–186; of New Zealand 159–160; principles underpinning Japan's foreign policy 73–74
FPA (Force Posture Agreement) 5
FPDA (Five Power Defence Arrangements) 60–61, 128, 158, 163
Framework for Security Cooperation 148
France: Adapted Military Service 56; agreement with UAE 57; air force 58; Djibouti, French military presence in 57; EEZs 56; FAZSOI 56–57; interests, objectives, and capabilities in the Indian Ocean 55–59; La Réunion 56; Mayotte 56; military power, ranking 58; multi-national operation in IO 58; New Zealand, relations with 158; overseas military personnel 58; territories held by 56
France and Security in the Asia-Pacific 57–58
France d'outre-mer 56
Freedom of Navigation Operations 24
frigates: *DAEGU*-class 91–92; *INCHEON*-class 91; Jiangkai-II 26; *Jiangwei II* 28; *KKF Ulsan*-Class Frigate Batch-II 110n31; *Oliver Hazard Perry*-class 214; RAN 145; *Steregushchy* 37; *ULSAN*-class 91
FSB (Federal Security Service) 40–41
FSO (Federal Protection Service) 41

GANGGYEONG-class coastal minehunters 95
GCC (Gulf Cooperation Council) 61, 208, 209; anti-piracy efforts 224–225; balance of forces in the Persian Gulf 202–203, **203**; collective naval military capabilities 222–223; Iranian naval threat 225–226; Iranian occupation of UAE Islands 211–212; key strategic developments 223–224; Kuwait naval force 214–215; maritime clashes 209–210; naval capabilities 213; North Dome settlement 212–213; *Operation Praying Mantis* 210; Qatar Amiri

258 *Index*

Navy 216–219; Royal Bahrain naval force 213–214; Royal Navy of Oman 215–216; Royal Saudi naval forces 219–221; UAE Navy 221–222
geopolitical importance of South Africa 231
A Global Strategy for the European Union's Foreign and Security Policy 63
global commons, impact on Japan's security 70–71
global economy, risks of 71
global security environment challenges to Japan's security: human security 71; international terrorism 70; risks to the global commons 70–71; shift in balance of power 70
GO JUN BONG-class landing ships 93
Grand Strategy of New Zealand 158–159
Gray, Colin 156
"gray-zone" situations 72
GSDF (Ground Self-Defense Forces) 73
Guam, U.S. maritime presence in 6
Gulf of Aden, piracy in 51
GUMDOKSURI-class patrol boats 90
gunboat diplomacy 38
guns vs. butter 172; South African debate on 239–242

HADR (humanitarian assistance and disaster relief operations) 4
Hae Sung anti-ship subsonic speed missiles 90
Hamad Port 217–218
HANTAE-class LCU 103
Hanwha Techwin 97
hardliner faction 40
Harris, Harry B., Jr. 5, 7, 9, 15
HDW (Howaldtswerke-Deutsche Werft) 93
helicopters: UH-60P 96; Westland Lynx Mark 99 96; Westland Super Lynx Mark 99A 96
heroin trafficking in Southeast Asia 132n3
Holmes, James 26
Hu, Jintao 27
human security, impact on Japan's security 71
hybrid warfare 38, 51; Russia's use of 39
Hyunmoo-3C cruise missiles 93

IGRC (Islamic Revolutionary Guard Corps) 200
IGRCN (Islamic Revolutionary Guard Corps Navy) 200–201
IISS (International Institute of Strategic Studies) 13
IKC2 (Integrated Knowledge Command and Control) 128
illegal fishing of China, ROK resolution of 106
Imjin War 86
impediments to India's maritime policy 187–190
import substitution 188
INCHEON-class frigates 91
India: "Act East" policy 125, 184–186; aircraft carrier program 187, 191n20; anti-piracy efforts 174; blue-water ambitions 179; China, relationship with 182–184; deep sea mining venture 174; EEZs 190; Framework for Security Cooperation 148; import substitution 188; interdiction capabilities 190; "Look East" policy 184–186; "Malabar" 19n67; maritime interests 175–176; maritime strategy 173–174, 189; maritime threats 180–181; military investment 174; military missions 176; national defence industry 177; naval threats 173; navy 176–177; navy, investment in 15; as nuclear power 174; Pakistan as maritime threat 180–181; port security 181; post-1991 developments 175; proactive maritime policy, impediments to 187–190; regional security 189–190; rivalry with China 50–51; Russia as supplier of weaponry 177–179; Sea Control 189–190; submarine program 189; UNCLOS 174; United States, relations with 179–180; U.S relationship with 7
'Indo-Pacific' region 144
informationization 23–24
INS Aridhaman 177
INS Arighat 177
interdiction capabilities of India 190
international disaster relief operations, SDF role in 82
international peace, Japan's contribution to 80–81, 81
international terrorism: impact on Japan's security 70, 76; international cooperation against 81–82
IO (Indian Ocean): BIOT 59; Britain's interests, objectives, and capabilities in 59–62; British "East of Suez" withdrawal 60–61; China's naval

posture in 25–29; France's interests, objectives, and capabilities in 55–59; "Malacca dilemma" 27; Middle East Force 17n5; NATO's coalition interests, strategy, and operations in 64–65; Persian Gulf states 182; PLAN's scope of operation in 14–15; Russian maritime strategy 50–51
IO-WestPac 17n1
Iran: *artesh* 200; balance of forces 202–203, **203**; conventional navy 201–202; denial strategy 198–199; Doha's pro-Iran policies 218–219; *Fars* 198; IGRC 200; Islamic Republic's naval strategy 198–199; maritime threats 195–198; naval capabilities 199–200; naval strategy 195–198; North Dome settlement 212–213; occupation of UAE Islands 211–212; *Operation Praying Mantis* 210; Qajar dynasty 197; Safavids 196; Tehran's claim to Bahrain 211; threat to GCC 225–226; Treaty of Turkmenchay 196; Yemen, importance to Red Sea operations 202
Iran-Iraq War 197–198
ISAF (International Security Assistance Force) 64
ISIL, British contribution to campaign against 61–62
Islamic Republic's naval strategy 198–199
ISMMS (Inter-Sessional Meeting on Maritime Security) 82
ISR (intelligence, surveillance and reconnaissance) 78
ITLOS (International Tribunal for the Law of the Sea) 129, 132
Izumo-class helicopter destroyer 78

Japan: administration of Senkakus, U.S. recognition of 8–9; alliance with U.S., strengthening 78–79; approximate naval strength **108**; Basic Plan on Ocean Policy 82; challenges to human security 71; comprehensive defense architecture, building 76; contribution to international peace and security 80–81; cyber security, strengthening 76; defense equipment and technology cooperation 77; disarmament and non-proliferation efforts 81; domestic foundations of policy approaches 84; efforts in resolving global issues 83–84;

ensuring stable use of outer space 77; escort activities 83; foreign policy objectives 75; GSDF 73; intelligence capabilities 77; international disaster relief operations, SDF role in 82; international peace, contribution to 81; international terrorism, impact on security of 70; JCG 73; "Malabar" 19n67; maritime security, ensuring 76; MSDF 73, 77–78; national interests 74; outer space, promoting utilization of 77; partnership with Southeast Asian states 130; principles underpinning foreign policy 73–74; proactive approach to diplomacy 76, 79–80, 80–81; risks to the global commons, impact on security of 70–71; rule of law, strengthening 81; SDF 73, 77–78, 82–83; shift in balance of power, impact on security of 70; strategic policies 75; technological capabilities, strengthening 77; territorial dispute with ROK 104–105; territorial integrity, protecting 76; Three Non-Nuclear Principles 73–74; U.S. presence in 5, 79
Japan-U.S. Defense Cooperation 78
JCG (Japan Coast Guard) 73
Jennings, Peter 143
Jiangkai-II frigates 26
Jiangwei II frigate 28
Jin-class submarines 188–189
Joint Strategic Vision of the Asia-Pacific and Indian Ocean Region 7
JS Izumo 78
jurisdictional disputes in South China Sea 11–13

KAAV7A1 Amphibious Assault Vehicle 97
KADIZ (Korean Air Defense Identification Zone) 105–106
Kadyrov, Ramzan 41
KAMD (Korean Air and Missile Defense System) 94–95
KDX-I destroyers 92
KDX-II CHUNGMUGONG YI SUN-SHIN-class destroyers 88
KDX-II destroyers 92
KDX-III destroyers 92–93
KDX-III SEJONG THE GREAT-class destroyers 88
Key, John 165
Khan, Reza 197
King, Ed R. 17n5

Kissinger, Henry, "Twin Pillar" policy 210
KKF Ulsan-Class Frigate Batch-II 110n31
Klub missiles 25
Knights, Michael 226
Kongo-class destroyers 78
Kremlin, factions in 40–41
KSS-I class submarines 94
KSS-II class submarines 94
KTO (Korea Theater of Operations) 90
Kuwait naval force 214–215
Kuznetsov 42

La Réunion 56
Lady Anelay 60
landing ships: *CHEON WANG BONG*-class 93; *GO JUN BONG*-class 93; ROKS *Dokdo* 93; ROKS *Marado* 93
Lavoy, Peter 7
LCS (Littoral Combat Ships) 5
LCU (utility landing craft) 103
Liancourt Rock, territorial dispute over 104–105
Liaoning 27, 47
liberal values of New Zealand 156
Liu, Huaqing 22
"Look East" policy 184–186
loyalist faction in Russia's Kremlin 41
Luyang I destroyers 28

"Malabar" 19n67
"Malacca dilemma" 27
Malaysia: FPDA 60–61; Piracy Reporting Center 126; territorial disputes in South China Sea 11–13; *see also* Southeast Asia
Mandela, Nelson 233
Manyier, David 241
Mao, Tse-tung 16
marines, ROK 97
maritime nations 1
Maritime Security in the Indian Ocean and the Western Pacific 247
maritime security strategies of Southeast Asian states 125–130; resource exploitation 125–126
maritime terrorism in Southeast Asia 124
Mattis, James 2
Mayotte 56
Mbeki, Thabo 237
MccGwire, Michael K. 17n4
MDGs (Millennium Development Goals) 71
Mediterranean Sea, Russian maritime strategy 44–46

Medvedev, Dmitry 40
Middle East Force 17n5
middle powers, Australia 138–139
Military Doctrine 39
mine and countermine, ROK 95
missile defense: ROK 94–95; THAAD 94–95
missiles: ASMs 25; BrahMos anti-ship missile 50; *Hae Sung* anti-ship subsonic speed missiles 90; Hyunmoo-3C cruise missiles 93; PAC-2 GEM-T 111n55; SM-2 Block IIIB 92; SM-3 95; Spike NLOS 96; YJ-ASM 25
modernization: of Chinese navy 48; of Russian navy 37–38
Mogherini, Federica 63
Montreux Convention 44
MSDF (Maritime Self-Defense Forces) 73, 77–78
MSI (Maritime Security Initiative) 128
MSP (Maritime Straits Patrol) 126

NAMPO-class minelayer support ship 95
"narrow seas," advantage of diesel attack submarines in 24–25
National Guard (Russia) 39
national interests: clashes involving, policy challenges of 249–250; of Japan 74; of South Africa 234–236
National Security Strategy 39
nationalism in Southeast Asia 131–132
NATO (North Atlantic Treaty Organization) 39; coalition interests, strategy, and operations in the Indo-Pacific region 64–65; ISAF 64
natural gas: North Dome settlement 212–213; South China Sea reserves 18n43
Nauru Agreement 161
naval capabilities as force multipliers 252
navies 43–44; area-denial doctrine 25; Australian 145–147; Baltic Sea Fleet 43–44; Black Sea Fleet 44–46; China's anti-access naval doctrine 24–25; China's naval posture in Indian Ocean 25–29; *Chosun Inmingun Haegun* 110n13; Freedom of Navigation Operations 24; IGRCN 200–201; India 176–177; India's investment in 15; informationization of 23–24; IO-WestPac maritime forces 19n69; Kuwait naval force 214–215; Middle East Force 17n5; modernization of Russian navy 37–38; Northern Fleet

42–43; Pacific Fleet (Russia) 46–50; PACOM 17n18; PLAN 13–16; Qatar Amiri Navy 216–219; RAN 144–145; RBNF 213–214; ROK, organization of 88–89, *89*; Royal Navy 61–62; Royal Navy of Oman 215–216; Royal Saudi naval forces 219–221; Russian navy, role in Syrian conflict 46; Russian-Indian projects 50; Russia's maritime strategy 36–39; SAN 232; surface combatants-coastal patrol, ROK 90–91; UAE Navy 221–222; U.S. superiority over China 18n42; *see also* ROK (Republic of Korea); U.S. maritime policy
NCC (Naval Component Command) 90
NDPG (National Defense Program Guidelines) 69
Nehru, Jawaharlal 173
New Zealand: Australia, relationship to 154–156; bilateral defence cooperation 166n27; building resilience in the economy 161; Canberra Pact of 1944 154–155; capacity-building focus 161–162; Closer Economic Relations and Closer Defence Relations agreements 157; cooperative relationships 163; defence policy 164; *Defence White Paper 2016* 156, 159–160; economy 156; EEZ 155–156; EEZs 161; ethnic identity mix 157; FPDA 60–61, 158, 163; France, relations with 158; Grand Strategy 158–159; liberal values of 156; maritime capabilities 164; national identity 156–158; Nauru Agreement 161; *New Zealand's National Security System* 159–160; *NZ Inc strategies* 163; *Oceania* 157; PIF 162; plug-and-play military interoperability 164–165; pursuit of national goals 160–165; Regional Assistance Mission to the Solomon Islands 160; regional perspective 156–158; regional response to Fiji coups 162; rules-based order 163; security objectives 160; South Pacific, relationship with 162; strategic outlook 155–156; United States, relations with 157–158; Washington Declaration of 2012 157–158; WCPFC 161; Wellington Declaration of 2010 157–158
New Zealand's National Security System 159–160

Nixon, Richard, "Twin Pillar" policy 210
"Nixon Doctrine" 210
NMCC (National Maritime Coordination Centre) 161
Non-Aligned Movement 50
non-proliferation, Japan's contribution to 81
North Korea: approximate naval strength **109**; Armistice of 1953 98; *Chosun Inmingun Haegun* 110n13; "Northern Limit Line" 98–100, *99*; provocative actions of 72; relations with Russia 49; ROK's strategy for defeating 101–104; U.S maritime strategy for 7; U.S. Navy assets for deterring 8; *YUGO*-class submarine 101
Northern Fleet 42–43
"Northern Limit Line" 98–100, *99*
Northwest Islands Defense Command 89–90
Novorossiya project 40
NSC (National Security Council) 69
NSS (National Security Strategy) 69
nuclear weapons: India as nuclear power 174; Japan's Three Non-Nuclear Principles 73–74
NZ Inc strategies 163

Obama, Barack 24; "Rebalancing" policy 1–2
objectives: Australia's contemporary maritime objectives 146–148; of Britain in the Indian Ocean 59–62; of France in the Indian Ocean 55–59; Japan's foreign policy objectives 75; New Zealand's pursuit of national goals 160–165; New Zealand's security objectives 160; of Russian maritime strategy 39; of U.S. maritime policy 3–4
occupation of UAE Islands 211–212
Oceania 157
'Offshore Constitutional Settlement' 146
"offshore water defense," China's naval posture in Western Pacific 22–25
oil: China's dependence on foreign oil 26; South China Sea reserves 18n43; Southeast Asian reserves 122
oligarchs 40
Oliver Hazard Perry-class frigates 214
"One Belt, One Road" 42, 183–184
"One China Policy" 10
Operation Allied Protector 64
Operation Ocean Shield 64
Operation Praying Mantis 210

opportunities and challenges for Southeast Asian states 130–132
origins of "pivot" toward Asia strategy 17n7
O'Rourke, Ronald 198
"Orthodox" faction 40–41
OSB (Operation Sovereign Borders) 146–147
outer space, Japan's promoting utilization of 77

PAC-2 GEM-T missile 111n55
Pacific Ocean, Russia's maritime strategy 46–50
Pacific powers 1
PACOM (Pacific Command) 17n18
Pakistan as maritime threat to India 180–181
Pannikar, K.M. 173
Paracel Islands, territorial disputes over 12
patrol boats: *CHAMSURI*-class 90; *GUMDOKSURI*-class 90; RAN 145; in the "West Sea" 101
"Pax Britannica" 207–208
PDRK (Peoples Democratic Republic of Korea) *see* North Korea
peace *see* international peace
peacetime roles of ROK 87
Pence, Mike 2
Permanent Court of Arbitration report 18n44
Persian Gulf states 182; balance of forces 202–203, **203**; Iranian navy 201–202
Pethiyagoda, Kadira 182
Philippines: ASG 120; EDCA 5; Kalayaan Island Group dispute 129; territorial disputes in South China Sea 11–13; *see also* Southeast Asia
PICs (Pacific Island Countries) 80
PIDF (Pacific Islands Development Forum) 162
PIF (Pacific Islands Forum) 162
piracy: *Atalanta* 63–64; "Code of Unplanned Encounters at Sea" 126; Combined Task Force 150 64–65; GCC's anti-piracy efforts 224–225; in Gulf of Aden 51; India's anti-piracy efforts 174; Japan's escort activities 83; in Southeast Asia 123
Piracy Reporting Center 126
"pivot" to Asia, origins of 17n7
PKX-A patrol boat 90
PLAN (People's Liberation Army's Navy) 251–252; air defense 28; area-denial doctrine 25; carrier operations 27–28; IO, scope of operation in 14–15; "Malacca dilemma" 27; modernization of naval forces 47–48; naval posture in Indian Ocean 25–29; naval posture in Western Pacific 22–25; supply ships 28; *see also* China
POHANG-class corvettes 91
policy: "Act East" 125; "Act East" policy 184–186; Basic Plan on Ocean Policy 82; challenges of national interest clashes 249–250; Doha's pro-Iran policies 218–219; domestic foundations of Japanese policy approaches 84; guns vs. butter 172, 239–242; impediments to India's maritime policy 187–190; "Look East" policy 184–186; New Zealand foreign policy 159–160; New Zealand's foreign policy 159–160; objectives of U.S. maritime policy 3–4; "One China Policy" 10; principles underpinning Japan's foreign policy 73–74; "Rebalancing" policy 13–14; sub-regions, U.S. policy approach to 252–253; Trump's U.S. Asia policy 2–3; "Twin Pillar" policy 210; U.S. maritime policy 4–16; U.S. "pivot" towards Asia 4–5; *see also* U.S. maritime policy
political instability as threat to regional security 248
political technology, Russia's use of 38–39
populist nationalism in Southeast Asia 131–132
port security, India 181
power projection 39
Pratas Islands, territorial disputes over 12
PRC (People's Republic of China) *see* China
Prince Edward Island Group 231
principles underpinning Japan's foreign policy 73–74
provocative actions of North Korea 72
PSI (Proliferation Security Initiative) 161
Pulau Ligitan, territorial dispute over 125
purpose of Russia's maritime strategy 40
Putin, Vladimir 38, 41, 51; Rotenberg brothers, association with 45

Qajar dynasty 197
Qatar 216–219; EEZs 218; Hamad Port 217–218; North Dome settlement 212–213
Qatar National Vision 2030 218

RAN (Royal Australian Navy) 144–145; patrol capabilities 145
RBNF (Royal Bahrain Naval Force) 213–214
RBNS Sabha 214
RCEP (Regional Comprehensive Economic Partnership) 2
"Rebalancing" policy 1–2, 4–5, 13–14, 69, 124–125; strategies for achieving 4–5
ReCAAP (Regional Cooperation Agreement on Combating Piracy and Armed Robbery against ships in Asia) 126, 133n35
Regional Assistance Mission to the Solomon Islands 160
regional perspective of New Zealand 156–158
regional security of India 189–190
resettlement of Chagossians 59–60
resource competition in Southeast Asia 122–123
Richards, Sir David 61
Richardson, John 14
RIMPAC (Rim of the Pacific) 14, 18n57
risks to the global commons, impact on Japan's security 70–71
ROK (Republic of Korea): approximate naval strength **108**; Armistice of 1953 98; Battle of *Daecheong* 100; blue-water navy 86–87; *CHAMSURI II*-class patrol boats 90; *CHAMSURI*-class patrol boats 90; *CHANG BOGO*-class submarines 94; CJCS 89; destroyers 92; expansionism of China, controlling 105–107; frigates 91–92; *GO JUN BONG*-class landing ships 93; illegal fishing of China, resolution of 106; interoperability with allies 97; KAAV7A1 Amphibious Assault Vehicle 97; KADIZ 105–106; Marine Corps 88; marines 97; mine and countermine 95; missile defense 94–95; *NAMPO*-class minelayer support ship 95; naval aviation 95–96; Navy, organization of 88–89, *89*; NCC 90; North Korea, defeating 101–104; North Korea, deterring 98–101, *99*; "Northern Limit Line" 98–100, *99*; Northwest Islands Defense Command 89–90; peacetime roles 87; *Sejong the Great* 107; SLOC protection 101–102; *SON WONIL*-class submarines 94; submarines 93–94; support to international missions 107; surface combatants-amphibious 93; surface combatants-coastal patrol 90–91; surface combatants-ocean going 91–93; territorial dispute with Japan 104–105; wartime roles 87–88; *YANGYANG*-class coastal minehunters 95; *Yulgok* Plan 91
ROKS *Cheonan* 91
ROKS *Daegu* 91–92
ROKS *Dokdo* 93
ROKS *Marado* 93
ROKS *Ulsan* 91
Romania, maritime cooperation with Russia 46
Rotenberg brothers 45
Royal Gurkha Rifles 61
Royal Saudi naval forces 219–221
rule of law, strengthening in the international community 81
rules-based order: Australia 139–140; New Zealand 163
Russia: annexation of Crimea 37–38; the Arctic, maritime strategy in 42–43; Atlantic maritime strategy 42–43; Baltic Sea, Russian maritime strategy 43–44; Black Sea, Russian maritime strategy 44–46; Chechen faction 41; export of military technology 39; FSB 40–41; hybrid warfare 38, 39, 51; Indian Ocean, maritime strategy 50–51; *Klub* missiles 25; Kremlin, factions in 40–41; loyalist faction 41; maritime strategy 36–39; *Military Doctrine* 39; modernization of naval forces 37–38; National Guard 39; *National Security Strategy* 39; Northern Fleet 42–43; Novorossiya project 40; objectives of maritime strategy 39; oligarchs 40; "Orthodox" faction 40–41; Pacific Ocean, Russian maritime strategy 46–50; political technology, use of 38–39; purpose of maritime strategy 40; regional developments 42; relations with North Korea 49; role in Syrian conflict 46; Rotenberg brothers 45; sources of maritime strategy 39–41; *Steregushchy* frigate 37; as supplier of weaponry to India 177–179; support for Chinese military modernization 47–48; Treaty of Turkmenchay 198; trends in Russian maritime power 51–52; Turkey, maritime cooperation with 45–46

SADC (Southern African Development Community) 233
Safavids 196

SAN (South African Navy): in African context 236–239; under-budgeting 232–233; categories of maritime military services 232; guns vs. butter 239–242; role in peace support operations 238–239
SANDF (South African National Defence Force) 235
Saudi Arabia: Iran as threat to 208–209; Royal Saudi naval forces 219–221; SNEP 219; Tehran's claim to Bahrain 211; "Twin Pillar" policy 210
SDF (Japan Self-Defense Force) 73, 77–78, 130; international disaster relief operations 82; overseas activities 82–83
sea control 101–102
A Secure and Prosperous United Kingdom 61–62
Sejong the Great 107
Senkaku Islands: impact on security of Asia-Pacific region 72–73; as maritime flashpoint 48–49; U.S. recognition of Japanese administration 8–9
Shah, Nadir 196
shift in balance of power, impact on Japan's security 70
Shogyu, Sergey 38, 40
Sibal, Kanwal 148
Singapore: FPDA 60–61; maritime capability 128; ReCAAP 126; Total Defense concept 131; *see also* Southeast Asia
Sipadan territorial dispute 125
SLOCs (Sea Lanes of Communication): Australian 142; ROK protection of 87–88, 101–102; in Southeast Asia 125–126; vulnerability of 71
SM-2 Block IIIB missiles 92
SMCM (surface mine countermeasures) 88
smuggling: OSB 146–148; as Southeast Asian security concern 121
SNEP (Saudi Naval Expansion Program) 219
Socotra Rocks, territorial dispute over 105–106
soft power index 167n45
SOLAS (Safety of Life at Sea) 125–126
SON WONIL-class submarines 94
sources of Russian maritime strategy 39–41
South Africa 230–231; defence forces 235–236; *Defence Review 1998* 231; *Defence Review 2015* 234–235;
geopolitical importance 231; maritime threats 233–234, 235–236; post-1994 maritime context 231–234; Prince Edward Island Group 231; *White Paper on South African Participation in International Peace Missions* 237
South China Sea: natural gas reserves in 18n43; oil reserves in 18n43; Permanent Court of Arbitration report 18n44; Russian maritime strategy 49–50; U.S. maritime policy in 11–13
South Pacific, New Zealand's relationship with 162
Southeast Asia: China as security concern 129; COLREGS 126; cooperative defense activities 127; core security concerns 120–125; domestic politics 131; economic growth of 122; EEZs 231; "everyday security concerns" 132n1; heroin traffickers 132n3; maritime capabilities of states 128; maritime geography 121; maritime safety 126; maritime security strategies 125–130; maritime terrorism 124; military modernization programs 127–128; national interests 234–236; opportunities and challenges 130–132; partnerships with middle powers 129–130; piracy 123; populism 131; power competition in 124–125; resource competition 122–123; resource exploitation 125–126; smuggling in 121; terrorism in 121–122; unregulated fishing 123; *see also* ASEAN (Association of Southeast Asian Nations)
Soviet invasion of Afghanistan 208
Soviet Union, bastion defense 37
SPHINX-D Radar System 94
Spike NLOS missiles 96
Spratlys, territorial disputes over 11–12
SSBNs (U.S. strategic missile submarines) 6
stability, threats to in the Indian Ocean 248–249
Steregushchy frigate 37
Strait of Hormuz 207
Strategic Defence and Security Review 62
strategic policies of Japan 75; building a comprehensive defense architecture 76; cyber security, strengthening 76; defense equipment and technology cooperation 77; enhancing intelligence capabilities

77; maritime security, ensuring 76; measures countering international terrorism 76; promoting utilization of outer space 77; strengthening diplomacy 76; strengthening technological capabilities 77; territorial integrity, protecting 76
submarines: *CHANG BOGO*-class 94; *Collins*-class 145; diesel attack submarines 24–25; India's submarine program 189; *Jin*-class submarines 188–189; in MSDF 78; ROKN 93–94; *SON WONIL*-class 94; SSBNs 6; *YUGO*-class 101
sub-regions, U.S. policy approach to 252–253
Suez Canal 207
Sun-Shin, Yi 86
supply ships, Chinese 28
surface combatants-amphibious, ROK 93
surface combatants-coastal patrol, ROK 90–91
surface combatants-ocean going, ROK 91–93
Swaine, Michael D. 19n54
Sweden as potential NATO member 44
Syrian conflict, role of Russian navy in 46

Taiwan: territorial disputes in South China Sea 11–13; U.S. maritime policy towards 9–11
Takeshima 104
technocratic faction 40
technology: political technology, Russia's use of 38–39; Russian export of military technology 39
territorial disputes: Bubiyan Islands 210–211; Diaoyu Islands 48–49; expansionism of China, controlling 105–107; North Dome settlement 212–213; Pulau Ligitan 125; ROK-Japan 104–105; Senkaku Islands 48–49; Socotra Rocks 105–106; in South China Sea 11–13; Tehran's claim to Bahrain 211; Warbah Islands dispute 210–211
terrorism: ASG 120; British contribution to campaign against ISIL 61–62; "Code of Unplanned Encounters at Sea" 126; CSI 126; international terrorism, impact on Japan's security 70; as Southeast Asian security concern 121–122; *see also* piracy

THAAD (Terminal High Altitude Area Defense) missile system 8, 92–93, 94–95
threats to South Africa's maritime security 233–234
Three Non-Nuclear Principles 73–74
Ticonderoga-class guided missile cruisers 8
Tillerson, Rex 2
Total Defense concept 131
trade routes, China's dependence on foreign oil 26
traditional security concerns of Southeast Asia **121**
Trans-Pacific Partnership 2
Treaty of Turkmenchay 198
Treaty on Basic Relations 104
Trump, Donald 2, 24; National Security Strategy 17n9; U.S. Asia policy 2–3
Tsai, Ing-wen 10
Turkey, maritime cooperation with Russia 45–46
"turn to Mahan" 26
"Twin Pillar" policy 210
Type-901 supply ship 28

UAE (United Arab Emirates): agreement with France 57; UAE Navy 221–222
UH-60P helicopters 96
Ukraine conflict, hybrid warfare 38
ULSAN-class frigates 91
UN (United Nations): Japan's efforts to strengthen diplomacy 80–81; MDGs 71
UNCLOS (United Nations Convention on the Law of the Sea) 3, 163; India as pioneer member 174; territorial disputes in South China Sea 11–13
United Kingdom: Bahrain, naval presence in 61; "East of Suez" British withdrawal 60–61; fight against ISIL 61–62; interests, objectives, and capabilities in the Indian Ocean 59–62; national security strategy 61; "Pax Britannica" 207–208; Royal Navy 61–62; *A Secure and Prosperous United Kingdom* 61–62; Strategic Defence and Security Review 62
United States: alliance with Japan, strengthening 78–79; Arab Gulf states, relations with 6–7; Brexit 63; "burden-sharing" 129; "forward presence" 6; FPA 5; Freedom of Navigation Operations 24; as guarantor of security

250–251; India, relationship with 7, 179–180; national interests 2–3; national objectives in the IO-WestPac region 3–4; New Zealand, relations with 157–158; "One China Policy" 10; *Operation Praying Mantis* 210; "pivot" to Asia 4–5; policy approach to sub-regions 252–253; "Rebalancing" policy 1–2, 13–14, 69, 124–125; superiority over China's navy 18n42; Trump's U.S. Asia policy 2–3; *see also* U.S. maritime policy; U.S. Navy
unregulated fishing in Southeast Asia 123
U.S. maritime policy 4–5; deterring North Korea 8; increased regional presence of U.S. naval assets 5–6; Joint Strategic Vision of the Asia-Pacific and Indian Ocean Region 7; recognition of Japanese administration of Senkakus 8–9; in South China Sea 11–13; towards China 13–16; towards Taiwan 9–11; working with friends, allies, and potential adversaries 6–7
U.S. Navy: assets for deterring North Korea 8; "Malabar" 19n67; Middle East Force 17n5; PACOM 17n18
USPACOM (U.S. Pacific Command) 5
USS Curtis Wilbur 12
USS Decatur 12
USS John Stennis 18n46
USS Lassen 12

Vego, Milan 24–25
Vietnam: maritime economic development 131; territorial disputes in South China Sea 11–13
Vikramaditya 178
vulnerability of sea lanes of communication 71

Wang, Lidong 27
Warbah Islands dispute 210–211
wartime roles of ROK 87–88
Washington Declaration of 2012 157–158
WCPFC (Western and Central Pacific Fisheries Commission) 161
weapons: informationization of 23–24; Russian-Indian projects 50
Wellington Declaration of 2010 157–158
Western Pacific: China's anti-access naval doctrine 24–25; China's naval posture in 22–25
Westland Lynx Mark 99 helicopters 96
Westland Super Lynx Mark 99A helicopters 96
White, Hugh 140
White Paper on South African Participation in International Peace Missions 237
WPNS (Western Pacific Naval Symposium) 126
Wu, Shengli 14

Xi, Jinping 2, 14, 16, 48
xinxihua 23

YANGYANG-class coastal minehunters 95
Yemen, importance to Iran's Red Sea operations 202
YJ-ASM 25
Yoshihara, Toshi 26
YUGO-class submarine 101
Yulgok Plan 91

Zenko, Michael 201
Zhang, Jie 27
Zumwalt-class stealth destroyers 6